PROBLEMATIC REBEL

PROBLEMATIC
REBEL

Melville, Dostoievsky, Kafka, Camus

Revised Edition

Maurice Friedman

The University of Chicago Press

Chicago and London

A first edition of this study was published in 1963 by Random House under the title *Problematic Rebel: An Image of Modern Man.* ©1963 by Maurice Friedman.

SBN: clothbound 226-26395-9; paperbound 226-26396-7
Library of Congress Catalog Card Number: 72-101360

The University of Chicago Press, Chicago 60637
The University of Chicago Press, Ltd., London

Revised edition ©1970 by The University of Chicago
All rights reserved. Revised edition published 1970
Printed in the United States of America

To my Mother
and
To the memory of
my Father

Contents

PREFACE TO REVISED EDITION   xi

PREFACE TO FIRST EDITION   xiii

PART I   *Between Prometheus and Job*

1   The Biblical Rebel and the Greek Rebel   3
     Biblical Man   5
     The Biblical Exile   6
     Job: The Biblical Rebel   12
     Oedipus, Antigone, and Prometheus: The
     Greek Exile and the Greek Rebel   22
2   Doctor Faustus and Faust   37

PART II   *Herman Melville*

3   *Moby Dick*: The Sundering of Truth and
     Reality   51
4   Ishmael, Bartleby, and the Confidence Man:
     The Modern Exile   67
5   Captain Ahab: Modern Promethean   95
6   Ahab, Bartleby, and Billy Budd: Freedom and
     Compulsion and the Divided Man   129
7   A Job's Whale   142

PART III   *Fyodor Dostoievsky*

8   Exiles of the Underground   151
     The Underground Man   151

	Raskolnikov: Isolation and Rebellion	161
	Stavrogin: The Divided Man as Exile	171
9	Dostoievsky's "Man-God"	182
	Kirilov	182
	Raskolnikov	189
	Ivan and the Grand Inquisitor	193
10	Personal Freedom, Psychological Compulsion, and Guilt	217
	The Underground Man and Raskolnikov	217
	Stavrogin and Versilov	220
	Prince Myshkin	227
	Raskolnikov and Father Zossima	235
11	Fathers and Sons	238
	The Raw Youth and *The Brothers Karamazov*	238
12	Dmitri, Ivan, and Alyosha: The Three Faces of Job	267

PART IV *Franz Kafka*

13	Kafka as Hunger Artist	285
	"A Report to an Academy"	292
	"The Burrow"	293
	"The Metamorphosis"	296
	"The Hunter Gracchus" and "A Country Doctor"	300
	"The New Advocate" and "A Hunger Artist"	304
	"Investigations of a Dog" and "The Great Wall of China"	307
	The Castle	312
14	Psychological Mirror-Writing	328
	Personal Freedom and Psychological Compulsion	328
	Kafka's "Escape from Father"	335
15	*The Trial:* The Problematic of Guilt	346
16	The Paradox of the Person in the Modern World	374
	"A Hunger Artist"	375

	The Castle	378
	The Call	382
	The Land-Surveyor	387
	K. and the Authorities	390
	Kierkegaard's Single One	393
	The Village as Means or Obstacle to the Castle	396
17	Kafka: The Suffering and Contending Job	400

PART V *Albert Camus*

18	Encounter with the Absurd	413
	Caligula, The Misunderstanding, The Fall: From the Absurd Exile to the Absurd Rebel	413
	The Fall: The Crisis of Motives	425
	The Plague: From the Modern Promethean to the Modern Job	427

PART VI *A Depth-Image of Modern Man*

19	Melville, Dostoievsky, Kafka, and Camus	437
20	The Problematic Rebel: An Image of Modern Man	455
	The "Death of God" and the Alienation of Modern Man	456
	The Modern Exile	461
	The Modern Promethean: Nietzsche's Zarathustra	466
	The Problematic of Modern Man	469
	The Problematic Rebel	483
	From the Modern Promethean to the Modern Job	483
	The Modern Job	485

BIBLIOGRAPHY OF WORKS BY AND ABOUT MELVILLE, DOSTOIEVSKY, AND KAFKA	495
INDEX	513

Preface to Revised Edition

In its original form, this book consisted of intensive studies of Melville, Dostoievsky, and Kafka prefaced by sections on Biblical, Greek, and Renaissance images of man. Before it was printed, however, I revised this form, bringing in Camus and subsuming the interpretations under the headings of the Modern Exile, the Modern Promethean, the Problematic of Modern Man, and the Modern Job. Through this the meaning of my dialogue with these authors emerged in an explicitness that has set me on a path followed in *To Deny Our Nothingness: Contemporary Images of Man.* Meanwhile it has become clear to me that with no sacrifice of the depth-image of modern man and a decisive gain in the faithfulness to the literature, the headings could be subsumed under the authors.

It will be evident to the reader from its relatively small size and the absence of bibliography that the Camus section of this reorganized *Problematic Rebel* by no means represents the intensive study given the other three novelists. Nonetheless, the Camus section is not only important for me personally but is indispensable to the depth-image of modern man that emerges from this portrayal of the "problematic rebel." For this reason also, I have added to the original material some pages on the early Camus from my book *To Deny Our Nothingness: Contemporary Images of Man.*

I have not attempted to bring my bibliographies of Melville, Dostoievsky, and Kafka up to date since the first edition, published in 1963, because I have not read any literature that has altered my readings or that seems to me essential to include; the bibliographies represented in the first place only the works I had consulted, not a comprehensive list. The one exception is the startling and gratifying discovery that Dostoievsky in his journals explicitly speaks of having divided Job, exactly as I said he did, into the Job of faith of Father Zossima and the rebellious Job of Ivan Karamazov!

I wish to acknowledge my indebtedness to Richard Huett and the Delacorte Press for permission to use material from *To Deny Our Nothingness: Contemporary Images of Man* (1967), and to Howard P. Vincent and the Kent State University Press for permission to use material from my essay "Bartleby the Modern Exile" in *The Melville Annual 1965, A Symposium: Bartleby the Scrivener*, edited by Howard P. Vincent (Copyright 1966 by Kent State University Press).

MAURICE FRIEDMAN

Temple University
October 1969

Preface to First Edition

This book grows out of years of concern with the problem of the modern image of man, a concern which has led me to teach such courses as "The Image of Man in Modern Thought" at Sarah Lawrence College, "The Rebel and the Exile in Literature" at the New School for Social Research, and "The Image of Man and Psychotherapy" at the Washington (D.C.) School of Psychiatry and the William Alanson White Institute of Psychiatry, Psychoanalysis and Psychology. Specifically, *Problematic Rebel* is based on an intensive study of three modern writers—Herman Melville, Fyodor Dostoievsky, and Franz Kafka—as well as a more extensive study of the novels of Albert Camus and a number of other literary works, both ancient and modern. It integrates these studies around such themes as the Modern Exile, the Modern Promethean, and the "problematic" of modern man, and it derives from this combination of studies and themes an image of modern man—the Problematic Rebel and the Modern Job.

The image of modern man that grows out of this book is, above all, a product of the meeting of philosophy and literature. It is at once philosophy *of* literature and philosophy *through* literature. More precisely, it is the product of approaching literature in terms of the "image of man" that emerges when a character is portrayed in sufficient depth that he speaks to us, through his very uniqueness, not only of the man of a certain period but of man as such. The image of man represents a mid-point between novel, play, or poem regarded as art and the same regarded as idea. It is particularly important, as a result, in dealing with so-called "novels of ideas," such as those of Melville, Dostoievsky, Kafka, and Camus. The image of man is not a purely literary approach, concerned with literature as a goal in itself. But neither does it use literature as a mere illustration of ready-made philosophical concepts and categories. It goes *through* the faithful interpretation of literature to discover what new understanding of man this literature gives us. Thus it guards the wholeness of many types of fiction, drama, and poetry as most modern schools of literary theory do not.

If one wishes to make a decisive break with the universal "human nature" of earlier philosophy and attain a picture of man in his uniqueness and his wholeness, one must move from *concepts* about man, no matter how profound, to the *image* of man. Our primary source of understanding man is not Berdyaev's systematic presentation of Dostoievsky's thought on man, but Dostoievsky's novels themselves with their completely unsystematic, paradoxical, contrary, but infinitely rich presentation of individual men. The novel or drama which presents an image of man is not *less* but *more* precise than an abstract treatise on the nature of man or an existentialist analysis of the human condition. It says something that cannot be adequately paraphrased in conceptual terms or translated into symbolic meanings, something that cannot be said better, therefore, in some other form. In its very particularity the image of man in literature gives us the wholeness of man as more abstract disciplines cannot. Next to the lives of actual men, literature comes closest to retaining the concrete uniqueness of individual men while at the same time enabling us to enter into a sufficiently close relationship with these men that they can speak to us as bearers of the human—as exemplification of what it does and can mean to be a man.

In the years during which I have been working on *Problematic Rebel* I have become more and more concerned with the *problematic* of a modern image of man—what would be necessary in order for such an image to represent both man as man and modern man. When I speak of "the problematic of modern man," I do not mean simply something that is doubtful or ambiguous or in balance. I mean something that contains such contradictions and paradoxes that I find myself impelled to single out the problematic element by speaking of "the problematic" as such rather than leave it a mere adjective. The problematic is vital in the progression of the book, which proceeds from the discussion of the Modern Exile to two types of rebels—the Modern Promethean and the Modern Job—yet splits up the discussion of these two types by a long section on the Problematic of Modern Man. This is because the Modern Promethean reveals himself on deeper examination to be not only romantic but also problematic, and because it is necessary to go *through* this problematic and to take it up into the more complex figure of the Modern Job for our image of modern man—the Problematic Rebel—to emerge.

I am indebted to John and Betty Musser of St. Paul, Minnesota, for a grant which enabled me to spend the summer of 1958 writing the first draft of the Melville section of this book. I am also indebted to the Lucius N. Littauer Foundation and to its president, Harry Starr, for a grant which helped make it possible for me to spend the academic year of 1959-1960 in Israel and Europe, where I wrote the first drafts of the Dostoievsky and Kafka sections.

I am grateful to Professors William Charvat and M. O. Percival of the Ohio State University, and to Muriel Rukeyser, my colleague at Sarah Lawrence, for their helpful suggestions in connection with the Melville sections and to Professor Lea Goldberg of the Hebrew University, Jerusalem, for reading the Dostoievsky sections. I want also to express my gratitude to my friend Professor Martin Buber for many hours of stimulating discussion of Dostoievsky and Kafka during the weekly visits that my wife and I made to his home in Jerusalem from January to May of 1960. I also owe to my stay in Israel the opportunity to discuss Kafka with three of Kafka's close friends, Dr. Max Brod of Tel Aviv, Dr. Felix Weltsch and Professor Hugo Bergmann of the Hebrew University, Jerusalem. I must express my gratitude, too, to my

friend Morris Philipson of Vintage Books for his encourage-
ment and suggestions over a number of years.

What I owe to my wife, Eugenia, cannot be stated in a
catalogue of acknowledgments. She has given me aid far
beyond what any husband has a right to expect. For the past
three years she has worked unstintingly, assisting me with
the bibliography, selection of significant material, discussion
of ideas, the style, editing, and proofreading. She has been
my partner and co-worker throughout. Without her devoted
help and her belief in this book, it would not have been
possible.

I hope that *Problematic Rebel* is worthy of her devotion.
I hope too that it is not unworthy of Melville, Dostoievsky,
Kafka, and Camus—the four men of integrity and courage
through my dialogue with whom this "depth-image" of modern man has come into being.

MAURICE FRIEDMAN

Sarah Lawrence College
January 1963

——————————

PART ONE

BETWEEN PROMETHEUS AND JOB

1

THE BIBLICAL REBEL
AND THE GREEK REBEL

An "image of man" is neither an ideal nor a mere description but the tension between the two: it is at once "hero" and "everyman." Those either-ors that divide mankind into simple classes or groups are essentially alien to it. For the same reason, a depth-image of modern man can be reached only on the far side of such easy oppositions as "average man" and "superman," "insider" and "outsider," "conformist" and "nonconformist," "organization man" and "loner," "beat" and "square." From a surface, statistical point of view, the vast majority of modern men are not rebels. Many of those who are, moreover, are so obviously dependent upon what they are rebelling against that it is easy to dismiss them as of little significance in themselves. A depth-image of modern man, nonetheless, shows him to be both exile and rebel—not in his relation toward any particular social structure but in his stance toward existence itself. He is, at the same time, a *problematic* rebel. Although his rebellion is neither dubious nor unreal, it is not a simple, heroic rebellion which can be glorified in the image of the romantic hero. It is, rather, a complex, contradictory set of attitudes and actions that reflects his problematic; it is his response to his exile that gives rise to his problematic—his reaction to his alienation and inner division.

Herman Melville, Fyodor Dostoievsky, Franz Kafka, and Albert Camus offer us a depth-image of modern man in his dynamic and complexity. More than any other writers of the nineteenth and twentieth centuries, these men help us to understand the man who knows existence emptied of God and himself as alienated and divided. Melville shows the world in which modern man now finds himself—that of the "death of God"; Dostoievsky sets forth the problematic rebel who lives in this world and tries to find a way out of exile; Kafka depicts a later, more pervasive stage of exile and an unromantic, more deeply problematic man; Camus moves from the Modern Exile who affirms himself *despite* the absurd to the Modern Job who stands in dialogue with the absurd. Taken together they give us many of the most important aspects of an image of modern man. In whatever form we meet this image, it remains a complex and contradictory figure through whom our understanding of the problematic of modern man is deepened—and with it our understanding of ourselves.

To understand what is distinctively modern in this image we must go back to some of the images of man as exile and as rebel that we have inherited from the Greek, Biblical, and Renaissance worlds, in particular those of Prometheus and Job. Modern man stands between Job and Prometheus— not merely in the sense of our double heritage of "Hebraism and Hellenism" to which Matthew Arnold pointed in his essay of that title, but also in an almost directly contrary sense:

modern man has uprooted the figures of Job and Prometheus from the soil which nourished them and gave them meaning. For a poet like Shelley, a novelist like Melville, or an essayist like Camus, Prometheus has become simply the modern rebel, without the order that gave the original Prometheus his strength. Similarly, Nietzsche in *The Birth of Tragedy* understands Prometheus as the symbol of noble Greek disobedience, opposed to the slavish "Semitic" obedience represented in the myth of Adam and Eve. Thomas Hardy, on the other hand, uses the figure of Job, divorced from his dialogue with God, to express modern man's sense of being abandoned in a cold, impersonal universe, while Archibald MacLeish converts Job into a symbol of modern, non-religious humanism. Over the works of Melville, Dostoievsky, and Kafka stand the shadows of both Job and Prometheus. It is not possible to understand the image of modern man without understanding—in their original context and their subsequent transformation—these prototypes that modern man has carried over from the ancient worlds.

BIBLICAL MAN

The crucial difference between the Greek and the Biblical image of man lies in the context in which they are set. In the Greek view the cosmos is already there: gods and men unfold their drama within a self-sufficient world order that is superior to them both—an uncreated reality that maintains and regulates itself. In the Biblical view, in contrast, God really transcends his creation while remaining in relation to it. The Biblical God is not a First Cause or Prime Mover—the initiator and regulator of a universal order. He stands in direct relation to each concrete particular and "sees the fall of every sparrow."

He who removes mountains, and they know it not, . . .
who commands the sun, and it does not rise;
   who seals up the stars;
who alone stretched out the heavens,
   and trampled the waves of the sea; . . . (Job 9:5-8)[1]

[1] Unless otherwise indicated, all references to the Old and New Testaments are from the Revised Standard Version.

Creation does not take place once and for all: God creates
the world anew every day and sustains it at every moment.
Creation is not identical with God; it is the word of God
through which he speaks to man. The mountains, the whirlwind, the animals and flowers are themselves the word of the
creator. They speak to man as what they are, and in this
speech he recognizes the address of God:

The heavens are telling the glory of God;
   and the firmament proclaims his handiwork.
Day to day pours forth speech,
   and night to night declares knowledge.
There is no speech, nor are there words;
   their voice is not heard;
yet their voice goes out through all the earth,
   and their words to the end of the world. (Psalm 19:1-4)

The existence of Biblical man is rooted in hearing and responding. Within this dialogue man has real freedom and
spontaneity. He does not have to choose between being an
Oedipus who must resign himself to his fate or a Prometheus
who rebels against Zeus without hope of a positive response.
Through man's freedom he helps shape history. History is not
here, as in Greek thought, a cyclical process: it is a linear
movement from creation to redemption. The particular, concrete present is the unique moment of revelation, the moment
in which redemption takes place. God speaks to man in the
events of history, and man responds with his existence.

THE BIBLICAL EXILE

The Hebrew Bible begins, if not with an act of rebellion,
at least with an act of disobedience: that act whereby man
became man. In eating of the tree of knowledge of good and
evil, Adam and Eve did not commit evil, since they did not
know what evil was, but they disobeyed the injunction which
protected them against this knowledge and through this disobedience left their existence as children within the Garden
of Eden for the confusion and responsibility of the adult
world. From innocence they moved into experience, from

timelessness into history. Although they were banished from paradise, this first exile does not mean that they were abandoned by God, who remains with them in history as in the Garden. Man enters into exile with the "world all before him," as Milton movingly depicts at the end of *Paradise Lost:*

> They, looking back, all the eastern side beheld
> Of Paradise, so late their happy seat,
> Waved over by that flaming brand; the gate
> With dreadful faces thronged and fiery arms:
> Some natural tears they dropped, but wiped them soon;
> The world was all before them, where to choose
> Their place of rest, and Providence their guide:
> They, hand in hand with wandering steps and slow,
> Through Eden took their solitary way. (Book XII, ll. 641-
>   649)

This first exile is followed by a second when Cain, having slain his brother Abel, is exiled from the very ground from which his brother's blood cries out to God. "When you till the ground, it shall no longer yield to you its strength; you shall be a fugitive wanderer on the earth" (Genesis 4:12). Even in this second, more terrible exile Cain is not abandoned by God, who sets a limit to his suffering.

> Cain said to the Lord, "My punishment is greater than I can bear. Behold, thou hast driven me this day away from the ground; and from thy face I shall be hidden; and I shall be a fugitive and a wanderer on the earth, and whoever finds me will slay me." Then the Lord said to him, "Not so! If any one slay Cain, vengeance shall be taken on him sevenfold." And the Lord put a mark on Cain, lest any who came upon him should kill him. Then Cain went away from the presence of the Lord, and dwelt in the land of Nod, east of Eden. (Gen. 4:13-16)

Another, still more dreadful exile is that reported in the story of the Tower of Babel, when men wished to reach heaven and overcome all the created limits to human existence. As a punishment for this attempt of men to deify themselves and deny any reality transcending them, God doubly exiles them

—from that place and from one another—by confusing their languages and scattering "them abroad from there over the face of all the earth."

At the center of Biblical faith stands not belief, in the ordinary sense of the term, but trust—a trust that no exile from the presence of God is permanent, that each man and each generation is able to come into contact with reality. In the life of individual man, as of generations of men, it is the movement of time—the facts of change and death—which most threatens this trust. Every great religion, culture, and philosophy has observed that "all is flux" and that man himself is a part of this flux. The conclusions that have been drawn from this fact, however, are as different as the world views of those who have drawn the conclusions. The response of Biblical man has not taken the form of a cyclical order of time or an unchanging absolute, like the Greek, nor of the dismissal of time and change as *maya*, or illusion, like the Hindu, nor of the notion that one may flow with time, like the Taoist. He stands face to face with the changing creation and receives each new moment as an address of God—the revelation that comes to him through the unique present.

To stand before eternity is to be aware of one's own mortality:

> For a thousand years in thy sight
> are but as yesterday when it is past, . . .
> men . . . are like a dream, like grass . . .
> in the morning it flourishes and is renewed;
> in the evening it fades and withers. . . .
>   our years come to an end like a sigh. . . .
> yet their span is but toil and trouble;
>   they are soon gone, and we fly away. (Psalm 90:4-10)

This is the universal human condition—a condition which has tempted some men to see existence as unreal or as an ephemeral reflection of reality and others to "eat, drink, and be merry, for tomorrow we die." The psalmist, in contrast, prays that he may withstand this reality and heighten it, that he may make his existence real by meeting each new moment with the wholeness of his being:

So teach us to number our days
That we may get a heart of wisdom. (Psalm 90:12)

In Ecclesiastes, however, the product of a later stage of
Hellenistic wisdom literature, we find that the trust of Biblical man has declined in exact proportion as the movement of
time has come to seem to him an exile in which he is cut off
from the presence of God. Although the author of Ecclesiastes
still believes in God, he no longer believes that he can meet
God and find reality in his everyday life. Time for him is no
longer a succession of concrete presents in each of which one
may meet God, but a never-ending flow from future to past in
which "nothing is new under the sun" and "all is vanity." The
very repetition of seasons and of situations makes time a
meaningless cycle for him and all human effort vain:

For everything there is a season, and a time for every
matter under heaven:
a time to be born, and a time to die; . . .
a time to kill, and a time to heal; . . .
a time to weep, and a time to laugh;
a time to mourn, and a time to dance; . . .
a time to keep silence, and a time to speak;
a time to love, and a time to hate;
a time for war, and a time for peace.
What gain has the worker from his toil? . . .
That which is, already has been; that which is to be, already has been. (Eccl. 3:1-15)

The conclusion of Ecclesiastes is "Remember also your
Creator in the days of your youth, before the evil days come,
and the years draw nigh, when you will say, 'I have no pleasure in them.'" The emphasis is not on the relationship with
God, however, but on the melancholy sadness of the passing
away of youth and of life:

Before the sun and the light, and the moon, and the stars
are darkened and the clouds return after the rain; in the
day when the keepers of the house tremble, and the strong
men are bent, and the grinders cease because they are few,
and those that look through the windows are dimmed,
and the doors on the street are shut; when the sound of

the grinding is low, and one rises up at the voice of a
bird, and all the daughters of song are brought low; . . .
and terrors are in the way; the almond tree blossoms, the
grasshopper drags itself along and desire fails; because
man goes to his eternal home, and the mourners go about
the streets; before the silver cord is snapped, or the
golden bowl is broken, or the pitcher is broken at the
fountain, or the wheel broken at the cistern, and the dust
returns to the earth as it was, and the spirit returns to
God who gave it. Vanity of vanities, says the Preacher;
all is vanity. (Eccl. 12:1-8)

The increasing sense of exile which leads from Psalm 90 to
Ecclesiastes is paralleled in the movement from the Psalms
to the Book of Job, though in Job, in contrast to Ecclesiastes,
the heightening of the exile ultimately results in a deepening of trust. At first sight, the trust of Biblical man seems to
be based on the expectation that his relationship with God
will protect him from the ordinary vicissitudes that beset
other men:

He who dwells in the shelter of the Most High,
who abides in the shadow of the Almighty,
will say to the Lord, "My refuge and my fortress;
    my God, in whom I trust."
For he will deliver you from the snare of the fowler
    and from the deadly pestilence;
he will cover you with his pinions,
and under his wings you will find refuge; . . .
You will not fear the terror of the night,
    nor the arrow that flies by day,
nor the pestilence that stalks in darkness,
    nor the destruction that wastes at noonday. (Psalm
    91:1-6)

Yet the psalmist does not actually see God as guaranteeing
him against danger. He trusts *in spite of* the evils of life, for
his relationship with God is the very meaning of his life—
more important than evil or death:

The Lord is my shepherd, I shall not want;
    he makes me lie down in green pastures.
He leads me beside still waters;

he restores my soul. . . .
Even though I walk through the valley of the shadow of
 death,
 I fear no evil;
for thou art with me. (Psalm 23:1-4)

It is not only man's mortality, however, but the suffering of
the innocent and the prosperity of the wicked that leads to
the tempering of trust in Job and in the Psalms. The reaffirmation of trust takes place out of an immediate sense of exile:

My God, my God, why hast thou forsaken me?
 Why art thou so far from helping me, from the words
 of my groaning?
O my God, I cry by day, but thou dost not answer;
 and by night, but find no rest. . . .
. . . I am a worm, and no man;
 scorned by men, and despised by the people.
All who see me mock at me, . . .
 they make mouths at me, they wag their heads;
"He committed his cause to the Lord; let him deliver
 him . . . !"
Be not far from me,
 for trouble is near
 and there is none to help. (Psalm 22:1-11)

When God no longer prepares a table for the good man in
the presence of his enemies; when the good man sees, not the
recompense of the wicked, but their prosperity and their ar-
rogance, his trust is shaken. He cannot bear the fact that the
presence of God is emptied out of the world, that the sinners
who cannot stand in the judgment are nonetheless confirmed
by the congregation, and divine and social reality are split
asunder. He confesses that his feet had almost stumbled out
of envy of the arrogant:

 They are not in trouble as other men are;
  they are not stricken like other men.
 Therefore pride is their necklace;
  violence covers them as a garment. . . .
 They scoff and speak with malice;
  loftily they threaten oppression. (Psalm 73:5-8)

Yet he regains his trust when he realizes that the wicked are set "in slippery places," that they have deprived themselves of true existence. It is the wicked who are in exile and not he, for they are far from God:

> My flesh and my heart may fail,
> but God is the strength of my heart and my portion for
> ever.
> For lo, those who are far from thee shall perish;
> thou dost put an end to those who are false to thee.
> But for me it is good to be near God . . . (Psalm
> 73:26-28)

In Psalm 73 the wicked "are like a dream when one awakes." But in Psalm 82 the wicked remain all too real, and it is God who must awake and judge them. The earth is given over to the hands of unjust judges—"gods and sons of the most high" who "show partiality to the wicked" rather than aiding the weak and the fatherless and maintaining "the right of the afflicted and destitute." These judges "have neither knowledge nor understanding, they walk about in darkness," and through them, "all the foundations of the earth are shaken." As in the myths of the ancient Gnostics, the world is given over to evil archons and God is beyond reach. The psalmist can no longer take comfort from the inauthentic existence of the wicked and the nearness to God of the good. Rather, he calls upon God to arise and judge the earth so that the wicked may "die like men" and "fall like any prince." Although he has not lost his trust, he cannot dispel the reality of exile.

On the ground of this exile stands Job—the Biblical rebel.

JOB: THE BIBLICAL REBEL

It is not theology but anthropology, not the metaphysical problem of evil but the problem of man, which is the real starting point of the Book of Job. Job, too, asks "What is man that Thou art mindful of him?" He does not ask it out of wonder, however, like the psalmist, but out of despair over the paradox of man's existence as at once an unreflecting animal immersed in the flow of sensation and a self that is called into being and that recognizes the demand which its existence places on it.

> "What is man, that thou dost make so much of him,
>   and that thou dost set thy mind upon him,
> dost visit him every morning,
>   and test him every moment?" (Job 7:17-18)

In cursing the day of his birth, Job does something far worse than cursing God, as his wife urges him to do in Chapter 2: he denies the creator who made him and the creation in which he is set. This denial is not primarily rebellion, however; it is exile. Job experiences the most terrible exile that Biblical man can know: that sense of abandonment by God that undermines the very meaning of his existence. The abyss has opened beneath Job; his life has become insupportable to him, and the only relief he can imagine is death.

> "Why did I not die at birth,
>   come forth from the womb and expire? . . .
> Why is light given to him that is in misery,
>   and life to the bitter in soul,
> who long for death, but it comes not,
>   and dig for it more than for hid treasures . . .
> Why is light given to a man whose way is hid,
>   whom God has hedged in?
> For my sighing comes as my bread,
>   and my groanings are poured out like water.
> For the thing that I fear comes upon me,
>   and what I dread befalls me.
> I am not at ease, nor am I quiet;
>   I have no rest; but trouble comes." (3:20-26)

In contrast to Job, his three friends begin with the general proposition that God rewards the good and punishes the evil, and deduce from it the particular—the assertion that Job suffers because he is guilty. Although they know that Job is the most upright and God-fearing of men, that he was "eyes to the blind and feet to the lame," and that he sought out the cause of him he did not know, they accuse him of having mistreated the widows, the orphans, and the poor. They look away from the existential reality of Job's unique situation rather than face the question raised by his suffering. The god that they argue for, as a result, is not the real God whom Job encounters, but an idol—the product of their own rationalized theology. They see neither Job nor God as he really is, and Job in rebuking them witnesses not only for himself but for the God who transcends all their conceptions of his nature.

> "Will you speak falsely for God,
>   and speak deceitfully for him?
> Will you show partiality toward him,
>   will you plead the case for God?
> Will it be well with you when he searches you out?
>   Or can you deceive him, as one deceives a man?
> He will surely rebuke you
>   if in secret you show partiality.
> Will not his majesty terrify you,
>   and the dread of him fall upon you?
> Your maxims are proverbs of ashes,
>   your defences are defences of clay." (13:7-12)

Eliphaz the Temanite, one of the three friends, begins his speech to Job with the reaffirmation of the orthodox formula:

> "Think now, who that was innocent ever perished?
>   Or where were the upright cut off?
> As I have seen, those who plow iniquity
>   and sow trouble reap the same." (4:7-8)

But he continues with a genuinely numinous vision of transcendence, a fascinating and terrifying encounter with the *Mysterium Tremendum* that leaves in its wake a sense of the Wholly Otherness of God and the creatureliness of man:[2]

---

[2] I use here the terminology of Rudolph Otto's classic study of religion, *The Idea of the Holy*, trans. John W. Harvey (New York: Galaxy Books, 1960). Speaking of the manifestation of the divine as, to begin with, irrational and impersonal, Otto writes, "It has its wild and demonic forms and can sink to an almost grisly horror and shuddering. . . . It may become the hushed, trembling, and speechless humility of the creature in the presence of . . . that which is a *Mystery* inexpressible and above all creatures." (Chap. IV, pp. 12 f.)

"Dread came upon me, and trembling,
  which made all my bones shake.
A spirit glided past my face;
  the hair of my flesh stood up. . . .
  there was silence, then I heard a voice:
'Can mortal man be righteous before God?
  Can a man be pure before his Maker?
Even in his servants he puts no trust,
  and his angels he charges with error;
how much more those who dwell in houses of clay,
  whose foundation is in the dust,
  who are crushed before the moth.
Between morning and evening they are destroyed;
  they perish for ever without any regarding it.'"
  (4:14-20)

Job recognizes the transcendence of God and the mortality of man as clearly as his friends. But he does not stop there. His very knowledge that he will die makes him demand all the more insistently that God come near to him again and recognize the justice of his plaint:

"Remember that my life is a breath . . .
  while thy eyes are upon me, I shall be gone." (7:7-8)

It is out of the ground of his very exile that Job rebels, and his personal sense of exile is intensified by his bitter knowledge that man's days are numbered and that he must spend his limited life in "months of emptiness" and "nights of misery."

"The eye of him who sees me will behold me no more . . .
  he who goes down to Sheol does not come up . . .
Therefore I will not restrain my mouth:
  I will speak in the anguish of my spirit;
  I will complain in the bitterness of my soul." (7:8-11)

Scared by dreams and terrified by visions, Job "would choose strangling and death rather than my bones." His very loathing of his life makes him beg God to let him alone, "for my days are a breath."

"How long wilt thou not look away from me,
    nor let me alone till I swallow my spittle?
If I sin, what do I do to thee, thou watcher of men?"
    (7:19-20)

Yet in words of the utmost pathos Job pleads that God pardon his transgression and take away his iniquity for the sake of that very dialogue which Job seems to have just denied.

The basic paradox of the Hebrew Bible is the dialogue between eternal God and mortal man, between the imageless Absolute and man who is created in God's "image." If that dialogue is to take place, it must take place not in eternity but in the present—in the unique situation of a limited man who was born yesterday and will die tomorrow. Like Jacob wrestling with the angel, Job wrestles with God to receive the blessing of this dialogue on which the very meaning of his existence depends. Job demands of God that he not let his days slip away like a breath, "for now I shall lie in the earth; thou wilt seek me, but I shall not be" (7:21).

But Job also knows that he cannot speak with God as with a man like himself, that he is crushed by God's very transcendence. He cannot appeal from God to some order ultimately stronger than God, as does Prometheus,

"For he is not a man, as I am, that I might answer him,
    that we should come to trial together.
There is no umpire between us,
    who might lay his hand upon us both." (9:32-33)

Even if Job summoned him and he answered, Job would not believe that God was listening to his voice,

"For he crushes me with a tempest,
    and multiplies my wounds without cause;
he will not let me get my breath,
    but fills me with bitterness. . . .
Though I am innocent, my own mouth would condemn
    me;
    though I am blameless, he would prove me perverse."
    (9:17-20)

It is on the ground of this utter hopelessness that Job stands and contends, and indicts God with a bitterness unequaled in the Bible or any other scripture:

> "I am blameless; I regard not myself;
>   I loathe my life.
> It is all one; *therefore I say,*
>   he destroys both the blameless and the wicked.
> When disaster brings sudden death,
>   he mocks at the calamity of the innocent.
> The earth is given into the hand of the wicked;
>   he covers the faces of its judges—
> if it is not he, who then is it?" (9:21-24, italics mine.)

In Psalm 82 the psalmist sees the earth as given over to the hands of unjust judges, but he does not accuse God himself of injustice, far less suggest that, like some grinning devil or evil Gnostic creator god, he "mocks at the calamity of the innocent." Job never gives up his trust in the creator who is also his redeemer, but he can only recognize him as the God of the real world in which the innocent suffer while the wicked prosper. Were Job to experience an evil so terrible that he could not recognize the voice of God in it, he would no longer be able to trust in God; for trust in God, at its deepest level, means trust in existence. Job's "temptation" is that he may not be able to go beyond the cursing of his own existence—that he may find it impossible to bring his suffering, his loathing, and his horror into his dialogue with God.

Job's temptation is equally, however, that he will not stand his ground and witness for his own innocence when no one else will do so.

> "Let him take his rod away from me,
>   and let not dread of him terrify me.
> Then I would speak without fear of him,
>   for I am not so in myself." (9:34-35)

In the end Job withstands *both* temptations—that which comes to him from his bitterness and that which comes from his dread: he neither denies God nor ceases to contend with him. "He may indeed slay me, I am ready to accept it," [3] says Job, "yet I will defend my ways to his face" (13:15).

Job speaks for man because he speaks for himself. He penetrates so deeply into the uniqueness of his own situation that his protest becomes a protest against the suffering of all men, his witness for himself a witness for man as such. Job is the true existentialist. He does not begin with any theories of the nature of God or of the nature of man. He holds fast to his trust in the real God whom he meets in the dreadful fate that has befallen him, and he holds fast to the facts of his innocence and his suffering. At the heart of the Book of Job stands neither "blind faith" nor denial of God, but trusting *and* contending, recognizing his dependence on God yet standing firm on the ground of his created freedom.

Job's most famous statement of trust—"I know that my Redeemer lives"—refers to a future, but not, as is commonly thought, one beyond the grave. It is not disembodied that he will see God,[4] but in this life at that future hour when God has come near to him again: "whom I shall see for myself,[5] and my eyes shall behold, and not another" (19:25-27). It is precisely this that happens to Job at the end of the poem, and he expresses this happening in the identical words: "I had heard of thee by the hearing of the ear, but now my eye sees thee" (42:5).

"The fear of the Lord," quotes Job, "that is wisdom" (28: 28). Like the typical modern man, Job does not have the security that may be derived from a belief in personal immortality,

---

[3] My own translation, with Martin Buber's help, from Buber's German, "Wohl, er mag mich erschlagen, ich harre dessen," in which "harre," as Buber himself explains, has something of awaiting in it—accepting and being ready at once. (*Die Schrift*, trans. from Hebrew into German by Martin Buber in co-operation with Franz Rosenzweig, IV, *Die Schriftwerke* [Köln and Olten: Jakob Hegner Verlag, 1961.]) Buber's translation seems to me to strike the right middle point between the King James Version's "Yea though he slay me, I will trust in him" and the Revised Standard Version's "He will slay me; I have no hope."

[4] Martin Buber has explained to me the phrase that is ordinarily translated "without my flesh" as "from my flesh" or "without my skin." Job's skin is peeling off because of his sickness.

[5] Again Buber's rendition.

"For there is hope for a tree,
  if it be cut down, that it will sprout again . . .
But man dies, and is laid low;
  man breathes his last, and where is he?" (14:7-10)

If only there were immortality, Job would wait eagerly until
his release should come and he could enter again into the
dialogue with God:

"Thou wouldest call, and I would answer thee;
  thou wouldest long for the work of thy hands.
For then thou wouldest number my steps,
  thou wouldest not keep watch over my sin." (14:15-16)

But Job knows that such a hope would be vain. Job is also
like modern man in that he does not think of the earth either
as the center of the universe or as planted on secure foundations.

"He stretches out the north over the void,
    and hangs the earth upon nothing." (26:7)

Job shares the wonder before the "heavens" that leads the
psalmist to question "What is man?" the wonder whose modern expression is Pascal's terror before the silence of the infinite spaces.

"The pillars of heaven tremble,
  and are astounded at his rebuke. . . .
Lo, these are but the outskirts of his ways;
  and how small a whisper do we hear of him!
But the thunder of his power who can understand?"
  (26:11-14)

For all this, the words of the Lord that reach Job out of
the whirlwind come in the form of a rebuke for "darkening
counsel without knowledge." Job has wanted a dialogue with
God, but when this dialogue comes it dismays him by forcing
him to recognize that the partner with whom he speaks is the
creator who "laid the foundation of the earth."

"Gird up your loins like a man,
  I will question you, and you shall declare to me.
Where were you when I laid the foundation of the earth?

Tell me, if you have understanding . . .
when the morning stars sang together,
and all the sons of God shouted for joy?" (38:3-7)

The reality of creation is the reality of the otherness that Job
cannot remove into his rational comprehension of the world.
Job has presumed to do what no man can properly do—to
grasp the whole of creation in such a way that he might pro-
nounce not merely on his own innocence and his suffering,
but also on the injustice God has done to him and to the innocent in general. Instead of seeing God's justice in terms
of his unique relationship with God, he has sought to objec-
tify and measure it, to set his suffering and his merits on a
comparative scale with that of other men. He has sought to
"anthropomorphize" creation—to rationalize reality to fit
the moral conceptions of man. Despite man's power to "comprehend" the world, it has a reality independent of him
which makes it ludicrous to speak, like Thomas Gray, of a
flower that "wastes its sweetness on the desert air."

"Who has cleft a channel for the torrents of rain,
and a way for the thunderbolt,
to bring rain on a land where no man is,
on the desert in which there is no man;
to satisfy the waste and desolate land,
and to make the ground put forth grass?" (38:25-27)

The real God is not the God whom man removes into the
sphere of his own spirit and thought, but the creator who
speaks to man through creatures that exist for their own sake
and not just for human purposes. The hippopotamus and
the crocodile confront man with a terrifying reality of otherness that he cannot ignore and remind him that their creator
is more terrible still.

"Behold, Behemoth,
which I made as I made you; . . .
His bones are tubes of bronze,
his limbs like bars of iron.
He is the first of the works of God. . . .
Can you draw out Leviathan with a fishhook,
or press down his tongue with a cord? . . .

None is so fierce that he dares to stir him up.
  Who then is he that can stand before me?
  Who has given to me, that I should repay him?
    Whatever is under the whole heaven is mine." (40:15,
      18-19; 41:1, 10-11)

Job despises himself and repents in dust and ashes because
he "uttered what I did not understand, things too wonderful
for me, which I did not know" (42:3). This does not mean
that he repents of his contending itself. On the contrary, the
Lord upholds Job and rebukes his hypocritical friends, "for
you have not spoken of me what is right, as my servant Job
has" (42:7). What Job repents of is stated with utmost precision in God's answer itself:

  "Will you even put me in the wrong?
    Will you condemn me that you may be justified?"
    (40:8)

Job is wrong not because he has witnessed for himself and
contended with God but because he could not justify himself
without condemning God, because he had to put God in the
wrong in order that he might feel more securely in the right.
He substituted for his desire to know God directly in dialogue the Gnostic's attempt to comprehend the whole of creation as if he were not himself a part of it.

  Job's repentance does not mean the end of his dialogue
with God but its real beginning.

    " 'Hear, and I will speak;
      I will question you, and you declare to me.'
    I had heard of thee by the hearing of the ear,
      but now my eye sees thee." (42:4-5)

This is the real answer which Job receives and not the Epilogue which restores to him his health, his riches, and another
set of children. When God comes near to Job again, this suffering, without being any less real, is taken up into the dialogue that stands at the center of his existence. Through his
very rebellion he has received an answering response which
leaves him no longer an exile.

  Whereas Ecclesiastes tells us only of the universal human

condition, the Book of Job penetrates so deeply into the unique situation of one man that it offers an image for all men. This image includes the existential situation of a man who suffers and despairs, the question about man and about the meaning of his own existence that this situation produces, and the courage and strength of the Biblical rebel who both trusts and contends. What it does *not* include, in any objectifiable form, is the answer to Job's question. This answer is not found in the speeches of the Lord from the whirlwind—these set the limits on Job's presumption, but they cannot restore his trust. It is found in God's coming near to him again, in God's entering into dialogue with him. This event cannot be translated into a general truth that may be applied to the situation of other men, much less an assurance that others who trust and contend will receive an answer as Job has. The answer that Job receives as to the meaning of his suffering cannot be detached from his unique relationship with God. No objective metaphysical solution to the problem of evil, correspondingly, can be an answer to Job's personal, existential question as to whether he can once again see God in the midst of the darkness that overwhelms him. That Job does once again experience immediacy with God enters, nonetheless, into the image of exile and deepened trust which Job presents us; for this experience belongs to Job's uniqueness, and it is his very uniqueness that makes him an image of man.

OEDIPUS, ANTIGONE, AND PROMETHEUS: THE GREEK EXILE AND THE GREEK REBEL

In speaking of "slavish Semitic obedience," Nietzsche, of course, ignores the figure of Job, who contends with God as no one before or since. He also ignores the figure of Oedipus, who submits to fate in a way that would be unthinkable to Job. Still more important, for our purposes, he ignores the fact that Oedipus is not only much more typical of the Greek world view than Prometheus but also lays the foundation for a proper understanding of the latter. In Sophocles' presentation of the tragedy of Oedipus the King, Aristotle found the classical pattern for tragedy, and in it, too, we find the classic expression of the Greek world view. The Greek world view begins with an already existent cosmos—an order of existence which is more powerful than Zeus himself, an order (*moira*) in which impersonal fate is the final determinant. Man is free to rebel against this order, but only at the cost of *nemesis*—that destruction which the order visits on those who violate it—or of a reconciliation attained through his own suffering and perhaps death. The hopeful element in the Greek view is that there *is* an order in which man can find a place. The tragic element is that to remain in harmony with this order he must pay the price of the loss of something of his humanity, something of his full possibility of personal existence. The Greek virtues of moderation (*sophrosiné*) and goodness (*arêté*) reflect that same emphasis upon keeping one's place in the order. This is what underlies Heraclitus' assertion that if the sun stepped out of its appointed orbit, the *Erinyes* (or Furies) would pursue it. But for a man to subsume himself under an order means something different than for an inanimate object to do so, even one as great as the sun. For man does so not through impersonal law but through his character and consciousness itself.

"Character," said Heraclitus, "is destiny [$\delta\alpha\iota\mu\omega\nu$] for man." It is his *daimon*. Although the Greek concept of fate is of an all-pervasive force, this does not mean, as in modern determinism, that man is determined by the past as a link in a chain of cause and effect. Although it is predestined that Oedipus will kill his father and marry his mother, as the oracle predicts, this in no way means a limitation of his free *will*. His every move is not conditioned, as in modern determinism; nor is he a puppet pulled by strings. If the fate that has been predicted is inescapable, it is he himself who works out his fate through his own character and free act.

Oedipus is the tragedy of the human person in relation to the order—the hero whose fall is at once the penalty for an individual overstepping of the limits and the taking upon himself of the responsibility for the group. The very superiority which sets Oedipus above ordinary men as an exemplar for them also brings his downfall. This downfall comes not only through the fact that he oversteps the limits of success

allowed to man, but also that his knowledge of his own superiority breeds a pride and impatience that contribute to
his peripety. When Oedipus goes to the oracle, disturbed by
the assertion of a drunken companion that the king and
queen of Corinth are not his true parents, he does not receive any answer to his question but instead is told that he
will kill his father and marry his mother. Yet he rushes away
from home in order to avoid fulfilling the oracle, and precisely
thereby meets his real father, Laius, on the road. When he
kills Laius, this action too takes place through his own im-
petuous character. A lone youth, on foot, he refuses to make
way for Laius' equipage, and when the latter brings his goad
down on his head, he kills Laius and five of his six servants.
Again, when he learns that the plague has been brought on
Thebes through the sin of one man, he is quick to accuse the
blind sage Tiresias and after him his own brother-in-law
Creon. He decides not to have Creon killed but to exile him,
stating at the same time that he will hate him wherever he
goes. Creon's reply aptly describes the "tragic flaw" through
which Oedipus' own character becomes his destiny:

> I see thy mercy moving full of hate
> And slow; thy wrath came swift and desperate.
> Methinks, of all the pain that such a heart
> Spreadeth, itself doth bear the bitterest part. (vv. 673-
> 676)[6]

" 'Tis Apollo, all is Apollo," says Oedipus after the horrible
truth has been revealed to him.

> . . . 'tis he long time hath planned
> These things upon me evilly, evilly,
> Dark things and full of blood.
> I knew not; I did but follow
> His way. . . .
> What man saith
> God hath so hated him? (vv. 1329-1334, 1345-1346)

Yet Apollo did not intervene at all. It is Apollo's doing only in
the sense that the Delphic oracle of Apollo predicted what

6 Sophocles, *Oedipus, King of Thebes*, trans. Gilbert Murray (New York:
Oxford University Press, 1911).

was to happen and that this prediction amounts to an inescapable fate. Oedipus knows that he did the whole thing himself—"but mine the hand/And mine the anguish"—and he did it not as a mere automaton but of his own free, if ignorant, will. Therefore to Oedipus there is no contradiction in blaming Apollo and at the same time taking on himself full responsibility for his action. It is his own hand that has wronged his parents "too deep for man to understand."

> I that was chief in Thebes alone, and ate
> The King's bread, I have made me separate
> For ever. Mine own lips have bid the land
> Cast from it one so evil. . . .
> My misery
> Is mine, and shall be borne by none but me. (vv. 1380-
>   1383, 1414-1415)

When Oedipus sees Creon, moreover, he recognizes how the evil that he has committed unknowingly has been crowned by the conscious evil that he has been impelled to by his character.

> Alas, what word to Creon can I speak,
> How make him trust me more? He hath seen of late
> So vile a heart in me, so full of hate. (vv. 1419-1421)

What is more, although the same pollution that taints him taints the children who are at once his sisters and his daughters, he wants all the punishment and ill effects to rest on him and none on them.

Oedipus' character is his destiny. There is, indeed, the prophecy, but the prophecy does not in itself compel his actions. That Oedipus himself works out the destiny that is fated for him is much more terrible than if he had been simply acted upon by external mechanisms, for in the latter case one need not identify with the power that shapes one's fate, whereas in the former case one must. It would be unthinkable for Oedipus to defy the order as separate from him and hostile to him, since he recognizes his place in the order and knows that the order acts through him and not just on him. But for this reason, too, Oedipus' fate is much more deeply significant in relation to the whole than any modern, purely external determinism could be. In direct contrast to the modern man, who, on the plea of an "Oedipus complex," sometimes denies responsibility for deeds he has knowingly committed, Oedipus reasserts his personality in the face of the order by taking responsibility for his actions even when he was unaware of their true meaning. From being a mere pawn, impersonally moved or acted upon by the order, he faces the universe once more as a person who freely accepts his fate and, to that extent, shows himself superior to it.

Like Aristotle's tragic hero for whom Oedipus served as a model, Oedipus' fate is worse than he deserves. His "tragic flaw" does not compare to the terrible misery of his swift downfall. Sophocles' *Oedipus the King* is pervaded, in fact, by a sense of evil that goes beneath all moral questions to an original separation between the holy and the profane, the clean and the unclean, the permitted and the taboo. Oedipus does not speak of his crime in moral terms but in terms of purity and pollution. He speaks of his "polluting arms" and asks, "Am I a thing born evil? Am I foul in every vein?" Both Oedipus and the Chorus appeal to the cleanness of God to purify what has been here defiled, and both plumb the depths of the problem of evil with the question of whether there is uncleanness and impurity at the very heart of the order itself. After Oedipus has blinded himself, the Chorus wails, "Do there crawl/Live Things of Evil from the deep/ To leap on man?" and Oedipus himself says, "Where, Thing of Evil, where/Endeth thy leaping hither?" Is there something evil in the nature of the universe itself? Even before the full revelation, the horror that lies in wait is reflected in the weakening of the Chorus' faith in the goodness of the order:

> In a world where such things be,
> What spirit has shield or lance
> To ward him secretly
> From the arrow that slays askance?
> If honour to such things be,
> Why should I dance my dance? (vv. 893-898)

This problem is deepened by the fact that although the Chorus separates itself from the unclean Oedipus and wishes that it had never seen his face, it not only pities Oedipus but is terrified by him as well. This terror, as Aristotle points out in the *Poetics,* is the result of our identification with the tragic hero. It is not so much an individual identification, however, as it is the clear vision that Oedipus is an image of man for all men, that his fate is a commentary on human existence in general.

> Nothingness, nothingness,
> Ye Children of Man, and less
> I count you, waking or dreaming!
> And none among mortals, none,
> Seeking to live, hath won
> More than to seem, and to cease
> Again from his seeming.
> While ever before mine eyes
> One fate, one ensample lies—
> Thine, thine, O Oedipus . . .
> What thing is human more
> Dare I call blessed? (vv. 1186-1198)

The very fact that Oedipus stood so high above men makes his fall so far below them all the more terrifying.

> Straight his archery flew
> To the heart of living; he knew
> Joy and the fulness of power. . . .
> But now, what man's story is such bitterness to speak?
> What life hath Delusion so visited, and Pain,
> And swiftness of Disaster? (vv. 1199-1201, 1209-1210)

From being the loved one of Fortune and the mightiest of mortal men Oedipus plummets to the miserable outcast who has put out his own eyes and has been led out of Thebes as one too foul to be looked upon by men. This same peripety is emphasized in the final chorus, and the moral for man's fate is drawn still more explicitly:

> Therefore, O Man, beware, and look toward the end of
>   things that be,

The last of sights, the last of days; and no man's life account as gain
Ere the full tale be finished and the darkness find him
without pain. (vv. 1528-1530)

Man's life as such is a life of pain and disaster. It is not a
life without meaning, but the meaning is a tragic one—the
reconciliation of the human person with the order through a
loss that is terribly real. Sophocles does not look away from
the true tragedy of human existence, but neither does he see
man's fate as a bitter or ironic one. The Greek order is not
the spatial, quantitative one of the modern scientific cosmos
—an order that works upon man externally. It is a moral order in the deepest sense of the term—a qualitative order in
which man finds his place again and again through discovering his potentialities and his fateful limitations. These two together—man's potentialities and his limits—constitute the
Greek tragic vision.

Oedipus the tragic hero is also Oedipus the exile. He undergoes three separate exiles, in fact. The first comes when
his parents, in a futile attempt to avoid the fate predicted by
the oracle, give him to a shepherd who, instead of leaving
him to die on the mountain, gives him to another shepherd
who takes him to the king and queen of Corinth. The second
comes when he leaves his home in Corinth in another futile
attempt to avoid his predestined fate. The third comes when
he discovers the truth about himself, puts his eyes out, and
asks to be led out of Thebes as an unclean being unfit to remain in the community. In *Oedipus at Colonus* we learn that
this last exile, from being a voluntary one, becomes an en-
forced one when Oedipus himself becomes reconciled to his
fate and is ready to remain in Thebes but his sons insist that
he be sent away. Oedipus dies in exile, moreover, cursing his
son Polyneices and his brother-in-law Creon who come to
bring him back in order to have the good fortune that his remains will bring the land in which he lies.

Underlying all of these exiles, however, is the exile of the tragic hero himself: the exile of the man who must be brought low just because he has been high, of the hero who tests the limits of human potentialities and becomes thereby a gloomy object lesson of the limitations which the order sets to human fulfillment. At an even deeper level is the exile that Oedipus experiences as a member of the house of the Labdacidae whose sorrows, in the words of the Chorus of *Antigone*, are "from olden time . . . heaped upon the sorrows of the dead; and generation is not freed by generation, but some god strikes them down, and the race hath no deliverance." This exile is still more terrible than that of the tragic hero who commits *hybris* and suffers a downfall through the realization of his potentialities as a person and a human being. Here something has gone wrong within the order itself —something has become "out of order" and cannot be set right. As a result of this flaw within the order, Oedipus is *destined* to violate the order, to become the "unclean" man whose actions have placed him outside the order. The basis of all tragedy to the Greeks is the violation of the order, and the "pity and terror" occasioned by the downfall of the tragic hero reflect both the "tragic flaw" through which this downfall has come and the undeserved fate that has overtaken the hero. But to the Greeks there could be no more horrible tragedy than that of the man who is destined to cut himself off from the order, for this man is an exile from his very birth.

Antigone, the daughter of Oedipus, inherits this same state of exile. She too must suffer the fate that inexorably dogs her family. She goes into exile with Oedipus and returns only to find herself in the impossible situation created by the division between her brothers, each of whom has slaughtered the other—Eteocles in defending the city, Polyneices in attacking it. Her uncle Creon, who now succeeds to the throne of Thebes, decrees that Eteocles is to be buried in honor while Polyneices is to be left unburied, an object of shame to be eaten by the vultures. In defying this decree and attempting to bury her brother with her own hands, Antigone goes a step beyond Oedipus and becomes not only an exile but also a rebel. Unlike the modern rebel, however, she is rebelling not against the past in the name of the present, but against the present in the name of the past. The laws of the gods ordain that a dead man must be buried, so that his soul may not wander forever but go down to the underworld which now has jurisdiction over him. Creon, in violating this law for the sake of political necessity as he sees it and in insisting on putting Antigone to death rather than suffer any challenge to his authority, is laying bare and intensifying a rift in the order itself.

This rift, in the first instance, takes the form of a conflict between family and state in which Creon has no hesitation in sacrificing family ties for loyalty to the state, while Antigone sees nothing shameful in defying the state and separating herself from all of her fellow citizens out of loyalty to her brother. More basically, it is a conflict between the laws of the gods—the laws of the older tradition which Antigone upholds—and the laws of the state—the decrees which the tyrant proclaims and enforces. In such a situation, Antigone is, on the face of it, necessarily in the wrong. When she asks her sister Ismene to join her in her action and the latter refuses, Antigone says, "If *thou* wilt, be guilty of dishonouring laws which the gods have stablished in honour," to which Ismene replies, "I do them no dishonour; but to defy the State,—I have no strength for that." Antigone sees the situation as one necessitating choice: she cannot both obey the gods and obey Creon. Ismene is content to rest on good intentions to the gods coupled with compliance to the state.

The Chorus goes further, however, and makes Antigone herself responsible for her fate. Her character, like that of her father, is the tragic flaw which will bring about her downfall: "The maid shows herself passionate child of passionate sire, and knows not how to bend before troubles." Even when Antigone is going to her death and the Chorus bestows on her a grudging admiration, it still makes her entirely to blame in her conflict with Creon. Since he represents the state, her action is necessarily "self-will."

Reverent action claims a certain praise for reverence; but an offence against power cannot be brooked by him who hath power in his keeping. Thy self-willed temper hath wrought thy ruin. (vv. 861-911)[7]

Antigone herself complains that through being pious she finds herself impious—the one singled out for violation of the state and the divine order which it represents. That her piety could have such a result leads her, like the Chorus in *Oedipus,* to doubt the order itself: "What law of heaven have I transgressed? Why, hapless one, should I look to the gods any more,—what ally should I invoke,—when by piety I have earned the name of impious?"

The Greek tragic view is thus bound up in the deepest sense with the problem of evil. This problem in *Antigone* is that of the relation of man to the order, the abyss that opens up beneath the feet of the man who stands on the ground of faithfulness to the divine laws. Antigone, however, is not a tragic hero in the traditional sense of the term, despite her pride and inflexibility. It is, rather, Creon who embodies the tragic flaw and who points once again the moral of the man who commits *hybris* and is punished with *nemesis.* Creon is as arrogant and tyrannical in his dealings with Antigone as he is unsure. "While I live, no woman shall rule me," he exclaims. Later he explicitly identifies loyalty to the state with ignoring the fact that Antigone is his niece, and the cause of order with not suffering a woman to worst him. His son Haemon, who is engaged to Antigone, points out to him the emptiness and danger of an attitude which refuses to recognize any point of view other than his own: "Think not that thy word, and thine alone, must be right. For if any man thinks that he alone is wise,—that in speech, or in mind, he hath no peer,—such a soul, when laid open, is ever found empty." Haemon's words only move his father to further intransigence, however, even though he points out that the people are all on the side of Antigone.

CREON: Am I to rule this land by other judgment than mine own?

[7] Sophocles, *Antigone,* trans. R. C. Jebb, in *The Complete Greek Drama,* eds. Whitney J. Oates and Eugene O'Neill, Jr. (New York: Random House Inc., 1938), I.

HAEMON: That is no city which belongs to one man.
CREON: Is not the city held to be the ruler's?
HAEMON: Thou wouldst make a good monarch of a desert. . . .
Thou wouldest speak, and then hear no reply? (vv. 736-739, 757)

Creon carries his *hybris* to the uttermost limit when, informed of the sickness that is visiting the state because of the unburied corpse and charged by the blind seer Tiresias with self-will, he replies, "No, though the eagles of Zeus should bear the carrion morsels to their Master's throne—no, not for dread of that defilement will I suffer his burial." Eventually Creon reluctantly yields to pressure with the pious statement, "We must not wage a vain war with destiny. . . . My heart misgives me, 'tis best to keep the established laws, even to life's end." His change comes too late, however. He finds open the cave where Antigone has been sealed up, Antigone hanging by the neck, and Haemon embracing her. Haemon rushes at his father and, missing him, drives the sword into his own breast. Eurydice, Haemon's mother and Creon's wife, kills herself when she learns the news, and Creon is left alone, asking to be led out of the sight of men, and bewailing his own blind stubbornness and folly. The conclusion of the leader of the Chorus leaves no doubt that it is now Antigone's point of view that has prevailed and that the decrees of the state may not stand against the eternal laws: "Wisdom is the supreme part of happiness; and reverence towards the gods must be inviolate. Great words of prideful men are ever punished with great blows."

The tragic meaning of *Antigone* is not limited, however, to the cost in suffering and death that man must pay for the violation of the order. Antigone, as we have seen, has herself been led to question the order when she finds that piety toward the established laws can lead her to being impious in the eyes of men. Though Antigone's view is justified in the end, meanwhile she has died a martyr's death and in so doing has made visible for all time the rift within the order itself—between family and state, between the laws of the gods and the laws of man. Although Antigone is not a "tragic hero" in Aristotle's sense of the term, she is a tragic figure in her conflict with Creon, who can budge from his position no more than she can from hers. Between these two people—each in his own situation and with his own unyielding temperament —no reconciliation is possible. Antigone is called "self-willed" because she is strong and proud, but equally because her will is guided by loyalty to her brother and piety to the gods. Creon's "self-will" more genuinely deserves the name, and Haemon puts his finger on that which from Creon's side makes the conflict unavoidable when he points out that Creon allows no voice other than his own. Here the tragic dimension is not just in the tragic hero and his relation to the order, as it is with Oedipus, but in the conflict between *two* tragic figures, each of whom must do as he does because he is as he is. The tragedy here lies in the relationship between man and man rather than between man and what is not man.

Oedipus is an exile but in no sense a rebel. Antigone is a rebel, yet one who rebels in the name of the established tradition. Only Prometheus rebels against the present in the name of the future, against the gods in the name of man. For this reason and because of his heroic, indomitable nature, Prometheus has always been the rebel par excellence, and the "Promethean" the very symbol of rebellion. Defying the reign of Zeus out of love for mankind, Prometheus gave men "honors beyond their due": fire and with it all those things that make man man as we know him—all the arts and crafts of civilization, such as reading, numbers, metals, knowledge of the seasons. Through Prometheus, the sly god, men have ceased to be dreaming children and have become adults, forever building a civilization which each generation bequeaths to the one that follows. Although Prometheus is not a man but a Titan—one of that older race of gods dispossessed of their rule by the Olympians—he does for man what no Oedipus can do.

It is Prometheus who helped Zeus overthrow his father Cronos and gain dominion over the heavens, but now Zeus punishes Prometheus for helping the race of man that Zeus had planned to destroy, and Prometheus must remain chained to a rock, his liver eaten out anew by an eagle each day.

Zeus is unmerciful: his mind "knows no turning, and ever harsh the hand that newly grasps the sway." But Prometheus, with his gift of foresight that Zeus does not possess, knows that there will come a time when Zeus must humble himself and turn to Prometheus for protection against the destiny which will overthrow him if he consummates his union with Thetis and she bears a son who will serve him as he served his father. "All toil alike in sorrow, unless one were lord of heaven," says Power; "none is truly free, save only Zeus." Although man has free will, it comes to nought in the face of destiny, and even the gods are limited by Zeus's sway. But Zeus himself remains subject to destiny, for all his great power, and in this lies Prometheus' hope.

> PROMETHEUS: Not yet hath all-ordaining Destiny decreed my release; but after many years, broken by a world of disaster and woe, I shall be delivered. The craft of the forger is weaker far than Necessity.
> LEADER: Who then holds the helm of Necessity?
> PROMETHEUS: The Fates triform and the unforgetting Furies.
> LEADER: And Zeus, is he less in power than these?
> PROMETHEUS: He may not avoid what is destined. (vv. 507-513)[8]

Zeus himself is subject to destiny. Prometheus' rebellion against him, as a result, is not a rebellion against the order of things, but, like that of Antigone, a rebellion within the order and in conformity with it. Although now the order gives the power to Zeus, Prometheus knows that Zeus is only "the ruler of the day": "Let him act, let him reign his little while as he will; for he shall not long rule over the gods."

Prometheus, as a result, is no more a modern rebel defying the order in the name of man than Antigone. What is more, unlike her, he has the wherewithal to resist that no human being has. He is immortal and equipped with the gift of foresight denied even to Zeus. Yet there are two heritages that he bequeaths to the rebel of later ages. One of these is

[8] Aeschylus, *Prometheus Bound*, trans. Paul Elmer More, in *The Complete Greek Drama*, I.

his heroic and unyielding nature. When Hermes, "the lackey of Zeus," comes to browbeat him into submission, Prometheus says:

> Do I seem to cower and quail before these new gods? Hardly, I think; there is no fear in me. . . . Be assured I would not barter my hard lot for your menial service. . . . Dream not that ever in fear of Zeus's will I shall grow womanhearted, and raise my supine hands in supplication to my hated foe for deliverance from these bonds;—it is not in my nature. (vv. 954-956, 959, 1002-1004)

The other heritage is the cause of mankind as the ground for rebellion. Through Prometheus man's potentialities have been indefinitely extended, and even Zeus is powerless to reverse the current which brings each successive generation of men to ever new power and achievement. "Wonders are many," says the Chorus in *Antigone*, "and none is more awesome (δεινός) than man." The order must stretch, as it were, to include this new, dynamic element that continually pushes back the boundary denoting man's place in the universe.

But Prometheus is also a tragic figure, and this the Modern Promethean tends to forget. His heroic rebellion and his knowledge that Zeus will not destroy him must be held in the balance with his unremitting suffering, his exposure on the rock, his exile from his own true existence as the cunning god, the Contriver. Aeschylus highlights this side of the picture when he gives Prometheus as temporary companion Io, the virgin changed into a heifer by the jealous ire of Hera, Zeus's wife, and pursued unrelentingly by a stinging fly. Though Prometheus is fixed in one place while Io is "an exile doomed in solitary ways to wander to the confines of the world," they are both exiles. Nor does Prometheus' love for mankind and the new powers that he has given man mean that the Greeks saw man as possessing unlimited potentiality. With man in general, as with the tragic hero in particular, the fulfillment of human potentialities inevitably leads to a fatal overstepping of the limits prescribed to man by the order and with it an inevitable fall.

Prometheus is a symbol of man not only in his knowledge and craft, his role as the extender of human potentialities and the father of human science. He is also the symbol of man as the being in between, the one who is not all-powerful like Zeus yet knows and sees the future. He is man wresting room for himself from a jealous creation. Fate is more powerful than Zeus, and this margin of power leaves space for man, but it is a space that has to be conquered in the teeth of Zeus's hostility. Prometheus, like man, combines the finitude of limited power with the knowledge that transcends that limit in the very act of knowing it. Only through the fact that man's knowing is both finite and infinite can he know not only the limits of his power but also those of his knowledge.[9] Prometheus is not simply the symbol of man's knowledge and science down through the generations. He is the very symbol of the ambiguity of science which extends man's dominion and at the same time brings him closer to *hybris* and self-destruction.

[9] Indissolubly connected with the finitude which is given by the ability to know *only* this, there is a participation in infinity, which is given by the ability to know at all. . . . When we recognize man's finitude we must *at the same time* recognize his participation in infinity, not as two juxtaposed qualities but as the twofold nature of the processes in which alone man's existence becomes recognizable." Martin Buber, *Between Man and Man*, trans. Ronald Gregor Smith with an Introduction by Maurice Friedman, 2d ed. (New York: Macmillan Paperbacks, 1965), "What Is Man?" p. 121.

2

DOCTOR FAUSTUS AND FAUST

Perhaps the most significant form in which the Prometheus myth has been carried into the modern world, apart from its many direct resurrections, is the Faust legend. Reaching back to the Gnostics of New Testament times and in particular to Simon Magus whose uncle was a Faustus, this legend moves forward through the Middle Ages, taking with it an ever greater accretion of stories surrounding man's use of forbidden knowledge for the acquisition of illicit power, until it is embodied once again in a fourteenth-century alchemist and necromancer of the same name. The legends surrounding this man's life were incorporated in Johann Spies's

Faustbuch of 1587 which Christopher Marlowe drew on for his *Tragical History of Doctor Faustus*. Doctor Faustus is a Promethean figure in the strange dual context of medieval Christianity and Renaissance Humanism. While Christianity saw man's life on earth solely as a preparation for heaven or a fall to hell, Renaissance Humanism taught that man is a little world that contains all the potentialities of the great—potentialities clearly to be realized in this life rather than sacrificed for the world to come. Thus *Doctor Faustus* stands under the double aegis of knowledge as sinful overstepping of human limitation and, in the phrase of Francis Bacon, "knowledge as power." The ambiguity of man's knowledge in Aeschylus' *Prometheus Bound* is here reproduced in an entirely different setting.

Hell, according to Mephistopheles' definition of it, is nothing other than exile from heaven. However, Doctor Faustus cannot understand this exile since he imagines hell to be a place rather than a state of being: when Mephistopheles says that he himself is in hell, Faustus replies that hell cannot be so bad then. But Faustus does glimpse the possibility that if heaven be made for man, as Mephistopheles asserts, then he is in danger of exiling himself from true human existence. "If it were made for man, 'twas made for me:/I will renounce this magic, and repent." Later, however, Doctor Faustus seeks "real life" in the lips of Helen of Troy who will make him "immortal with a kiss," thereby excluding from his soul the grace of heaven. Faustus himself eventually realizes what he has done and asserts that, though the Serpent that tempted Eve may be saved, his offense can never be pardoned. He laments that he has ever seen his college or "read book" since this knowledge has led him to exchange "eternal joy and felicity" for twenty-four years of "vain pleasure."

In his famous final soliloquy Faustus finds himself a prisoner of that very passage of time for which he had surrendered any existence more deeply rooted than the flux of sensation. The flow of future into present that formerly brought him happiness now brings him eternal damnation: since he has for so many years abandoned himself to this dimension, there is now no escaping it. Nonetheless, he imagines himself as leaping up to God and points to Christ's blood streaming in the firmament: "One drop, one half a drop would save my soul."

All possibility of immediacy is lost, however: the God who comes near to Job again in dialogue does not exist for Faustus. Faustus knows only the wrathful creator God of the Gnostics, a just rather than an evil God, to be sure, but one who cuts him off from the redeemer Christ and hands him over to hell.

> . . . see where God
> Stretcheth out his arm, and bends his ireful brows:
> Mountains and hills, come, come, and fall on me,
> And hide me from the heavy wrath of God. (vv. 1436-
> 1439)[1]

Not even for Christ's sake, "whose blood hath ransomed me" will there be a limit to Faustus' eternal torment. He has divided his life into external sensations of pleasure, knowledge, and power, and an inner soul that has had no connection with them, and now he must face into the reality of the soul that he has left empty. He wishes, like Job, that he could escape from the human condition that makes man both animal and person, that he could change to "some brute beast" that has no soul. Like Job too, he curses his birth—in this case the parents who engendered him. But the next moment he redirects this curse to himself and Lucifer "that hath deprived thee of the joys of heaven." In quick succession his thoughts turn from heaven to the wrathful God—"My God, my God, look not so fierce on me"—and from God to hell— "Ugly hell gape not, come not Lucifer."

Faustus cannot repent and receive the benefit of Christ's sacrifice, for he is given over to harsh judgment, cut off from the grace of God. To the Christianity that *Doctor Faustus* represents, the human world is a temporary exile that may lead either to salvation in heaven or permanent exile in hell. To Faustus this world is now what Mephistopheles earlier declared it to be—a place where the man who is cut off from

[1] Christopher Marlowe, *The Tragical History of Doctor Faustus,* in *Plays* (New York: E. P. Dutton, Everyman's Library).

heaven is already in hell, beyond the reach of Christ's mercy and redeeming love. Faustus has cut himself off from authentic existence by dividing his experiencing from the self that experiences, with the result that his inner self is now utterly empty and beyond the hope of any last-minute reclamation. Even apart from this, however, his repentance itself is never, in fact, sincere and whole-hearted. Faustus' very last words before he is carried off by the devils are "I'll burn my books, ah Mephistophilis." It is as if he were holding his books behind him the whole time and only at the last moment is ready to give them up. Even then, it is not because he repents of having sought power through knowledge, but only a final hopeless attempt to save himself.

The final chorus attempts to reproduce not only the form but also the world view of classical tragedy. Yet this world view is interfused both with medieval Christian morality and with the fascination that knowledge held for the Renaissance man.

> Cut is the branch that might have grown full straight,
> And burned is Apollo's Laurel bough,
> That sometimes grew within this learned man:
> Faustus is gone, regard his hellish fall,
> Whose fiendful fortune may exhort the wise,
> Only to wonder at unlawful things,
> Whose deepness doth entice such forward wits,
> To practise more than heavenly power permits. (vv. 1478-
>   1485)

Although the Chorus points to Faustus as a warning, exactly as the final Chorus of *Oedipus the King* pointed to Oedipus, Faustus' fall is not the limited fall of fortune that a man may experience within the world but a "hellish fall" which brings with it unlimited damnation. Faustus is not put before the people as an image of the human condition, as is Oedipus, but as a moral object lesson "to wonder at unlawful things." His fate, moreover, is not seen as that which lies in wait for every man, but as the special temptation exerted by the "deepness" of forbidden knowledge on "forward wits." In Marlowe's age, however, these "forward wits" were no longer the alchemists and necromancers of the Faust legend but the scientists, scholars, and explorers who were pushing back the horizons of the known world. So far from believing that heavenly power had set a limit to what men might practice, as the Chorus asserts, they believed that man's possibilities were unlimited and that his highest duty was to realize them.

In the end, Faustus is neither a Greek nor a Christian, but a Renaissance tragic hero—a man whose comet-like career is not checked by the overstepping of set limits but by burning himself out in the cosmic night. His end makes a glorious spectacle, to which the grand rhetoric of Faustus' final soliloquy provides the proper accompaniment. Man is destroyed not by his finitude but by his infinity, and, at this stage in the parabola that sweeps upward from the Renaissance to the modern age, this progress into the unlimited seems not terrifying but heroic. The ambiguity underlying this Renaissance Prometheus is discernible only when we look back to the Christian morality in which his "fall" is set or forward to those further stages of exile when man and the natural world in which he lives come apart.

A significant step on this road to exile is reflected in Goethe's *Faust.* The "Prologue in Heaven," written in conscious imitation of the Prologue to the Book of Job, presents a dialectic view of reality and of evil closer to the Book of Job, in which Satan is the servant of God, than to *Doctor Faustus* in which God and the devil are irreconcilable opposites. The archangels praise creation, whose "rival tempests . . . storming from sea to land, from land to sea" form "a chain of deepest action" the very interaction and desolation of which serves as the base for "the gentle movement" of God's Day. Mephistopheles cannot join in this praise of creation. His concern is with man, "the little god o' the world" whose reason enables him "to be far beastlier than any beast." "Of suns and worlds I've nothing to be quoted;/How men torment themselves, is all I've noted." Man is no longer quite the grand figure that he was for the Renaissance. He is, instead, a "wretched creature," a "microcosmic fool" who is constantly trying to raise himself to the level of a god but who is as constantly brought up short by his human limitations.

What is at stake in the temptation of Faust, according to both the Lord and Mephistopheles, is not the integrity of a unique man but the nature of man in general. "While Man's desires and aspirations stir,/He cannot choose but err," says the Lord and adds that after he has led Faust downward by means of his traps and snares, Mephistopheles himself will be forced to admit that "A good man, through obscurest aspiration,/Has still an instinct of the one true way." The hope of man is now neither in the knowledge which gives him power over the world around him, as in the Renaissance, nor in the reason which brings him into harmony with the universal order, as in the Age of Enlightenment, but in the creative life force stirring in the depths. Even though this force leads to evil, as long as it keeps moving it cannot help but lead man eventually to the good—no longer seen as any external state or moral action, but as a fulfillment of the creative force that surges through the self. Even the "evil" to which Mephistopheles tempts man serves the purposes of the Lord by actualizing this creative life force that might otherwise lie dormant.

> Man's active nature, flagging, seeks too soon the level;
> Unqualified repose he learns to crave;
> Whence, willingly, the comrade him I gave,
> Who works, excites, and must create, as Devil. ("Prologue")[2]

Mephistopheles defines himself in the same way as "Part of that Power, not understood/Which always wills the Bad, and always works the Good." But Faust sees Mephistopheles in a less dialectical manner as that negation which works counter to the upward surge of life.

> So, to the actively eternal
> Creative force, in cold disdain
> You now oppose the first infernal,
> Whose wicked clench is all in vain! ("The Study")

Faust begins where Doctor Faustus leaves off. Instead of wishing to use magic for power over the world, like Doctor

2 All quotations from Goethe's *Faust*, Part I, are from the Bayard Taylor translation (New York: Croft's Classics, 1948).

Faustus, Faust wants to use it to escape from the human condition that oppresses his heart with some unknown need. Caught up to mystic ecstasy by the "sign of the Macrocosm," he feels himself a god before whose soul "Creative Nature" unfolds. "How grand a show!" cries Faust, only to add the next moment, as he falls back into the role of the observer, "but, ah! a show alone." Unable to make "boundless nature his own," he realizes once again man's exile: the "Founts of all Being" flow and feed yet man's "withered heart" vainly aspires to them. Faust now turns instead to the titanic vitality of the sign of "the Earth Spirit" and through a Dionysian rapture escapes once again from the limitations of the human condition:

> I glow, as drunk with new-made wine: . . .
> The woe of earth, the bliss of earth invite me . . .
>   ("Night")

When the Earth Spirit itself shows up, however, Faust cannot bear it, and the Earth Spirit ridicules the man who so lately thought himself a god:

> What mean perturbation
> Thee, superhuman, shakes? Thy soul's high calling,
>   where?
> Where is the breast, which from itself a world did
>   bear, . . .
> A writhing worm, a terror-stricken form?

Faust is like the spirit he conceives, the Earth Spirit points out, not like the reality which, precisely because it is unlimited, is too terrible for limited man to endure! Faust does not fail to grasp the ignominy of his position:

> I, image of the Godhead, who began—
> Deeming Eternal Truth secure in nearness— . . .
> And laid aside the earthly man . . .
> Enjoying in creation the life of Gods . . .
> A thunder-word hath swept me from my stand. . . .
> When that ecstatic moment held me,
> I felt myself so small, so great;
> But thou hast ruthlessly repelled me
> Back upon man's uncertain fate.

Thrown "back upon man's uncertain fate," Faust recognizes his condition, and that of every man, as one of change and anxiety in which every deed and sorrow impedes the march of life, an exile in which "some alien substance" increasingly cleaves "to all the mind conceives of grand and fair."

Faust tries once more to escape "man's fate"—this time through suicide. Although man cannot overcome the limitations of life, his dignity may still vie with the gods through daring to fling asunder "those gates which every man would fain go slinking by!" Like Sartre's Orestes, he is prepared to take on himself the whole burden of a world emptied of meaning—"To take this step with cheerful resolution/ Though Nothingness should prove the ultimate conclusion!" As Faust puts the beaker of poison to his lips, however, he hears a chorus of angels singing Easter music. Overcome by childhood nostalgia for the faith in which he no longer believes, Faust melts, his "tears gush forth: the Earth takes back her child!" The only alternative that is left to Faust now is to set out to experience "man's uncertain fate," and this he does through his pact with Mephistopheles.

What impels Faust to leave his study and go out into the world with Mephistopheles is his inner suffering, his "frenzied crazed unrest." Faust complains that he has "two souls," one of which embraces the world "in love and clinging lust," while the other leaves the dust of earth below for the rarefied spiritual realities of "the high ancestral spaces." This inner conflict produces an alienation from the flow of time and experience entirely foreign to Doctor Faustus and leaves Faust disillusioned with all possibility of fulfillment. Like Job when he curses the day of his birth, Faust complains that his existence has become meaningless and fraught with terror to the point that he longs for death:

> In very terror I at morn awake,
> Upon the verge of bitter weeping,
> To see the day of disappointment break,
> To no one hope of mine—not one—its promise keeping:—
> That even each joy's presentiment . . .

With grinning masks of life prevent
My mind its fairest work to finish!
Then, too, when night descends . . . comes no rest to
  me,
But some wild dream is sent to fray me. . . .
Death is desired, and Life a thing unblest! ("The Study")

Unlike Doctor Faustus, Faust sets a condition on whether Mephistopheles will get his soul for hell in return for the service which he renders Faust on earth. Whenever Faust stands still and stretches himself in quiet on an idler's bed, whenever he says to the passing moment, "Stay, thou art so fair!" then Mephistopheles shall have him. For Faust, as for the Lord, this is a question of his inner nature and not of any external good and evil between which he must choose. "If I stand still, I'm slave to you, Or whom?" says Faust, "—why should that be debated?" But Faust does not think that he will stand still, for experience offers him no lasting pleasure or satisfaction:

A game whose winnings no man ever knew,—
A maid, that, even from my breast,
Beckons my neighbor with her wanton glances . . .

It is not joy that Faust expects to get from Mephistopheles but experience—experience which puts aside the Renaissance fascination with knowledge in favor of a romantic identification with the stream of human life.

I take the wildering whirl, enjoyment's keenest pain,
Enamored hate, exhilarant disdain.
My bosom, of its thirst for knowledge sated,
Shall not, henceforth, from any pang be wrested,
And all of life for all mankind created
Shall be within mine inmost being tested:
The highest, lowest forms my soul shall borrow,
Shall heap upon itself their bliss and sorrow,
And thus, my own sole self to all their selves expanded
I too, at last, shall with them all be stranded!

That this entering into the joys and sorrows of all mankind represents still a fourth attempt on Faust's part to escape from the limitations of "man's uncertain fate" is evident from

his very words, "my own sole self to all their selves expanded."
That it does not represent any actual going beyond his own
experience to that of any other person becomes evident
from the Gretchen tragedy which dominates the rest of Part
One.

After Faust, through the resourcefulness of Mephistopheles, has seduced Gretchen, a simple village girl, he falls
in love with her. Now Faust can no longer be satisfied with
the sensual pleasure which he gets from Gretchen, for he
knows he is leading her to ruin; nor can he look on her merely
as a content of his own experience as he had when he originally seduced her. "Though I be glowing with her kisses,
do I not always share her need?" Seeking refuge from his conflict in romantic communion with nature, Faust complains
that the very wonders of nature which elevate him show
him his own self and with it the consciousness "that nothing
can be perfect unto Man." He no longer sees his inner conflict as that between the material and the spiritual. Now it
is the unreconcilable opposition between the ecstasy which
uplifts him and the cold cynicism and denial of the now indispensable Mephistopheles who demeans him to himself.
Mephistopheles is Faust's second self, the outward symbol
of his inner conflict. Though Faust tells Gretchen in the
scene in "Martha's Garden" that "feeling is all in all," there
is one part of Faust that cynically holds back at the very
point when the rest of him is enthusiastically entering in.

Mephistopheles exhibits a calm detachment from Gretch-
en's ruin which leads him to see it only objectively and en
masse. "She is not the first," he comments, to which Faust
responds with an anguished indictment of God reminiscent
of Job:

> Not the first! O woe! woe which no human soul can grasp,
> that more than one being should sink into the depths of
> this misery,—that the first, in its writhing death agony
> under the eyes of the Eternal Forgiver, did not expiate
> the guilt of all others! The misery of this single one
> pierces to the very marrow of my life; and thou art
> calmly grinning at the fate of thousands! ("Dreary Day")

When Faust enters the prison with Mephistopheles to try to free Gretchen, he is overwhelmed by "mankind's collected woe," and Gretchen herself sees her situation as an image of man's fate in general: "Now over each neck has quivered/ The blade that is quivering over mine." Gretchen refuses to escape with Faust to what could only be for her a permanent and unbearable exile. She has become exactly what Faust foresaw when he pictured himself as the wanderer and exile uprooting her from her settled and traditional life:

> I am the fugitive, all houseless roaming,
> The monster without aim or rest,
> That like a cataract, down rocks and gorges foaming,
> Leaps, maddened, into the abyss's breast!
> And sidewards she, with young unwakened senses,
> Within her cabin on the Alpine field
> Her simple, homely life commences,
> Her little world therein concealed.
> And I, God's hate flung o'er me, . . .
> She and her peace I yet must undermine. ("Forest and
>   Cavern")

Faust concludes this earlier speech with the wish that her fate will crush him too, so that one ruin may overwhelm them both. At the end of Part One, however, he does not share her fate but abandons her in order to save himself. Faust could not stay with Gretchen any more than Doctor Faustus could repent. He entered into relationship with her as the experiencing self who regards the world with which he comes into contact as contained within his experience. Now, even though he loves her, he leaves her to go on to still other experiences.

At the end of Part Two, Faust is saved because, "He who ever strives/Him can we save." "Striving" is thereby elevated to a value in itself, independent of the goal or even the direction of the striving, as of the effect of that striving on other persons. We are told, moreover, that the true meaning of earthly events is not found in concrete human existence but in that mystic fulfillment which completes it:

All things transitory
But as symbols are sent:
Earth's insufficiency
Here grows to Event.[3]

Gretchen's unhappy death no longer seems a tragedy but an event which, regarded in its true symbolic light, assumes its proper place in that striving through which Faust is saved! Yet in the context of Part One, Gretchen's fate *is* a tragedy, not only from the standpoint of the reader but of Faust himself. Faust's love for Gretchen breaks through the romantic circle of the glorification of feeling and experience to real concern about another person as an independent center of reality, and despair that his love has brought her ruin. The inner conflict that Faust experiences in this tragedy, like that which originally drove him from his study, points us from "feeling is all in all" to the "death of God," from romantic self-fulfillment to the problematic of modern man.

[3] Johann Wolfgang von Goethe, *Faust. A Tragedy*, trans. Bayard Taylor (Boston: Houghton Mifflin, 1888).

PART TWO

HERMAN
MELVILLE

3

"MOBY DICK":

THE SUNDERING OF TRUTH

AND REALITY

Herman Melville's *Moby Dick* includes both explicitly and implicitly the Greek, Biblical, and Renaissance images of man—Prometheus and Job, Doctor Faustus and Faust—and it leads through them to the Modern Rebel and the Modern Exile. It weaves them into one grand story which tries out all possibilities, tests out all the directions, and at the same time has its own drama, its own unique setting, its own unique hero and observer. Perhaps more than any other book it shows us the image of man set over against as well as within the reality in which we live—over against the nonhuman whale as well as within the dual opposites of land and sea.

Moby Dick, as no other work of our times, presents the basic situation within which the problematic of modern man develops: the "death of God" and the alienation of man. It explores the limits of human and of modern existence as few books before or after it have done. If *Moby Dick* gives us no answer, it has never been excelled in the way in which, dynamically progressing from image to image, suggestion to suggestion, action to action, it has stated its question—a question concerning existence itself. The very form in which the question is put produces an insistent suggestion of dualism, yet one that does not take refuge in a philosophical system or religious dogma—one that is contained in the poetic flesh and bones of the book.

To understand *Moby Dick*'s significance for the "death of God" and the image of man we have to treat it as a gigantic poem in which each stanza, each image, is of significance in itself, and which at the same time moves along from image to image and from chapter to chapter in such a way that we will never find the meaning of the poem simply through taking a particular image or chapter except as it is set in the dynamic, dramatic progression of the whole. *Moby Dick* is a metaphysical novel, but we must distinguish between the explicitly metaphysical passages which Melville so liberally strews throughout for poetic and symbolic purposes and the implicit metaphysics which we touch on only when we have gone through the dramatic situation and the characters into the basic attitude toward existence that we glean from the interplay of symbolic suggestion, action, and point of view. Thus the change of point of view follows and is an integral part of the going out to sea, the long journey around the world up to the point where the White Whale has been sighted, and the chase.

It is in the problem of point of view more than any other that the metaphysical dimension of *Moby Dick* is found. This metaphysical dimension is not the picture of what reality *is,* but of man's relation to that reality. The changing, ever-shifting point of view in *Moby Dick* is representative of the ever-changing, ever-shifting attitude of man toward the reality that confronts him. This variation in point of view is brought about, in the first place, by the fact that Melville at times seems to identify with Captain Ahab and at times with Ishmael. This is further complicated by the fact that Ishmael is at once participant and observer, taken up in the chase yet able to take time out to meditate on whaling and the sea and comment on what is happening. Ishmael is the narrator, and in the early chapters of the book he is the protagonist. What is more, his is the point of view from which the book and the quest of Moby Dick both begin. If Ahab sees Moby Dick from one unvarying standpoint, Ishmael sees every aspect of the White Whale, and he sets them all before us. Common to both Ahab and Ishmael is the tension between "truth" and reality. In *Moby Dick* it is the changing relationship of truth and reality which takes us out to sea and in the end turns us back toward home. It is this relation which is the very dynamism of the book, correlative with the basic symbolism of sea and land. The land is the harbor, the sea is the open perilous part of the world. The sea is that toward which we go in search of truth till we are no longer able to face the truth, or until truth is sundered from reality, and our only choices are to be drowned in reality or to retreat to land without our full share of the truth. This is the paradox through which Melville expresses the "death of God," and this paradox provides the context for both Ahab the Modern Promethean and Ishmael the Modern Exile.

Chapter XXIII, "The Lee Shore," is a "thumbnail epitaph" for Bulkington, the godlike hero who sails forth on the search for truth and scorns to take shelter in the comfortable half-truths and falsehoods of the "treacherous, slavish shore." Although land is haven, it is also the greatest peril; on its rocks the ship that has launched forth can easily be dashed to pieces. And this is the greatest peril for the soul that wishes through "deep, earnest thinking" to preserve "the open independence of her sea." For this soul knows that the truth it seeks is no finite truth, no truth that can be kept in deep-freezes or safe-deposit boxes. It is Truth with a capital T, infinite truth. It is not God, or even God's truth, but it partakes of God's absoluteness. "As in landlessness alone resides the highest truth, shoreless, indefinite as God—so better it is to perish in that howling infinite, than be ingloriously dashed upon the lee, even if that were safety!" This truth is so much the meaning of man's life that not just the attainment of it, but the seeking of it is the only true goal of human existence. Bulkington, the sailor who returns from a long voyage only to ship out again immediately and drown in a gale, is glorious in his very perishing because he perishes in the search for truth.[1] The truth for which he seeks is outside and above him, and through its quality of godlike absoluteness it is identical with reality. This is an essentially Platonic image of truth as itself the ultimate reality combined with a romantic, Faustian conception of the search for truth as itself the highest value.

In Chapter XXXV, "The Mast-Head," the relation of truth and reality undergoes a highly disconcerting transformation. The mast-head is the station high up on a mast that is manned by a member of the crew on the lookout for whales, and the purpose of the voyage is seeking for whales. But this purpose is completely frustrated when the mast-head is manned by "the sunken-eyed young Platonist" who looks inward to his thoughts rather than outward for whales. He also has gone to sea, like Bulkington, but unlike Bulkington he now sees the truth as essentially within rather than above. He too values the sea, but he values it as a symbol of the

---

[1] A closely comparable passage appears in *Mardi:* "The verdict be, the golden haven was not gained;—yet, in bold quest thereof, better to sink in boundless deeps, than float on vulgar shoals." Herman Melville, *Mardi* in *The Complete Works of Herman Melville,* II, 277. How fully Melville himself saw Bulkington as an image of man is evident in his reflections on "usable truth" in his discussion of Hawthorne's *House of Seven Gables:* "There is a certain tragic phase of humanity which, in our opinion, was never more powerfully embodied than by Hawthorne. We mean the tragedies of human thought in its own unbiassed, native, and profounder workings. We think that into no recorded mind has the intense feeling of the usable truth ever entered more deeply than into this man's. By usable truth, we mean the apprehension of the absolute condition of present things as they strike the eye of the man who fears them not, though they do their worst to him." Letter to Nathaniel Hawthorne, Pittsfield, Wednesday morning (March ? 1851). Willard Thorp, *Herman Melville, Representative Selections,* American Writers Series, ed. Harry Hayden Clark (New York: American Book Co., 1938), pp. 387-88.

soul, and though the soul is ultimately identical with the universal soul that underlies all, this universal soul is reached directly only by going within.

The sunken-eyed young man is, of course, the philosophical idealist. His philosophical patrimony is not Plato but German idealism refracted through Emersonian transcendentalism, a movement which held attraction for the young Melville too. His identification of the soul within with the soul underlying all is greatly aided by nature at that point: the summer day, the beautiful sea, the ship rocking gently to and fro produce a "blending cadence of waves with thought" in which he loses his own identity. In truth, he has no identity as a personal, an individual being, for the very soul within him is the soul of the absolute, and the "other"—the world outside him—is only the visible symbol of this invisible soul: "He takes the mystic ocean at his feet for the visible image of that deep, blue, bottomless soul pervading mankind and nature." The cleavage between mankind and nature which modern man has more and more come to feel, the split which even the Renaissance idea of man as a microcosm linked to the macrocosm could not stop, is here done away with. So far from seeing man as set opposite hostile nature, the young idealist knows that in essence both are really thought or soul, that one spirit or consciousness underlies both. "Every strange half-seen, gliding beautiful thing that eludes him; every dimly-discovered, uprising fin of some undiscernible form, seems to him the embodiment of those elusive thoughts that only people the soul by continually flitting around it." The cannibalistic sharks are nothing more than thoughts; therefore we need not be in terror of them.

> In this enchanted mood thy spirit ebbs away to whence it came, becomes diffused through time and space, like Cranmer's sprinkled Pantheistic ashes, forming at last a part of every shore the round globe over. There is no life in thee, now, except that rocking life imparted by a gently rolling ship, by her, borrowed from the sea; by the sea, from the inscrutable tides of God.[2]

[2] All quotations from *Moby Dick* are from the Newton Arvin edition (New York: Rinehart, 1948).

There is nothing in the world that can stand opposite you and face you; for all is simply part of the one.

"But while this sleep, this dream is on ye, move your foot or hand an inch, slip your hold at all, and your identity comes back in horror." If your identity had been truly lost, Melville implies, it could not have come back; if it had been at one with all reality, then it could not have troubled you even though your foot did slip and you fell into the ocean. But what you discover in a lightning flash of illumination is that what you took to be the whole of reality, seemingly unbounded in its compass, really resides in your own consciousness—that the world is more than your consciousness, even though your consciousness is able to include in its scope the farthest stars, the farthest reaches of time. Beyond that infinite with which you are in tune is another, hostile infinite that destroys you. Your consciousness, instead of being universal, coincident with the whole of reality, is a point of view limited by the ground on which you stand, the very conditions of your human existence as a unique person who will die and who knows that he will die. (We are reminded here of Faust thrown back from the signs of the Macrocosm and the Earth Spirit on "man's uncertain fate.") Therefore, you hover "over Descartian vortices," crushed by a reality you have chosen to ignore, a reality essentially "other" than you. "Perhaps, at midday, in the fairest weather, with one half-throttled shriek you drop through that transparent air into the summer sea, no more to rise for ever. Heed it well, ye Pantheists!" [3] The young Platonist's "half-throttled shriek"

[3] That Melville himself shares Ishmael's attitude toward pantheism and that he himself was once just another such "sunken-eyed young Platonist" is clearly suggested by the autobiographical statement with which Ishmael prefaces his warning to the pantheist: "Let me make a clean breast of it here, and frankly admit that I kept but sorry guard. With the problem of the universe revolving in me, how could I—being left completely to myself at such a thought-engendering altitude." The same warning against letting the *"all* feeling" become identical with the universe is contained in the famous passage in one of Melville's letters to Hawthorne: "In reading some of Goethe's sayings, . . . I came across this, *'Live in the all.'* That is to say, your separate identity is but a wretched one—good; but get out of yourself, spread and expand yourself, and bring to yourself the tinglings of life that are felt in the flowers

has irreparably sundered thought and reality, and the very existence of truth as a meaning linking reality and thought has been put in question. Whatever "truth" is left is merely a shadow of our thought: this is not a truth which can "make us free" by bringing us into meaningful relation with a reality outside us.

In "The Whiteness of the Whale" (XLII) the whiteness of Moby Dick is subsumed under the all-encompassing paradox of whiteness in general. Whiteness is at once the very color of the divinity and the color of everything that is most terrifying. At first "the visible world seems formed in love," but then the revelation comes that "the invisible spheres were formed in fright"—and it is all the more horrible because it is a later revelation. Whiteness is "the most meaning symbol of spiritual things, nay, the very veil of the Christian's Deity," and yet it is "the intensifying agent in things the most appalling to mankind." The evil, which at first seems a small part of our existence, turns out to be its great underlying reality. Either we must deny it or we must ascribe it to God, neither of which we can do. Therefore, the universe breaks apart; it is no longer a *uni*verse at all, but simply man and the "inscrutable malice" opposite him. Whiteness is "the colorless, all-color of atheism." Like the traveler to Lapland who refuses to use colored glasses, "so the wretched infidel gazes himself blind at the monumental white shroud that wraps all the prospect around him." If one looks at reality without rose-colored glasses, if one looks the truth in the face, one must go blind. One cannot see the truth and live; or rather there is no longer any truth, for reality is too much for us.

---

and the woods, that are felt in the planets Saturn and Venus, and the Fixed Stars. What nonsense! Here is a fellow with a raging toothache. 'My dear boy,' Goethe says to him, 'you are sorely afflicted with that tooth; but you must *live in the all*, and then you will be happy!' . . . This 'all' feeling, though, there is some truth in it. You must often have felt it, lying on the grass on a warm summer's day. Your legs seem to send out shoots into the earth. Your hair feels like leaves upon your head. This is the *all* feeling. But what plays the mischief with the truth is that men will insist upon the universal application of a temporary feeling or opinion." Pittsfield, June (?) 1951. Thorp, *op. cit.*, p. 393.

. . .

In the middle sections of *Moby Dick* we see a growing intensity of the revelation of evil as the heart of reality, and good as the appearance that first obscures and overlays evil and later on is stripped aside, as it were, so that the evil is laid bare. This middle section of *Moby Dick* is made up of bits and pieces: every type of whale, every part of the whale, everything to do with the whale or whaling is exploited by the author to the full to suggest what he wishes to suggest without ever taking responsibility for any of these suggestions in such a way that one can say of any of them, *This* is what Melville believes. The key to understanding this cumulative suggestion is given us by Ahab himself in "The Sphinx" (LXX), "O Nature, and O soul of man! how far beyond all utterance are your linked analogies! Not the smallest atom stirs or lives on matter, but has its cunning duplicate in the mind." If Melville could no longer believe, with the sunken-eyed young Platonist, that man is a microcosm of the macrocosm— a being with a secure place in the cosmos—this much at least of his transcendentalism he could retain: a correspondence between the inner world and the outer. "Some certain significance lurks in all things," says Ishmael in "The Doubloon" (XCIX), "else all things are little worth, and the round world itself but an empty cipher!" Every single thing which Ishmael says about the whale, down to the minutest details, he can also use as a symbol of the inner life of man, or the soul of man, or the destiny of man.

This certainly implies no universal soul, or "Oversoul," that makes man safe in nature, no monism of truth and reality. Yet at least one last link, or thread, still exists between truth and reality, for we can in some sense know reality. We can encounter infinity even if we cannot paint it, even if we realize that it is hostile to us and will destroy us. This knowledge at any rate goes a step beyond that aspect of the Gnostic world in which the ordinary man cannot even face the evil of reality and does not know he is in a world of darkness. But this step still leaves us in a Gnostic world—that of the Elect who know that man *is* not and cannot be at home in this world.

"Of the Monstrous Pictures of Whales" (LV) takes us a step further in this whole problem of truth and the relation of reality to appearance: "Any way you may look at it, you must needs conclude that the great Leviathan is that one creature in the world which must remain unpainted to the last." We have the suggestion of the whale as an almost mystic absolute that cannot be comprehended by our concepts and our symbols, an ineffable reality which one cannot describe but only point to: "True, one portrait may hit the mark much nearer than another, but none can hit it with any very considerable degree of exactness." They all fall short because by its very nature the whale is a thing you cannot get hold of and see all the way around: "There is no earthly way of finding out precisely what the whale really looks like."

"The only mode in which you can derive even a tolerable idea of his living contour," Ishmael continues, "is by going a-whaling yourself." The truth with which Melville is concerned is not the truth about man and nature that can be known by the detached observer. It is "existential truth" which can be verified only through participation—the truth that discovers the limits of reality through going out to encounter them. How vain and foolish it is "for timid untravelled man to try to comprehend aright this wondrous whale, by merely poring over his dead attenuated skeleton," says Ishmael. "No. Only in the heart of quickest perils; only when within the eddyings of his angry flukes; only on the profound unbounded sea, can the fully invested whale be found out." In order to know, one must participate, but to participate means to risk oneself. If you do go whaling yourself, "you run no small risk of being eternally stove and sunk by him. Wherefore, it seems to me, you had best not be too fastidious in your curiosity touching this Leviathan." Here is the central paradox of the whole book: to know the whale, this living reality that confronts us, you have to go whaling yourself; yet if you go forth to meet that reality, it is very likely to destroy you—because it is absolute and infinite or because it is malicious and hostile or because it is cold and indifferent, or all three. "The dead, blind wall butts all inquiring heads at last," meditates Ahab.

Ishmael loses no chance to reinforce this paradox. "Unless you own the whale, you are but a provincial and sentimentalist in Truth. But clear Truth is a thing for salamander giants only to encounter; how small the chances for the provincials then?" The whale is greater than I can ever describe, says Ishmael. The whale, however, is reality; and unless you own this reality, you have got to renounce any possibility whatsoever of finding the truth. When Ishmael tries to read the Sperm Whale's brow in "The Prairie" (LXXIX), he cannot do it. "Human or animal, the mystical brow" signifies the creator: "God: done this day by my hand." The Sperm Whale is itself almost a god:

> In that full front view, you feel the Deity and the dread powers more forcibly than in beholding any other object in living nature. For you see no one point precisely; not one distinct feature is revealed; no nose, eyes, ears, or mouth; no face; he has none, proper; nothing but that one broad firmament of a forehead, pleated with riddles; dumbly lowering with the doom of boats, and ships, and men.

But the Sperm Whale is a silent god, a god of "pyramidical silence," an unrevealed and unrevealing god who stands ready in an era of the "death of God" to fill the now absent place of divinity.

> If hereafter any highly cultured, poetical nation shall lure back to their birthright, the merry May-day gods of old; and livingly enthrone them again in the now egotistical sky: in the now unhaunted hill; then be sure, exalted to Jove's high seat, the great Sperm Whale shall lord it.

"I but put that brow before you," Ishmael concludes. "Read it if you can."

If we cannot hope to decipher the whale's brow, there is still less hope of knowing his spout. "I have ever found your plain things the knottiest of all," says Ishmael in "The Fountain" (LXXXV). "And as for this whale spout, you might al-

most stand in it, and yet be undecided as to what it is precisely." Besides which, to know it you must get near it, and if
you get near it, it may poison or blind you. "The wisest thing
the investigator can do then, it seems to me, is to let this deadly
spout alone." In this same chapter, however, the whale
becomes for once not the ineffable reality that baffles the
truthseeker but the truthseeker himself, "the mighty, misty
monster," whose head is "overhung by a canopy of vapor, engendered by his incommunicable contemplations, and that
vapor . . . glorified by a rainbow, as if Heaven itself had put
its seal upon his thoughts." Here speaks what is left of the
young Platonist in Ishmael, only now a balance has been
reached between earthly doubts and heavenly intuitions:

> And so, through all the thick mists of the dim doubts
> in my mind, divine intuitions now and then shoot, en-
> kindling my fog with a heavenly ray. And for this I
> thank God; for all have doubts; many deny; but doubts
> or denials, few along with them, have intuitions. Doubts
> of all things earthly, and intuitions of some things heav-
> enly; this combination makes neither believer nor infidel,
> but makes a man who regards them both with equal eye.

This passage invites contrast with the end of "The Whiteness
of the Whale" where the wretched infidel gazes himself
blind because he will not use colored glasses. There the
choice seems to be between looking at a reality that blinds
one and retaining one's eyesight only through voluntarily
blinding oneself to reality. Here there seems to be a third
possibility: the balance of intuition and doubts that enables
Ishmael to view all the horrors of Moby Dick and all the
dreadful aspects of whiteness with an equal eye. The sunken-
eyed young Platonist, who rested in mystic intuition alone,
was completely the prey of Cartesian doubt once his foot
slipped and he fell into the ocean. But the man who combines intuition with doubt, he is, perhaps, the strongest of all
men.

Ishmael does not preserve this balanced point of view,
however. The very next chapter, "The Tail" (LXXXVI),
returns with heightened intensity to the central paradox of

truth and reality. "Excepting the sublime *breach*," says Ishmael, the "peaking of the whale's flukes is perhaps the grandest sight to be seen in all animated nature."

> Out of the bottomless profundities the gigantic tail seems spasmodically snatching at the highest heaven. So in dreams, have I seen majestic Satan thrusting forth his tormented colossal claw from the flame Baltic of Hell.

"The more do I consider this mighty tail, the more do I deplore my inability to express it," laments Ishmael. "Dissect him how I may, then, I but go skin-deep"—a not surprising conclusion to an undertaking that he described earlier as "the classification of the constituents of a chaos," the fearful attempt "to have one's hands among the unspeakable foundations, ribs, and very pelvis of the world." "I have undertaken to manhandle this Leviathan," says Ishmael in "The Fossil Whale" (CIV), thus stating as explicitly as he can not only his own aim as observer but Ahab's aim as actor-revenger—that of anthropomorphizing the whale, dissecting him into human categories, reducing him to manageable size, divesting him of all terror and mystery, punishing and destroying him for his earlier insubordination to man. But Ishmael is not without proper respect for his "mighty theme."

> Friends, hold my arms! For in the mere act of penning my thoughts of this Leviathan, they weary me, and make me faint with their outreaching comprehensiveness of sweep, as if to include the whole circle of the sciences, and all the generation of whales, and men, and mastodons, past, present, and to come, with all the revolving panoramas of empire on earth, and throughout the whole universe, not excluding its suburbs.

"I know him not, and never will," Ishmael concludes in "The Tail." I have told you everything about this whale, he seems to say: what he is made of, his blubber, his head, his flukes, the ambergris from the sick whale. Yet I cannot begin to grasp him, for my understanding gives me only the surfaces and not the depths of reality.

In "Brit" (LVIII) the whole symbolism of land and sea

undergoes a complete reversal and becomes the contrast between good and evil, innocence and experience, appearance and reality. The sea, at first, has the appearance of good, but when we look beneath the surface beauty we discover that the sea is a savage, murderous, cannibalistic force. The beauty of the sea makes all the more horrible the horrors that we subsequently discover. "This green, gentle, and most docile earth," in contrast, is now the place of real shelter rather than the false lure of safety, as in "The Lee Shore." In "The Lee Shore" Ishmael praises that "deep, earnest thinking" which "is but the intrepid effort of the soul to keep the open independence of her sea." Now, in "Brit," the sea stands for an element essentially antithetical to man and hostile to human existence.

For as this appalling ocean surrounds the verdant land, so in the soul of man there lies one insular Tahiti, full of peace and joy, but encompassed by all the horrors of the half known life. God keep thee! Push not off from that isle, thou canst never return!

That "insular Tahiti" is the South Seas paradise which Melville contrasted in his earlier works with the modern civilization that he did not like. It is also the "Tahiti" which every one of us experiences in the original innocence of childhood, and loses forever as we cast off into a world of experience. It is perhaps, too, an almost mystic center of inward joy and peace that some souls can carry a little way intact into the world of experience. When confronted with the dark horror outside, however, or when confronting the dark horror within, it is soon irretrievably lost: one can return to it only in reminiscence, but never in reality.

Yet "Brit" does not give us the final word on the human condition. In "The Grand Armada" (LXXXVII), in a truly breath-taking picture, Ishmael's whaleboat is towed into the center of a whole herd of sperm whales and there at the becalmed center where the boat glides after the whale breaks loose they see below the surface of the water the mother whales nursing their young and other whales engaging in play. From this Ishmael draws an analogy with himself, reminiscent of "The Fountain" two chapters before it—one that reveals his inner core as, after all, intact even in the world of experience:

> And thus, though surrounded by circle upon circle of constemations and affrights, did these inscrutable creatures at the centre freely and fearlessly indulge in all peaceful concernments; yea, serenely revelled in dalliance and delight. But even so, amid the tornadoed Atlantic of my being, do I myself still for ever centrally disport in mute calm; and while ponderous planets of unwaning woe revolve round me, deep down and deep inland there I still bathe me in eternal mildness of joy.

"Deep down and deep inland"—this phrase, set in contrast with "the tornadoed Atlantic of my being," recalls "the insular Tahiti encompassed by all the horrors of the half known life" at the end of "Brit." Yet here we have, in fact, the opposite of that image. In "Brit" one sets out into the world of experience at the cost of losing one's original intactness. But now, in "The Grand Armada," Ishmael preserves a calm and joyful center inside despite the fact that "ponderous planets of unwaning woe" revolve around him. This is a modification of the point of view of "Brit" which does not dismiss it, does not attempt to return to the idealism of the young Platonist, but does suggest that there is some hope for man, after all, since even in the world of experience and horror, he can, like Ishmael, retain this central core intact. In "The Blanket" (LXVIII) Ishmael even proposes the whale as an image of man, for the whale suggests how man may protect this central core by a thick wall of blubber to make room for "interior spaciousness" and "strong individual vitality," retaining "in all seasons a temperature of thine own." A man of great inwardness has to have "thick walls"; he cannot be open to every wind that lashes and retain his "interior spaciousness." He has to have a wall between inner and outer for there to be an "inner" at all. This is what the young Platonist, who thought his inwardness was one with all reality, failed to see.

To be protected from the incursion of reality, however, means to be protected from the full truth. It is the diabolism of the natural world that makes "truth" so inhuman, so impossible for man to bear. In "Stubb's Supper" (LXIV), through a comparison between Stubb eating a whale steak above decks and the sharks eating whale meat below, Melville extends the cannibalism of the sea to the cannibalism of men, producing, as in this parallel between sharks and pirates that he draws along with it, a picture of "a shocking, sharkish" world all around:

> Though amid all the smoking horror and diabolism of a sea-fight, sharks will be seen longingly gazing up to the ship's decks, like hungry dogs round a table where red meat is being carved, ready to bolt down every killed man that is tossed to them, and though while the valiant butchers over the deck-table are thus cannibally carving each other's live meat with carving knives all gilded and tasselled, the sharks, also, with their jewel-hilted mouths, are quarrelsomely carving away under the table at the dead meat; and though, were you to turn the whole affair upside down, it would still be pretty much the same thing, that is to say, a shocking sharkish business enough for all parties; and though sharks also are the invariable outriders of all slave ships crossing the Atlantic, systematically trotting alongside to be handy in case a parcel is to be carried anywhere, or a dead slave to be decently buried; and though one or two other like instances might be set down, touching the set terms, places, and occasions, when sharks do most socially congregate, and most hilariously feast; yet is there no conceivable time or occasion when you will find them in such countless numbers, and in gayer or more jovial spirits, than around a dead Sperm Whale, moored by night to a whale-ship at sea. If you have never seen that sight, then suspend your decision about the propriety of devil-worship, and the expediency of conciliating the devil.

Having discovered that evil is the reality lurking under the appearance of the good, you might well worship a devil-god, as Melville has Ahab's mysterious harpooner Fedallah do, who in this respect is not a Parsee at all but a Gnostic. Contrary to the balance between good and evil suggested by "The Whiteness of the Whale," evil is the one real power in the world.

This suggestion of the sharks as image of man and the universe is reinforced in "The Shark Massacre" (LXVI). The sharks viciously snap not only at each other's disembowelments but also at their own entrails. Even in their corpses there lurks "a sort of generic or Pantheistic vitality." This is no longer the pantheism of the young Platonist who saw man and nature as at one with God, but a pantheism of universal, diabolic, demonic evil. Evil is not only real; it is a fully alive, universal, all-encompassing reality, enough to evoke from the shark-bitten Queequeg the exclamation: "Queequeg don't care what god made him shark, wedder Fejee god or Nantucket god; but de god wat made shark must be one dam Ingin." What sort of a god *could* create this evil world? "Did he who made the Lamb make thee?" when "thee" is no longer even a dreadful yet symmetrical tiger but these voracious, horrible sharks—and voracious, horrible man?

4

ISHMAEL, BARTLEBY,
AND THE CONFIDENCE MAN:
THE MODERN EXILE

Ahab is the Modern Promethean, Ishmael the Modern Exile. Ishmael's exile is perhaps no greater than Ahab's, yet he accepts and lives within his exile as Ahab, the romantic rebel, does not. *Moby Dick* begins with the statement, "Call me Ishmael," and the Ishmael of the whaling world is, indeed, another such exile from home and wanderer in the "wilderness of waters" as the Biblical Ishmael who is driven forth into the wilderness by his father Abraham. As Melville's Ishmael describes himself, so the Lord describes the Biblical Ishmael: "He shall be a wild ass of a man, his hand against every man and every man's hand against him" (Gen. 16:12).

"No man is an island entire of itself; every man is a piece of the continent, a part of the main," says John Donne in his famous Meditation (XVII). In explicit contrast to Donne, Ishmael begins as an *"Isolato,"* "not acknowledging the common continent of men, but . . . living on a separate continent of his own." The world itself to Ishmael is not a voyage complete—a harmony or an order—but "a ship on the passage out."

Ishmael the contemplative knows that "meditation and water are wedded for ever" and that "the tormenting, mild image" that Narcissus grasped at in vain is the fountain "we ourselves see in all rivers and oceans": "It is the image of the ungraspable phantom of life; and this is the key to it all." Ishmael's narcissism lies not in contemplating his own mirrored image but the image of life and the world, and if he is as likely to drown as Narcissus, it is not from reaching for himself but for "the undeliverable, nameless perils" of the great whale. "Not ignoring what is good, I am quick to perceive a horror, and could still be social with it," says Ishmael. At the heart of horror is wonder, and horror and wonder are wedded, as nowhere else, in *Moby Dick.* It is Ishmael, the contemplator, not Ahab, the mad avenger, who gives us in "Loomings" (I), our first, archetypal glimpse of the great White Whale:

> The great flood-gates of the wonder-world swung open, and in the wild conceits that swayed me to my purpose, two and two there floated into my inmost soul, endless processions of the whale, and, mid most of them all, one grand hooded phantom, like a snow hill in the air.

In "The Whiteness of the Whale" Ishmael is no longer so ready to be sociable with horror. The ultimate terror, to him, is the indifference of an absolute that excludes man: "Is it that by its indefiniteness," Ishmael asks, that whiteness "shadows forth the heartless voids and immensities of the universe, and thus stabs us from behind with the thought of annihilation, when beholding the white depths of the milky way?" Here we have the exact opposite of "The Lee Shore" in which truth was "shoreless, indefinite as God." Now indefiniteness is not a characteristic of truth but of an irra-

tional force that threatens us with annihilation. When Bulkington drowns, he is not "annihilated": part of him leaps up
from the ocean spray a demigod, a Promethean tragic hero
whose search for truth makes him immortal even when he
perishes in the quest. Not so the young Platonist's drowning,
similar though it might seem, for there is no relationship possible to the indifferent adversary that destroys him—that
purely quantitative infinite of sheer nonlimitation that has
no respect for human limitations. Here we have evil in its
second major form of indifference, an evil as terrible or more
terrible than the first form of intelligible malignity. In the end
these two types of evil fuse in such a way that the book receives the full cumulative force of both: the inscrutability
of the malignant whale joins with the indifference of the infinite universe; while the hostile whale comes toward the
sailor and tears him to bits, the sun and the sea smile on
indifferently "as at a birth or bridal." There is, however, an
important difference between these two types of evil, symbolized by Ahab's concentration on Moby Dick himself and
Ishmael's concentration on the whiteness of his hump. In Ahab
all evil focuses *in* to Moby Dick. In Ishmael the whiteness of
the whale points *out* to the whole universe. Ishmael can tolerate diffuse anxiety and Ahab cannot. In the language of modern
psychiatry, Ahab is analogous to the paranoiac, Ishmael the
neurotic. Ahab personalizes all evil—for him even the intangible is malignant. Ishmael depersonalizes it—behind the
universe there is, perhaps, not an evil god but a heartless
and indifferent void.[1] While Ahab has a more terrible alone-

[1] William Charvat offers us an important caution at this point. Melville's
object, he observes, "was to get the reader to entertain the *possibility*—
not the certainty—that behind the immensities of the universe there is
a blank void of nothingness, of No-God, from which emanate terrors beyond our comprehension. . . . After a long list of the accepted benign
associations of whiteness, he tried to lead the reader, example by example, to the realization that white is also the symbol of terror, and that
therefore malignity and benignity are inseparably one. The climactic
paragraph, in which the appalling proposition is put, is not assertion but
question. The reader is told not that evil is absolute, but that *if* we
grasp imaginatively all the associations of whiteness, then we are in a
position to understand a madman's 'fiery hunt' for the source of evil. But
we are also warned that he who sees nothing but the 'colorless, all-color

ness and isolation from other men than Ishmael, his belief that in attacking Moby Dick he is rebelling against the evil that torments him makes his exile less profound than that of Ishmael who cannot come up against, much less hate, the indifferent evil that oppresses him.

In "The Fossil Whale," in a horror reminiscent of "The Whiteness of the Whale," Ishmael obtains "dim shuddering glimpses" into the "Polar eternities" of "preadamite" time and is "horror-struck at this antemosaic, unsourced existence of the unspeakable terrors of the whale, which, having been before all time, must needs exist after all humane ages are over." What Copernicus and Pascal stated of space, Ishmael here states of time: that man is not its center, that human life shrinks into itself in terror before the vision, pre-eminently accorded to modern man, of time stretching indefinitely into the past and the future. The chapter that begins with man-handling the Leviathan leaves us at the end with our categories abandoned, our inquiring mind stilled in silent worship before the "wholly other," numinous reality of the Whale.

"If I know not even the tail of this whale," says Ishmael in "The Tail," "how understand his head? Much more, how comprehend his face, when face he has none? Thou shalt see my back parts, my tail, he seems to say, but my face shall not be seen." Moses was only allowed to see the back of God, for "no man can see God's face and live." Yet this did not prevent God from speaking "to Moses face to face, as a man speaks to his friend" (Exodus 33:11, 18-23). Ishmael's god is faceless in a terrible sense: "Hint what he will about his face,

---

of atheism' is a 'wretched infidel' who 'gazes himself blind.'" William Charvat, "Melville and the Common Reader," *Studies in Bibliography, Papers of the Biographical Society of the University of Virginia,* XII (1959), p. 53. Our approach differs from Charvat's, however, in that he seems to see Ishmael's only purpose as helping us imaginatively to understand Ahab's chase rather than as also presenting what the White Whale meant to him, as he announces at the beginning of the chapter. Nor can the warning with which the chapter ends be understood as anything less than the danger arising from the contact with truth. This contact is intolerable *because of the very nature of that truth.* It is in this same form of a warning that Ishmael has commented on the terrible nature of reality throughout the rest of the book.

I say again, he has no face." We cannot say "Thou" to this god, because he is no "Thou," not even in relation to man: he is the blank indifferent "It." The special terror in the modern vision of evil is that it is completely impersonal. "Le silence éternel de ces espaces infinis m'effraie," says Pascal. Behind Ishmael's imageless god is not the God of Job who can speak to man out of the whirlwind but the "dead God" who cannot speak at all—the god who is no god. Melville gives still more explicit expression to this in *Pierre* in his criticism of the "delusion" of idealist philosophers and their transcendentalist followers:

> That profound Silence, that only Voice of our God . . . from that divine thing without a name, those impostor philosophers pretend somehow to have got an answer; which is absurd, as though they should say they had got water out of stone; for how can a man get a Voice out of Silence? [2]

Ishmael's evil of indifference is echoed by Ahab when he complains of the "frozen heavens" and "creative libertines" who abandoned poor Pip, the Negro cabin boy, to insanity on the immense ocean—"the omniscient gods oblivious of suffering man." In "The Castaway" (XCIII) poor little Pip, the cabin boy, who has gone out on one of the whaleboats, foolishly jumps over the side and is left by Stubb, who assumes that he will be picked up by one of the two boats in his wake. But they turn before spying him, and only by merest chance is he picked up later on by the ship itself. The "awful lonesomeness" of the open, shoreless ocean "is intolerable," says Ishmael. "The intense concentration of self in the middle of such a heartless immensity, my God! who can tell it?" The "heartless immensity" of the ocean, no less than "the heartless voids and immensities of the universe," forces us to realize our own limitedness, our own mortality. When a man loses his limits, when he can no longer retain his inwardness and at the same time relate to the world outside, he has lost that condition that makes human existence possible. Even if he

[2] Herman Melville, *Pierre, or the Ambiguities* (New York: Grove Press, 1957, Evergreen E-55), p. 290.

remains alive, he ceases to be really human, and this is what happens with Pip: "The sea had jeeringly kept his finite body up, but drowned the infinite of his soul." He has gone mad.

"The Carpenter" (CVII) begins with a distinction between the tragic dimensions of man regarded singly and the triviality of man in the mass:

> Seat thyself sultanically among the moons of Saturn, and take high abstracted man alone; and he seems a wonder, a grandeur, and a woe. But from the same point, take mankind in mass, and for the most part, they seem a mob of unnecessary duplicates, both contemporary and hereditary.

The Pequod's carpenter, though no duplicate himself, embodies "a certain impersonal stolidity" that makes him look indifferently not only on men, but on all reality, as interchangeable parts of some general mechanism. "Teeth he accounted bits of ivory; heads he deemed but top-blocks; men themselves he lightly held for capstans." If he is not a mere machine, he is a robot with the humming soliloquy of an unreasoning wheel for a soul, "a pure manipulator" who works "by a kind of deaf and dumb, spontaneous literal process." He has no history and no organic relation to the world of man and nature: "He was a stript abstract; an unfractioned integral; uncompromised as a new-born babe; living without premeditated reference to this world or the next." Yet, even so, he represents a principle at the heart of reality, for his impersonal stolidity seems "one with the general stolidity discernible in the whole visible world," a stolidity that indifferently "ignores you, though you dig foundations for cathedrals."

In "Ahab and the Carpenter" (CXXVII) Ahab equates the carpenter's indifference with that indifference of which he accuses the gods when he is confronted by the insane Pip:

> "Then tell me; art thou not an arrant, all-grasping, intermeddling, monopolizing, heathenish old scamp, to be one day making legs, and the next day coffins to clap them in, and yet again life-buoys out of those same coffins? Thou

art as unprincipled as the gods, and as much of a jack-of-all-trades."

"But I do not mean anything, Sir. I do as I do."

"The gods again."

The indifference of the gods means the annihilation of all human value, for it is a denial of human personality in its unrepeatable uniqueness. The carpenter is "alike indifferent and without respect in all," even as Ahab's image of the gods —"deaf Burkes and blind Bendigoes."

Apart from Ishmael, only Starbuck sees the mad chase as a progress into exile. "Is this the end of all my bursting prayers? all my life-long fidelities?" Starbuck cries when he is facing death. The world is given over to this fiend Ahab. God exists, but he does not show himself, he does not intervene and help. He is an "indifferent God" who leaves the whole crew to their fate. For Starbuck, as for the Manxman, "the skewer seems loosening out of the middle of the world." [3] "I misdoubt me that I disobey my God in obeying him!" Starbuck murmurs to himself at the beginning of the last day of the chase. But as the crew's "fear of Ahab was greater than their fear of Fate," Starbuck's sense of the reality of Ahab is more distinct and compelling than that of his hiding God. "Great God, where art thou? Shall I? Shall I?" Starbuck exclaims when he stands in Ahab's cabin with Ahab's musket trying in vain to bring himself to kill the sleeping Ahab so that he "may survive to hug his wife and child again." In the world of the Pequod, God is in eclipse and Ahab is the moon that hides that sun. This divine indifference comes into the sharpest focus in the cry of anguish and protest with which Starbuck responds to Ahab's boast in "The Chase—Second Day" (CXXXIV), "I'll ten times girdle the unmeas-

[3] Nathalia Wright in *Melville's Use of the Bible* (Durham, N.C.: Duke University Press, 1949), rightly points out the startling resemblance between this statement and W. B. Yeats' poem "The Second Coming": "Things fall apart; the center cannot hold;/Mere anarchy is loosed upon the world." There is also an amazing similarity between the ending of "The Second Coming"—"And what rough beast, its hour come round at last,/Slouches towards Bethlehem to be born?"—and a passage from Melville's *Clarel*—"Is faith dead *now?* . . . /Then what's in store? what shapeless birth?/Reveal the doom reserved for earth?"

ured globe . . . I'll slay him yet!":

> "Great God! but for one single instant show thyself . . .
> Shall we keep chasing this murderous fish till he swamps
> the last man? Shall we be towed by him to the infernal
> world? Oh, oh,—Impiety and blasphemy to hunt him
> more!"

There is, Ishmael repeatedly suggests, no such thing as a
normal, safe, objective reality that can be held up in contrast
to the demonic world of "crazy Ahab." In "The Line" (LX)
Ishmael speaks of the whaleboats setting out after a whale
and the harpoon lines whizzing along that might at any point
catch one by the neck and throw one out of the boat into the
sea. But for Ishmael the whale line is not a symbol of the
dangers of whaling alone, nor even of the sea or the search
for truth. Rather, it is the true symbol of human existence in
general, of the human condition on land or sea:

> All men live enveloped in whale-lines. All are born with
> halters round their necks; but it is only when caught in
> the swift, sudden turn of death, that mortals realize the
> silent, subtle, ever-present perils of life. And if you be
> a philosopher, though seated in a whale-boat, you would
> not at heart feel one whit more of terror, than though
> seated before your evening fire with a poker, and not a
> harpoon, by your side.

Even the land now offers no real shelter from the "horrors of
the half known life."

Ishmael begins "The Try-Works" (XCVI) with a suggestion
of the predominance of evil similar to that in "The Shark
Massacre." This sense of rampant diabolism is strengthened
by the impression Ishmael receives at the helm, as described
in a remarkable accumulation of powerful images that captures in a single symbolic sentence both the ship's dramatic
progress to destruction and the intense, single-minded driving of Ahab's soul:

> As they narrated to each other their unholy adventures,

their tales of terror told in words of mirth; as their un-
civilized laughter forked upwards out of them, like the
flames from the furnace; as to and fro, in their front, the
harpooneers wildly gesticulated with their huge pronged
forks and dippers; as the wind howled on, and the sea
leaped, and the ship groaned and dived, and yet stead-
fastly shot her red hell further and further into the blackness of the sea and the night, and scornfully champed the
white bone in her mouth, and viciously spat round her
on all sides; then the rushing Pequod, freighted with
savages, and laden with fire, and burning a corpse, and
plunging into that blackness of darkness, seemed the
material counterpart of her monomaniac commander's
soul.

This ship is a little world that, like the great one, has neither meaning nor purpose, as, like some gigantic horse, it
bears its burning freight into the night. The picture of the
ship driven by furies to a relentless doom and the implicit
suggestion that this is also the ship of the world "on its passage out" is reinforced by the impression uppermost in Ishmael's mind as he stands at the helm, "that whatever swift,
rushing thing I stood on was not so much bound to any
haven ahead as rushing from all havens astern." The unsur-
passable image of chaos that these passages afford suggests
not only the diabolism of the ancient Gnostics but also modern man's sense of the earth hurtling through the empty
space of the heavens on its meaningless progress to extinc-
tion. Even the sentence which seems to imply a purpose to
the voyage—"The burning ship drove on, as if remorselessly
commissioned to some vengeful deed"—actually gives us a
foreboding of the predestined end of Ahab's quest and
hints at the chaos which is at the core of his cosmos.

Caught up in this vision, Ishmael gets turned around at
the wheel and almost capsizes the ship. The terror and inse-
curity which this incident causes Ishmael leads him, in
marked contrast to Captain Ahab, to a general injunction
against turning away from the known guides—the helm, the
compass, and the tiller—to look into "the artificial fire when
its redness makes all things ghastly." The warning to Ishmael,

the steerer of the ship, becomes, through Ishmael the narrator, a warning to all men who are steering a direction into the unknown future: "Look not too long in the face of the fire, O man! Never dream with thy hand on the helm!" The young Platonist fell to his death because he dreamed on the mast-head when he should have been looking for whales and watching his footing. Ishmael's vision of evil at the helm of the fire ship in the night is the very opposite of the young Platonist's sense of oneness with all the universe, but it is just as much a dream, just as much a partial reality which will destroy man if he fails to see its proper limits and allows it to become the whole. "Believe not the artificial fire . . . To-morrow, in the natural sun, the skies will be bright." The unnatural fire that "glared like devils in the forking flames" will show up in gentler relief in the light of "the glorious, golden, glad sun, the only true lamp—all others but liars!"

But if the fire is artificial, the ocean is all too real, and the same sun which disperses the night and all false lamps can only light up, not hide, this dark two-thirds of the earth. To face reality means to recognize the predominance of evil and suffering: "That mortal man who hath more of joy than sorrow in him . . . cannot be true, not true, or undeveloped . . . The truest of all men was the Man of Sorrows, and the truest of all books is Solomon's and Ecclesiastes is the fine hammered steel of woe. 'All is vanity.' ALL."

In the "Epilogue" we are told that after Moby Dick has "stove in" the Pequod and it has sunk, Ishmael falls into the water too far from the vortex to be sucked down into it. He is pulled near enough to the "vital center" to reach Queequeg's "coffin life-buoy" when it is thrown up by the bursting bubble. In a remarkable suspension of hostilities the cannibalistic sea refrains from devouring Ishmael until, on the second day, he is picked up. "The unharming sharks, they glided by as if with padlocks on their mouths; the savage sea-hawks sailed with sheathed beaks." The destruction which engulfs not only mad Ahab but right-minded Starbuck, jolly Stubb, and the whole anarchic crew, spares Ishmael, the man who has gone forth to look into the fire but who has turned back before "the wisdom that is woe" could descend into "the woe that is madness."

Ishmael's survival is obviously more than a technical device for getting the story told—Melville has often dispensed with Ishmael as narrator, particularly in this whole last section leading up to and during the chase. Nor is Ishmael saved because he is a man of equal stature to Ahab who shows the right way to oppose the demonic. At its simplest, his being spared suggests youth's privilege of flinging itself into a terrible experience and yet emerging from it to new life. Ishmael experiences without commitment. He is not a mere observer, but neither is he a full participant. At a deeper level, however, distinct overtones of resurrection sound forth.[4] In "Loomings" (I) Ishmael links his impulse to take ship with thoughts of death and suicide:

> Whenever I find myself growing grim about the mouth; whenever it is a damp, drizzly November in my soul; whenever I find myself involuntarily pausing before coffin warehouses, and bringing up the rear of every funeral I meet; . . . then I account it high time to get to sea as soon as I can. . . . With a philosophical flourish Cato throws himself upon his sword; I quietly take to the ship.

Now, at the very end of the book, Ishmael is saved by a coffin that his friend Queequeg, the cannibalistic South Sea Island harpooner, had the ship's carpenter make for him when he thought he was going to die. When Queequeg unexpectedly recovered, the coffin was used as a life-buoy, a fact which leads Ahab himself in "Ahab and the Carpenter" (CXXVII) to a meditation that brings out clearly its significance as a symbol of resurrection, while stressing the fact

---

[4] Ishmael's resurrection is prefigured in "The Hyena" (XLIX) where he expresses the "genial desperado philosophy" bred by the perils of whaling by making a will and then feeling that "the days I should now live would be as good as the days that Lazarus lived after his resurrection; a supplementary clean gain of so many months or weeks as the case might be. I survived myself. . . . Now then, thought I, . . . here goes for a cool, collected dive at death and destruction, and the devil fetch the hindmost."

that it is no longer possible for him to have a share in any redemption.

> "Oh! how immaterial are all materials! What things real are there, but imponderable thoughts! Here now's the very dreaded symbol of grim death, by a mere hap, made the expressive sign of the help and hope of most endangered life. A life-buoy of a coffin! . . . Can it be that in some spiritual sense the coffin is, after all, but an immortality-preserver! I'll think of that. But no. So far gone am I in the dark side of earth, that its other side, the theoretic bright one, seems but uncertain twilight to me."

In the "Epilogue" the coffin suggests resurrection still more clearly by the way in which it emerges from the sea after the ship has sunk. Everything had been pulled down into the great vortex, including the coffin itself.

> Till, gaining that vital centre, the black bubble upward burst; and now, liberated by reason of its cunning spring, and owing to its great buoyancy, rising with great force, the coffin life-buoy shot lengthwise from the sea, fell over, and floated by my side. Buoyed up by that coffin, for almost one whole day and night, I floated on a soft and dirge-like main.

This resurrection symbol gains still further content—some critics would say its most important content of all—through the fact that the coffin is Queequeg's and that Queequeg and Ishmael have what Ahab and Starbuck fail to achieve— a friendship, a relationship of genuine mutuality, of reciprocal help, love, and care. This friendship begins even in "The Spouter-Inn" (III) and is what leads the two men to sail on the same ship. Once established in the early chapters, it receives relatively little attention throughout the book, as does Ishmael the participant himself. In "The Monkey Rope" (LXXII), however, the working relationship between the two men becomes an image of man for Ishmael, as Queequeg balances himself on the whale's back in the water, amidst the sharks, beginning the work of cutting in and stripping, while Ishmael, on the deck above, is joined to him by a "monkey rope" made fast to the belts of both men.

I seemed distinctly to perceive that my own individuality was now merged in a joint stock company of two: that my free will had received a mortal wound; and that another's mistake or misfortune might plunge innocent me into unmerited disaster and death . . . I say that this situation of mine was the precise situation of every mortal that breathes; only, in most cases, he, one way or other, has this Siamese connexion with a plurality of other mortals.

This is indeed "the precious image of each and all of us men in this whaling world." Man's free will cannot be understood—as the *cogito ergo sum* philosopher and the nineteenth-century individualist would wish to understand it—as a function of independent, primarily isolated individuals; or even, as the Greeks understood it, as the freedom of the individual to work out his fate within a larger destiny. We are linked directly to other men, to the other man; we move with him, and our free will is dependent on his so that together they become a common destiny. This destiny is not an impersonal necessity but a shared interhuman reality— "a joint stock company of two," at once economic co-operation and reciprocal relationship. Ishmael is free to pull on his end of the rope, but he also "cannot possibly forget that, do what I would, I only had the management of one end of it."

This interpretation is given still further weight if we add to Ishmael's statement in "Loomings" of why he took to sea the sentence we formerly omitted—"And especially whenever my hypos gets such an upper hand of me, that it requires a strong moral principle to prevent me from deliberately stepping into the street, and methodically knocking people's hats off"—and recall that this inner state begins to change even before he has sailed on the Pequod, at the point when he and Queequeg become friends: "I felt a melting in me. No more my splintered heart and maddened hand were turned against the wolfish world. This soothing savage had redeemed it." "We cannibals must help these Christians," Ishmael has Queequeg say, as it were, after he has saved a man from drowning, and it is Cannibal Queequeg who saves

Christian Ishmael—both members of "the First Congrega-
tional Church" of mankind—when the coffin-canoe that was
to bear the dead body and tranquil spirit of the one becomes
the coffin-life-buoy that bears the live body and the resur-
rected spirit of the other. Ishmael does not offer an alternative point of view to Ahab nor succeed in the quest for
truth where Ahab fails, but he discovers in the sphere of
the interhuman the means for overcoming a sterile isolation
and entering into a trusting and meaningful relationship
with existence.

As the Biblical Ishmael is saved from death in the wilderness to become the father of a great nation (Gen. 21:9-21),
so Melville's Ishmael is saved from death in the ocean to return to the society of the land. The ship that picks up Ishmael at the end is the Rachel. When the Pequod meets the
Rachel (CXXVIII), just before the final case, the Rachel has
lost one whaleboat containing the captain's twelve-year-old
son. Ahab refuses the captain's earnest plea to go in search
of her with all the hardness of inexorable fate. "Even now I
lose time," says Ahab, too preoccupied with his attack on the
nonhuman to be willing to turn aside, even momentarily, to
help the human. In contrast to the unswerving progress of
the maniacally captained Pequod, the Rachel's departing
course is the very picture of the faltering, groping path of human misery: "By her still halting course and winding, woeful
way, you plainly saw that this ship that so wept with spray,
still remained without comfort. She was Rachel, weeping
for her children, because they were not." But the Rachel suggests human compassion as well as human suffering, the moth-
erly compassion that Ahab necessarily excludes from his com-
fortless masculine world. If the Rachel does not find the
captain's son and Ishmael is not picked up by his own ship,
still it is of more than stepmotherly moment when the sail that
draws ever nearer to the floating Ishmael turns out to be
"the devious-cruising Rachel, that in her retracing search
after her missing children, only found another orphan." It is
with these words that *Moby Dick* ends—not with a merely
aesthetic enclosure, as when the sea rolls on indifferently
over the sunken Pequod, not with the peaceful harmony of

Shakespeare's *Tempest* in which "the sea change" is after all a dream one can wake up from, but with the chastened comfort experienced by the lonely exile who has found at least a temporary haven.

Although Ishmael partly overcomes his isolation in his friendship with Queequeg and his return to the society of the land, he is still an "orphan." Ishmael's rescue by the *Rachel* suggests overtones of the redemption of the Shekina —the immanent Glory of God of the Talmud and the Kabbala.[5] But it reminds us still more strongly that prior to that redemption, the Shekina is traditionally pictured as in exile. If the modern corollary of the exile of the Shekina is the "death" or "eclipse" of God, the modern corollary of the Biblical Ishmael is Ishmael the Modern Exile. "Ishmael is not merely an orphan," writes Alfred Kazin:

> He is an exile, searching alone in the wilderness, with a black man for his only friend . . . This agony of disbelief *is* his homelessness . . . He is man, or as we like to think, modern man, cut off from the certainty that was

[5] The symbol of Rachel weeping for her children is employed by Jeremiah in the Hebrew Bible, and Jeremiah's passage is quoted by Matthew in the New Testament (Matthew 2:17-18). Melville was deeply concerned with the Prophet Jeremiah, as Nathalia Wright points out, and he marked in his text not only these verses of "lamentation and bitter weeping" (Jeremiah 31:15) but also the verses of comfort that precede and follow them. (Wright, *op. cit.*, pp. 91-93. Cf. pp. 84-90.) Jeremiah, the prophet who above all refused to soften the word of disaster with the preachment of safety, couples his vision of Israel's exile with a vision of its redemption from exile when the remnant in the wilderness are saved and Israel's children return to their own country (Jeremiah 31: 2-13). Melville, who read not only in the "Old" Testament but in the' Talmud—the Aramaic Targum—may also have known from there, or from Christian sources, that in normative and mystical Judaism the exile of Israel became a central symbol not only for the destiny of the people but for the complementary destiny of God. In the Talmud, the holy spirit is hypostatized as the Shekina, the form of the divine immanence, the indwelling Glory of God. In intentional parallel with the exile of Israel from the Holy Land, the Shekina is pictured as in exile from God and redemption as the reunification of God and his exiled Glory. Nathalia Wright points out Melville's use of the Shekina in passages as widely separated in his career as Babbalanja's vision in *Mardi* and the first draft of the ending of *Billy Budd*. "Billy took the full Shekina of the dawn." (*Ibid.*, pp. 117, 135, 160 f.) In the Kabbala the *Ein Sof*, God's infinite transcendence, is identified with the husband, the Shekina

once his inner world . . . What Melville did through Ishmael was to put man's distinctly modern feeling of "exile," or abandonment, directly at the center of the stage.[6]

In his story "Bartleby the Scrivener" (1853) Melville carries the Modern Exile a stage beyond his representation in Ishmael. In its paradoxical strangeness and its portrayal of a condition of alienation utterly devoid of romantic pathos, "Bartleby" is a remarkable anticipation of Kafka and Camus. Bartleby himself bears an amazing resemblance to many of Kafka's heroes in the sense that he gives of being afforded existence only on the narrowest and most restricted terms.

The true story is not Bartleby in himself but his employer's relation to him. The employer is not only the narrator of the story and the point of view; he is also in himself the representative of that humanity on which Bartleby impinges through his uncommon yet "common" humanity. The employer, by his own confession, is a man filled from his youth upwards "with a profound conviction that the easiest way of life is the best." His first grand point was prudence, his second method, according to John Jacob Astor, who but confirmed thereby the general opinion that he was "an eminently safe man." This complete unwillingness to venture is reflected in his practice which never calls him forth to address a jury but leaves him "in the cool tranquility of a snug retreat," to "do a snug business among rich men's bonds, and mortgages, and title-deeds." Even his law chambers of Wall Street offer a tame view, deficient in "life," namely the soot-blackened square cistern made by the walls of the surrounding high buildings. In similar fashion, he ex-

---

with the wife who wanders in exile, suffering the misery of the world and yearning to be reunited with her husband. This feminine Shekina was also identified in the Kabbala with Jeremiah's Rachel weeping for her children. (Cf. Gershom G. Scholem, *Major Trends in Jewish Mysticism* [revised ed. New York: Schocken Books, 1950] p. 230.) It is possible that Melville himself knew this, in which case the rescue of Ishmael by the Rachel takes on still another depth-dimension.

[6] Alfred Kazin, "Ishmael and Ahab," *The Atlantic Monthly*, LXCVII (Jul.-Dec. 1956), Nov. 1956, pp. 82 f.

ploits his law clerks, or scriveners, to the fullest, but, "being a man of peace," does not insist when they refuse to take off work during their "fits." Since Nipper's fit is on when Turkey's is off and vice versa, the narrator accepts this as "a good natural arrangement, under the circumstances."

It is against this background that we first meet Bartleby, who comes in answer to an advertisement and stands, "a motionless young man," upon his office threshold—"pallidly neat, pitiably respectable, incurably forlorn!" At the same time he is described as "so singularly sedate" in aspect that the employer is glad to have him among his corps of copyists. Instead of placing him with the others he assigns him a corner on his side of the folding doors, "so as to have this quiet man within easy call, in case any trifling thing was to be done." Bartleby presents all the aspect of an efficient office machine which the employer is glad to take advantage of without troubling over the eclipsed humanity that this quiet efficiency purports. Bartleby's window commands no view at all, though it gives some light through a small opening between buildings. To make his enclosure more complete still, the employer put up a high green folding screen which entirely isolates Bartleby from his sight while not removing him from his commanding voice. Bartleby fits into this "satisfactory arrangement" with machine-like compliance, writing by sunlight and candlelight. The only thing that mars the employer's delight in Bartleby's application is the fact that he is not "cheerfully industrious" but writes on "silently, palely, mechanically."

Even so, one may imagine that this arrangement would have gone on indefinitely had not Bartleby one day surprised his employer by the quiet words "I prefer not to" when asked to compare a copy sheet. Without anger, impatience, or impertinence, Bartleby sets a limit to the employer's ready willingness to relate to him as a non-human machine. At the outermost margins of personal existence without active rebellion or "anything ordinarily human," Bartleby asserts through his passive resistance that he does after all exist as a self, even if only in this entirely negative form.

The employer is flabbergasted, to say the least. In the face of this mild but unmovable wall, he feels helpless and unable to act. "I should have as soon thought of turning my pale plaster-of-paris bust of Cicero out of doors," he confesses. With any other man he would have flown into a rage and thrust him ignominiously away, but Bartleby not only strangely disarms him, "in a wonderful manner" he touches and disconcerts him. What touches and disconcerts the employer? The curious mixture of the human and the inhuman. The ordinary picture of the exploiter is that of a ruthless man. The narrator of our story, in contrast, is an "easy-going" man who combines exploitation with ruth. The very nature of his exploitation, in fact, is his willingness to take advantage of Bartleby's eccentricities without raising too much fuss or demanding for Bartleby what he can or will not demand for himself. After his surprise at Bartleby's failure to fulfill duties which are customary for copyists, the employer quickly becomes reconciled to the new situation, again on the basis of his own advantage.

> His steadiness, his freedom from all dissipation, his incessant industry (except when he chose to throw himself into a standing reverie behind his screen), his great stillness, his unalterableness of demeanour under all circumstances, made him a valuable acquisition. One prime thing was this—*he was always there*—first in the morning, continually through the day, and the last at night. I had a singular confidence in his honesty.[7] (18)

This adjustment on the part of the employer to what is so manifestly his own best interests does not prevent him from "falling into sudden spasmodic passions" with Bartleby. But the passion is not so much anger as it is irritation at something that troubles routine and makes it necessary for him to think in unaccustomed ways: "It was exceedingly difficult to bear in mind all the time those strange pecularities, privi-

[7] All page references are to William Plommer's edition of "Bartleby" in Herman Melville, *Four Short Novels* (New York: Bantam books, 1959).

leges, and unheard-of exemptions, forming the tacit stipulations on Bartleby's part under which he remained in my office."

It is a strange reversal of situation that allows the employee rather than the employer to stipulate the terms of work, especially when this stipulation is not based on any contractual agreement or mututal bargaining but upon an entirely unexplained and undefended "I prefer not to." That the employer puts up with such a fiat from his employee seems to be due to the fact that Bartleby's paleness and lack of life "touch" him while his "wonderful mildness" disarms and unmans him. The employer confesses to a strange and superstitious knocking at his heart, threatening to denounce him for a villain if he dares "to breathe one bitter word against this forlornest of mankind."

This still does not adequately explain why Bartleby so disconcerts the employer. He is continually at a loss as to what response he can make to Bartleby's quiet setting of limits, which finally extends to preferring not to do any work at all, at the same time preferring not to quit the office. This rupture of the climate of social expectation catapults the nineteenth-century Bartleby into the absurd world of Camus's *The Stranger* and Kafka's "The Judgment." If Bartleby had sought to justify his refusal to comply with some rational or emotional argument, if he had even said I *will* not instead of I *prefer* not, the employer would have known how to respond. As it is, Bartleby, destroys the common world of mutual expectation within which the easy-going employer exploits and indulges his employees.

> It is not seldom the case that, when a man is browbeaten in some unprecedentedly and violently unreasonable way, he begins to stagger in his plainest faith. He begins, as it were, vaguely to surmise that, wonderful as it may be, all the justice and all the reason is on the other side. (13 f.)

The language that the employer uses here is entirely inappropriate. Bartleby browbeats nobody, and there is nothing violent even about his unreasonableness. Nor is there any reason to suppose that what is in question here is whether reason and justice are on one side or the other, since these terms are utterly irrelevant to the situation. But the situation *is* an unprecedented one, and the employer does stagger in his plainest faith—the faith that rests on a common social world, a common social expectation that Bartleby no longer shares.

The employer continues to stagger in his plainest faith as Bartleby's "I prefer not to" becomes ever more absolute. Bartleby is a human being who has placed himself outside the realm of the human—the interpersonal and interhuman relations between man and man. His actions no longer exist in living interchange with those of other men. He exercises his subjectivity in becoming a thing, or as the employer labels him, an office "fixture." When the employer orders Bartleby to be gone by the next morning, he is at first charmed by the fact that "without loudly bidding Bartleby depart—as an inferior genius might have done— I *assumed* the ground that depart he must; and upon that assumption built all I had to say." But the cold light of morning brings to him the awareness that an assumption means nothing when the common ground of social expectation and reciprocal interaction is no longer present.

> It was truly a beautiful thought to have assumed Bartleby's departure; but, after all, that assumption was simply my own, and none of Bartleby's. The great point was, not whether I had assumed that he would quit me, but whether he would prefer so to do. He was more a man of preferences than as-assumptions. (27)

It is this world of ruptured expectations and mistaken assumptions that makes it necessary for the jury in Camus's *The Stranger* to convict Meursault of not weeping at his mother's funeral. Threatened by the fact that Meursault's murder of the Arab was completely unmotivated and absurd, they attempt to portray Meursault as a fiend. They thereby only widen the gap of the absurd that separates Meursault, who expects nothing, from the society that judges and executes him. It is an absurd world too that leads Georg Bendemann to drown himself without protest when, in Kafka's story "The Judgment," his father sentences him to death by drowning.

Although from time to time the employer burns "to be rebelled against again," he gradually gives up any attempt to get Bartleby to do anything and acknowledges to himself "that wondrous ascendancy which the inscrutable scrivener had over me." One cause of this ascendancy is the fact that this "easy-going" man does not know how to relate to a man who is the opposite of easy-going, to someone, in fact, who stands on the outermost rim of human existence. The employer has spent his entire life shutting out whatever is not comfortable, safe, and snug, and now he is confronted with an "incubus" that places before him an augury of death from which he cannot escape. Bartleby's "mild effrontery" is spoken of, in almost the same breath, as a "cadaverously gentlemanly *nonchalance*," and everything about Bartleby suggests not life but death. He is installed behind the screen before the others arrive and remains after they leave. He never eats anything but ginger-nuts, is never seen to leave the office, and the employer discovers that he even lives there, sleeping on his chair at night.

This revelation of the "miserable friendlessness and lone-liness" of Bartleby's life places before the reluctant employer an image of a solitude which is even more horrible than Bartleby's poverty. His aloneness in the midst of the deserted Sunday Wall Street—"sole spectator of a solitude which he has seen all populous"—conjures up in the employer's mind the image of an "innocent and transformed Marius brooding among the ruins of Carthage!" As a result of this image, the employer is seized, *for the first time in his life*, by a "feeling of overpowering stinging melancholy." All he had ever experienced before was "a not unpleasing sadness," but now "the bond of a common humanity" draws him "irresistibly to gloom." Far out as Bartleby is from everything that is normal and human, he is still, like the employer, "a son of Adam." The revelation of his horrible aloneness arouses a feeling of "fraternal melancholy" which causes the employer to reflect, in language reminiscent of Ishmael's "wisdom that is woe," that "happiness courts the light, so we deem the world is gay; but misery hides aloof, so we deem that misery there is none." He has presentiments of Bartleby's corpse laid out among uncaring strangers, and he recalls "all the quiet mysteries" that set Bartleby off from other men—that he never speaks except to answer, that he never reads anything, not even a newspaper, but spends his leisure time staring out of a window in a dead reverie, that he never goes out for a walk, that he declines to give the least information about himself. Concluding that "the scrivener was the victim of innate and incurable disorder"—a disorder not of the body but of the soul—the employer tries to throw off the ghost that haunts him by inuring himself to a suffering which he cannot reach or help. His fraternal melancholy finally merges into fear and his pity into repulsion "just in proportion as the forlornness of Bartleby grew and grew to my imagination."

The forlornness of the Modern Exile is not only that of loneliness. It is also that of existence as a self surrounded by an oppressive, infinite reality of non-self that threatens at every moment to blot out the self. This oppressiveness can be experienced in two quite different worlds. One is the world of *Moby Dick* in which both Ahab and Ishmael stand facing a hostile and/or indifferent nature. The other is the world of Bartleby, a world in which the self stands without relation to other selves, without any assertion of its own existence or demand placed upon the existence of others, other than the sheer negative self-assertion of "I prefer not to." These two worlds come together in the employer's horrified reaction to the revelation of Bartleby's non-social existence. "I was sorry for him," he confesses. "He seemed absolutely alone in the universe. A bit of wreckage in the mid-Atlantic," like poor little Pip, the cabin boy who had to spend hours in the open sea without contact with any limit through which he could preseve his sense of himself as a person. In an entirely different sense, this is what happens with Bartleby. When the employer finally does tell Bartleby that he must go, he answers not a word. "Like the last column of some ruined temple, he remained standing mute and solitary in the middle of the otherwise deserted room."

The employer manages to reconcile himself to seeing Bartleby as a fixture in his office, an object "harmless and noiseless as any of these old chairs." Bartleby is a non-present presence whose being "always there" is no longer reassuring because of the work that he does—he does none—but because the employer never feels so private as when he knows Bartleby is there. After a time, however, the employer no longer sees Bartleby as a man—most of his links with common humanity are severed, indeed—but as an "intolerable incubus," a ghost who casts "a general gloom over the premises." Yet he cannot bring himself to call a constable "and commit his innocent pallor to the common jail." Even in his object-like shut-in-ness Bartleby retains enough humanity to trouble the employer's conscience. And the employer is too far inside Bartleby's situation to be able to settle, like Meursault's prosecutors, for the common-sense absurdity of the law. Upon what ground, he asks himself, could he have Bartleby jailed?

> . . . a vagrant, is he? What! he a vagrant, a wanderer, who refuses to budge? It is because he will *not* be a vagrant, then that you seek to count him *as* a vagrant. That is too absurd. No visible means of support: there I have him. Wrong again: for indubitably he *does* support himself, and that is the only unanswerable proof that any man can show of his possessing the means so to do. (33)

Since Bartleby will not quit him and since he cannot bring himself to have him removed, the employer takes the remarkable step of moving to other offices. He leaves his own ground altogether rather than dislodge the man who stands that ground. Yet even for this action something within him upbraids him. When he says goodbye to Bartleby, he has to tear himself away from the man whom he had so

longed to be rid of. Sent for by the new tenants as the last
person who knew anything about the still unbudging Bartleby, the employer even offers to take Bartleby home with
him, only to be met by the decisive, "No, at present I
would prefer not to make any change at all."

The relationship between Bartleby and the employer pre-
figures, in a curious distorted fashion, the relationship between Billy Budd and Captain Vere. When the employer
moves away and cuts off Bartleby's last link to human
existence, he condemns him to death only indirectly and
against his will. Captain Vere, in contrast, condemns Billy
Budd to death directly, in full knowledge of what he is
doing and with good conscience. Yet both men stand in a
kind, fatherly relationship to the young man whom they cut
off, and both find it necessary to sacrifice the heart to impersonal duty or business respectability. Not that the judgment that can be entered against Captain Vere can be
entered against Bartleby's employer. We can hardly see what
else he can do and remain the person and lawyer that he is.
Yet there is some reality, however distorted, behind the
guilt that the employer feels when he comes to visit Bartleby
in the Tombs. "I know you," Bartleby says in answer to
the salutation of the employer, "and I want nothing to say
to you." Although the employer denies any guilt, he follows
this denial by a singularly lame rationalization calculated to
relieve himself rather than Bartleby:

> "It was not I that brought you here, Bartleby,"
> said I, keenly pained at his implied suspicion. "And
> to you, this should not be so vile a place. Nothing
> reproachful attaches to you by being here. And
> see, it is not so sad a place as one might think.
> Look, there is the sky, and here is the grass." (38)

Sky and grass are more than the employer's office afforded,
but this is nonetheless a jail—a jail appropriately named
The Tombs, for to Bartleby it means the final triumph of
the world of death. Bartleby's reply leaves nothing to be
said: "I know where I am."

Although we may not wish to judge the employer, his very relationship to Bartleby places an inescapable judgment upon him. This is a judgment in the first instance on his safe and snug way of life, on his readiness to exploit his employees insofar as they do not protest or make trouble, on his impersonal law practice, and on the anonymous social and economic world to which it belongs. On a deeper level, it is the monstrously unfair but nonetheless inescapable judgment that is placed upon him as the one person upon whom Bartleby depends, the one person to whom Bartleby relates. No rational accusation of guilt could be brought against the employer for setting a limit to Bartleby's absolute demand. Yet a residue of existential guilt inevitably remains. The fact that he alone stands in relation to Bartleby justifies his feeling that he is held to "terrible account." Cutting Bartleby off not only means killing him; it also means the final exclusion of the exile from the bond of "common humanity." It is this bond that the employer has recognized all along as preventing him from taking action against "this forlornest of mankind," and it is this bond that is now severed in letting Bartleby go to his lonely death. The guilt of the employer is here no moral one. It is the guilt of human existence itself, the guilt that every man feels when his responsibility for another is unlimited while his resources are limited.

When the narrator visits Bartleby again, a turnkey points out where "the silent man" has been lying for the last twenty minutes. The employer goes over to the inert figure, strangely huddled against the wall, and discovers he is dead. To the grub-man's question, "He's asleep, ain't he?" the employer replies, "With kings and counselors." This is a phrase from the speech in which Job curses the day of his birth.

> Why died I not from the womb?
> . . . .
> For now should I have lain still and be quiet. I
>   should have slept; then had I been at rest,
> With kings and counselors of the earth,

which built desolate places for themselves.
. . . .

Wherefore is light given to him that is misery,
  and life unto the bitter in soul? (RSV 3:11, 13,
  14, 20)

Although no certain facts about Bartleby ever come to
light, a rumor does reach the ear of the narrator that Bartleby had once "been a subordinate clerk in the Dead Letter
Office at Washington, from which he had been suddenly removed by a change in the administration." The impersonality
of the Dead Letter Office, combined with the attempts at
personal communication which come to nought there, make
Bartleby's derangement understandable to the narrator, if
not very convincingly so to us. "By nature and misfortune
prone to a pallid hopelessness," Bartleby became permanently disordered through working where he had to consign
such letters to the flames by the cartload.

> Sometimes from out the folded paper the pale clerk takes
> a ring:—the finger it was meant for, perhaps, moulders
> in the grave; a bank-note sent in swiftest charity:—he
> whom it would relieve, nor eats nor hungers any more;
> pardon for those who died despairing; hope for those
> who died unhoping; good tidings for those who died
> stifled by unrelieved calamities. On errands of life, these
> letters speed to death. (41)

. . .

The bitter and savage ironies of Melville's second novel
after *Moby Dick—The Confidence Man* (1857)—recapitulate some of the motifs of *Moby Dick* in a way that brings to
the fore the problematic of modern man. In *The Confidence
Man* the metaphysics of White-Whale-hating is replaced by
"the metaphysics of Indian-hating," Ahab by the "Indian-
hater par excellence," who renounces "the pomps and glories
of the world" for the sake of his revenge deep in the wilderness which eventually swallows him. "An intenser Hannibal,
he makes a vow, the hate of which is a vortex from whose
suction scarce the remotest chip of the guilty race may rea-

sonably feel secure." Only a little less extreme than the story of the Indian-hater is the story of "China Aster the Candlemaker whose career was an example of the truth of Scripture, as found in the sober philosophy of Solomon the Wise; for he was ruined by allowing himself to be persuaded against his better sense, into the free indulgence of confidence and an ardently bright view of life, to the exclusion of that counsel which comes by heeding the opposite view."

The Confidence Man, to be sure, rejects this story along with Indian-hating and Ecclesiasticus—the Apocryphal book of Jesus ben Sirach which, more than any book he has read, seemed "calculated to destroy man's confidence in man." The whole book, however, is one elaborate and tirelessly repeated pun on the word "confidence" and its synonym "trust." The very Confidence Man who, in his various disguises, preaches trust in man is the one who undermines man's trust by the swindles he practices upon them in its name. And lest we feel that what is in question here is only a matter of trust in business, or, taken on a broader level, of trust between man and man, the Confidence Man himself explicitly draws the connection with trust in existence itself: "From what you say," an old man says to the Confidence Man, "I see you are something of my way of thinking—you think that to distrust the creature, is a kind of distrusting of the Creator." These are indeed corollaries, as we saw in *Moby Dick*—to trust in man one must trust in existence and vice-versa. ("Knowing you persuades me more than the Bible of our immortality," Melville wrote to Hawthorne in November 1851.) [8] Nor can there be any doubt here of Melville's own point of view. The book is one long exercise in misanthropy, and this misanthropy is clearly linked to the distrust of creation:

> "You rather jumble together misanthropy and infidelity."
> "I do not jumble them; they are co-ordinates. For misanthropy, springing from the same root with disbelief

[8] Letter to Nathaniel Hawthorne dated "Pittsfield, Monday afternoon," [November (?), 1851]. Thorp, *op. cit.*, p. 396.

of religion, is twin with that . . . set aside materialism and what is an atheist, but one who does not, or will not, see in the universe a ruling principle of love; and what a misanthrope, but one who does not, or will not, see in man a ruling principle of kindness? . . . In either case the vice consists in a want of confidence." [9]

A century later Martin Buber described the modern "eclipse of God" in precisely these terms. The waning of genuine dialogue between man and man is the symptom, writes Buber, but a pervasive "existential mistrust," such as has never before existed, is the disease itself:

> The existential mistrust is indeed basically no longer, like the old kind, a mistrust of my fellow-man. It is rather the destruction of confidence in existence in general . . . At its core the conflict between mistrust and trust of man conceals the conflict between the mistrust and trust of eternity.[10]

For Melville both mistrust of man and mistrust of eternity are expressions of the existential mistrust that is the daily bread of the Modern Exile.

[9] Herman Melville, *The Confidence-Man: His Masquerade* (New York: Grove Press), p. 187.

[10] Martin Buber, *Pointing the Way: Collected Essays*, ed. and trans. with Introd. by Maurice Friedman (New York: Harper Torchbooks, 1963), "Hope for This Hour," pp. 223 f., 229. Alfred Kazin's analysis of *The Confidence Man* suggests as far-reaching and profound a pessimism as my own: "*The Confidence Man* marks the full eruption of Melville's wrath against the American belief—liberal, conservative, and radical—that reality is always calculable, that things are never as desperate as they seem, that the world is a moral constant in the mind of History or God . . . the heart of it is anguish, an almost unbearable sense of betrayal . . . It is an attack on the spirit of consolation . . . of 'moderation,' on 'the picked and prudent sentiments,' . . . it is an embittered, tense, splintery book . . . And it is not simply an attack on the naïveté of the old American liberalism, on the strut-and-brag of American commercialism, on the innocence of transcendentalism; it is a great cry against the deception appearance practices upon reality." (Alfred Kazin, *The Inmost Leaf. A Selection of Essays* [New York: Harcourt Brace, 1955], "On Melville as Scripture," p. 206.) Melville's concern for the "eclipse of God" is even more explicit in his long poem *Clarel* (1876), but here it is focused on the conflict between science and faith. (Herman Melville, *Clarel. A Poem and Pilgrimage in the Holy Land*, II, Part III, Chap. V, pp. 21 f. and Part IV, Chap. XXV, Epilogue—*The Works of Herman Melville*, XV [London: Constable & Sons, 1922].)

5

─ ─ ─ ─ ─ ─ ─

CAPTAIN AHAB:

MODERN PROMETHEAN

Captain Ahab, the hero of Melville's *Moby Dick*, we are told, is a godly, ungodlike man. Like every hero, he is a mixture of the divine and the demonic. His very opposition to the order of things gives him a certain grandeur and nobility; he is to some extent in the line of Milton's Satan in *Paradise Lost*, of Byron's Manfred, and, of course, Prometheus, all of whom win our admiration by grandly defying.

Ahab's Modern Prometheanism is both set in perspective and foreshadowed by the sermon that Ishmael hears when, at the beginning of the story, he wanders into a strange chapel, the pulpit of which is constructed like the prow of a whaling boat. "The Sermon" that Father Mapple, the old whaling preacher, gives from this pulpit-prow is about Jonah, the man who fled before the Lord's word to go to Nineveh, who is thrown off the ship in a storm, and who is swallowed for forty days in the belly of the whale. In it there are prophetic overtones of Captain Ahab in the service of the Lord, Ahab as the rebellious prophet refusing the message of the Lord. But Father Mapple's image of man is actually not Biblical but Calvinist. In contrast to the Book of Jonah, his sermon is founded on a stern, transcendent God, a sinful world, and the moral duty of self-denial. This is the God the Gnostics and Doctor Faustus call the redeemer God, and it really is the world of the Gnostics and Doctor Faustus rather than the world of the Hebrew Bible that we see here. The basic contrast here is between the dark wrath below and the redemption above. Here is man "deepening down to doom," sinking down in "black distress" into the "opening maw of hell" and the redeemer God coming as a "radiant dolphin" shining "bright as lightning" to deliver the helpless and undeserving sinner.

The two "lessons" that Father Mapple draws from the story of Jonah show consequences of this dualism that could not have followed from the original context. In the Book of Job, Job neither commits himself to God with blind faith, nor does he feel that in order to exist as an "I" he must destroy God, like the Modern Promethean—Dostoievsky's Kirilov, Nietzsche's Superman, or Sartre's Orestes. He finds his very existence in the relationship with God, and at the same time he rebels within that relationship, contending, standing his own ground, meeting God from his own unique position. In Father Mapple's sermon the relationship of this "I" to God has essentially changed. Man's self can no longer exist in Job's sense— as a partner, standing in dialogue with God. Now at the core of the self is sinful man, man born in depravity, man who must choose between affirming himself and affirming God. This already points us toward Ahab, who makes that same choice. Both must choose: there is no room any longer for both self and God, for the self is sinful and to obey God it must disobey itself. This is the first lesson that Father Mapple draws from Jonah: "It is in disobeying ourselves that the hardness of obeying God consists."

Father Mapple finds a second moral in Jonah. Jonah is not an ordinary man but a prophet who finally did the Almighty's bidding, and the bidding of the Almighty was "to preach the truth in the face of falsehood."

> "This, shipmates, this is that other lesson; and woe to that pilot of the living God who slights it! Woe to him whom this world charms from Gospel duty! Woe to him who seeks to pour oil upon the waters when God has brewed them into a gale! Woe to him who seeks to please rather than to appall! . . . who, in this world courts not dishonor! *Woe to him who would not be true, even though to be false were salvation.*" (Italics mine.)

The truth as given by God, and Jonah, as the mouthpiece of God going forth to speak the truth, this truth a clear line of division between good and evil and this world an evil world against which the prophet must witness, the temptation to let this world charm one from Gospel duty and the consequent hostility to this world—this is the view of truth and of the prophet of truth in Father Mapple's sermon.

This is, at first glance, just a further extension of the first lesson, since Jonah does not want to obey God and to obey God he must disobey himself and preach God's word to the Ninevites. Yet without any clear transition another note enters in: "Woe to him who would not be true, even though to be false were salvation." It is one thing to say that one must be true and not give in to the charms of this world. It is quite another to say that one must be true *even* at the cost of salvation and set these two in opposition to each other. Although it is unthinkable that a Calvinist preacher would mean this, Father Mapple's words seem to suggest a certain absoluteness of truth that transcends even salvation—man's relation to God. As Father Mapple continues, moreover, it begins to appear that quite a different self is here than that of his first lesson. "But oh! shipmates! on the starboard hand of every woe there is a sure delight . . . Delight is to him

—a far, far upward, and inward delight—who against the proud gods and commodores of this earth, ever stands forth his own inexorable self." The self that a moment before was to be denied and disobeyed in obedience to God is now suddenly enthroned in the highest place, identified with truth or with the serving of truth. This is Prometheus, enduring endless agonies, yet standing forth his own inexorable self, against Zeus—the proud god of this world.

"Delight is to him when the ship of this base, treacherous world has gone down beneath him," adds Father Mapple. The relationship to God means the denial of the world. God is no longer the creator. The world is given over to the evil God, and the redeemer God redeems man not *in* the world but *from* the world. The paradoxical result of this dualism between man's relation to God and his relation to the world is that this "prophet" at once enjoys the profound humility of disobeying himself to obey God and the equally profound pride of being the spokesman of God who stands forth his own inexorable self against all the world. This "pilot of God" "gives no quarter in the truth and kills, burns, destroys all sin though he pluck it out from under the robes of senators and judges." "Delight,—top-gallant delight is to him, who acknowledges no law or Lord but the Lord his God and is only a patriot to heaven." The world is evil, and he, the bearer of truth, has the sanctified task of destroying evil, giving no quarter in the truth. Yet he does not even bear a word of truth, as does Jonah, a word of God that calls men to turn back to true existence. Rather, he simply takes it on himself to attack and destroy in the name of God.

When Ahab, unlike Father Mapple's Jonah, cuts himself off from God and identifies himself with truth, this sanctification of the task of destroying evil remains. "The Sermon" is not merely a moral and Biblical framework within which to judge the sinfulness of Captain Ahab—an unrepentant Jonah who takes on himself the vengeance which should belong to God and does not know the mercy for God's creation that the God of the Book of Jonah has for his creatures. It also contains the Promethean note which, when it is freed from the relationship to God, can sound forth, in Ahab, in that absolute affirmation of self which identifies the truth and the good with oneself, the false and the evil with what stands opposite one.

Not too long after Ishmael reports that "reality outran apprehension; Captain Ahab stood upon his quarter-deck," and immediately following the destruction of the young Platonist by an infinite that his finiteness cannot endure, we arrive at the central dramatic incident from which all the rest flows—Ahab's announcement in "The Quarter-Deck" (XXXVI) that the true goal of the voyage is the chase of Moby Dick. Here is the first real drama of the book; here the meaning is not merely symbolic but derives from the total situation—Ahab's coming on deck, his rousing the men, the Black Mass in which the harpooners drink from their inverted harpoons,[1] his almost magical success in bringing the crew along with him in his purpose, the clash with Starbuck, the one man who tries to stand against him.

Starbuck, the first mate, is a right-minded man representing mere unaided virtue. He is a strong man and he is a good man, but he lacks Ahab's passion and power, his depth and intensity. Therefore, his mere right-mindedness cannot stand against the demonry of Ahab. "Vengeance on a dumb brute! that simply smote thee from blindest instinct! Madness!" cries Starbuck. "To be enraged with a dumb thing, Captain Ahab, seems blasphemous." It seems blasphemy to Starbuck because he assumes, first, that this "dumb brute" is part of the natural world and second, that nature is the creation of God and therefore is essentially good. He recognizes that whales can bring death to men, but he cannot recognize that there could be any personal malice in Moby Dick's sheering off Ahab's leg. He cannot see Moby Dick, as Ahab does, as an incarnation of the ultimately hostile nonhuman power that confronts man.

Just before he speaks of blasphemy, Starbuck makes quite

---

[1] Cf. M. O. Percival, *A Reading of Moby Dick* (Chicago: University of Chicago Press, 1950), pp. 9-13. Percival rightly points out the organic link between this scene and the later one where Ahab baptizes his own new-forged harpoon "non . . . in nomine patris, sed in nomine diaboli!" ("The Forge," CXIII).

a different statement: "I came here to hunt whales, not my commander's vengeance. How many barrels will thy vengeance yield . . . it will not fetch thee much in our Nantucket market." Here everything is turned into dollars and cents, everything is measured by the cash premium. "My vengeance will fetch a great premium here!" replies Ahab, smiting his chest. Starbuck, after all, has no intrinsic values to oppose to Ahab's. His fear of blasphemy and his concern for barrels of oil all too comfortably fit together in the God-fearing, money-earning Puritanism from which he comes. No reverence for the whale as a part of God's creation enters into Starbuck's attitude toward killing whales for money. Here "creation" becomes merely a collection of natural objects which are there for man to exploit without limit. There is no suggestion of the wonder before the independent otherness of creation that runs through the Book of Job and in particular the speeches of the Lord, who brings "rain on a land where no man is, on the desert in which there is no man; to satisfy the waste and desolate ground." In its place we find the mid-nineteenth-century rapacity of the American frontiersman, of which the American whaling industry was one of the greatest examples. "Duty and profit hand in hand!" says Starbuck at the time of the first lowering for a whale.

One of the mysteries of this chapter is how Ahab gets the rest of the crew to go along with him and "hunt his vengeance," rather than the oil they came out for. Ahab brings the whole ship and the whole crew into his demonic inner world, into his maddened consciousness; it is a powerful, an archetypal world, but it is his own personal world. Aside from observer Ishmael's, there is essentially only one point of view from now on, and that is Ahab's. There are feeble attempts to resist Ahab's spell, Starbuck making his occasional protest, Ishmael from time to time falling into doubt. But there is not really another active and positive standpoint which can compete with Ahab's. Even the parade of ships that exchange greetings with the Pequod only serve to throw Ahab's attitude into symbolic relief. These ships are other worlds, indeed, with sharply contrasting attitudes toward Moby Dick; nonetheless, with the exception of the Rachel, they are only "ships that pass in the night." The world of *Moby Dick* is the Pequod, and Ahab is both its captain and its soul. "There is one God that is Lord over the earth, and one Captain that is lord over the Pequod," Ahab says to Starbuck.

But where a single point of view dominates, truth becomes identical with it and with him who holds it. Ahab's response to Starbuck's charge of blasphemy indicates a decisive new stage in the relationship between truth and reality. "Hark ye yet again,—the little lower layer," says Ahab. Ahab also has his Platonism; like the "sunken-eyed young Platonist," he too sees all visible things as only symbols of the reality behind them: "All visible objects, man, are but as pasteboard masks." But unlike the symbols of the young Platonist, they do not relate integrally to what they symbolize. Rather, they are, like pasteboard masks, thin, empty, flimsy things that cover a very different reality; they remind us, indeed, of that sunken-eyed young Platonist himself, fallen through the pasteboard mask of a fair day, a beautiful sky, and a summer sea, to his horrible·death. Despite Ahab's famous transcendentalist cry, "O Nature, and O soul of man! how far beyond all utterance are thy linked analogies," Ahab's symbolism is not one of correspondence but of antagonism between the appearance and the reality that lies behind it: "In each event—in the living act, the undoubted deed—there, some unknown, but still reasoning thing puts forth the mouldings of its features from behind the unreasoning mask." The mask is not the face of reality but the façade; it is the *persona*—the mask that the characters wore in ancient plays. What really acts and moves behind it one can never know.

The horror that "the little lower layer" opens to Ahab is that what seems irrational is really rational yet unknowable, that it is both inscrutable and malicious. "Inscrutable malice" brings together two meanings of evil that are played on again and again in the course of this book: on the one hand, the personal malignancy that lies behind the seemingly impersonal or ordinary natural reality; on the other hand, the impersonal, and therefore the inhuman and antihuman, reality that confronts us in the world if we see it as it is, and not through the sunken eyes of the young Platonist.

The only thing one can do in the face of this hostile reality is to strike out at it.

> If man will strike, strike through the mask! How can the prisoner reach outside except by thrusting through the wall? To me, the white whale is that wall, shoved near to me. Sometimes I think there's naught beyond. But 'tis enough. He tasks me; he heaps me; I see in him outrageous strength, with an inscrutable malice sinewing it.

Ahab's sense of impotence, after his leg is cut off and he himself is tied down to his bunk for many months, is given full expression here. He feels himself suffocated by this mask "shoved near" to him; the only way he can live is to break through it and destroy it. "That inscrutable thing is chiefly what I hate; and be the white whale agent, or be the white whale principal, I will wreak that hate upon him." Whether Ahab is striking through the whale at God or whether there is "naught beyond," it is Ahab's hatred of the inscrutability of reality that compels him to sail around the world to pursue Moby Dick even though, as Starbuck says to him, "The white whale seeks thee not."

"Talk not to me of blasphemy, man," Ahab continues. "I'd strike the sun if it insulted me. For could the sun do that, then could I do the other; since there is ever a sort of fair play herein, jealousy presiding over all creations." The Prometheanism of that passage is rather like that of the original Prometheus of Aeschylus: a defiance not of the order but in the name of the order—the "fair play" that jealously presides over the whole. But in his next statement Ahab goes beyond the Aeschylean Prometheus: "But not my master, man, is even that fair play. Who's over me? Truth hath no confines." Ultimately there is not even an order which is over Ahab!

Here is the essential breakthrough to the Modern Promethean. Ahab arrogates to himself all the authority of truth which resided before either in God and our relationship to God, as it does for Father Mapple, or in the Platonic or idealistic absolute, as it does for Bulkington and the young Platonist. For modern man neither of these truths is any longer possible, since "God is dead." The "death of God" means the death of both the Biblical image of man face to face with God and the Greek-Platonic image of an absolute order and an absolute good in harmony with which man can live. In the face of a basically inscrutable reality, the only way left to man to find any meaning in his existence is to identify truth with himself and with his attack on the reality that appears to be fair and beautiful and is really malignant and hostile to man.

"I, Ishmael, was one of that crew," says Ishmael at the beginning of "Moby Dick" (XLI). "My shouts had gone up with the rest, my oath had been welded with theirs. A wild, mystical, sympathetical feeling was in me; Ahab's quenchless feud seemed mine." Ishmael and the crew are now entirely involved in Ahab's purpose. "With greedy ears," Ishmael confesses, "I learned the history of that murderous monster." This highly subjective statement turns out to be merely the prelude to what seems at first an entirely objective history, a scientific account of whales and sperm whales and even of the White Whale himself. Ishmael puts every intimation off on "crazy old Ahab," yet he ever more powerfully suggests that maybe there is something to it after all. Each section of the chapter tells the reader something of sperm whales or Moby Dick and then says, in closely similar formulations of the same idea, "Small wonder, then, that men react to it thus."

As the sea surpasses the land in its dangers, so the whale fishery surpasses every other sort of fishery, the sperm whale every other sort of whale, and Moby Dick every other sort of sperm whale. In this one animal, therefore, we have reached the apex of the danger man encounters when he sets out to face the hostile reality of the universe. Moby Dick, we are told, is a sperm whale of uncommon magnitude and malignity, great ferocity, cunning and malice. "No wonder, then, that ever gathering volume . . . the outblown rumors of the White Whale did in the end incorporate themselves with all manner of morbid hints, and half-formed foetal suggestions of supernatural agencies, which eventually invested Moby Dick with new terrors unborrowed from anything that visibly appears." It is "the invisible spheres" attaching them-

selves to Moby Dick that help to build up such wild "sug-
gestings" and "unearthly conceits" as that of his ubiquitous-
ness—that he is to be found at the same time in two different places. To some he seems "not only ubiquitous, but
immortal." "Though groves of spears should be planted in his
flanks, he would still swim away unharmed." What particularly invests the White Whale with terror, however, is "that
unexampled, intelligent malignity which . . . he had over
and over again evinced in his assaults."

Now that his ubiquity and immortality are combined with
his malignity and intelligence, Moby Dick can be characterized by that very quality which Ahab says he cannot bear
in "The Quarter-Deck"—inscrutable malice." Due to his
"treacherous retreats" and his "infernal aforethought of ferocity," the dismemberings and deaths that he caused were "not
wholly regarded as having been afflicted by an unintelligent
agent."

> Judge, then, to what pitches of inflamed, distracted fury
> the minds of his more desperate hunters were impelled,
> when amid the chips of chewed boats, and the sinking
> limbs of torn comrades, they swam out of the white
> curds of the whale's direful wrath into the serene, exas-
> perating sunlight, that smiled on, as if at a birth or a
> bridal.

Here the horror is not only the maiming and death itself, but
also the contrast between the appearance of serenity and
beauty and the horrible reality. "Linked analogies" notwith-
standing, "nature" does not correspond here to what is happening to man; or rather, one part of nature—the intelligent
malignity of Moby Dick—destroys, while the rest of nature
looks on with "benign indifference," to use Camus' phrase
in *The Stranger*.

In the face of this malignity and indifference of nature,
Ahab is, indeed, Promethean and defiant, but rather piti-
fully so. We are told of one captain who, like an Arkansas
duelist, blindly sought "with a six-inch blade to reach the
fathom-deep life of the whale." That captain was Ahab, we
learn, and we sense again the impotence that lies behind

Ahab's need to strike through the wall that is suffocating him. Having lost his trust in existence, Ahab's only choice is either to go down submitting or to go down defying. It is this blind Prometheanism of Ahab's that leads to Moby Dick's "reaping away" his leg: "No turbaned Turk, no hired Venetian or Malay, could have smote him with more seeming malice." It was not to Ahab alone that the White Whale seemed malicious, but to everybody, and this suggestion of social objectivity is reinforced by the recurrence here of the same formula as that used in the more "objective" accounts of sperm whales and of Moby Dick—"no wonder then," "judge then": "Small reason was there to doubt then that ever since . . . Ahab had cherished a wild vindictiveness against the whale, all the more fell for that in his frantic morbidness he at last came to identify with him not only all his bodily woes, but all his intellectual and spiritual exasperations."

Now Ishmael tells us exactly what Moby Dick symbolizes to Ahab, and, prepared by the whole of what has gone before, we cannot dismiss it as merely the aberration of a distracted, inflamed mind: "The White Whale swam before him as the monomaniac incarnation of all those malicious agencies which some deep men feel eating in them, till they are left living on with half a heart and half a lung." The next statement, certainly, is made as an entirely objective one even if at the end it is linked with Ahab:

That intangible malignity which has been from the beginning; to whose dominion even the modern Christians ascribe one-half of the worlds; which the ancient Ophites of the east reverenced in their statue devil;—Ahab did not fall down and worship it like them; but deliriously transferring its idea to the abhorred White Whale, he pitted himself, all mutilated, against it.

Ishmael in no way suggests that "that intangible malignity" itself exists only in the mind of Ahab or that it is a merely psychological phenomenon. On the contrary, "it has been from the beginning," and even the modern Christian, like the ancient Gnostic, sees that evil as at least as powerful as good, and probably more powerful. The Gnostic Ophites drew the logical conclusion that it is the devil, or snake, that should be worshiped and propitiated, not God. We do not find here, as in Zoroastrianism, the almost equal conflict of good and evil, with good bound to win out in the end with the aid of the free and rational decision of man. Rather, as in Gnosticism, evil is radically real, more real, in fact, than good on the plane of this world.

By the time that Ishmael has built up the White Whale for us, it is not an unworthy or inadequate symbol of that metaphysical evil with which Ahab identifies it.

> All that most maddens and torments; all that stirs up the lees of things; all truth with malice in it; all that cracks the sinews and cakes the brain; all the subtle demonisms of life and thought, all evil, to crazy Ahab, were visibly personified and made practically assailable in Moby Dick.

The protagonists have now clearly reached mythical and metaphysical dimensions. As Moby Dick represents all evil in life, so Ahab represents all of humanity: "He piled upon the Whale's white hump the sum of all the general rage and hate felt by his whole race from Adam down." Ahab's identification of himself with truth now manifests itself in his belief that he is man fighting what is hostile to man, protesting for the sake of his own humanity before it goes down to inevitable defeat.

The entrance of the Pequod into "The Pacific" (CXI) heralds the encounter with Moby Dick. The "serene Pacific" lulls the "meditative Magian rover" into the ocean pantheism of the young Platonist: "Lifted by those eternal swells, you needs must own the seductive god, bowing your head to Pan." But to Ahab the Pacific is not a votive offering to Pan but the approach to the hated White Whale that swims within its waters. "In his very sleep, his ringing cry ran through the vaulted hull, 'Stern all! the White Whale spouts thick blood!'" As the book picks up momentum, the choice has crystallized into the polar opposites of a pantheistic illusion or a Promethean "woe that is madness." Just when we might wish to give ourselves to the seductive sea and sky and the fragrant musk from the Bashee isles, Ahab's cry suddenly sweeps us beyond all moderation and balance into the final stages of the chase in which, with ever heightened pace, the drama rolls unrelentingly to its end.

In "The Quadrant" (CXVIII) Ahab throws down and tramples on his quadrant, saying that if God had meant man to look upward, he would not have put our eyes level with the horizon. Ahab, who has been defying the world of nature all along, suddenly wants to follow the natural way, or so it would seem. At this very point we see pass over the Parsee's face "a sneering triumph that seemed meant for Ahab, and a fatalistic despair that seemed meant for himself." This incident gives us the clue to the difference between the Prometheanism of Ahab and that of both the original Prometheus and his Renaissance counterpart, from Doctor Faustus on. Ahab's defiance is based neither on an order which will eventually bear him out, nor on the mastery of "fire," that power stolen from the gods through which man builds his civilizations. On the contrary, not only in the case of the quadrant, but finally in that of the compass and all his other guides, Ahab throws away science, that form of co-operation with nature which man has used to gain his greatest dominion over it. "Science! Curse thee, thou vain toy," shouts Ahab as he flings down the quadrant. Science, the very essence of man's Prometheanism in the modern world, science, the key symbol of man's unlimited power since the Renaissance, no longer suffices to assure Ahab of his victory over nature and the gods. As Ishmael himself says in "Brit" (LVIII):

> However baby man may brag of his science and skill, and however much, in a flattering future, that science and skill may augment; yet for ever and for ever, to the crack of doom, the sea will insult and murder him, and pulverize the stateliest, stiffest frigate he can make.

Ahab abandons the central belief of Bacon and Renaissance man that the way to the realization of one's humanity is through the knowledge that gives one power over nature.

For Ahab, co-operation with the impersonal world means submission to it. Ahab's Modern Prometheanism, in contrast to Greek and Renaissance Prometheanism, means the defiance of the impersonal in the name of the personal, as he himself makes explicit in his "worship" of the fire when the masts are set ablaze with the "corposants," or "St. Elmo's fire," in "The Candles" (CXIX).

> Oh! thou clear spirit of clear fire, whom on these seas I as Persian once did worship, till in the sacramental act so burned by thee, that to this hour I bear the scar; I now know thee, thou clear spirit, and I now know that thy right worship is defiance. To neither love nor reverence wilt thou be kind; and e'en for hate thou canst but kill; and all are killed. No fearless fool now fronts thee. I own thy speechless, placeless power; but to the last gasp of my earthquake life will dispute its unconditional, unintegral mastery in me. In the midst of the personified impersonal, a personality stands here. Though but a point at best; whencesoe'er I came; wheresoe'er I go; yet while I earthly live, the queenly personality lives in me and feels her royal rights.

Here then is the secret of Ahab's defiance: he is what this "clear spirit of fire" can never be—a person, and as a person he is conscious and aware of himself, as the fire is not. "Thou knowest not how came ye, hence callest thyself unbegotten; certainly knowest not thy beginning, hence callest thyself unbegun. I know that of me, which thou knowest not of thyself, oh, thou omnipotent." This fire resembles an absolute, in fact the absolute just as it is described by the Buddha—"unborn, unbegotten, uncreated"—but it is something short of absolute after all. This ostensible absolute that has confronted us throughout the book—the absoluteness of Moby Dick, of the sea, of the indifferent universe—turns out to lack one essential dimension, and that is personality. Personality is not only consciousness of oneself as a self; it is also the ability to stand as a person and hold one's ground in the face of the reality confronting one, as Ahab defies the fire and as Job contends with God.

Ahab has found something in man which gives him that

inwardness, that stance from which to relate to the outer, that makes him not just a helpless atom in an infinite world, not just little Pip cast away on the immense, indifferent ocean. Ahab's fight as the representative of the human against all that "heaps" and maddens man now becomes the fight for man as person against the vast, seemingly omnipotent impersonal. Ahab knows of something that stands at the origin of both the person and the impersonal, something which man can face as a person, something which gives him the power to defy the impersonal. "There is some unsuffusing thing, beyond thee, thou clear spirit, to whom all thy eternity is but time, all thy creativeness mechanical. Through thee, thy flaming self, my scorched eyes do see it."

There is another absolute, after all, which is really absolute in a way in which this seeming absolute of nature is not. There is an eternity which is something more than an infinity of time. There is a creativity which is something more than this enormous, seemingly unlimited power. The very nature of that eternity is such that while it gives birth to the personal and impersonal there is a closer, more "integral" kinship between it and the personal. It bears up the person in the face of the impersonal even when physically he is so helpless, so limited, so easily destroyed. Ahab does not respect the courage of Stubb, because it partakes of the nature of the impersonal. "Ay, thou art brave as fearless fire, and as mechanical," Ahab says to Stubb during the final chase, taking us back to his speech to the corposants in "The Candles." Stubb, like them, is a "personified impersonal," a creature that wears the mask of personality but lacks its real creativity.

This is the one point in the book where the overall dualism seems to be qualified by the glimpse of something which perhaps, after all, underspans and overarches the gap between the human personal and the nonpersonal. Yet a dualism is implicit here too—between Ahab's "fiery father" whom he recognizes in the "clear spirit of clear fire" and his "sweet mother" whom he knows not. Since the "fiery father" seems to stand for the ineffable source of personality, there is also implicit here a Gnostic dualism between darkness and light, wrath and love, the evil "creator God" and the good "redeemer God" of the Marcionites and other Gnostics. Thus Ahab says to the fire:

> "To neither love nor reverence wilt thou be kind; and e'en for hate thou canst but kill; and all are killed . . . War is pain and hate is woe. Come in thy lowest form of love, and I will kneel and kiss thee; but at thy highest, come as mere supernal power; and though thou launchest navies of full-freighted worlds, there's that in here that still remains indifferent. Oh, thou clear spirit, of thy fire thou madest me, and like a true child of fire, I breathe it back to thee."

Man is a child of nature as well as spirit, but he may use his natural force to defy nature; he may, and Ahab does, "fight fire with fire."

In his speech in "The Candles," Ahab seems to acknowledge a transcendent with which he identifies himself in his fight against the hostile world. If Ahab resembles the Gnostics in this and other respects, it is not because Melville is under Gnostic "influence," as some critics think.[2] Melville is a modern man who makes use of Gnostic symbolism to say something essentially different from what the Gnostics were saying: different, first, in that the "creator God" he is accusing is much closer to the power of nature, absolutized and personified, than to the God of the Bible, even in the grossly caricaturized form given him by the Gnostics; second, in that, unlike the Gnostics, he does not appeal to transcendent spirit but to the personality, as no ancient Gnostic would.[3] Man, to the Gnostic, is a fallen creature made in the image of the evil creator God, and man's body and psyche, in other words most of what goes into making up his personality, are corrupt and evil as well. Only the pneuma, the hidden, essentially impersonal spirit, still retains kinship with the transcendent

[2] Cf. William Brasswell, *Melville's Religious Thought: An Essay in Interpretation* (Durham, N.C.: Duke University Press, 1943), p. 62.

[3] In the modern Gnostic personalism of the existentialist philosopher Nicholas Berdyaev, however, the personal is identical with a transcendent spirit dualistically divided from the external world of "objectification."

redeemer God. Ahab is not an ancient Gnostic but the late continuation of the Renaissance man, now disillusioned in the essential Renaissance belief that man fulfills himself as a person through his knowledge of and control over nature. Ahab can no longer affirm himself as a person except in defiance of the impersonal.

As the novel takes its inexorable course, however, we realize that the personal is precisely what Ahab more and more gives up and betrays until he ends by utterly denying it and making himself a part of the very impersonal that he has here defied. Ahab takes his heroic stance at the meeting point of the personal with the impersonal. But he goes too far. He sacrifices the meeting of person and person through which alone he could remain a person. Ahab fights evil and becomes it, as has been remarked so often. He becomes it because he gives up the one ground on which he could fight it—his real human existence as a person in actual relation to other persons.

As a consequence, even the "personality" that he affirms is not, in him, a whole person but only one aspect of a person —a heroic ego rather than a self, as Newton Arvin points out, a "proud and defiant will" rather than "a human being in all his wholeness and roundness." [4] In "The Deck, Ahab and the Carpenter" (CVIII) Ahab moves from likening the carpenter who fashions him a new wooden leg to "that old Greek, Prometheus, who made men" to his own Promethean prescription for "a complete man after a desirable pattern," an image of man which leaves out not only everything unique and personal in man, but the heart itself.

> Imprimis, fifty feet high in his socks; then, chest modelled after the Thames Tunnel; then, legs with roots to 'em, to stay in one place; then, arms three feet through the wrist; no heart at all, brass forehead, and about a quarter of an acre of fine brains; and let me see—shall I order eyes to see outwards? No, but put a sky-light on top of his head to illuminate inwards.

[4] Newton Arvin, *Herman Melville*, The American Men of Letters Series (New York: William Sloane Ass., 1950), pp. 176 f.

Ahab's "complete man" fills us with all the horror of the Golem or Frankenstein monster that it resembles. Yet the pseudo-human image that Ahab's monster wears makes us suspect that this "man" is for Ahab not only instrument but ideal—illuminated inward, without real contact with others, of superhuman intelligence, devoid of heart—a self-portrait, in fact; Ahab as he has increasingly become and as he wants to be! That Melville intends Ahab's image of man as a reflection of Ahab's own loss of humanity becomes eminently clear when we recall that Ishmael has described Ahab as "a Prometheus" whose "intense thinking" has created a vulture that feeds forever upon his heart. This is not Prometheus the noble rebel but Prometheus the exile, exiled by his very rebellion which cuts him off from his own self. "I stand for the heart," writes Melville. "To the dogs with the head! I had rather be a fool with a heart, than Jupiter Olympus with his head." [5]

Ahab is "queenly," indeed, but not a person in the full sense of the term. Yet, unlike his monstrous model and despite his overweening will, Ahab has a great heart, and from his first description of Ahab as "a man of greatly superior natural force, with a globular brain and a ponderous heart," Melville never lets us forget it. In Ahab, Melville created a demonic romantic figure who appeals, and is meant to appeal to us, through his noble suffering and dark grandeur. "Moody stricken Ahab stood before them with a crucifixion in his face; in all the nameless regal overbearing dignity of some mighty woe," recounts Ishmael, describing Ahab's first appearance. "Oh, my captain, my captain!—noble heart," says Starbuck in his last appeal. "See, it's a brave man that weeps; how great the agony of the persuasion then!" Starbuck still hopes that a brave man's tears can reach that "noble heart." Ahab himself contrasts his wild suffering with the lesser woe of the blacksmith: "Thy shrunk voice sounds too calmly, sanely woeful to me. In no Paradise myself, I am impatient of all misery in others that is not mad." That this distinction between superior and inferior suffering is shared

[5] Letter to Nathaniel Hawthorne, Pittsfield, June ? 1851, Thorpe *op. cit.*, p. 392.

by Melville is made clear beyond doubt by his comment on the Ahab who lies crushed and broken at the bottom of Stubb's boat after the mishaps of "The Chase—First Day" (CXXXIII):

> Far inland, nameless wails came from him, as desolate sounds from out ravines. But this intensity of his physical prostration did but so much the more abbreviate it. In an instant's compass, great hearts sometimes condense to one deep pang, the sum total of those shallow pains kindly diffused through feebler man's whole lives. And so, such hearts, though summary in each one suffering; still, if the gods decree it, in their life-time aggregate a whole age of woe, wholly made up on instantaneous intensities; for even in their pointless centres, those noble natures contain the entire circumferences of inferior souls.

We must distinguish between two types of "heart"—the romantic-demonic and the human. The former remains strong in Ahab till the end; the latter disappears. Ahab mistakes romantic defiance, as a result, for the affirmation of human personality. The hedonistic and sadistic Stubb is characterized by Fleece as "more of shark dan Massa Shark hisself." Ahab is above any vulgar enjoyment or mere meanness. "Gifted with the high perception, I lack the low, enjoying power," he says of himself. Just for this reason, it is he, and not Stubb, who recognizes sharkish, cannibalistic nature as evil and goes forth to attack it. Yet he does not really recognize any independent "other." His "woe" goes over to madness just at this point, when he projects all evil onto Moby Dick. Ahab is not mad merely in any prosaic sense; he is romantically mad. "I'm demoniac," he boasts, "I am madness maddened! That wild madness that's only calm to comprehend itself!" Prophet and fulfiller in one, he is more than the great gods ever were. "I laugh and hoot at ye, ye cricket-players, ye pugilists . . . ye've knocked me down, and I am up again; but *ye* have run and hidden." The gods themselves cannot swerve Ahab from his fixed purpose. Like a giant locomotive, "over unsounded gorges, through the rifled hearts of mountains, under torrents' beds, unerringly I rush!" Thus in Ahab the image of man finally becomes the image of a locomotive! This is the ultimate irony of Ahab's "iron way."

In "The Candles" Ahab speaks of a personal existence that he does not live. In "The Symphony" (CXXXII) he lives it— for a brief moment—in a relation to Starbuck that is, for once, person-to-person, rather than captain-to-mate. In the opening of "The Symphony" the dualism that is so often suggested throughout *Moby Dick* is replaced by a dialectic. Until now the very substance of a terrifying dualism, the gentle air and cannibalistic sea become partners in a male-female dialectic, and their antagonism disappears in their harmonious sexual intercourse. But Ahab appears on the scene with his own dualism intact: "Tied up and twisted; gnarled and knotted with wrinkles; haggardly firm and unyielding; his eyes glowing like coals, that still glow in the ashes of ruin; untottering Ahab stood forth in the clearness of the morn; lifting his splintered helmet of a brow to the fair girl's forehead of heaven." Yet even Ahab, as he leans over the deck, is not entirely impervious to the caressing of the "glad, happy air" and "winsome sky." For a moment the lovely aromas seem to dispel "the cankerous thing in his soul." From beneath his slouched hat he drops a tear into the ocean, and Starbuck, who stands near, hears "in his own true heart the measureless sobbing that stole out of the centre of serenity around him."

This is another Ahab, not the "grand, ungodly godlike man" of whom Captain Peleg, the ship's owner, speaks to Ishmael, but the Ahab whom Peleg characterizes, "Stricken, blasted, if he be, Ahab has his humanities!" This is the Ahab who says to the shoals of fishes who swim away from the Pequod when its wake crosses with a stranger ship, "Swim away from me, do ye?" in a tone which we are told, "conveyed more of deep helpless sadness than the insane old man had ever before evinced." "I feel deadly faint, bowed, and humped," Ahab says to Starbuck in "The Symphony," "as though I were Adam staggering beneath the piled centuries since Paradise." Ahab, the self-appoined representative of mankind in its fight against the hostile nonhuman world now acknowledges himself, for once, the frail human being burdened beyond his endurance: "God! God! God!

crack my heart!—stave my brain!—mockery! mockery! bitter biting mockery of grey hairs, have I lived enough to wear ye, and seem and feel thus intolerably old?"

Ahab asks Starbuck to stand close and says, "Let me look into a human eye, it is better than to gaze upon sea and sky, better than to gaze upon God." Ahab now longs for the personal and in the only way in which it can really be present —person in relation to person, eyes looking into eyes, face responding to face. "By the green land; by the bright hearth stone! this is the magic glass, man; I see my wife and my child in thine eye." This link with Starbuck is also a link with the land and with all that Ahab has of humanity in him. Starbuck takes advantage of the moment to plead: "Oh, my Captain! my Captain! noble soul! grand old heart, after all! why should anyone give chase to that hated fish!" But Ahab's glance is averted. The moment of openness is followed by bitterness, irony, despair, and defeat. "Like a blighted fruit tree he shook, and cast his last, cindered apple to the soil!" From now on Ahab will only be the old man on the chase—with this difference; that he has, for once, acknowledged weakness. Ahab's sense of the futility of his life quickly turns into a sense of fate—at first his own inner compulsion, but later the external, "predestinated" universe. Since Ahab does not now identify himself with this compulsion, he sees it as external to him and projects it onto fate and to God, the judge who "himself is dragged to the bar" for creating the evil of the world.

> "If the great sun move not of himself; but is as an errand-boy in heaven; nor one single star can revolve, but by some invisible power; how then can this one small heart beat; this one small brain think thoughts; unless God does that beating, does that thinking, does that living, and not I. By heaven, man, we are turned round and round in this world, like yonder windlass, and Fate is the handspike."

"The mild, mild wind" and the fragrant air make Ahab think of mowers sleeping among new-mown hay in the Andes, but he ends with a bitter reflection on death: "Aye, toil we how we may, we all sleep at last on the field. Sleep? Aye, and rust amid greenness: as last year's scythes flung down, and left in the half-cut swaths." No sooner is the sweet moment of peace experienced than man is caught up again in the flow that inexorably takes him on to his death. It is the sense that he cannot rest in any such moment that is the bitterness which drives Ahab on, that hands him back helpless to his compulsion. What in Goethe's *Faust* is romantically meaningful and itself the guarantee of salvation—that Faust will not rest in any moment but "ever strives"—in "The Symphony" is a dreadful fate that drives man mercilessly to his end.

"The Symphony" is the only real break that we see in Ahab's mad progress toward destruction. Does this mean that there is a real chance for Ahab to turn back? No, for all his strength lies in the demonic side of his character, while the human is weak and unrealized. Ahab's "humanity" is more passive emotion than active attitude. The one moment of freedom, of real dialogue with another person, quickly dissolves into the monologue of a man who can never really listen and respond to another person. Starbuck steals away "blanched to a corpse's hue with despair" and Fedallah, Ahab's Mephistophelian *alter ego*, is left looking up at Ahab from where his eyes are reflected in the water.

F. O. Matthiessen has called Melville's account of the three days of the actual chase of Moby Dick "the finest piece of dramatic writing in American literature." [6] The first essential of the drama is the appearance of Moby Dick himself. In "The Chase—First Day," "the grand god revealed himself" with all the "terrors of his . . . trunk" and "the wrenched hideousness of his jaw."

A gentle joyousness—a mighty mildness of repose in swiftness, invested the gliding whale . . . Not Jove, not that great majesty Supreme! did surpass the glorified White Whale as he so divinely swam.

[6] F. O. Matthiessen, *The American Renaissance* (London and New York: Oxford University Press, 1941), p. 421.

The other essential of this archetypal drama is the legendary hero, the Prometheus who not only withstands but goes forth to attack this leviathanic Zeus. Once "The Symphony's" moment of weakness is passed, Ahab resumes his defiance, and these last chapters resound with the leitmotif of Ahab's unconquerable soul. Although Ahab confesses to Starbuck that it is "sweet to lean sometimes," yet "even with a broken bone" he claims himself "untouched": "Nor White Whale, nor man, nor fiend, can so much as graze old Ahab in his own proper and inaccessible being." When Stubb laughs at a wreck of a boat, Ahab exclaims, "What soulless thing is this that laughs before a wreck? Man, man! did I not know thee brave as fearless fire (and as mechanical) I could swear thou wert a poltroon." But when Starbuck draws near and says, "Aye, Sir, 'tis a solemn sight; an omen, and an ill one," Ahab rejects Starbuck's omen with the same scorn as Stubb's "soulless laughter": "If the gods think to speak outright to man, they will honorably speak outright; not shake their heads, and give an old wives' darkling hint." Men who look for omens are men who passively resign themselves to fate, and this will never be Ahab—the man who converts the omen-fraught terror of the corposants into his own magic fire with which he welds the crew once more to his purpose. "Begone! Ye two are the opposite poles of one thing; Starbuck is Stubb reversed, and Stubb is Starbuck, and ye two are all mankind." Mankind is made up, on the one hand, of those fearless dolts who are able to act because they have no true sense of what they are confronting and, on the other, of those solemn, passive beings who are afraid to act at all because they see man at the mercy of fate and wish, like Shakespeare's Brutus, to blame their being "underlings" on their stars. Ahab insists on both full awareness of the hostile reality that confronts man and fully active confrontation of it. As a result, "Ahab stands alone among the millions of the peopled earth, nor gods nor men his neighbors! Cold, cold—I shiver!" Here stands the lonely Superman, the Titan Prometheus towering over the lesser breed of men.

When Starbuck pleads with Ahab to abandon the chase in "The Chase—Second Day" (CXXXIV), Ahab replies: "Star buck, of late I've felt strangely moved to thee, ever since that hour we both saw—thou know'st what, in one another's eyes." The dialogue with Starbuck that recalled his own humanity is still present to Ahab, but while the chase continues this dialogue can have no significance for him. It cannot affect or even in the slightest way deflect his onrushing course: "In this matter of the whale, be the front of thy face to me as the palm of this hand—a lipless, unfeatured blank." The confrontation with what is not man transcends and submerges the dialogue with man. It does not even preserve man's personality from what threatens to destroy it, as in "The Candles." If Ahab's next statement to Starbuck is the Promethean "Ahab is forever Ahab, man," it is followed by a total surrender to the impersonal power that he was originally fighting:

> "This whole act's immutably decreed.[7] 'Twas rehearsed by thee and me a billion years before this ocean rolled. Fool! I am the Fate's lieutenant; I act under orders. Look thou underling! that thou obeyest mine."

Even mad little Pip, whom Ahab has befriended, can no longer reach Ahab when he calls to him and warns him against the sharks. "Ahab heard nothing; for his own voice was high-lifted then." Ahab is the most thoroughgoing example of the "monological man" that one can find, short of the psychotic. He can hear no other human voice because his own is "high-lifted." In the end it is just this that most drastically betrays the destruction of his own humanity. "Ye are not other men," says Ahab to his crew, "but my arms and my legs and so obey me." There can be no human dialogue because there is only one person, one consciousness present, and this consciousness exists only in relation to the impersonal. "They were one man, not thirty . . . the individualities of the crew . . . were all directed to that fatal goal which Ahab their one lord and keel did point to." This is

---

[7] That on occasion Ishmael, and perhaps Melville too, shares this Calvinist attitude toward predestination is suggested by Ishmael's statement in "The Town-Ho's Story" (LIV): "Gentlemen, a strange fatality pervades the whole career of these events, as if verily mapped out before the world itself was charted."

humanity at its height and at its depth—standing bravely confronting what is not man, yet denying the individuality and the free interrelationship of men in so doing.

Ahab's betrayal of the personal for the impersonal is an integral part of his denial of dialogue in favor of that overweening monologue in which all people and things become subsumed under his own ego. To this world-subjectivizing individualism Ahab clings to the last. The crew are only part of his consciousness and purpose: Starbuck must not die because he reminds Ahab of his wife and child; Moby Dick must be destroyed because he did not passively submit to being converted into oil. When Ishmael says in "The Monkey-Rope," "Another's mistake or misfortune might plunge innocent me into unmerited disaster and death," his "innocent me" is ironic. He knows that human existence is essentially, and not just secondarily, interdependent and reciprocal. Ahab's "innocent me" is paranoid—the inverted idealist's accusation against the world that does not conform to his inwardness and subject itself to his purposes. When the carpenter makes a new leg for Ahab, the latter bewails:

> "Here I am, proud as a Greek god, and yet standing debtor to this blockhead for a bone to stand on! Cursed be that mortal interindebtedness which will not do away with ledgers. I would be free as air; and I'm down in the whole world's books." (CVIII)

Ahab's monological consciousness is nowhere more evident than in his reaction to the encounter with other worlds that have not come under the domination of his mad chase as has the little world of the Pequod. This encounter takes the form of the Pequod's nine "gams"—its meeting and exchange of greetings with the succession of symbolically named whaling ships that pass it in the course of the book's action—the Albatross, the Town-Ho, the Jeroboam, the Virgin, the Rose-Bud, the Samuel Enderby of London, the Bachelor, the Rachel, and the Delight. Ordinarily, we are told, the meeting of two whaling ships at sea, one perhaps outward bound, the other coming home after a long voyage, is the occasion for "friendly and sociable contact," exchange of letters and news, exchange of visits—in short, a "gam." Ahab's unsociability and his singleness of purpose stand out all the more starkly in the face of this natural and customary sociability, "for . . . he cared not to consort, even for five minutes, with any stranger captain, except he could contribute some of that information he so absorbingly sought." When the Pequod meets another ship, Ahab's one question is, "Hast seen the White Whale?"

The captain of the Samuel Enderby has not only seen the White Whale, but has lost his arm as a result of him. But he refuses to lower for Moby Dick again, not wishing to give him another arm. " 'There would be great glory in killing him, . . . but, hark ye, he's best let alone; don't you think so, Captain?'—glancing at the ivory leg." But to Ahab it is just that which makes Moby Dick irresistible: "He is. But he will still be hunted, for all that. What is best let alone, that accursed thing is not always what least allures. He's all a magnet!" Moby Dick's evil magnetism cannot hold the English captain, who will not even go along with Ahab as to the character of Moby Dick: "What you take for the White Whale's malice is only his awkwardness." To such superficiality and levity Ahab can only turn his back: "In vain the English captain hailed him. With back to the stranger ship, and face set like a flint to his own, Ahab stood upright till alongside of the Pequod." But the Samuel Enderby at least has encountered Moby Dick. The jolly Bachelor, like jolly Stubb, will not even take him seriously. The Bachelor's captain stands erect on his quarter-deck enjoying "the whole rejoicing drama" of his "glad ship of good luck." Ahab, in "striking contrast," stands on the quarter-deck of "the moody Pequod," "shaggy and black, with a stubborn gloom."

"Come aboard, come aboard!" cried the gay Bachelor's commander, lifting a glass and a bottle in the air.

"Hast seen the White Whale?" gritted Ahab in reply.

"No; only heard of him; but don't believe in him at all," said the other good-humoredly. "Come aboard!"

"Thou art too damned jolly. Sail on." (CXV)

Perhaps the finest single symbol of Ahab's monological life is the doubloon which he nails to the mast as a prize for the first man who raises the White Whale. When one after the other Ahab, Starbuck, Stubb, Flask, and the Manxman read the markings on the doubloon, "to each and every man in turn," it "but mirrors back his own mysterious self," as Ahab says himself. But only Ahab sees it as himself. "Look here,— three peaks as proud as Lucifer. The firm tower, that is Ahab; the volcano, that is Ahab; the courageous, the undaunted, and victorious fowl, that, too, is Ahab; all are Ahab." Each sees reality from his own perspective, as little Pip indicates with his grammatical recitation, "I look, you look, he looks; we look, ye look, they look." But only Ahab identifies himself with reality to such an extent that he can recognize no independent "other." It is fitting that it is Ahab himself who first raises Moby Dick and claims the doubloon for his own, and he does not fail to draw the proper conclusion from this happening:

> "I saw him almost that same instant, Sir, that Captain Ahab did, and I cried out," said Tashtego.
> "Not the same instant; not the same instant; not the same—no, the doubloon is mine, Fate reserved the doubloon for me. I only; none of ye could have raised the White Whale first." (CXXXIII)

If Ahab sounds more like a grasping child here than a noble hero, he leaves us in no doubt that his natural superiority to all men is destined by "Fate" itself. The passage in "The Chase —Second Day" in which he characterizes himself as "Fate's Lieutenant" not only begins with "Ahab is forever Ahab," as we have seen, but ends with "Ahab's hawser tows his purpose yet." Ahab is Fate's lieutenant, not its underling. If, after "The Symphony," he no longer has the strength to fight the nonhuman in the name of the human, he now finds in "Fate" the support for the Promethean self-affirmation that enables him to pit himself against the hated White Whale. Fate is no longer, for him, the merely external power that it was in "The Symphony." Rather, it is the larger order with whose purposes he co-operates, even as he once saw Fate as co-operating with his purposes when he said, in "The Sunset"

(XXXVII), "The path to my fixed purpose is laid with iron rails, whereon my soul is grooved to run."

Ahab obeys Fate, but he still defies the Whale. When Moby Dick finally turns to destroy the ship that is harassing him, "retribution, swift vengeance, eternal malice" are "in his whole aspect," recalling all the hints about his inscrutable malice that are piled up in earlier chapters as well as the accounts of other sperm whales destroying large ships with "judicious" malice and "decided, calculating mischief." Ahab, certainly, does not look on the White Whale at the last as his partner in a predestined drama. His relation to him, more intensely personal even than that with Starbuck or any other human being, is one of pure hatred. "To the last I grapple with thee; from hell's heart I stab at thee; for hate's sake I spit my last breath at thee . . . while still chasing thee, though tied to thee, thou damned whale! *Thus*, I give up the spear!" Ahab goes down defying to the last. Unlike the dying whale who even as a representative of the "dark Hindu half of nature" still turns his body toward the natural sun, Ahab turns his body *from* the sun. He denies his link with nature even while he sinks his harpoon into the whale who the next moment carries him down to his death. "Towards thee I roll, thou all-destroying but unconquering whale," Ahab cries in this same speech. The whale, like the fire, has the power to destroy, but it cannot conquer Ahab; it cannot conquer that personality that he still retains to the last, if only in his defiance.

It is not nature alone that Ahab is cut off from, however, but all mankind. "Oh lonely death on lonely life!" says Ahab. "Oh, now I feel my topmost greatness lies in my topmost grief." There is no positive sense in which Ahab can be called great—even for Melville he cannot be an image of man in the full sense of the term—but he is great in his grief, in his proud aloneness, in his Promethean defiance. He is a man who pours all his life's searching and fighting into this one moment, who insists on giving his death the very meaning his life has had.

If Moby Dick is "all-destroying," he is still "unconquering." In Ahab's final hate-spitting, "from hell's heart"-stabbing defiance of the White Whale to whom he is tied, the note of self-affirmation rings out clear and undaunted. That Ahab responds to the hostility of the world with defiance does not represent a moral choice on his part in any ordinary sense of the term: he has to defy to exist. Ahab is the last stage of the romantic hero who turns his defiant despair into a barricade against God and man alike and settles down to live in the heightened reality of his own agonized self with its narrow intensity of meaning. His isolation is not that of the albino who is ejected by his fellows from the herd but, in Melville's own image in "The Cabin-Table" (XXXIV), that of the grizzly bear who shuts himself up in sullen self-reliance:

> Though nominally included in the census of Christendom, he was still an alien to it. He lived in the world, as the last of the Grisly Bears lived in settled Missouri. And as . . . that wild Logan of the woods, burying himself in the hollow of a tree, lived out the winter there, sucking his own paws, so, in his inclement, howling old age, Ahab's soul, shut up in the caved trunk of his body, there fed upon the sullen paws of its gloom!

Ahab is not only the best example in literature of Kierkegaard's "demonic shut-inness." [8] He is also the best example of Martin Buber's "second stage of evil," in which man reaches the threshold of self-deification and absolute self-affirmation. The man in this stage denies all order and reality that might call him to account and says, "What I do is good because *I* do it" and "What I say is true because *I* say it." [9]

Here the final stage of the isolated romantic hero merges with the end-term of the Modern Promethean who, as the only means of overcoming man's alienation and recovering

---

[8] W. H. Auden, *The Enchafèd Flood, or the Romantic Iconography of the Sea* (London: Faber & Faber, 1951); M. O. Percival, *op. cit.*, pp. 16-18, 34-36, 42, 100-102. Cf. Sören Kierkegaard, *The Concept of Dread* and *The Sickness unto Death*.

[9] Martin Buber, *Good and Evil. Two Interpretations* (New York: Charles Scribner's Sons, 1953) II. "Images of Good and Evil," trans. Michael Bullock, Part Two and Part Three, Chaps. IV, V, pp. 99-114, 133-143. Cf. Maurice Friedman, *Martin Buber: The Life of Dialogue* (New York: Harper Torchbook, 1960), "The Nature of Evil," Chap. XV.

his creative freedom, denies any reality that transcends him. Ahab is a proud romantic figure, Milton's Satan[10] and Byron's Manfred, but he is also a tragic and pitiable figure shivering in the cold on his outpost on the jutting cliff. Behind the lineaments of the romantic rebel we can dimly discern the face of the Modern Exile; behind the noble despair lurks the quotidian.

Through Ishmael, Melville is able to express with some precision the sense in which he does and does not identify with Ahab. Ishmael's warning to those who discover the dark side of life and plunge remorselessly on in their knowledge of it expresses Melville's own reservations as to his hero Ahab. "Give not thyself up, then, to fire," concludes Ishmael in "The Try-Works" (XCVI), "lest it invert thee, deaden thee; as for the time it did me. There is a wisdom that is woe; but there is a woe that is madness." Somewhere between the foolish optimist and the too-wise madman, Ishmael, and without question Melville too, hoped to find the truly wise man who could face the evil and suffering of the world without being overwhelmed by it: "There is a Catskill eagle in some souls that can alike dive down into the blackest gorges, and soar out of them again and become invisible in the sunny spaces." One must have the wisdom that is woe to be man, really to be man, and yet one has to stop short of immersing oneself in that woe, stop short of madness. Man cannot prove himself man through the attitude of a "jolly Stubb," who grins at Moby Dick and will not take him seriously. But neither can he authenticate himself in the way of Ahab, who, like an inverted idealist, turns the natural rebellion of the whale against being killed into a universal, metaphysical evil; who captures the crew within his own inner world and his own purpose; and who refuses, even on encountering other ships, to recognize any reality other than that of his monomaniac hunt.

If one must choose, however, between the superficial optimist and the man who looks only into the depths of life, Ish-

<hr>

[10] Cf. Henry F. Pommer, *Milton and Melville* (Pittsburgh: University of Pittsburgh Press, 1950), pp. 96 f.

mael and Melville choose the latter: "Even if he for ever flies within the gorge, that gorge is in the mountains; so that even in his lowest swoop the mountain eagle is still higher than other birds upon the plain even though they soar." The fire is a symbol not only of evil, but also of suffering, of the search for truth, of the full and intense use of man's spiritual energies, and of that elemental sphere in which the human mind cannot long sojourn without madness. There is an admiration here for the Promethean hero, the seeker for truth, reminiscent of the apotheosis of Bulkington in "The Lee Shore." There is admiration for the profundity, for the courage, heroism, and defiance of the mad Ahab. But there is also a word of warning. Ahab's defiance is not a romantic pose. Ahab acts as he does because no other relation to existence is open to him.

Moby Dick abounds with evidence that Melville intended Ahab to be seen within the context of tragedy. He proclaims that "democratic dignity" which enables him to "ascribe high qualities" and "weave tragic graces" around "meanest mariners, and renegades and castaways." Although Ahab lacks the "outward majestical trappings" of emperors and kings, he is still fit subject for "the tragic dramatist who would depict mortal indomitableness in its fullest sweep": "Oh, Ahab! what shall be grand in thee, it must needs be plucked at from the skies, and dived for in the deep, and featured in the unbodied air!" Ahab, "a poor old whale-hunter," can occupy the throne of the tragic hero that in ancient times might only be held by kings and those of noble blood.

The mediator between Ahab and the tragic hero of old, and the patent of Ahab's tragic nobility, is the romantic hero with his titanic suffering and his dark morbidity. In almost his first, oblique reference to Ahab in "The Ship" (XVI), Ishmael leaves us in no doubt that Ahab is cast in the dimensions of the romantic tragic hero:

> When these things unite in a man of greatly superior natural force, with a globular brain and a ponderous heart; who has also by the stillness and seclusion of many long night-watches in the remotest waters . . . been

led to think untraditionally and independently; receiving all nature's sweet or savage impressions fresh from her own virgin voluntary and confiding breast, and thereby chiefly . . . to learn a bold and nervous lofty language—that man makes one in a whole nation's census—a mighty pageant creature, formed for noble tragedies. Nor will it at all detract from him, dramatically regarded, if either by birth or other circumstances, he have what seems a half wilful over-ruling morbidness at the bottom of his nature. For all men tragically great are made so through a certain morbidness.

Nor does Melville fail to provide us with Ahab's tragic flaw: "In his fiery eyes of scorn and triumph, you then saw Ahab in all his fatal pride." Melville's intention is also evident in modes and motifs from Shakespearean tragedy, in particular *Lear* and *Macbeth*, with which the final chapters are permeated, as well as in the heightened tone throughout, which enables Melville to "spread a rainbow" over Ahab's "disastrous set of sun."

Ahab, for all that, is not a tragic hero in the traditional Aristotelian sense of the term. There is too little real fate, despite Ahab's reference to it; there is too much that grows, almost arbitrarily, out of Ahab himself. Nor can we identify with Ahab as with the Greek tragic hero. Despite the fact that "Ahab has his humanities" in his relation to Starbuck and mad Pip, toward the end he becomes almost inhuman. Our rare glimpses of his human emotions only reinforce the sense of the dominance of the inhuman will in which they are submerged. Ahab ends his dialogue with Starbuck with his statement that, in the predestined matter of the whale, Starbuck's face is to him but as the palm of his hand, "a lipless, unfeatured blank." When Ahab refuses to help hunt for the son of the Rachel's captain, his language still contains a touch of the human—"God bless ye, man, and may I forgive myself"—but it begins with "I will not do it. Even now I lose time," and ends with "I must go." Pip's offer in "The Cabin" (CXXIX) to serve as Ahab's leg touches Ahab and threatens to melt his stern determination. But he puts Pip away from him with all the more energy therefore, even while blessing him:

"Lad, lad, I tell thee thou must not follow Ahab now. The hour is coming when Ahab would not scare thee from him, yet would not have thee by him. There is that in thee, poor lad, which I feel too curing to my malady. Like cures like; and for this hunt, my malady becomes my most desired health . . ."

". . . Sir; do ye but use poor me for your one lost leg . . ."

"Oh! spite of million villains, this makes me a bigot in the fadeless fidelity of man!—and a black! and crazy! . . ."

". . . I will never desert ye, Sir . . . I must go with ye."

"If thou speakest thus to me much more, Ahab's purpose keels up in him. I tell thee no; it cannot be . . . Weep so, and I will murder thee! have a care, for Ahab too is mad . . . Thy hand!—Met! True art thou, lad, as the circumference to its centre. So: God for ever bless thee; and if it come to that,—God for ever save thee, let what will befall."

Ahab's "Weep, so, and I will murder thee!" is, in reality, his final word to little Pip, who dies shut up in Ahab's cabin because Ahab has gone to hurl his harpoon at Moby Dick. Although the reader may feel Ahab's humanity in "The Symphony" and "The Cabin," it is difficult for him to identify with the Ahab of the final chase or experience at Ahab's death the catharsis of "pity and terror" that the spectacle of the tragic hero's downfall is traditionally supposed to induce.

Even if this were not the case, there could be no emotional catharsis and no tragic resolution in Aristotle's sense of the term. Ahab does not in any way become reconciled to the order of the universe as the Greek tragic hero, including Prometheus, invariably does: instead, as we have seen, he goes down defying to the last. What is more, for Melville himself there is no order with which man can become reconciled, even through tragic suffering and death. The very heart of *Moby Dick*, indeed, is the denial of just this order. Ahab's defiance of Moby Dick is succeeded by the tranquil indifference of the sea that at the end, when the other two protagonists have disappeared, looks on with detachment just as it has all along. If the sea at the end of *Moby Dick* is a tranquil rather than a raging one, it is, nonetheless, the "masterless ocean" that "overruns the globe." Although the final picture of the sea rolling on "as it rolled five thousand years ago" suggests an attitude of acceptance, there is here no true tragic reconciliation. The aesthetic enclosure is that provided by the artistic form: it does not answer any of the questions that the book has raised, but it holds in powerful equilibrium the still unsilenced torment of the Modern Promethean.[11]

Yet Ahab *is* a tragic figure, for he possesses true tragic grandeur. We cannot dismiss him as merely romantic, merely psychotic, merely a mid-nineteenth-century American individualist, no matter how we study Melville's sources, describe the social history of the time, and psychoanalyze Melville and his characters. If ancient Greek tragedy is based on the positing of an order and man's reconciliation with it, a truly modern tragedy must be based on the modern view of the world, and not Aristotle's—a fact largely ignored by those literary scholars who dutifully carry over Aristotle's world view, along with his *Poetics*, to every analysis of modern tragedy. The modern tragedy must mean the recognition of the absence of any such order, and it *may* also mean the hero's defiance in the face of a hostile world. Ahab is not simply the victim of psychological determinism, like Lavinia in Eugene O'Neill's *Mourning Becomes Electra* and Blanche in Tennessee Williams' *Streetcar Named Desire*. His defiance grows out of freedom as well as compulsion, and in this sense at least, he is, in his very character as a Modern Promethean, a modern tragic hero.

---

11 "If Ahab persists in the face of an obvious dilemma, and is thereby destroyed, the dilemma is the same as Melville's own, and Melville has not resolved it for himself . . . Ahab's fury is the last stage of Melville's malaise. Actually, no final condemnation is possible. The largest paradox in *Moby-Dick*, prior to any moral judgment, is the necessity of voyaging and the equal necessity of failure." "Just as the method of *Moby-Dick* is a paradox, the theme of the book is an unresolved question." (Charles Feidelson, Jr., *Symbolism and American Literature* [Chicago: University of Chicago Press, 1953], pp. 34 f., 185.)

6

AHAB, BARTLEBY, AND
BILLY BUDD:
FREEDOM AND COMPULSION AND
THE DIVIDED MAN

AHAB

Melville's Captain Ahab is a Modern Promethean, but in a sense quite different from the merely symbolic Prometheanism of the drowned Bulkington. What makes Ahab really modern, as Bulkington is not, is the deep inner division in him. We are told that Ahab's intense thinking has made him into a Prometheus whose own mind creates a vulture that feeds upon his heart—a very different consequence of "deep, earnest thinking" than is suggested with the apotheosized Bulkington. In Ahab, Melville has depicted the problematic of modern man—the alienation, the divided nature, the unresolved tension between personal freedom and psychological compulsion which follow on the "death of God."

Melville himself never lets us forget how much of.Ahab's Prometheanism must be ascribed to psychological illness. Ahab cannot be dismissed as *merely* projecting evil on the nonhuman world, for Ishmael himself provides us with an enormous accumulation of suggestions that the world is hostile to man either in a personal-malignant or a cold-indifferent way. What makes Ahab "crazy" is the fact that he personifies this evil in Moby Dick. Melville explicitly ascribes this association of all evil with the White Whale to Ahab's delirium and his "transference," a term which Melville uses in a manner not unlike its modern psychoanalytical usage.

In "Moby Dick" Melville actually appears to "psychoanalyze" his hero. We are told of the stages of Ahab's monomania, being constantly reassured throughout that this *is* a monomania. The first stage was the "sudden, passionate, corporal animosity" which led him to drive his knife into the whale; the second stage was "the agonizing bodily laceration" that he felt when his leg was sheared off; the third came when "Ahab and anguish lay stretched together in one hammock" for "long months of days and weeks"; the fourth was that period when "his torn body and gashed soul bled into one another; and so interfusing made him mad"; by the fifth stage he became "a raving lunatic . . . unlimbed of a leg," yet possessing enormous "vital strength." This coupling of impotence and vital strength recurs again and again with Ahab. His sense of impotence is expressed in his terrible rage and frustration, but he is the only really vital person in the whole boat, the only one with full depths of vitality, and this is why everything centers on him. In the sixth stage Ahab hid his madness. "The direful madness" was gone from the outside, but "Ahab, in his hidden self, raved on." His "full lunacy subsided not but deepeningly contracted," and yet, at the same time as his "broad madness" had not been left behind, so "not one jot of his great natural intellect had perished." His vital intelligence is not only preserved in madness but enormously enhanced: "Far from having lost his strength, Ahab, to that one end, did now possess a thousand fold more potency than ever he had sanely brought to bear upon any one reasonable object."

Ahab's madness has given him sources of almost unlimited strength: he has gone down to a deeper level not only than ordinary men can reach, but than he himself could reach so long as he was sane. He is, in fact, a sort of negative super-man; he has achieved what the rest of humanity vainly strives for: the full working of the mind, the great clarity of intellect, the fullness of passion and vitality—all harnessed in one direction. And the whole process is mad. Yet at just this point we are told: "This is much, yet Ahab's larger, darker, deeper part remains unhinted. But vain to popularize pro-fundities, and all truth is profound." Here, despite all the disclaimers about Ahab's madness, Ishmael clearly tells us that there is reality in this man which, far from our being able to dismiss it, is too deep for us to begin to comprehend. Moreover, and equally important, the location of "truth" is no longer "up there," where Bulkington sought it, nor is truth the young Platonist's one soul underlying all; truth is now found inward—not in consciousness and thoughts, as the idealist holds, but in that deep unconscious force, that vitality and inner purpose that Ahab embodies. This means not only that truth has been removed inward and thus divorced from its marriage with external reality; it has now also been inex-tricably merged with madness. The startling question arises as to whether the search for truth is not necessarily madness, whether sanity is possible only if one abandons the search for truth. Commenting in "The Albatross" (LII) on Ahab's "progress" round the world "through numberless perils to the very point where we started," even Ishmael questions the rationality of this search:

In pursuit of those far mysteries we dream of, or in tor-mented chase of that demon phantom that, some time or other, swims before all human hearts; while chasing such over this round globe, they either lead us on in barren mazes or midway leave us whelmed.

Ahab's inner division and the complex relation between his

personality and his psychological illness come to the surface most clearly during that brief interlude in "The Symphony" in which Ahab recognizes his compulsion for what it is. There, as we have seen, he identifies himself, for once, not with the monomaniac drive to chase the whale, the rage and passion to pursue, but with the person who is driven by that compulsion, the man who is old and tired and knows it. "What mad thing has made me run the seas these forty years!" he exclaims. The very nature of the compulsion that possesses Ahab has always in the past made him identify with it. The symptoms of his inner dualism that he manifests up till now are not so much a sign of the weakness of his resolve, we are told in "The Chart" (XLIV), "but the plainest tokens of its intensity." When Ahab's intolerably vivid nightmares become an insufferable anguish that force him to "burst from his state room, as though escaping from a bed that was on fire," the agent is not "crazy Ahab, the scheming, unappeasedly steadfast hunter of the White Whale" who had gone to the hammock. The agent is "the eternal, living principle or soul in him" which, becoming dissociated in sleep, "spontaneously sought escape from the scorching contiguity" of that supreme purpose which "by its own sheer inveteracy of will, forced itself . . . into a kind of self-assumed, independent being of its own" which "could grimly live and burn, while the common vitality to which it was conjoined, fled horror-stricken from the unbidden and unfathered birth."

Therefore, the tormented spirit that glared out of bodily eyes, when what seemed Ahab rushed from his room, was for the time but a vacated thing, a formless somnambulistic being, a ray of living light, to be sure, but without an object to color, and therefore a blankness in itself.

Now, however, in "The Symphony," it is the fully conscious Ahab, rather than a dissociated vacant, inner blankness, who does not identify himself with his compulsion.

"The madness, the frenzy, the boiling blood and the smoking brow with which for a thousand lowerings old

Ahab has furiously, foamingly chased his prey—more a demon than a man!—aye, aye! what a forty years' fool—old fool, has old Ahab been! Why this strife of the chase?"

"Locks so grey did never grow but from out some ashes," Ahab adds, reinforcing the image of an extinct volcano implicit in Melville's earlier phrase, "the burnt-out crater of his brain." Perhaps it is because his volcanic fire has temporarily gone out, or at least burnt low, that Ahab now knows his compulsion for what it is. Ahab's inner compulsion is fate itself for him. "With little external to constrain us," says Ishmael commenting on Ahab, "the innermost necessities in our being, these still drive us on." After Ahab has ceased to identify with his compulsion and before he projects it on God, he has a moment of genuine doubt as to his own self which makes him question whether there really is an "I," a person behind his actions and not some objective, impersonal force.

"What is it, what nameless, inscrutable, unearthly thing is it, what cozening, hidden lord and master, and cruel, remorseless emperor commands me; that against all natural lovings and longings, I so keep pushing, and crowding, and jamming myself on all the time; recklessly making me ready to do what *in my own proper, natural heart, I durst not so much as dare? Is Ahab, Ahab? Is it I, God, or who, that lifts this arm?* (Italics mine.)

How startling this confession of weakness on the lips of the man who said, "Who's over me? Truth hath no confines"!

Although we may assume that Ahab's inner division continues, "The Symphony" represents the only moment of his awareness of it. Throughout the rest of the book it manifests itself all too clearly in the contradiction between his end—the personal—and his means—the impersonal. The authoritarian personality, or "sado-masochist," as Erich Fromm points out, never merely dominates others. He is always either dominated by some person or, like Napoleon and Hitler, sees himself as following the orders of Destiny, Necessity,

History, of Nature.[1] This is Ahab, who exchanges the fellowship on an equal level for the vertical chain of command: on
the one hand, Starbuck now exists for him only as a dog, an
underling, a faceless instrument of his will; on the other, he
himself is only an instrument of "Fate."

BARTLEBY

Is there any justification aside from death for the explicit
link between Bartleby and the image of man that is made by
the narrator's despairing cry "Ah Bartleby! Ah humanity!"?
Is not Bartleby so eccentric, so sick, that he stands as the
exception to mankind rather than as its representative? We
may pity him, but can we also recognize ourselves in him?
To answer this question we must look at the nature of Bartleby's sickness. If he can be dismissed as simply sick, then
his significance is exhausted by his sickness and he has
nothing to say to us about man as man. In point of fact,
however, no man is "simply sick," for sickness is itself a
deficient mode of being human. Just for that reason, it constitutes an enormously significant commentary on the very
meaning of health. If a sick person were completely determined and a normal person completely free, then the pallid
Bartleby would not be so troubling to his employer. Actually,
man is both free and not free at once. One of the most important aspects of the problematic of modern man, in particular, is the complex intermixture of personal freedom and
psychological compulsion.

If we apply this approach to an analysis of Bartleby's "I
prefer not to," it becomes unmistakably clear that Melville
has intentionally placed at the very heart of his story the
question of whether Bartleby's "sickness" is to be understood as involuntary compulsion, willful self-isolation, or
both. When the employer tries to tempt Bartleby to open
rebellion with the question, "You *will* not?" Bartleby answers, "I *prefer* not." What is the difference between not
willing and not preferring? We are more accustomed to the
distinction between "I will not" and "I cannot," and these

[1] Erich Fromm, *Escape from Freedom* (New York: Rinehart, 1941),
pp. 234-237.

are the terms in which the employer thinks when at leisure intervals he looks into "Edwards on the Will" and "Priestly on Necessity." But "I *prefer* not" cannot properly be equated either with "I *will* not" or "I *can* not," and this is what 'at bottom most deeply disconcerts the employer. He oscillates between seeing Bartleby as a free and voluntary agent and as a helpless victim of an incurable disorder because he cannot get him into steady focus the one way or the other.

Reflecting upon the fact that Bartleby lives on ginger-nuts and that ginger is a hot and spicy thing while Bartleby is not, the employer concludes, "Ginger, then, had no effect upon Bartleby. Probably he preferred it should have none." The statement suggests a triumph of human will over natural cause and effect. In the next paragraph the employer remarks that "Nothing so aggravates an earnest person as a passive resistance," and proceeds to explain this "passive resistance" as the result of involuntary eccentricities. Yet he goes on to confess that this view of Bartleby enables him to "cheaply purchase a delicious self-approval" through humoring Bartleby "in his strange wilfulness." Thus the involuntary is paradoxically equated by the employer with the willful.

Bartleby's "I prefer not" is actually third position between "I will not" and "I can not," a position exactly indicated by the narrator's term "willful." The American psychiatrist Leslie H. Farber distinguishes between the "will" of genuine dialogue and the "willfulness" of hysteria. The willful man "is the image of the eternal stranger: that condition of man in which he is forever separated from his fellows, unknown and unaddressed. . . . When wholeness eludes us in its proper setting—in dialogue," man's separate will poses as his total self. "The life of the will becomes distended, overwhelming, and obtrusive at the same time that its movements become increasingly separate, sovereign, and distinct from other aspects of the spirit."[2] Bartleby is willful in pre-

[2] *The Worlds of Existentialism: A Critical Reader,* ed. with Introductions and Conclusion by Maurice Friedman (New York: Random House, 1964), p. 455 f. Cf. Leslie H. Harber's *The Ways of the Will* (New York: Basic Books, 1966 ; Harper Colophan Books, 1968).

cisely this sense. He might pose as a model for Farber's image of the schizophrenic as the eternal stranger, "forever separated from his fellows, unknown and unaddressed." But if this is so, we can neither reduce Bartleby to a well man who does what he does knowingly or a sick man who is simply acted upon by nature. He retains responsibility for his will, but it is the will of willfulness, the will of the man who is sick in his relations to others and to himself.

"I prefer not to" may now be understood more exactly. It means, in the language of the German psychiatrist Viktor von Weizäcker, not "I would if I could," but "I *could* do it if I *would*, but I cannot will to do so."[3] Hence it means an intermixture of *can* and *will*, rather than the one or the other by itself. We are none of us as free of compulsion *or* of responsibility as we would like to think. We all of us walk a narrow, difficult road in the tension between the two. In Bartleby, we see a man who has run aground on that tension.

FATHERS AND SONS: THE DIVIDED MAN

In Newton Arvin's view, Melville, who lost his father at an early age and went to sea to escape from the women in his family, was seeking for the father in all his writings. Melville's own relation to his dead father is mirrored, certainly, in Ishmael and Ahab, Pierre and his father, Bartleby and his employer, Billy Budd and Captain Vere. This is not to say, however, that these relationships have a merely psychological significance. On the contrary, the absence of the father so deeply affected Melville's world view that the most profound metaphysical and existential questions take root in this soil. Ultimately the absence of the father meant for Melville the shattering of trust and the search for the father the search for renewal of trust.

BILLY BUDD

Melville's last, posthumously published novel, *Billy Budd, Foretopman* (1891), shows clearly Melville's inability to give

---

[3] *The Worlds of Existentialism*, p. 405.

up the search for the father and at the same time the mistrust that lies beneath the apparent renewal of trust—in short, Melville as the divided man. Many critics hold that, in contrast to *Moby Dick*, *Billy Budd* represents an acceptance, a "truce," a resignation on Melville's part.[4] Certainly the events of this novel are presented with a detachment and calm objectivity in marked variance with the tone of *Moby Dick*, *Pierre*, and *The Confidence Man*. In what is more of an allegory than a novel, Melville presents the story of the "Handsome Sailor" Billy Budd, who is falsely accused of fostering mutiny by the malicious master-at-arms Claggart and who is sentenced to hang by the just and fatherly Captain Vere when, prevented from finding words by his speech defect and his anger, Billy strikes out and kills Claggart during a confrontation in the Captain's cabin.

Billy is man before the fall, without the knowledge of good and evil. He is also the figure of Christ, and his rising in "the halter" is an ascension to heaven:

> It chanced that the vapory fleece hanging low in the east was shot through with a soft glory as of the fleece of the Lamb of God seen in mystical vision and simultaneously therewith, watched by the wedged mass of upturned faces, Billy ascended; and, ascending, took the full rose of the dawn. (XXII) [5]

The earlier version, "took the full Shekinah of that grand dawn," makes the identification still clearer, if possible. What is more, Billy's last words are "God bless Captain Vere!" a cry which the crew, almost reluctantly, echoes. Captain Vere stands to Billy not in the relation of the crucifiers whom Jesus asks his "Father" to forgive, but of the Father himself, to

---

[4] "No longer does Melville feel the fear and dislike of Jehovah that were oppressing him through *Moby-Dick* and *Pierre*. He is no longer protesting against the determined laws as being savagely inexorable. He has come to respect necessity . . . Melville has gained a balance that was lacking to his angry defiance in *Pierre* and *The Confidence Man*. . . . Melville could now face incongruity; he could accept the existence of both good and evil with a calm impossible to him in *Moby-Dick*." (F. O. Matthiessen, *op. cit.*, pp. 500-514.)

[5] Herman Melville, "Billy Budd, Foretopman," in *Four Short Novels* (New York: Bantam Classic, 1959).

whom Jesus says, "Not my will but Thine be done." Although Billy's response may reflect Melville's own greater acceptance of the father against whom he earlier rebelled and of the Father God whose justice he formerly questioned, Billy's childlike relation to the fatherly Vere can hardly be taken seriously as Melville's own image of man. Fusing innocent man and divine man, it leaves no room for man as such—for man after the fall, the man of experience who knows both good and evil.

"Struck dead by an angel of God. Yet the angel must hang!" Captain Vere says when he discovers Claggart has been killed by Billy's blow. Billy has found a kind and just father in Captain Vere as Ishmael could not in Captain Ahab. Strong and compassionate, a sympathetic figure, Captain Vere brings together the two worlds of the heavenly truth—"chronologicals"—and earthly truth—"horologicals"—as no other figure in Melville's works has done. Captain Vere understands Billy's innocence and Claggart's malice and finds a way to live in the world of experience without losing his intellectual profundity and emotional fullness. Yet it is as difficult for the reader to share Billy's attitude toward Captain Vere as it is for the crew. Vere makes a complete split between the claims of the head and the claims of the heart. "Let not warm hearts betray heads that should be cool," he says to the drumhead court. The heart "here denotes the feminine in man, . . . and hard though it be, she must here be ruled out."

Vere has no hesitation whatsoever about the rights and wrongs of the situation. In matters of the English Navy, with its recent experience of the Great Mutiny and the regulations of the Mutiny Act, the head must rule alone and with it Vere's strict "justice." In his private relation to Billy, however, Vere is the compassionate and merciful father. The dualism of Melville's earlier works thus reappears here in the split between an objective social world completely given over to the laws of the state and a "natural," private, and interhuman world in which the heart, compassion, and human fellowship may play their part.

From Melville's earlier writings on the heart and the head,

we might expect him to have had some question himself about this dualism, and there are several indications that he did. Although Captain Vere's opposition to social innovations is a disinterested one based on his belief that they are "incapable of embodiment in lasting institutions, but at war with the peace of the world and the true welfare of mankind," Melville strongly hints, at Vere's death, that his relation to the English Navy is not, after all, a purely disinterested one: "The spirit that spite its philosophic austerity may yet have indulged in the most secret of all passions, ambition, never attained to the fulness of fame." We cannot help suspecting that this ambition contributes to the, after all not very admirable, simplicity with which Vere handles the "justice" of Billy's case. It is surely permissible to doubt that hanging the "Handsome Sailor," the man admired and loved by every member of the crew, is the best way of quelling any tendencies to mutiny that may exist. We might also question whether it is purely a concern for naval regulations that leads Vere to the unusual procedure of setting up a drumhead court on the ship rather than waiting to have Billy tried back at port, of himself taking over at the drumhead court and imposing his decision upon it, and of ordering Billy to be hanged the very next morning. That Melville himself had some question about this whole matter becomes evident from his reference in the same chapter to a similar incident on "the U.S. brig-of-war *Somers*" in 1842. Melville's own cousin was a member of the drumhead court later widely criticized for the summary trial and execution at sea of three sailors "though in a time of peace and within not many days sail of home"—"An act," Melville continues, "vindicated by a naval court of inquiry subsequently convened ashore. History, and here cited without comment."

Billy Budd itself is presented as "history . . . cited without comment," other than the psychological analysis of the three main characters that the author gives us. Nonetheless, there are indications that Melville's "acceptance" is not so complete as the critics have held. The report of this whole affair in a naval chronicle, which the author quotes, pictures a depraved, foreign, mutinous Billy stabbing to death a respectable, discreet, responsible, faithful, and patriotic Claggart. "The above," writes Melville, ". . . is all that hitherto has stood in human record to attest what manner of men respectively were John Claggart and Billy Budd." In an author's note crossed out in the original manuscript Melville wrote of this chronicle: "Here ends a story not unwarranted by what happens in this incongruous world of ours—innocence and infirmity, spiritual depravity and fair respite."

The devastating irony of this chapter not only assures us that something of the old Melville dualism is still present in *Billy Budd;* it also reflects back, indirectly, on Melville's own attitude toward the action of Captain Vere. After its statement about Claggart's "strong patriotic impulse," the record adds:

> "In this instance, as in so many other instances in these days, the character of this unfortunate man signally refutes, if refutation were needed, that peevish saying attributed to the late Dr. Johnson, that patriotism is the last refuge of a scoundrel." (XXV)

Claggart is a scoundrel and no patriot. Vere is a patriot and no scoundrel. But Melville's heavy irony carries over to Vere's patriotism, for Vere has made loyalty to the state an absolute and duty to its laws the sole criterion of justice and morality. Vere is killed in a duel between his vessel, the Indomitable, and a ship of the French Revolutionary fleet originally named St. Louis but later rechristened the Athéiste. Melville's comment on the name of this warship is equally a comment on the god that Captain Vere serves:

> Such a name, like some other substituted ones in the Revolutionary fleet, while proclaiming the infidel audacity of the ruling power was yet, though not so intended to be, the aptest name, if one consider it, ever given to a war-ship; far more so indeed than the *Devastation,* the *Erebus* (the Hell) and similar names bestowed upon fighting-ships. (XXIV)

The "Athéiste" is a fit name for a warship because the worship of the state implicit in the inexorable rule of military law is an idolatry that denies any absolute above the state. Melville makes this point in all explicitness in his remarks on the actions of the chaplain who comes to prepare Billy to meet his God:

> Marvel not that having been made acquainted with the young sailor's essential innocence (an irruption of heretic thought hard to suppress) the worthy man lifted not a finger to avert the doom of such a martyr to marital discipline. So to do would not only have been as idle as invoking the desert but would also have been an audacious transgression of the bounds of his function, one as exactly prescribed to him by military law as that of the boatswain or any other naval officer. Bluntly put, a chaplain is the minister of the Prince of Peace serving in the host of the God of War—Mars. As such, he is as incongruous as that musket of Blücher etc. at Christmas. Why then is he there? Because he indirectly subserves the purpose attested by the cannon; because too he lends the sanction of the religion of the meek to that which practically is the abrogation of everything but brute Force. (XXI)

The chaplain kisses the "felon" Billy; Captain Vere offers him some hours of fatherly companionship and consolation. Both hand him over to his death for the sake of "the God of War," a "martial discipline" which Melville divests of its dignity and glory and lays bare as "brute Force." Billy, citizen of Eden and of heaven, may accept without protest Vere's sacrifice of innocence to an objectified and evil social world. We cannot, and neither, we may now venture, could Melville himself. Thus, in the very work which seems at first glance to represent Melville's reconciliation with the order of things, we discover the link between the historical situation in which the problematic of modern man develops—the "death of God" and the alienation of man (in this case the double betrayal of the Father God, represented by the chaplain and the dualistic father Vere)—and the inner division which characterizes that problematic!

7

A JOB'S WHALE

MOBY DICK

In *Moby Dick,* Melville makes the motif of Job quite obvious, even as that of Prometheus. Ishmael summarizes the chapter "Moby Dick" with a statement that places the whole mad chase within the context of the Book of Job: "Here, then, was this grey-headed, ungodly old man chasing with curses a Job's whale round the world." Job's protest against the injustice of his innocent. suffering here becomes the outrageous suffering and evil experienced by mankind and piled by Captain Ahab on the hump of the White Whale, and it is this which makes Moby Dick a "Job's whale."

Moby Dick is also a "Job's whale" in another sense: Melville repeatedly associates this dismaying creature with the Leviathan of the Lord's speeches in the last chapters of the Book of Job. Not only Moby Dick, but the Sperm Whale in general is a "Job's Whale" to Ishmael: The soldier who has freely marched up to a battery "would quickly recoil at the apparition of the Sperm Whale's vast tail, fanning into eddies the air over his head. For what are the comprehensible terrors of man compared with the interlinked terrors and wonders of God!" If the *appearance* of the whale is too much for you, how much more what he *really* is, the reality we cannot grasp? If you, Job, cannot face Leviathan, whom I made with you, how much less can you understand me who created him and whom you cannot see? If the Leviathan compels Job to recognize that he is a limited creature who cannot put his arms around the world and comprehend the purposes of creation, the White Whale compels Ahab to recognize the limits to his freedom that he wishes to override or to ignore. For Ahab and for Ishmael alike, Moby Dick remains "a Job's whale" to the end. Ishmael speaks of "the awful taunt-ings in Job." "What am I that I should essay to hook the nose of this Leviathan!" Ishmael writes. " 'Will he (the Levia-than) make a covenant with thee? Behold the hope of him is vain!' " he quotes from Job. What is implicit in both these references to Job becomes clear when we turn to the full context from which Ishmael quotes, and this context reveals to us, as perhaps nothing in the book itself, the profoundest irony underlying *Moby Dick:*

Canst thou draw out leviathan with an hook? or his tongue with a cord which thou lettest down?

Canst thou put an hook into his nose? or bore his jaw through with a thorn?

Will he make many supplications unto thee? will he speak soft words unto thee?

Will he make a covenant with thee? wilt thou take him for a servant for ever?

Wilt thou play with him as with a bird? or wilt thou bind him for thy maidens?

Shall the companions make a banquet of him? shall they

part him among the merchants?

Canst thou fill his skin with barbed irons? or his head with fish spears?

Lay thine hand upon him, remember the battle, do no more.

Behold, the hope of him is in vain: shall not one be cast down even at the sight of him?

None is so fierce that dare stir him up: who then is able to stand before me? (Job, 41: 1-10)[1]

At first glance, the "tauntings in Job" do not seem so terrible since, even in Melville's time, the whaling industry had succeeded in doing just what the Book of Job said man could not do: filling the Leviathan's skin with harpoons, doing battle to him, dividing him up and bargaining over him. In "The Pequod Meets the Virgin" (LXXXI), Ishmael even returns the taunts with uproarious laughter:

Seems it credible that by three such thin threads the great Leviathan was suspended like the big weight to an eight day clock. Suspended? and to what? To three bits of board. Is this the creature of whom it was once so triumphantly said—"Canst thou fill his skin with barbed irons? or his head with fish-spears? The sword of him that layeth at him cannot hold, the spear, the dart, nor the habergeon: he esteemeth iron as straw; the arrow cannot make him flee; darts are counted as stubble; he laugheth at the shaking of a spear!" This the creature? this he? Oh! that unfulfilments should follow the prophets. For with the strength of a thousand thighs in his tail, Leviathan had run his head under the mountains of the sea, to hide him from the Pequod's fish-spears!

Ishmael depicts the Leviathan, Starbuck hunts him for cash, and Ahab seeks to kill him for revenge: each in his own way

---

[1] I have used the King James Version in this case, rather than the Revised Standard Version as elsewhere, since the former is the version that Melville used, as can be seen from the next quotation.

lays hands on him in battle and "dares to stir him up." Yet Ishmael repeatedly discovers that "dissect him how I may, I but go skin deep." Indeed, all his laborious cetology, with its detailed accounts not only of the kinds and habits of whales and whaling but also of the various processes of butchery after the whale is killed and the many uses to which parts of the whale are put, only serves to underscore this final sense of bafflement in his attempt to understand the Leviathan. Flicking off all Ishmael's anthropomorphizing categories with a shrug of his flukes, the "grand god" reveals himself once again, in the end, as the independent, destroying reality he always was. Starbuck's common-sense search for cash fares no better, and Ahab discovers that having laid hands once on Moby Dick he will not do it again and live. If *Moby Dick* is, indeed, a celebration of the American whaling industry and of expanding American civilization, it is also, at a profounder level, a deep recognition of the tragedy of such expansion— the inevitable, tragic limitations that are encountered by the American frontiersman, the giant industrialist, or, for that matter, modern man in all his forms since the Renaissance. These are the limits of existence, the limits of creation with which God "taunts" Job.[2]

Ahab sees Job's whirlwind, but he does not hear the voice

[2] A similar thought is expressed by Nathalia Wright: "One of the great Hebrew messages of doom . . . reverberates throughout *Moby-Dick*. It is the prophecy that the commercial states of Phoenicia, Tyre, and Sidon, would be destroyed (Isaiah 23:1, 15; Ezekiel 26-28)—a prediction the more remarkable because history had not thus far pointed to the precarious nature of a mercantile economy or to its possible downfall. Melville later marked Stanley's discussion on this subject in his copy of *Sinai and Palestine,* and in his own Bible he underscored the word 'merchants' in Job 41:6 '. . . shall they part him (leviathan) among the merchants?' " (Wright, *op. cit.,* p. 81.)

Richard Chase, in contrast, sees the tragedy of *Moby Dick* as lying in the fact that Ahab gives up his task as leader of civilization to become a tyrant and a machine. "Melville's central idea of tragedy is this self-defeat of leadership, . . . the degeneration of the potential hero, 'mystically illumined' by his withdrawal from the world and by his spiritual ordeal, into the sultan who leads his followers to destruction instead of leading them along the path of civilization." (Chase, *op. cit.,* pp. 54 f.) Although Ahab's tyrannical progress to destruction is certainly a part of his tragedy, Chase misses Melville's deep irony at the expense of "the path of civilization" taken as an ultimate value.

that speaks to Job through the whirlwind. Ahab contends with existence but can have no real dialogue with it. Ahab has stood his ground before Moby Dick as Job before the God who created Leviathan together with him. But Ahab lacks that experience of an answering response to his cry that gives Job back his humanity and gives meaning to his suffering. All Ahab has at the end of *Moby Dick* is defiance, and even this has to be bolstered up by impersonal fate. Job's dismay before Leviathan begets in him a still greater dismay before the creator of Leviathan. But Job, even in the depths of his bitterness, has a trust in the creator and his creation that Ahab cannot have. Job and Ahab share the same question: How is it possible to look existence full in the face and accept it as it is? But their answers are necessarily different because of the difference in their basic attitudes toward reality. In this similarity of question and difference of answer lies the profoundest problem in *Moby Dick:* Is Job's trust impossible in the modern era, the era of the "death of God"? What is at stake here is not simply faith or the problem of evil, but man himself: Job and Ahab are both men *in extremis*—explorers of the limits of human existence—but Job stands his ground and still trusts while Ahab can only defy.

If Ahab is something of a Modern Job as well as a Modern Promethean, he is also something of a modern Ahab, the wicked Biblical king after whom he is named. And *Moby Dick* has its own Elijah—a caricature of the Biblical prophet in the shape of a mad fanatic. In *Moby Dick*, God's judgment on present history reappears in the form of the White Whale itself, as is clearly hinted in "The Town-Ho's Story" (LIV), in a secret part of that tragedy which never reaches Captain Ahab's ears but "which seemed obscurely to involve with the whale a certain wondrous, inverted visitation of one of those so called judgments of God which at times are said to overtake some men." It is Moby Dick himself who revenges the lakeman Steelkilt on Radney, the mate whom Steelkilt was planning to kill. Again, in the Pequod's meeting with the Jeroboam, the mad Gabriel, who has brought both crew and captain of the Jeroboam under his domination, at once warns Ahab of divine judgment and prophesies his end. Gabriel has pronounced "the White Whale to be no less a being that the Shaker God incarnated; the Shakers receiving the Bible," and the death of Macey, the chief mate, who dares, nonetheless, to hunt Moby Dick, confirms Gabriel's dire predictions and solidifies his power. Though Ishmael makes the usual disclaimer—"Nor is the history of fanatics half so striking in respect to the measureless self-deception of the fanatic himself, as his measureless power of deceiving and bedevilling so many others"—there is a shadow of the Biblical prophet behind the fanatic caricature when Gabriel cries to Ahab, "Think, think of the blasphemer—dead, and down there!— beware of the blasphemer's end!" Gabriel's prophecy and Ishmael's disclaimer recall to us the conversation in "The Ship" (XVI) in which Captain Peleg first tells Ishmael about Ahab:

"*He's Ahab*, boy; and Ahab of old, thou knowest, was a crowned king!"

"And a very vile one. When that wicked king was slain, the dogs, did they not lick his blood?"

"Come hither to me—hither, hither," said Peleg, with a significance in his eye that almost startled me. "Look ye, lad; never say that on board the Pequod. Never say it anywhere. Captain Ahab did not name himself. 'Twas a foolish, ignorant whim of his crazy, widowed mother, who died when he was only twelvemonth old. And yet the old squaw Tistig, at Gayhead, said that the name would somehow prove prophetic. . . . It's a lie."

Melville does not mean by these overtones that in Ahab's fatal encounter with Moby Dick a transcendent God is calling him to account. The judgment of Ahab is the judgment of his self-absolutization and his self-destruction, but it comes through his meeting with a reality independent of him, a reality that he cannot, in the end, deny.

PART THREE

FYODOR DOSTOIEVSKY

8
————

EXILES OF THE UNDERGROUND

THE UNDERGROUND MAN

The situation from which both Dostoievsky's rebels and his exiles start and which they try either to escape or to affirm is that of the alienation of modern man. Some try to escape this alienation by destroying the transcendent reality that crushes them, others by destroying themselves. Dostoievsky brings both his exiles and his rebels to the dead end of isolation and inauthentic existence. Yet he begins where they begin—with alienation and inner emptiness, the "death of God," and the absence of an image of meaningful personal and social life. Dostoievsky's rebel-exiles carry their alienation with them in the contradictions and inner divisions of their own existence—the problematic of modern man. The alienation that underlies both rebel and exile in Dostoievsky issues in time into Dostoievsky's own contrast between the "man-god" and the "god-man."

This alienation is made fully explicit in Dostoievsky's *Notes from the Underground.* In Part I—"Underground"—the Underground Man begins with a description of his own character that gives us a key to his philosophy. He presents himself to us as a divided man, and his division is always one of the heights and the depths. "The more conscious I became of goodness and all that was 'sublime and beautiful,' the more deeply did I sink into the mire and the more ready I was to sink into it altogether." On the other hand, "The feeling of delight was there just because I was so intensely aware of my own degradation." He is an inverted superman. As a result of being more conscious, more intelligent, more aware than other people, he is not superior to them but infinitely inferior, and the only role open to him, as a result, is that of the masochist. Vain, suspicious, "as quick to take offence as a hunchback or a dwarf," he would have derived positive pleasure from someone's slapping his face. But even this intense delight would be spoiled by the inevitable conclusion that it was his own fault to begin with:

> What hurt most of all was that though innocent I was guilty and, as it were, guilty according to the laws of nature. I was guilty, first of all, because I was cleverer than all the people round me. (I have always considered myself cleverer than any one else in the world, and sometimes, I assure you, I've been even ashamed of it. At last, all my life I looked away and I could never look people straight in the face.) (114)[1]

Our masochist is no ordinary masochist. He does not feel inferior because he is inferior but because he is˙ superior. This seeming contradiction is explained by the Underground Man himself when he speaks of the man of intense sensibility

[1] All quotations from *Notes from the Underground* are from *The Best Short Stories of Dostoievsky,* trans. David Magarshack (New York: Modern Library).

who considers himself a mouse and not a man. "I grant you it is an intensely conscious mouse, but it's a mouse all the same, whereas the other is a man." The Underground Man cannot look anyone in the eyes because he is not himself a person and cannot meet others as persons. His superior cleverness is expended in endless introspection and fantasy and in a consciousness of himself and of others that reduces both to objects. His need to be a superman does not represent the strong position of the nonconformist, but the utter social dependence of the man who must compare himself with others in order to obtain any feeling of his own existence. The Underground Man is not really a self in the full sense of the term—someone who can stand his ground and meet others. He is a consciousness and a social role. Hence, precisely in his need to be superior he really is inferior to those persons who are men and not mice, and it is for this reason that he is ashamed before them.

We are hardly prepared after this to meet the Underground Man in the role of philosopher, in particular as the man who expresses Dostoievsky's own philosophy. Yet the protest which he makes against the utilitarian philosophy that accompanies the new era of mass industrialization is without question Dostoievsky's own. The utilitarians base everything upon the laws of twice two makes four, but the Underground Man doesn't care for the laws of nature and arithmetic—"as though such a stone wall were really the same thing as peace of mind." The stone wall is the objective reality that is foisted upon man in the name of science or society, but the Underground Man begins with the self, the knowing and experiencing subject, and he is unwilling to surrender this ground even though consciousness means for him pain and unlived life. "Can a man of acute sensibility respect himself at all?" he asks, and confesses that he is horribly bored, crushed by doing nothing, reduced by intensified consciousness to thumb-twiddling. Where other people can stop at secondary causes, he must keep pursuing one cause after another *ad infinitum* till his life is dominated by inertia and complete inaction. Yet for all that, he does not envy those who try to subsume subjective consciousness under twice-two and make human existence into a material affair seen from the outside by some logical supermind.

The "gentlemen" to whom the Underground Man addresses his ironic confession believe that if man "were enlightened, if his eyes were opened to his real, normal interests, he would at once cease behaving dishonourably . . . he would see that his advantage lay in doing good." "Oh the babe," cries our hero, "the pure innocent babe." What is to be done with the millions of facts that show that man knowingly goes against his own self-interest? "You, gentlemen, have . . . drawn up your entire list of positive human values by taking the averages of statistical figures and relying on scientific and economic formulae" but these, like so many of the moral philosophies of the twentieth century that base moral values entirely on need, interest, or logical analysis, are "mere exercises in logic." Let's send all these logarithms to the devil, says our hero, so that we can again live according to our foolish will. Man often not only does but *positively should* choose something against his own advantage.

One's own free and unfettered choice, one's own whims, however wild, one's own fancy, overwrought though it sometimes may be to the point of madness—that is that same most desirable good which we overlooked and which does not fit into any classification, and against which all theories and systems are continually wrecked. . . . All man wants is an absolutely *free* choice, however dear that freedom may cost him and wherever it may lead him to. (131)

There could be no stronger statement of freedom than that. It is the protest of a man against being transformed into a mere object to be played upon by external forces. The ego, says Freud in *The Ego and the Id,* is a passive servant that is *lived* by elemental forces rather than living itself. But this is the death of the "I" as "I," and in the face of this threat, already present in the "pleasure principle," the Underground Man goes to the other extreme of absolute subjectivity and absolute freedom. Like Nietzsche, he sees human existence as expressed primarily in will, not reason.

Will is not an opposite to reason but a greater whole which includes it, "a manifestation of the whole . . . of human life, including reason with all its concomitant head-scratchings." The focal point of recapturing and retaining freedom, for the Underground Man, is consciousness and will, *seen from within:* "The whole meaning of human life can be summed up in the one statement that man only exists for the purpose of proving to himself every minute that he is a man and not an organ-stop!"—a subject and not an object. Those who make the laws of logic into human laws reduce society to the ant hill and life to death. Logic cannot of itself tell us what man is, for logic begins with abstraction: it leaves out the wholeness of man. The "normal" and the "positive," prosperity and material welfare, are the goal of man only when seen from without. Seen from within, suffering is more precious than any Crystal Palace,[2] for suffering is the cause of consciousness and consciousness "is infinitely superior to twice-two."

The "gentlemen" whom the Underground Man attacks assume the necessary harmony between one's own interests, if intelligently understood, and the good of society. This "harmony" meant, in practice, that children worked for thirteen to fifteen hours a day in coal mines, that eighteen to twenty people had to live in one room without facilities of any sort, that the British "poor laws" were abolished in order not to interfere with the "natural" control of population through war and famine. It was, in fact, a "harmony" only for one class—the industrial and capitalist class, who identified their own interest with the welfare of society as a whole. Even if this harmony had been for the welfare of all, Dostoievsky would have been utterly repelled by this purely materialistic politico-economic utopia. The utilitarian calculus left no meaning to human life outside the smooth economic and political functioning of society. This is the "ant heap"—the closed, collective society of organic unanimity. This universal "ant heap" recurs in the ideal communist dictatorship set forth by

[2] The at that time remarkable building constructed for the British Exhibition of 1851 when Britain was the center of the rising industrial world.

Shigalyov in Dostoievsky's novel *The Devils* and in the harmonious "ant heap" which the Grand Inquisitor propounds in *The Brothers Karamazov*. The reduction of human society to the society of ants is the logical conclusion of the utilitarian standpoint, which sees men from the outside as objects constituted with such and such needs and interests rather than from within as persons.

I cannot help suspecting, says the Underground Man toward the end of Part I, that, although I do believe, I am "lying like a cobbler." Part II, "Apropos of the Wet Snow," reveals to us the meaning of this remark. The philosophy of the Underground Man, like his confessions of his character and his life, can neither be taken at its face value nor discarded. Rather, we must remember who is speaking, that he is aware of his own insincerity, and, in so far as we can perceive this, why he says what he does. Much that he says is undoubtedly true, yet there is another part of him looking on while he says it which the next moment will assure us that he was just lying, and there is a third part ready to give the lie to the second.

If in Part I the Underground Man was a mouse, in Part II he is a fly, and in both equally inhuman and masochistic.

> In the eyes of all those high society people I was just a fly, an odious, obscene fly, more intelligent, more highly developed, more noble than anyone else (I had no doubts about that), but a fly that was always making way for everyone, a fly insulted and humiliated by every one. (157)

Our great exponent of freedom and will reveals himself to us, in fact, as a person with neither freedom nor will. For two years, he tells us, he was preoccupied with how he might revenge his honor for the insult afforded him when an officer in a club lifted him aside in a way that seemed a slight on his dignity. Finally, after endless fantasies of duels and fights, he brushes the shoulder of the officer as they pass on the street and assumes that he has righted the balance thereby, though the latter hardly notices him.

Perhaps the closest he comes to real existence is his brief encounter with Lisa, and this is the experience that sticks in his mind years later and the one he must confess. He lives in a "funk hole," a depressing set of rooms, with a butler who always embarrasses and bullies him by demanding his wages. Otherwise he has no contact with anyone except for his superior at work. One day he is visited by a former schoolmate and takes advantage of the visit both to borrow money and to force his way into a small going-away party where he is obviously neither expected nor wanted. At the party he quickly gets into a quarrel with the three others and spends an hour pacing up and down in front of them while they eat. When they leave in a troika for a house of prostitution, he follows them in another, though they tell him they don't want him, and, arriving too late to catch them, goes in to sleep with a girl named Lisa. After their intercourse, he takes up the role of benevolent gentleman concerned with her sad plight, but overplays his part so that she accuses him of speaking as though he were reading from a book.

So far from stopping him, this spurs him on, and he describes for her the years that lie ahead of her—being kicked out of her house and sinking to ever worse ones, or, if she is lucky, dying of consumption in "the most foul-smelling corner of the cellar, in the damp and the darkness," buried in a cheap coffin by men who will not even bother to put the coffin in the dirt properly, visited by no one, remembered by no one.

> "Other women have children to visit their graves, fathers, husbands, but there will be neither tears, nor sighs, nor any remembrance for you. No one, no one in the world will ever come to you. Your name will vanish from the face of the earth as though you had never been born! Dirt and mud, dirt and mud, though you knock at your coffin lid at night when the dead arise as hard as you please, crying, 'Let me live in the world, good people! I lived, but I knew no real life. I spent my life as a doormat for people to wipe their dirty boots on. My life has been drunk away at a pub in the Hay Market. Let me live in the world again, good people!'" (211 f.)

"I lived, but I knew no real life." Within the unbelievable sadism of our masochist is a genuine note of pathos: the confession of inauthentic existence applies to his own present life quite as much as to the imagined future of the prostitute. Not to be remembered by others is here the tangible expression of not having existed at all. At every other moment in this book, the confession of the Underground Man takes place under the shadow of a self-irony which casts doubt on confession and philosophy alike. Here and here only is a direct emotion the sincerity of which cannot be doubted. Yet it comes unawares, in the form of an admonishment of someone whom he wants to think of as much beneath him. In this whole story, in fact, his one moment of real human contact is with Lisa, the girl whom he injures as much as he can.

Although he has invited Lisa to come and see him, this is the last thing he wants when the "disgusting truth" about all "those horrors and commiserations of last night" begins to blaze through his bewilderment. "Again to assume that dishonest, lying mask—again, again!" Fifteen years later, he confesses, he still sees in his mind's eye "the same pitiful, inappropriate smile" on Lisa's face that he saw that night. Yet Lisa does come to see him, and at the worst possible time, when he is in his old dressing gown and has just had a quarrel with his butler. Unable to forgive her for coming in on him then, he answers her pathetic confession that she wants "to get away from that —— place for good" by upbraiding her for coming and reducing his own motives to sheer sadomasochism:

> "To avenge my wounded pride on someone, to get my own back, I vented my spite on you and I laughed at you. I had been humiliated, so I too wanted to humiliate someone; they wiped the floor with me, so I too wanted to show my power . . . I wanted sport. I wanted to see you cry. I wanted to . . . make you hysterical." (231)

Even this is not the deepest layer. What I really wanted, he insists, "was that you should all go to hell!" Like a man who has been skinned, "every puff of air hurt me," and ˍven confessing all this to her now hurts so much that he will never forgive her for that. "I'm the most horrible, the most ridiculous, the most petty, the most stupid, the most envious of all the worms on earth who are not a bit better than me, but who—I'm damned if I know why—are never ashamed or embarrassed while I shall be insulted all my life by every louse." Our Underground Man is one of the best representatives in literature of the man of *ressentiment* against whom Nietzsche's Zarathustra inveighed—the man whose heart is corroded by poisonous resentment, hatred, and envy. His philosophy, as he says himself, is a "philosophy of malice."

It's only once in a lifetime that a man speaks his mind like this, he says, but in the hysteria that ensues a still deeper confession erupts from the depths. They throw themselves in each other's arms, and he sobs as he has never before sobbed in his life, "They—they won't let me—I—I can't be good!" Underneath his sado-masochism is his hatred, and underneath his hatred is his basic sense of alienation: he cannot be himself and be accepted and confirmed by others. Somewhere along the line he has come to feel himself confronted by the impossible choice between not being himself in order to be what others want him to be, on the one hand, and being himself and doing without the confirmation of others, on the other. To be both himself and good is impossible. Hence he must both criticize the "gentlemen" and depreciate himself, striking now outward, now inward, like the scorpion behind a rock which stings the passer-by and turns and stings itself.

What the Underground Man really wants is that Lisa disappear. She is too real a contact with the existence that he has turned his back on for him to be able to bear it. "I longed for 'peace.' I wanted to be left alone in my funk hole. 'Real life'—so unaccustomed was I to it—had crushed me so much that I found it difficult to breathe." Like T. S. Eliot's Prufrock and Camus' Jean-Baptiste Clamence, the Underground Man is making a confession from "hell"—the little world that he has built for himself to take the place of the real world. Their roles are now changed, he realizes, and he is ashamed to look at her: "She was the heroine now, while I was exactly the same crushed and humiliated creature as she had appeared to me that night." Because he is ashamed and because he wants to dominate her instead of she him ("I cannot live without feeling that I have someone completely in my power," he owns), he makes love to her as a sort of vengeance, an expression of "a personal, jealous hatred of her." Then he grins at her maliciously until she leaves of her own accord, and, to add the final and uttermost insult, he presses money into her hand, as if to say that he has been using her all along as a prostitute. "I did that cruel thing deliberately," he confesses, prompted by brain not heart. It was "so insincere . . . so deliberately invented, so *bookish*" that even he can't stand it and runs after her. But she has already disappeared.

His analysis of that moment is as much a product of the underground as the story itself. He wants to run after her in order "to fall on his knees before her, to sob with remorse, to kiss her feet, to beseech her to forgive me!" He feels as if his breast were being torn to pieces, nor can he ever after regard that moment with indifference. Yet the next moment he has already found a rationalization: he would only torture her, and is it not better for her anyway to carry away a purifying insult that will elevate her through suffering! An insult, after all, "is the most corrosive and painful form of consciousness!" And consciousness, as we have seen from Part I, is the highest value in itself.

> Tomorrow I should have bespattered her soul with mud, I should have wearied her heart by thrusting myself upon her, while now the memory of the insult will never die in her, and however horrible the filth that lies in store for her, the memory of that humiliaticɹ will raise her and purify her—by hatred, and, well, perhaps also by forgiveness. (238)

"Which is better: cheap happiness or exalted suffering?" he theorizes. "Well, which is better?" The painful self-irony of this whole passage cannot remove the disturbing questions that it raises. What are we to think now of the whole of the first part in which consciousness and suffering are put forward as the only truly desirable human goals while "cheap happiness" is scorned!

RASKOLNIKOV: ISOLATION AND REBELLION

It is not difficult to recognize in Raskolnikov, the hero of Dostoievsky's *Crime and Punishment,* the legitimate heir of the Underground Man, although one who takes the step that the Underground Man himself could not—the desperate attempt to break out of the underground through daring to act. There are a number of specific likenesses that leave no doubt of Raskolnikov's patrimony. The most striking of these is the relation to the prostitute that is carried over from the Underground Man and Lisa to Raskolnikov and Sonia. At the heart of this relationship lies the same motif of the prostitute's being the one person with whom the hero can enter into relationship. She is so low in the social scale that he can safely open himself to her as well as sadistically torture her, and her position outside of society seems to him so similar to his own that he can identify with her—the Underground Man unconsciously, Raskolnikov quite consciously. Thus Raskolnikov says to Sonia:

> "You, too, have transgressed . . . have had the strength to transgress. You have laid hands on yourself, you have destroyed a life . . . *Your own* (it's all the same!). You might have lived in spirit and understanding, but you'll end in the Hay Market. . . . But you won't be able to stand it, and if you remain alone you'll go out of your mind like me. You are like a mad creature already. So we must go together on the same road!" (323)[3]

Raskolnikov's sadism toward Sonia is as clear as the Underground Man's in relation to Lisa. He understands that she has difficulty in bringing herself to read to him from the New Testament because it is painful for her to betray and unveil her secret treasure and all that is really her own. But "the more he saw this, the more roughly and irritably he insisted

[3] All page references are to the Illustrated Modern Library edition of Dostoievsky's *Crime and Punishment,* trans. Constance Garnett (New York: 1945).

on her doing so." Knowing that she finds her sole strength in God, he suggests with a malignant laugh that there is perhaps no God at all. And in a speech worthy of the Underground Man he suggests that she has destroyed and betrayed herself for nothing and that "it would be better, a thousand times better and wiser to leap into the water and end it all!"

Like the Underground Man, it is not so much Raskolnikov's heart that is cruel as his mind. Raskolnikov's heart is given to positive, generous impulses, as the Underground Man's is not, but his mind is given over to inhuman theory. "He was young, abstract, and therefore cruel," his author says of him. This cruelty is with him, as with the Underground Man, a product of isolation, and his description of his life before his crime recalls vividly the Underground Man's confession, "I have spoilt my life by a moral disintegration in my funk hole, by my unsociable habits, by losing touch with life, and by nursing my spite in my dark cellar." " 'Razumihin works!' " says Raskolnikov to Sonia,

> "But I turned sulky and wouldn't. (Yes, sulkiness, that's the right word for it.) I sat in my room like a spider. You've been in my den, you've seen it. . . . And do you know, Sonia, that low ceilings and tiny rooms cramp the soul and the mind? Ah, how I hated that garret! And yet I wouldn't go out of it! I wouldn't on purpose! I didn't go out for days together, and I wouldn't work, I wouldn't even eat, I just lay there doing nothing. If Nastasya brought me anything, I ate it, if she didn't, I went all day without; I wouldn't ask, on purpose, from sulkiness! At night I had no light, I lay in the dark and I wouldn't earn money for candles. I ought to have studied, but I sold my books . . . I preferred lying still and thinking." (404 f.)

Like the Underground Man, too, Raskolnikov's philosophy is a "philosophy of malice" that grows out of resentment. "Why should I go to them?" Raskolnikov asks Sonia. "They destroy men by millions themselves and look on it as a virtue. They are knaves and scoundrels." The underground hero wants everybody to go to hell, and looks down with contempt on the "gentlemen" to whom he is talking. Raskolnikov on the very verge of his confession cries to himself:

> "Look at them running to and fro about the streets, every one of them a scoundrel and a criminal at heart and, worse still, an idiot. But try to get me off and they'd be wild with righteous indignation. Oh, how I hate them all!" (504)

What characterizes Raskolnikov more than anything is a divided nature which manifests itself as almost an alternation of two different characters—one proud and cruel, the other kind and generous. Thus his friend Razumihin characterizes him:

> "He is morose, gloomy, proud and haughty . . . He has a noble nature and a kind heart. He does not like showing his feelings and would rather do a cruel thing than open his heart freely. Sometimes, though, he is not at all morbid, but simply cold and inhumanly callous; it's as though he were alternating between two characters. . . . He never listens to what is said to him. He is never interested in what interests other people at any given moment." (211)

He is a monological man, par excellence, overbearing and nervously irritable, but one not incapable of generous impulses toward others. He is contemptuous of others and feels superior to them, yet even after his crime he still has a very strong sense of morality and of duty. Although capable of planning and executing a murder, he is discovered to have spent his last penny supporting a consumptive fellow student and his old father and, on another occasion, to have burned himself rescuing two little children from a fire.

After a month of morbid planning in which he is not sure whether he has any real intention of carrying out his plan or not, Raskolnikov leaves his bed, weak from fever, and murders the old pawnbroker woman Alyona, whom he has settled on as of no use to mankind or to any living person. But he also finds it necessary to murder her saintly sister Lizaveta, who returns unexpectedly, and the money and jewelry, for which he supposedly commits the murder, he puts under a stone and does not even examine. Lizaveta, like Sonia, is the meek person, the nag which is beaten to death in his dream. In his dream he is a child trying in vain to protect the nag from its cruel owner and is deeply distressed when she is whipped across the eyes. Now, without realizing it, though it is clear to us through what he says of the eyes, he sees himself as the exasperated owner who whipped the meek nag to death:

> "Poor Lizaveta! Why did she come in? . . . It's strange though, why is it I scarcely ever think of her, as though I hadn't killed her! Lizaveta! Sonia! Poor gentle things, with gentle eyes. . . . Dear women! Why don't they weep? Why don't they moan? They give up everything . . . their eyes are soft and gentle." . . . (270)

Raskolnikov has tried to relate to life through theory. His mind has become a separate, autonomous province, split off from his heart and intuitive awareness, and he has demanded of himself that he live according to the dictates of this autonomous entity and impose these dictates upon the reality with which he comes in contact. His mind thus becomes his means for denying not only the other parts of his own character but also the independent reality of other persons. Conversely, it is his isolation from others that has produced this detachment in which other people seem contained only in his thought and assessed only by his theories. "Here we have bookish dreams," the prosecutor Porfiry says to Raskolnikov, "a heart unhinged by theories." "If you'd invented another theory," he points out, "you might perhaps have done something a thousand times more hideous." Raskolnikov's theory is pure abstraction, an experimenting with life, for all its pretense at benefiting humanity or even himself.

Raskolnikov's isolation is self-reinforcing. Before his crime, as we have seen, he walled himself in in a voluntary isolation that even surpassed that of the Underground Man in his "funk hole." "He had gotten completely away from everything," the author says, "like a tortoise in a shell." This simile recalls to us Melville's description of Captain Ahab as a grizzly bear sucking its own paws, and the sentence that follows confirms us in the resemblance to this other monological man: "He was in the condition that overtakes some monomaniacs entirely concentrated upon one thing." In this condition even the servant girl irritates him, and the arrival of his mother and his sister Dounia is almost more than he can bear. "Nothing of all this would have happened," he says to himself just before he confesses, ashamed because he has responded to Dounia's fond care with an angry gesture, "if only I were alone and no one loved me and I too had never loved any one!" and he identifies this love as the thing that is forcing him to confess and meekly accept his punishment. He loves his mother and sister reluctantly because they pull him out of his isolation, which to him seems tantamount to forcing him to submit to the "others" whom he hates. It is at the end of this speech, after wondering whether in twenty years he will have grown "so meek that I shall humble myself before people and whimper at every word that I am a criminal," that he declares every one of "them" scoundrels and exclaims, "Oh, how I hate them all!" Raskolnikov, like the Underground Man, feels superior to everybody and yet threatened by the very existence of others, a resemblance which suggests that it is Raskolnikov's isolation that is the source of his "alternating characters" and of his theory of ordinary and extraordinary men.

Raskolnikov's crime may well be seen as a desperate attempt to break out of the underground and make contact with existence. In the first instance, however, his isolation after his crime is still more terrible than before—a fact that is repeatedly stressed throughout the book:

> If the whole room had been filled, not with police officers, but with those nearest and dearest to him, he would not have found one human word for them, so empty was his heart. A gloomy sensation of agonising, everlasting solitude and remoteness, took conscious form in his soul. (103)

Not only does he feel remote from others. He feels

> an immeasurable, almost physical, repulsion for everything surrounding him, an obstinate, malignant feeling of hatred. All who met him were loathsome to him—he

loathed their faces, their movements, their gestures. If any one had addressed him, he felt that he might have spat at him or bitten him. (110)

As he climbs the stairs to see his friend Razumihin, he realizes that this means meeting his friend *face to face*. "What he was least of all disposed for at that moment was to be face to face with any one in the wide world." He goes in, but choked with rage at himself, and immediately tries to leave. When he tells his mother that there will be "time to speak freely of everything," he is suddenly overwhelmed with confusion, pale, and chilled at the thought "that he would never now be able to speak freely of everything—that he would never again be able to *speak* of anything to any one."

At first glance, it seems to be Raskolnikov's crime itself that imposes silence on him because of the necessity of secrecy. But this crime has also cut him off from all real speaking, from all dialogue with others, and his sense of isolation, already so great before his crime, has now been absolutized. At one point he thinks of the man, condemned to death, who imagines that he would be willing to live in everlasting solitude on a square yard of space for all his life or eternity if only he did not have to die at once. "How true it is! Good God, how true!" Raskolnikov exclaims to himself. "Man is a vile creature! . . . And vile is he who calls him vile for that," he adds a moment later. Later in the book, however, he knows that he would prefer death to everlasting solitude.

> A special form of misery had begun to oppress him of late . . . there was a feeling of permanence, of eternity about it; it brought a foretaste of hopeless years of this cold leaden misery, a foretaste of an eternity "on a square yard of space." (414)

Even in Siberia this isolation continues. Raskolnikov seems "wrapped up in himself and, as it were, shut himself off from every one" while he is disliked and avoided by everyone as an infidel who "ought to be killed." *Raskol* means schism, division. By his theory and his crime he has completed the separation from the human race that already existed in strong measure before. But this absolute isolation is unbearable to him and itself forces him to confession and eventually to relationship with others. Raskolnikov's inner punishment is not the indictment of conscience, George Halperin holds, but the tragedy of freedom.

> He must have felt like a man who suddenly lost his sense of weight and solidity of the body; who no longer felt bounds or limitations, no bottom, no top, no support. This terrible vacuity, this separation from everything existing, this isolation was terrible. Can a man endure such freedom? Raskolnikov could not.[4]

It is isolation, then, rather than repentance or even guilt, that leads Raskolnikov to confess. His confession is an attempt to break through his absolute isolation to contact with others, and the contact he seeks is, without exception, that with women rather than men—Sonia, Dounia, his mother, even Mother Earth. The leitmotif that runs through this breakthrough is always the same—the softening of the hardened heart—and, strangely enough, Dostoievsky always suggests it is for the first time, as if to preserve the full effect of this acceptance of the feminine influence in the young man who has murdered two women under the dictates of an inhuman masculine theory. Thus, when he tells Sonia of his crime and she exclaims, "There is no one—no one in the whole world now so unhappy as you!," "a feeling long unfamiliar to him flooded his heart and softened it at once," and two tears start into his eyes. Again, when he goes to say good-by to his mother, we are told that "for the first time after all those awful months his heart was softened. He fell down before her, he kissed her feet and both wept, embracing." When he goes to the crossroads and remembers Sonia's words, "kiss the earth, for you have sinned against it too," he clutches "at the chance of this new unmixed, complete sensation. . . . Everything in him softened at once and the tears started into his eyes. He fell to the earth. . . . and kissed that filthy earth with bliss and rapture." At the

[4] George Halperin, *Tolstoy, Dostoievsky, Tourgenev* (Chicago: Chicago Literary Club, 1946), p. 50.

same time he thinks how Sonia "was with him for ever and would follow him to the ends of the earth, wherever fate might take him." When he tells Sonia of the murders, he repeatedly begs her never to leave him.

None of all this implies repentance or a feeling of guilt. In Siberia, almost at the very end of the book, he is complaining "if only fate would send him repentance," but he himself does not repent. What he is seeking in the breakthrough to the women is contact with others in the only form that he can bear it—the softening influence of the woman, the unthreatening companionship of the meek, who will tolerate his imperious pride and his irritable self-absorption. He is seeking at the same time an "unmixed, complete sensation" that will give him some relief from the tension between his "alternating characters." Kissing Mother Earth in unashamed tears of ecstasy is a central theme of Dostoievsky's that is repeated in *The Devils* and in *The Brothers Karamazov*. It is a concrete symbol of the overcoming of alienation through putting aside the masculine theory of the man-god in favor of the feminine emotion of the god-man.

Svidrigailov is at once father and double for Raskolnikov —the hopeless, but not entirely unsympathetic cynic who repels and frightens Raskolnikov by showing him, as in a mirror, the face of the man who really lives as if all things are permissible.[5] Svidrigailov is the logical end product of the meaningless freedom that Raskolnikov has embraced, the freedom purchased at the price of an ever more absolute iso-

---

[5] In his personality and manner of speech as in his confrontation of Raskolnikov with the end consequences of his own theory, Svidrigailov is a clear prototype of Ivan's poor-relation devil in *The Brothers Karamazov*. "I, too, am a man *et nihil humanum* . . ." he says, and when Raskolnikov exclaims that he is still trying to get around him, he laughs in the frankest way and says, "What of it? . . . this is what the French call *bonne guerre*." Ivan's devil also claims himself as image and prototype of man to whom nothing human is alien—"I put on a fleshly form and I take the consequences. Satan *sum et nihil humanum a me alienum puto*." Ivan's devil is also fond of urbane French phrases and he too, like Svidrigailov, is an unobtrusive poor relation of great personages who allow him into their company at times because he does not bore them. Like Ivan with his devil, Raskolnikov wonders whether Svidrigailov really exists or is a hallucination caused by madness.

lation.[6] "Svidrigailov is desperation, the most cynical," Dostoievsky writes in one of his notebooks, and adds that Raskolnikov is passionately attached to him.[7] They are, as Svidrigailov himself points out, "birds of a feather," only Svidrigailov has gone to the end of a road that Raskolnikov has only set out on. Svidrigailov has switched his wife, just as the nag is switched in Raskolnikov's dream. He is even more dependent on women than Raskolnikov and betrays terrible aloneness and despair in pressing after Dounia. When he has her physically at his mercy, it is really he who is at her mercy, for she is the strong person and he the essentially weak. After he lets her go, "a strange smile contorted his face, a pitiful, sad, weak smile, a smile of despair."

Svidrigailov has not murdered anyone, but he has been indirectly responsible for the death of his wife, of a servant whom he mocked, and of a little girl whom he raped and who later hanged herself (Stavrogin's crime in *The Devils* and one Dostoievsky originally planned to give to Dmitri in *The Brothers Karamazov*). All three of these deaths haunt him, the first two in the form of ghosts, the latter in the form of an ineradicable memory which appears in the depths of his consciousness in a dream that he has just before he shoots himself. He tells Raskolnikov his theory of ghosts as "shreds and fragments of other worlds" which the well man does not see because he lives only in this life but which the ill man comes into ever closer contact with until at death "he steps straight into that world." He pictures eternity not as something vast and beyond our conception but as the final term of hedged-in horror, Raskolnikov's "square yard of space": "What if it's one little room, like a bathhouse in the country, black and grimy and spiders in every corner, and that's all eternity is?" When Raskolnikov cries in anguish, "Can it be

[6] As J. A. L. Lloyd has pointed out on p. 112 of his book, *Fyodor Dostoievsky* (New York: Charles Scribner's Sons, 1947), Svidrigailov "is one of those victims of complete isolation . . . who have fled from humanity never to be reclaimed." Like Stavrogin in *The Devils*, "he has experimented with good deeds as with evil deeds, but he can no longer feel the faintest distraction in either."

[7] Ernest J. Simmons, *Dostoevsky, The Making of a Novelist* (London: John Lehmann, 1950), p. 131.

you can imagine nothing juster and more comforting than that?" Svidrigailov responds, "Perhaps that is just, . . . it's what I would certainly have made it." Svidrigailov is a mocking devil who horrifies Raskolnikov, and at the deepest level himself, by his vision of inner emptiness and desolation.

When Raskolnikov emerges from the office without confessing, after hearing of Svidrigailov's suicide, it is the sight of Sonia "pale and horror-stricken" with "a look of poignant agony, of despair, in her face" that turns him back. But there is nothing whole-hearted in this turning. It smacks rather of bitterness and defeat. "His lips worked in an ugly, meaningless smile. He stood still a minute, grinned and went back to the police office." In Siberia, where Sonia follows him and is loved by the very prisoners who hate and shun him, he recognizes that he is ashamed before Sonia even while he tortures her "with his contemptuous rough manner." Only at the very end of the book does he have a real breakthrough to Sonia through which a genuine mutual love is able to arise. This breakthrough too takes the form of the proud man softening and shedding the tears of the meek, the isolated man reaching for human contact, the rootless man flinging himself down on Mother Earth:

> All at once something seemed to seize him and fling him at her feet. He wept and threw his arms round her knees . . . she knew and had no doubt that he loved her beyond everything and that at last the moment had come. . . . They were renewed by love; the heart of each held infinite sources of life for the heart of the other. (530 f.)

This is a turning toward life, life identified with feeling as opposed to conscious analysis: "Life had stepped into the place of theory and something quite different would work itself out in his mind." But it is not "a full resurrection into a new life" either in the religious sense or in the sense of the attainment of a whole, authentic existence. "He did not know," comments the author, "that the new life would not be given him for nothing, that he would have to pay dearly for it, that it would cost him great striving, great suffering," and Dostoievsky concludes the book with the statement:

But that is the beginning of a new story—the story of the gradual renewal of a man, the story of his gradual regeneration, of his passing from one world into another, of his initiation into a new unknown life. That might be the subject of a new story, but our present story is ended. (532)

We do not see Raskolnikov's regeneration, nor can we even imagine what it will be like. Raskolnikov has not become a new man. At best he has experienced a rebirth that might set him on the road to becoming one. Even this is saying too much, for he has not overcome his inner dualism. The breakthrough from "theory to life" which gives feeling ascendancy over thought does not itself suggest an approach to wholeness so much as a compensatory stress on the emotional side that he has neglected and suppressed, now perhaps at the expense of the dominating intellect. Meekness and humility may be a way for Sonia. They cannot be an answer for Raskolnikov, for they represent only one of his two conflicting characters and not the other. This is why Raskolnikov's suggested "conversion" and "regeneration" is so unconvincing.

Yet in one essential respect a regeneration does take place! Raskolnikov moves for the first time into some kind of mutual relationship with another human being. He no longer merely clings to Sonia. He loves her. He has not really removed the dark abyss in his soul which Svidrigailov forced him to look at. He is still a man of "alternating characters" —a problematic man. But he is no longer imprisoned in a well-nigh absolute isolation. His breakthrough is not the defeat of the man from the underground. It is the emergence from the underground. It is not a religious conversion or resurrection, but it is perhaps the beginning of some measure of authentic existence, some contact with real life.

STAVROGIN: THE DIVIDED MAN AS EXILE

Nicholas Stavrogin, the hero of Dostoievsky's novel *The Devils*, or as it is sometimes translated, *The Possessed*, inherits and intensifies the alienation and inner division of the Underground Man and Raskolnikov. Stavrogin, more than any other of Dostoievsky's characters, represents the divided man as exile, and for this reason he embodies the problematic of modern man as perhaps no other of Dostoievsky's characters, unless it be Ivan Karamazov. The problematic of Stavrogin, however, remains hidden in, and refracted among, the relationships he has with men whose thinking he has himself largely formed.[8] As a result he must remain ambiguous and perplexing.

Stavrogin is, in his way, a heroic figure—seemingly purposeful, in complete control of himself, capable of great acts of daring and courage, sought after by all, loved or hated by all, attracting followers even though he has no place to lead them. Yet he is an utterly empty person. His nihilism

[8] According to the Russian literary critic M. M. Bakhtin, Dostoievsky never allowed one character or one point of view to dominate any of his novels, nor can Dostoievsky himself be identified with any one character or point of view. Dostoievsky's novels, therefore, are "polyphonic"—composed of a multiplicity of independent and discrete voices, each given its full value, each with its own separate world. The characters, or "voices," are not so much objects to their author as subjects, independent voices, each bearer of its own word. The word of a character does not express the ideology of the author, accordingly, nor can one reduce the ideology of the character to any systematic unity—as so many critics have tried to do!

This approach brings Bakhtin to a dialogical understanding of Dostoievsky, and the principal product of that dialogue, according to Bakhtin, is a never-completed image of man. The ideas in man are not the heroes of Dostoievsky's novels. Rather, the ideas reveal the man and are present in order that he may know himself. The conversation of the author is not *about* the character but *with* the character, whom Dostoievsky does not identify with, but relates to as the true artist, preserving their distance and at the same time preserving their reality as subjects with whom he enters into dialogue. Bakhtin's theory avoids the fatal tendency to reduce the novels of Dostoievsky to a system of ideas, on the one hand—of which Berdyaev's great book on Dostoievsky is only one out of many examples—or to objects of sociological or psychological inquiry, on the other. Bakhtin's approach is particularly helpful in dealing with the problematic relation of each of three entirely different characters in *The Devils*—Peter Verkhovensky, Shatov, and Kirilov—to the central figure, Stavrogin. Although as different from one another as is conceivable, they have all received their ideas from him and all look up to him as a man whose very existence gives meaning to their lives. Cf. M. M. Bakhtin, *Problemy Tovrcyestva Dostoeyevskovo* ("Problems of Dostoievsky's Writing") (Leningrad: "Priboi," 1929), summarized in Vladimir Seduro, *Dostoievski in Russian Literary Criticism 1846-1956* (New York: Columbia University Press, 1957), "M. M. Bakhtin on Dostoievski's Polyphonic Novel," Chap. 15. Cf. in particular Seduro, pp. 202 ff., 211-227.

is not a position or program, like that of Turgenev's Bazarov in *Fathers and Children*. It is a sheer vacuity of existence, which no amount of adventure, experiment, and sadistic cruelty can fill. He is the "demonic Thou" for countless others whom he himself is incapable of meeting as persons.

> Towards him everything flames, but his fire is cold. To him a thousand several relations lead, but from him none. He shares in no reality, but in him immeasurable share is taken as though in a reality.[9]

Stavrogin's fire is indeed cold, and this is the strange secret of this man who appears to others so full of life and passion and actually is consumed by emptiness and boredom. Son of a nobleman, voluntary exile, citizen of Switzerland (to Dostoievsky the country of Rousseau and shallow, rational liberalism), party to a secret marriage with a feeble-minded cripple performed almost as a joke—he is cut off from Russia, from the people, from the soil, from work, from any real existence. In him the "alienation" of modern man has reached its highest point.

Capable of great courage in the face of opposition or danger, Stavrogin acts nonetheless "without any sensation of enjoyment, but simply from unpleasant necessity, languidly, listlessly, and even with a feeling of boredom." Even his former ideas, repeated to him by the men who made them their own, Shatov and Kirilov, he greets only with annoyance and ennui. He has lost the distinction between good and evil and finds equal enjoyment and beauty in a "voluptuous and brutish act" and heroic self-sacrifice for the good of humanity. He has belonged, Shatov suggests, "to a secret society given up to a bestial sensuality." Shatov is at least partly right when he accuses Stavrogin of marrying in such a way "just because the infamy and absurdity of such a marriage reached the pitch of genius!"

[9] Martin Buber, *I and Thou*, 2nd ed. with a Postscript by the Author added, trans. Ronald Gregor Smith (New York: Charles Scribner's Sons, 1958), pp. 67 f. Buber uses Napoleon as his example of the "demonic Thou."

"Oh, you never walk at the edge of the abyss, but precipitate yourself over it boldly, head downwards. You got married because of your passion for cruelty, because of your passion for remorse, because of your moral turpitude. It was a case of morbid hysteria. . . . Stavrogin and a wretched, mentally deficient, destitute cripple! Did you feel a sensuous thrill when you bit the Governor's ear? Did you? You idle, loafing son of a nobleman, did you?"

"You're a psychologist," said Stavrogin, growing paler and paler, "though you're partly mistaken about the reasons for my marriage." (261)[10]

The secret of Stavrogin's boredom and his passionless indifference lies, more than anything, in the fact that he is not only cut off and detached but irreparably divided. He cannot do anything with his whole being and his whole heart. One part of him always looks on as the bored and listless observer, knowing that there is no extreme that can ever catch him up in such a way that he may really give himself to anyone or lose himself in anything. Even when the stunning Lisa, whom he thinks he loves, comes of her own to spend the night with him, voluntarily disgracing herself in the eyes of the town, he realizes in the morning that he cannot really love her. He knew this before, however. In his Confession that he gives Father Tikhon to read, he describes his attachment to Lisa not as love but as a fit of passion and confesses that he fled Switzerland on the advice of Dasha to whom he had confided the fact that he had no love for her whom he desired so much and could never love any one.[11]

The relationship between Stavrogin and Lisa, like that between Versilov and Anna in *The Raw Youth* and Dmitri and Katya in *The Brothers Karamazov*, is a maddening mixture of hatred and love. Lisa taunts Stavrogin in public and

---

[10] All quotations and page references other than Stavrogin's Confession are from the Penguin Classics edition of Fyodor Dostoievsky's *The Devils* (*The Possessed*), trans. David Magarshack, ed. E. V. Rieu (Harmsworth, England: 1953).

[11] Fyodor Dostoievsky, *Stavrogin's Confession and the Plan of the Life of a Great Sinner*, trans. S. S. Koteliansky and Virginia Woolf (Richmond, England: L. & V. Woolf, 1922), p. 68.

almost strikes him, yet when he admits publicly that he is married, she comes to him of her own free will. On the other hand, when Lisa does run to Stavrogin she will not stay with him despite his pleading and despite the fact that she has already ruined herself, for she knows that he does not love her and cannot marry her. He swears that he loves her even more after making love to her than before—a strange comparison, as Lisa remarks—and that he has paid with his life for "this new hope." But when she asks him whether he knew that she would leave him, he admits that it was so. He swears to her that he will not have one more "hour" of love than she, and like her he even sheds tears, but he cries to her in despair, "Torture me, kill me, work off your spite on me . . . I knew I did not love you, and I ruined you." When she came to him of her own accord he deluded himself, for a few hours—not with the hope that she loved him, but with the hope that he loved her! But what he has never been capable of, he is not capable of now, even for an hour. It is Lisa herself who foretells the gloomy future they would have together:

> "I always imagined that you would take me to some place where there was a huge, wicked spider as big as a man, and we should spend the rest of our lives looking at it and being afraid of it. That's what our love would be wasted on." (522)

Unlike Dostoievsky's "great sinner," Stavrogin undergoes no redeeming transformation and is incapable of any.[12] His visit to Father Tikhon and his confession are under the same

[12] In his plan for *The Life of a Great Sinner* Dostoievsky had projected the history of an unusual man who wavers between atheism and belief but eventually works through nihilism and crime to integrity and faith. "The main question," Dostoievsky wrote to A. Maikov (Mar. 25, 1870), "is the same which has tormented me, consciously and unconsciously, all my life—the existence of God. The hero is at different times in his life an atheist, a believer, a fanatic, and sectarian, now again an atheist." There is no question that Dostoievsky originally conceived Stavrogin (the man of the cross—*stavros*) in the light of this projected book. In particular there is the closest connection between Stavrogin's visit to Father Tikhon in the monastery and the second part of the plan which was to take place in a monastery and to center around the conversation between the Bishop Tikhon Sadonsky and a young nihilist boy.

shadow as his love for Lisa: they too are not, and cannot be, whole-hearted. In the conversation that takes place before Father Tikhon reads the written confession Stavrogin has brought with him, Stavrogin asks him to read the passage from the Apocalypse in which the man whose works are neither cold nor hot but only lukewarm is spewed out. This describes Stavrogin's own state, and he recognizes it. "It surprised you that the Lamb prefers a cold man to a merely lukewarm one," Tikhon says to him. "You don't want to be merely lukewarm." In an earlier version of the Confession Stavrogin says, "I did all this as an aristocrat, an idler, a man uprooted from the ground," and in the finished version Tikhon speaks of him as "uprooted." The Confession itself can be seen as a desperate attempt to break out of the "lukewarm" state—the indifference to good and evil—that has dominated him throughout the novel. But the very form of the Confession and his relationship to it make such a breakthrough impossible. Stavrogin's Confession, like his visit to Father Tikhon itself, is a moving but empty form—as fictitious as his own existence.

Stavrogin's Confession is a written, a literary confession, which he proposes to publish. Father Tikhon, when he has read it, shrewdly declares that Stavrogin will not publish it, since it will make people laugh at him—something he can bear far less easily than infamy. In the Confession he tells of how he kept several rooms in St. Petersburg where he used to make love first to a lady and then to her maid. The daughter of the landlady comes to his attention, a shy twelve-year-old girl to whom he is kind at first, only to let her be punished a short while later for something he has done himself, while he looks on. Still later, when she happens to be in the house alone, he seduces her. When she enters his room some time afterward and looks at him reproachfully, he turns away from her and waits in calm detachment while she goes into the next room and hangs herself. He is expecting just this, and he ascertains by peeping through a tiny crack that she has done as he expected.

Stavrogin tells how, for the first time in his life, he really felt fear after he had violated the little girl. After she has hanged herself, underneath his cheerfulness is the thought that he is "simply a low and despicable coward for my joy at having escaped and that I should never be an honest man."

It is just at this time that he takes it into his head to cripple his life, "but only in as disgusting a way as possible." The symbolic self-degradation of Stavrogin's marriage to Mary in no way relieves his guilt, however, any more than his later public confession of that marriage. In the Confession, Stavrogin tells of a dream of "the Golden Age" that he had, inspired by Claude Lorrain's picture, "Acis and Galatea." In this dream he sees the cradle of European man in a sunny green paradise in the Greek Archipelago inhabited by a beautiful and innocent race whose "virgin powers went out into love and into simple happiness." When he awakens, he finds his eyes full of tears for the first time in his life and his whole heart fills with an unfamiliar and even painful happiness. But when he closes his eyes to recapture the dream, he sees in the midst of the bright light a tiny point which takes on the form of the tiny reddish spider at which he had looked while waiting for Matryosha to hang herself. He sees the girl before him once again, shaking her head at him and threatening him with her tiny fist.

"Is this what they call remorse or repentance?" Stavrogin asks. "I do not know, . . . but it was intolerable to me, that image of her." Yet that image that he cannot bear returns to him every day since then, and he himself brings it of his own free will and will do so, he declares, until he goes mad. Like Svidrigailov, who also violated a little girl who killed herself, Stavrogin cannot get the image out of his mind. He is surprised at this himself since he has done many other equally bad things that do not bother him at all. His dream of the Golden Age gives us a clue. This vision, which Dostoievsky later reproduces word for word in Versilov's confession in *The Raw Youth*, also bears close resemblance to the vision of a lost paradise in the late story, "The Dream of a Ridiculous Man." As the "Ridiculous Man" is himself responsible for the corruption of the paradise that he discovers on another planet, so Stavrogin feels that, through his rape of Matryosha, an innocent child, he has irrevocably destroyed the possibility of innocence that mankind, and he as a child, once knew. Hence his moment of childlike happiness and tears is the precise moment when he is sufficiently open to what he has done that his guilt can become conscious.

Stavrogin's written Confession, his visit to Tikhon, and his plans to publish the Confession are all ways of attempting to handle the guilt that he has not been able to escape in any other manner. But Tikhon sees that, although sincere and "straight from the needs of a mortally wounded heart," this document does not represent a true repentance.

> "You have taken the great way, the rarest way. But you, it seems, already hate and despise beforehand all those who will read what is written here, and you challenge them. You were not ashamed of admitting your crime; why are you ashamed of repentance?"
> "Ashamed?"
> "You are ashamed and afraid!"
> "Afraid?"
> "Mortally . . . you seem to be luxuriating in your own psychology and clutch at each detail, in order to surprise the reader by a callousness which is not really you. What is this but a haughty defiance of the judge by the accused?" [13]

Stavrogin admits that he only wants the forgiveness of Tikhon and one or two others and that he prefers that the rest hate him. He foresees, in fact, that he will publish his Confession "unexpectedly, and, indeed, in a revengeful, hateful moment, when I hate them most." This is exactly the way in which he makes public his marriage to Mary, as we have seen. Stavrogin seeks "boundless suffering" so that he may forgive himself and the vision of Matryosha will disappear. "Don't make me afraid," he says, "or I shall die in anger." But when Tikhon tells him that everyone will laugh at him, he is afraid, and when Tikhon suggests that he go into retreat for a period of years as a lay novice to a holy man, he reacts with such aversion that Tikhon is horrified.

[13] *Ibid.*, pp. 71 f.

"I see . . . I see, as if it stood before me," Tikhon exclaimed in a voice which penetrated the soul with an expression of the most violent grief, "that you, poor, lost youth, have never been so near another and a still greater crime than you are at this moment . . . a day, an hour, perhaps, before the great step, . . . and you will commit it solely in order to avoid the publication of these pages."

Stavrogin shudders with anger and cries, "You cursed psychologist!" the same appellation he used for Shatov, and he angrily strides from the cell.[14]

The very acuteness of Stavrogin's self-awareness, reflected in his penchant for analyzing his motives in his Confession, stands in the way of a genuine repentance. Like the Underground Man, he tells us that he was overwhelmed by boredom. "I was so bored I could have hanged myself," he says in one version.[15] The corollary of this desire to escape boredom is his desire for sensation. In the St. Petersburg version, the narrator opines that the written Confession and its intended publication was "the same as the Governor's bitten ear," [16] that is, another "sensuous thrill," in Shatov's words. In the finished Moscow version Stavrogin says himself that "every . . .

---

[14] *Ibid.*, pp. 74-83. In a fragmentary sketch which he did not include in the finished chapter, Dostoievsky has Father Tikhon oppose the publication of the Confession on the ground that Stavrogin is trying to substitute a "leap" for the long work of setting himself to rights from within. "And would it be impossible to do it suddenly?" "Impossible? From the work of an angel it would become the work of a devil." . . . "Ah, that I already knew myself!" (*Der unbekannte Dostojewski* eds. René Fülop-Müller and Friedrich Eckstein [Munich: Piper & Co., 1926], p. 283). Stavrogin's desire to reach a new way of life through the "leap" he knows himself to be "the work of a devil" because this, too, for himself is inevitably just one more sensation, one more extreme action, with no more hope of personal wholeness and real relation to other people than any of his other actions. His guilt is real, but his overcoming of this guilt is not. "Stavrogin 'commits' the confession as he commits his crimes," writes Martin Buber, "as an attempt to snatch the genuine existence which he does not possess, but which—nihilist in practice but (in anticipation) existentialist in views—he has recognized as the true good." (Buber, *The knowledge of Man*, ed., with an Intro. Essay by Friedman [London: Allen & Unwin,1965]; New York: Harper & Row, 1966, "Guilt and Guilt Feelings," Chap. VI, trans. Friedman.)
[15] *Stavrogin's Confession*, pp. 46, 120.
[16] *Ibid.*, pp. 38 f., n. 2; *Der unbekannte Dostojewski*, pp. 403 f.

utterly degrading . . . ridiculous situation . . . always roused in me, side by side with extreme anger, an incredible delight." This is what he felt when he kept Matryosha in suspense and would not speak to her just before she hanged herself: "My heart thrilled with joy that I had kept up my character and waited for her to come first." [17] This desire for sensation does not mean that Stavrogin is indifferent or lacking in despair and a sense of guilt that might lead to repentance. But he is too split to bring all of himself into even this action of confessing. His problem is not that he does not believe in anything, but that he believes in opposites, that he is torn by extremes. Like love and self-degradation, confession cannot do for him what he cannot do for himself—make him give himself to life as a whole person.

In his last letter to Dasha, Stavrogin says he will never commit suicide: "I know that I ought to kill myself, to brush myself off the earth, like some loathsome insect; but I am afraid of suicide, because I am afraid of showing magnanimity." Yet he states with utmost clarity what are, in fact, the reasons why a short time later he does commit suicide. He kills himself out of despair—the despair of a man with strength but no direction, a man with passion and potentiality but with no image of authentic existence.

> "I've tried my strength everywhere. You advised me to do that so as to learn 'to know myself.' When I tried it for my own sake and for the sake of self-display, it seemed infinite . . . But what to apply my strength to—that's what I've never seen and don't see now. . . . My desires are never strong enough. They cannot guide me. . . . I tried wild debauchery and wasted my strength in it: but I do not like debauchery and I had no desire for it . . . from me nothing has come but negation, with no magnanimity and no force. Even negation has not come from me. Everything has always been petty and lifeless. Kirilov, in his magnanimity, could not compromise with an idea and—shot himself. But I can see that he was so magnanimous because he was insane. I can never lose my reason and I can never believe in an idea to the same extent as

[17] *Stavrogin's Confession,* pp. 43 f., 54 f.

he did. I cannot even be interested in an idea to the same extent. I can never, never shoot myself!" (666 f.)

Despite the grand theories which he lends to others, Stavrogin ends not as man-god or god-man but as a pitiful, bankrupt man. Whatever their differences, almost all the other characters in *The Devils* are alike in their desire to bring paradise on earth or their belief that the earth is already paradise if we but knew it. Only Stavrogin does not have this hope or this illusion. Only Stavrogin knows paradise as irretrievably lost, himself and mankind as in permanent exile. Yet in him the futility of those who have tried to find real existence through him is summed up and brought to its culmination. In Stavrogin the problematic of modern man has become explicit and unmistakable.

9

DOSTOIEVSKY'S "MAN-GOD"

KIRILOV

A direct road leads from Dostoievsky's alienated and divided exile—the Underground Man—to his Modern Promethean—the "man-god." Kirilov in *The Devils* is obsessed with suicide as the highest expression of human will which will free man from God and make him the "man-god." What keeps people from killing themselves is fear of pain and the after life, not love of life but fear of losing life. "Now man loves life," and "life is pain, life is fear, and man is unhappy." But "a new man will come, happy and proud. To whom it won't matter whether he lives or not." Having conquered pain and fear, this man will himself be a god. God does not exist but He is; the advent of the new man will mean the death of God:

> "Then history will be divided into two parts: from 'the gorilla to the annihilation of God, and from the annihilation of God to—"
> "To the gorilla?"
> ". . . to the physical transformation of the earth and man." (126)

But this transformation can only come about through suicide, suicide not through fear but to kill fear, for only through daring to kill oneself does one kill deception, do away with God, and become oneself a god.

In these words we seem to hear the echo of Zarathustra's, "If there were gods, how could I bear it to be no god. Therefore, there are no gods." Romano Guardini suggests that underlying Nietzsche's need to do away with the God who was too compassionate and saw too much and Kirilov's need to annihilate himself in order to annihilate God is the inability to live with an infinite "Other" that seems to crush finite man by his very existence.[1] As we have already seen in Captain Ahab, it is no longer possible for modern man to affirm both himself and the "Other," like Job—to contend with the Transcendent and yet remain in dialogue with it. Rather, he must become a Modern Promethean, doing away with the power that threatens to overwhelm him, substituting for I *and* Thou "either you or I but not both!" Kirilov goes even further than Nietzsche's Zarathustra. His will leads not to the Superman, but to his own self-deification.

> "If there is no god, then I am a god. . . . If there is a God, then it is always His will, and I can do nothing against His will. If there isn't, then it is my will, and I am bound to express my self-will . . . because all will has become mine." (612)

The "man-god" in Kirilov's theory does not kill himself out of fear. Yet since he kills himself in order to escape from pain and fear, is it not fear, just the same, that has led him to kill

---

[1] Romano Guardini, *Welt und Person, Versuche zur christlichen Lehre vom Menschen* (3rd unchanged ed.; Wurzburg: Werkbund-Verlag, 1950), "Got und 'der Andere,'" pp. 23-27.

himself? "I am terribly unhappy because I'm terribly afraid," Kirilov confesses to Peter just before his suicide. There is a similar paradox hidden in Kirilov's annihilation of God. He believes at one and the same time that God is necessary and so must exist and that he does not and cannot exist. With two such ideas a man cannot go on living, Kirilov says. Like Ippolit Terentyev in *The Idiot,* Kirilov sees himself as the rebel, the one man in thousands of millions "who won't put up with it and who will not want to." Man invented God so as to live without killing himself, says Kirilov. "That's the essence of universal history till now. I am the only man in universal history who for the first time refused to invent God." The logic of this statement is not that Kirilov is killing himself because he is free of God, but the exact opposite: he cannot and will not deceive himself that there is a God, and so, having no meaning in his life, he must kill himself. He sees his death as an absolute expression of his self-will, but he cannot see his life in this way. Underneath the rebel is the Modern Exile. Kirilov is a man who holds to Jesus but *cannot* believe him divine. He is a modern Gnostic who sees the universe as given over to an evil god—a cold, inhuman nature with no possibility of redeeming grace. "Listen to a great idea," Kirilov says to Peter:

"There was a day on earth, and in the middle of the earth were three crosses. One on the cross had such faith that He said to another, 'To-day thou shalt be with me in paradise.' The day came to an end, both died, and they went, but found neither paradise nor resurrection . . . that man was the highest of all on earth, He was that for which it was created. The whole planet, with all that is on it, is sheer madness without that man. There has never been anyone like Him before or since, and never will be. . . . If the laws of nature did not spare even *Him,* . . . and made even Him live in the midst of lies and die for a lie, then the whole planet is a lie and is based on a lie and a stupid mockery. So the very laws of the planet are a lie and a farce of the devil." (614)

Kirilov's "great idea" resembles the end of *The Idiot* where the Christlike man is dragged down into the darkness of a cruel nature. The resemblance is by no means fortuitous, for, despite his atheism, Kirilov, like Myshkin, is a mystic, and he too is at least a latent epileptic. Only his epilepsy is detected through his mysticism rather than his mysticism being manifested in his epilepsy as with Myshkin. In both we have the same ecstatic moments of eternal harmony worth a whole lifetime.

> "There are seconds—they come five or six at a time—when you suddenly feel the presence of eternal harmony in all its fullness . . . a man in his earthly semblance can't endure it. He has to undergo a physical change or die. . . . What is so terrifying about it is that it is so terribly clear and such gladness. . . . In those five seconds I live through a lifetime and I am ready to give my life for them, for it's worth it." (586)

Shatov, to whom Kirilov tells this experience, warns him that it is epilepsy and cites the identical illustration that Myshkin uses himself of the epileptic prophet Mohammed from whose pitcher "no drop of water was spilt while he flew round paradise on his horse."

Kirilov's ecstasy is of a slightly different flavor from Myshkin's, however, in its affirmation that everything is good. It is this mystical affirmation of the world as already paradise that Kirilov communicates to Stavrogin when he comes to see him. Kirilov quotes the apocalyptic saying that "time must come to a sudden stop." In his theory of the new beginning of history brought by the "man-god" who kills himself, he is indeed apocalyptic, and this note comes out again with utmost clarity in his conversation with Peter before he signs the letter prepared by Peter falsely attesting that it was he who killed Shatov: "I'm not afraid of the thoughts of supercilious slaves! You'll see for yourself that all that is secret will be made plain. And you'll be crushed. I believe! I believe!" In his conversation with Stavrogin, however, the end of time has a distinctly mystical character, and time is replaced, not by a new era of time, but by the eternal moment. It is true that Kirilov also sees this moment as in the future as far as all men are concerned: "When all mankind achieves happiness, there will be no more time, for there won't be any need for it. . . . Time is not an object, but an idea. It will be extinguished in the mind." But for Kirilov himself this eternal moment, and with it the goodness of everything, already exists. All is already divine, not in the general and the universal but in each particular.

> "Ever seen a leaf, a leaf from a tree? . . . I saw one recently, a yellow one, a little green, wilted at the edges. Blown by the wind. When I was a boy of ten I used to shut my eyes deliberately in winter and imagine a green leaf, bright green with veins on it, and the sun shining. I used to open my eyes and couldn't believe it because it was so beautiful . . ."
> "What's that? An allegory?"
> "N-no—why? Not an allegory, just a leaf, one leaf. A leaf's good. All's good." (243)

Kirilov is like Blake, who sees eternity in a wild flower and holds infinity in the palm of a hand. He is even closer to Zen Buddhism, however, with its enlightenment that leaves the "ten-thousand things" unchanged yet affirms them as reality apart from any moral distinctions, since to Kirilov, too, enlightenment makes man good without morality.

> "That mother-in-law will die, but the little girl will remain—all's good. . . ."
> "But what about the man who dies of hunger or the man who insults and rapes the little girl—is that good too?"
> "Yes, it is. And he who blows his brains out for the child, that's good too. . . . They are not good . . . because they don't know that they are good. When they find out, they won't rape a little girl. They have to find out that they are good, for then they will all at once become good, every one of them." (243 f.)

Even this mysticism is ultimately apocalyptic for Kirilov, however, since "he who teaches that all are good will bring about the end of the world." This man is the "man-god" whom Kirilov sets in conscious contrast with the god-man. "He who taught it was crucified," says Stavrogin. "He will come, and his name will be the man-god," replies Kirilov. "The god-man?" "The man-god; there is a difference there."

There is, indeed, a difference, yet the atheist-rebel Kirilov is, in his peculiar nihilistic way, a deeply religious man—an unbeliever who still lights the candle before the ikon and sees the whole meaning of existence in Christ, a denier who affirms everything and even prays to the spider crawling on the wall, "grateful to it for crawling," an inverted Christ who sacrifices himself to bring salvation to mankind, a man tormented all his life by God, a man whose passionate denial of God conceals the most desperate need of him. "If you found out that you believed in God, you would believe in Him, but as you don't know that you believe in God, you don't believe in Him," Stavrogin says to him.

The problematic of Kirilov is most clearly revealed by the context and manner of his suicide. Kirilov is a fanatic, a monomaniac, a completely monological man, who tells his great idea to whomever he talks to without discrimination but, apart from his relationship with Stavrogin two years before, has no real dialogue with anyone. One of the terrible ironies of his suicide is that it should be supervised by Peter Verkhovensky, a man whom he utterly despises, and that he should spend his last hours with this man. Another, more terrible irony, is that he should have offered his suicide to the revolutionary movement to use as it pleased and when it wished. This indifferent readiness to be a tool of a movement in which he does not himself believe contradicts his own statement that if one knows one is good, one at once becomes good. His theory has completely dehumanized him to the point where he is ready to aid in covering up the murder of his friend Shatov at the very time when the latter's wife has returned to him and has just had a baby, even though Kirilov himself has helped prepare for the delivery. Kirilov places great stress on the distinction between killing himself—"the most important" point of his self-will—and being useful to the movement by killing someone else—the least important point. But in practice the distinction is not so great as he makes out, since without being able to count on Kirilov's fake confession and his suicide, Peter undoubtedly would not have killed Shatov.

The most terrible irony, however, is the fact that the man who teaches that all is good, all already paradise, dies not a human being but, in Romano Guardini's phrase, a marionette. Kirilov's unhappiness, his terrible fear, and his fixed fanaticism fuse into a poison which transmutes him from a man into a jerking, grotesque monster that horrifies even the cold-blooded and inhuman Peter. When Peter enters the dark room, with gun drawn, to see whether Kirilov has perhaps escaped, he finds the latter rigid and erect, his body pressed against the wall. Overcome by blind rage, Peter dashes at him, shouting and stamping his feet, only to be stopped short again, "still more frozen with horror," when the figure remains completely unmoving with fixed, expressionless stare before his mad rush. Peter holds a candle to Kirilov's face and grips his shoulder, at which Kirilov knocks the candle out of Peter's hands and bites the little finger of his left hand. Peter hits Kirilov on the head with his revolver, tears his finger away, and rushes headlong from the house pursued by terrible shouts of "Now, now, now, now!" at the tenth of which he hears a loud shot. The "man-god" has ended neither god nor man but demon!

The "man-god" reappears in *The Raw Youth* in Versilov's interpretation of that identical vision of the Golden Age which his author has given to both Stavrogin and him. Awaking from the dream with his eyes wet with tears and an unfamiliar sensation of happiness, Versilov identifies his feeling as "the love of all humanity." He proceeds to interpret his vision as the death knell of European civilization and with it of God, of the "great idea of old" which had been its prime source of strength. Coming after this "death of God" is a harmony and love of men who, now realizing that they are not immortal, will love one another, work for one another, and all be happy since "everyone would tremble for the life and happiness of each." This vision of human harmony without God is very close to Kirilov's notion of the new age that the "man-god" will usher in and it is identical with the vision that Ivan's hallucinatory devil parrots back to him. It contains in seed the paradox brought to full bloom in Raskolnikov and Ivan, namely, that the "man-god" proclaims the loss of every basis for morality and love yet founds his vision of paradise on an apparent concern for the good of all humanity. With it is the twin paradox that Dostoievsky's problematic rebel divides mankind into two classes—the superior and the inferior —yet claims to act out of the love of all humanity.

RASKOLNIKOV

The Underground Man, as Walter Nigg points out, is a man who has lost all ground under his feet and is plunged into the abyss. Everything has become questionable to him, nothing stands fast any longer. This is not just a question of pathology or of an attack on rationalism, Nigg rightly asserts, but of the nihilistic man who stands in the void and finds himself face to face with nothingness. For him all traditional values have been destroyed. Raskolnikov, however, ventures into this abyss as the hero of *Notes from the Underground* does not. "All things are allowable" is the maxim on which he acts to discover whether there is an individual conscience that can stand above conventional social morality.[2] In so doing, as Ernest Simmons has remarked, he projects into society the same dualism of unlimited power and unlimited self-abasement that the Underground Man discovers in individual personalities.[3] As the Underground Man alternates between seeing himself as a conquering hero and as a mouse, so Raskolnikov sees all societies as divided into Napoleons and "louses."

The theory behind Raskolnikov's crime is one very similar to that which Nietzsche himself was later to espouse: the division of all people into extraordinary men to whom all is permitted because they are laws to themselves, men who benefit humanity just by overreaching its barriers, and ordinary men who must follow the "herd morality" and from whom no new idea or original impulse can ever be expected. Just who belongs to these two categories remains in some doubt, since the mediocre often mask as original, so that in the end one only proves oneself a superman by transgressing

[2] Walter Nigg, *Religiöse Denker. Kierkegaard, Dostojewskij, Nietzsche, Van Gogh* (Berlin-Munich: Gebrüder Weiss, 1952), pp. 131-138.
[3] Simmons, *op. cit.*, p. 128.

the common law and discovering whether one can do so without feeling guilty. This division between types of men, like that of Dostoievsky's Grand Inquisitor, is based on contempt for the ordinary man, or what Zarathustra calls "the last men." "What if I am wrong," cries Raskolnikov. "What if man is not really a scoundrel, man in general, I mean, the whole race of mankind—then all the rest is prejudice, simply artificial terrors and there are no barriers and it's all as it should be." Raskolnikov is a rebel. He cannot seriously entertain the thought that "it's all as it should be," for he cannot endure that he should have to remain in the relationship to the rest of society that he finds himself—the starving student in the garret, with cockroaches rustling through the wallpaper, knowing himself superior to all yet feeling looked down on by all, in short, the Underground Man!

Raskolnikov's theory is still moral to the extent of justifying those extraordinary people who commit breaches of morals by the benefit they bring mankind. Kepler, Newton, Lycurgus, Solon, Mohammed, and, above all, Napoleon are his images of man, and all of them are to him arch-criminals who are willing to bathe mankind in blood for the sake of a theory or a higher principle. One could call this the old argument that the end justifies the means were it not more concerned, in fact, with the romantic image of the criminal-benefactor than with the humanity to which he presumably dispenses benefits.

> "The vast mass of mankind is mere material, and only exists in order by some great effort, by some mysterious process, by means of some crossing of races and stocks, to bring into the world at last perhaps one man out of a thousand with a spark of independence." (258)

.What is more, this Promethean superman is great not only through what he does but, like Captain Ahab, through what he is. As Ahab is described as "a man of greatly superior natural force, with a globular brain and a ponderous heart," so Raskolnikov describes his superman as a man with "a large intelligence and a deep heart." And as Melville-Ishmael sees the suffering of such noble natures as in any moment containing "the entire circumferences of inferior souls," so

Raskolnikov sees pain, suffering, and "great sadness on earth" as always inevitable for "the really great men." The line between being a bloody Napoleon for the sake of humanity and drowning mankind in blood for the sake of being Napoleon is here so fine as to be invisible!

"I wanted to find out then and quickly," Raskolnikov says to Sonia, "whether I was a louse like everybody else or a man. Whether I can step over barriers or not . . ." His conclusion is that he is not Napoleon, but a louse. Whether he is Nietzsche's "pale criminal" who is up to the deed but not to the thought of it or whether, as Henri de Lubac suggests,[4] he must recognize the truth about the limits of being a man and give up trying to be God, he realizes that he cannot place himself alongside the "real *Masters*," such as Napoleon, "to whom all is permitted." "No, such people, it seems, are not of flesh but of bronze!" The Gnostic motif that Raskolnikov has taken up ends by revenging itself on him. Before, he resided in the underground unwillingly, a rebel only awaiting the chance to break out. Now he is forced to condemn himself to underground existence by his very nature and accept his essential inferiority according to the very division that he himself has erected. No wonder that up to the very end he is intermittently attacked by a rebellious doubt which makes him ask himself whether he has given up too soon and whether he is not, perhaps, a man and not a louse! Far from repenting for having killed the old woman, he is more concerned with the effect of the murder on himself: "Did I murder the old woman? I murdered myself, not her! I crushed myself once for all, for ever. . . . But it was the devil that killed that old woman, not I."[5] Raskolnikov suffers, not from

---

[4] Henri de Lubac, S. J., *The Drama of Atheist Humanism*, trans. Edith M. Riley (New York: Sheed & Ward, 1950), p. 189.

[5] Ernest Simmons see beneath Raskolnikov's "alternating between two characters" a fundamental opposition between self-will and submissiveness which Raskolnikov cannot harmonize either in himself or in his view of society. Unable to escape from this inner contradiction, he commits his murder out of "an unconscious desire to resolve his ambivalence," only to have to recognize that he is not a superior person and that his proper place, in fact, "is with the submissive people." (Simmons, *op. cit.*, p. 128.)

having killed, but from having failed in the role of the genius who can boldly overstep the law. "Killing her was atonement for forty sins. She was sucking the life out of poor people," he cries a short time before he goes to confess. "All men shed blood which flows in streams, and they are afterwards called benefactors of mankind. I only wanted to get the means to do a thousand good deeds."

Underneath this is the resentful hatred of the Underground Man for "you gentlemen": "They destroy men by millions themselves and look on it as a virtue. They are knaves and scoundrels." Even in Siberia he does not repent but looks on his crime in terms of the special prerogatives of the romantic hero, allowed what other men are forbidden because of his superior passionate nature.

> Mere existence had always been too little for him; he had always wanted more. Perhaps it was just because of the strength of his desires that he had thought himself a man to whom more was permissible than to others. (525)

Like the Underground Man, he attacks those "sceptics and halfpenny philosophers" who "halt half-way." He recognizes "his criminality only in the fact that he had been unsuccessful and had confessed it."

Raskolnikov's relationship with Svidrigailov is revelatory not only for Raskolnikov in particular but for the "man-god" in general. Not large freedom but existence shrunk to the nastiest and most limited dimensions conceivable is the final product of the romantic self-affirmation of the Napoleon who boldly oversteps the moral barriers that have linked him to his fellow man. Svidrigailov, like Ivan's devil, forces the rebel to face the problematic hidden within his theory and the ignoble emotions concealed beneath his noble rebellion. Raskolnikov still wants to think of his overstepping of morality as a higher morality. He has not recognized the consequences of the "death of God" except on the level of high theory and dramatic action. The petty, futile, stupid bathos of an empty existence, such as Svidrigailov embodies, is repulsive to him in the extreme, and he reacts to Svidrigailov's cynicism with a high moral tone hardly in keeping with his own position. He characterizes Svidrigailov's interest in women as "vice, a disease and a dangerous one," and later cries out, "Enough of your vile, nasty anecdotes, depraved, vile, sensual man!" Svidrigailov mocks him with being a "Schiller," an idealist, and throws in his face the fact that he has no moral vantage point from which to speak. "If you come to that, you are a thorough cynic yourself," says Svidrigailov, who is becoming "ruder and more sneering every moment." You are worried about moral questions, "duties of citizen and man." "Lay them all aside. They are nothing to you now, ha-ha! You'll say you are still a man and a citizen. If so you ought not to have got into this coil."

IVAN AND THE GRAND INQUISITOR

Ivan Karamazov stands in the direct line of descent from the Underground Man, Raskolnikov, Ippolit, Kirilov, Stavrogin, Versilov. In him the Underground Man reaches his subtlest psychological elaboration; in him the teaching of the man-god reaches its most persuasive philosophical culmination; in him the contradictions of the Modern Promethean who is at once Underground Man and "man-god" attain the most terrifying clarity.

Ivan is far less capable of action than either Raskolnikov or Stavrogin, he is essentially isolated from other people, and he is largely occupied with his own philosophical reflections. These reflections are not so quickly recognizable as the products of *ressentiment* as those of the Underground Man. In fact, they have a distinctly noble cast, and Ivan himself has considerable romantic charm. Yet Ivan is no romantic hero, and beneath his grand philosophizings is revealed depths of a soul that are neither beautiful nor profound but on the contrary nasty and mean. In Ivan, as in the Underground Man, the philosophical cannot be understood without the personal or the personal without the philosophical. The inner conflict of Ivan's ideas is as important a part of the dramatic progression of his character throughout the book as the outer events that develop from his hatred of his father and his rivalry with his brother Dmitri for the latter's fiancée Katya. At the same time the true meaning of this conflict is only revealed to us in the light of these actions themselves.

Characteristically, the first revelations we receive of Ivan are his dialectical ideas, in the form of a lecture of his recounted at the gathering at the monastery by the indignant Miusov. Ivan, according to Miusov, "solemnly declared . . . that there was nothing in the whole world to make men love their neighbours," that it was not natural law but simply the belief in immortality which had made men love one another, and that the loss of this belief would dry up love and every living force and leave nothing, not even cannibalism, immoral and unlawful. Here Ivan states even more explicitly than Raskolnikov or Zarathustra the moral consequences of the "death of God." If God is dead, then all is lawful. If there is no longer an absolute source of values, we can no longer assume the identity of the social order and the divine, and this means, as in the case of Raskolnikov, that the Underground Man is afforded a metaphysical rationale for his rejection of the hated society and its values. Ivan speaks not only for the Underground Man, however, but for modern man as such who, sooner or later, faces the personal and social crisis that arises from the loss of a source of values. The belief in immortality is crucial to Ivan, not, as might be supposed, because the source of moral action lies in the extrinsic value of the reward or punishment to be expected in the afterlife, but because for Dostoievsky, as Nicholas Berdyaev has pointed out, "it is inasmuch as he is an immortal creature that man has an absolute value and cannot allow himself to be used as a means or instrument of any 'interest' whatsoever: the denial of man's immortality is equivalent to a denial of man." [6] Raskolnikov kills Alyona, the pawnbroker, not only because she is of no social use but also because no man, to him, has any unique value in himself. If man has no unique or intrinsic value, there is nothing to prevent his being reduced to an object for the use of others, as Dostoievsky foresaw and our own day has abundantly illustrated. Liberalism which has no base except the sentimental love of

[6] Nicholas Berdyaev, *Dostoevsky*, trans. Donald Attwater (New York: Sheed & Ward, 1934; Meridian Books, Living Age Books: 1957), p. 105.

humanity in the end will give way before the most terrible tyranny, and nothing will stand in the way of one human being torturing and destroying another human being for power or profit or simply amusement.

The paradox of the man-god is illuminated if we look closely at his love of humanity. Ivan is a great lover of humanity in general, but he cannot love his neighbor. "It's just one's neighbours," he confesses to Alyosha, "to my mind, that one can't love, though one might love those at a distance." Another man will not admit my suffering, he adds by way of illustration, and why? "Because I smell unpleasant, because I have a stupid face, because I once trod on his foot." "One can love one's neighbours in the abstract, or even at a distance, but at close quarters it's almost impossible." Ivan is like the doctor of whom Father Zossima tells who found that the more he loved humanity in general the less he loved them in particular and, conversely, that the more he detested men individually the more ardent became his love for humanity.

> " 'I have often come to making enthusiastic schemes for the service of humanity, and perhaps I might actually have faced crucifixion if it had been suddenly necessary; and yet . . . as soon as any one is near me, his personality disturbs my self-complacency and restricts my freedom. In twenty-four hours I begin to hate the best of men: one because he's too long over his dinner; another because he has a cold and keeps on blowing his nose. I become hostile to people the moment they come close to me.' " (64)[7]

In this love for humanity in general, we hear the echoes of the Underground Man who, like Ivan and the doctor, restricts his services to mankind to his fantasy, where they serve to ennoble his own self-image, while he sets too absolute a value on his own detachment and isolation to suffer any actual person to come close to him.

Father Zossima tells the story of the doctor to Madame

[7] All page references are to the Modern Library edition of *The Brothers Karamazov*, trans. Constance Garnett, Introd. by Marc Slonim (New York).

Hohlakov whose head is also full of fantasies of noble service to others which she dare not carry out for fear she would not get the reward of gratitude that she deserves. "It is much and well that your mind is filled with such dreams and not others," Father Zossima responds with delightful realism. "Sometimes, unawares you may do a good deed in reality." But when she complains that she does not believe in God and immortality, Zossima draws the opposite conclusion from Ivan. Instead of saying that it is therefore impossible for her to love others, he says, on the contrary, that it is precisely through striving to love her neighbour actively and indefatigably that she can grow surer of the reality of God and of the immortality of the soul: "If you attain to perfect self-forgetfulness in the love of your neighbour, then you will believe without doubt."

Paradoxical as it may seem, Dostoievsky believes both and sees no contradiction between them: that one cannot love one's neighbor if one no longer sees one's neighbor as a man created in the image of God and yet that the way to rediscover the image of God when it has been lost is through the active love of one's fellow man. If it is Dostoievsky's hope that these two approaches will complement each other, Ivan's conclusions are of a very different sort. Like Raskolnikov and Nietzsche, Ivan proclaims the higher law of the higher man who knows that God is dead, and he fashions this law not simply on freedom from the "slave morality" but on the studied transgression of that morality.

> "He ended by asserting that for every individual, like ourselves, who does not believe in God or immortality, the moral law of nature must immediately be changed into the exact contrary of the former religious law, and that egoism, even to crime, must become, not only lawful but even recognised as the inevitable, the most rational, even honourable outcome of his position." (78 f.)

Ivan reveals himself here not as an amoral atheist nor even as a Nietzschean transvaluator of values, but as a modern Gnostic whose innermost teaching is the inversion of values. As Raskolnikov justifies his murder by appeal to a higher law, failing to recognize that in doing away with the universality of law he has also done away with law as such, so Ivan does not content himself with merely becoming amoral but constructs a new morality for the higher man who *knows* that there is neither God nor immortality. The antinomian Gnostics also believed in an elite, a group of the superior and the perfect predestined to salvation. This elite was characterized precisely by the fact that they *knew* and that, because they knew, they were not only above ordinary morality but were actually called upon to perform evil and sin in order to redeem and purify it by contact with their perfection. We do not have here, as appears at first glance, the mere secularization of religious values—this is what the enlightened liberals like Miusov have accomplished. We have the profane inversion of them proclaimed as the new religion, the higher law, the new morality.

The full implications of Ivan's Gnostic strain unfold in his conversations with Alyosha, with Smerdyakov, and with his devil. Ivan's self-revelation to Alyosha begins accidentally when he bursts out at Katerina Ivanovna's with "an expression of youthful sincerity and strong, irresistibly frank feeling" which leads Alyosha to say to him later that he is really "just a young and fresh and nice boy, green in fact!" Ivan readily acknowledges his "green youth" and his naïve love of life. Though he is wrestling with despair, he knows that his youth and his sheer love of life will conquer everything until he is thirty, including the Gnostic rejection of creation which plays so large a part in his thoughts.

"If I lost faith . . . in the order of things, were convinced in fact that everything is a disorderly, damnable, and perhaps devil-ridden chaos . . . still I should want to live . . . till I am thirty, I know that my youth will triumph over everything—every disillusionment, every disgust with life. . . . I have a longing for life, and I go on living in spite of logic. Though I may not believe in the order of the universe, yet I love the sticky little leaves as they open in spring. I love the blue sky, I love some people . . . I love some great deeds done by men, though

I've long ceased perhaps to have faith in them. . . ."
(273)

Alyosha echoes Ivan's declaration that one should love life more than the meaning of it, but this is precisely what Ivan is incapable of doing. His inner conflicts take all the joy out of his life long before he is thirty, and the conscious form in which these conflicts express themselves is his rebellion against an order that he cannot understand and accept.

Ivan joins Captain Ahab in a Gnostic rejection of creation as evil. Since he rejects creation, the God he affirms and accepts is not the creator but a Gnostic deity who has nothing essentially to do with the world. What this Gnostic affirmation of God and denial of the world comes to is revealed to us in the "Legend of the Grand Inquisitor" which Ivan now recites for Alyosha. The prelude to this recital, strangely enough, is the statement by Alyosha—for which Ivan is waiting—that "there is a Being and He can forgive everything, all and for all, because He gave His innocent blood for all and everything . . . it is to Him they cry aloud, 'Thou art just, O Lord, for Thy ways are revealed!'" Alyosha's statement is a curious echo of Ivan's own Gnosticism. Alyosha does not say, as does the Gospel of John of which Dostoievsky was so fond, that "God so loved the world that He gave his only-begotten Son." (Italics mine.) Rather, he speaks of Christ as giving himself, and when he says that, "It is to Him they cry aloud, 'Thou art just, O Lord'" (italics mine), he almost appears to be pointing to Christ in contrast to God!

To reject God the creator is to reject the Father and for Ivan, as Romano Guardini has pointed out, this rejection may be linked with the fact that he hates his own father and consciously desires his death.[8] It seems at first glance that he also rejects the Son, but his legend is really an affirmation of Christ—an utterly ambiguous affirmation of a Christ who is perhaps no less Gnostic than Ivan's Inquisitor.

The Christ in Ivan's legend, who reappears in Seville, Spain, in the time of the Inquisition and walks among the

[8] Romano Guardini, *Religiöse Gestalten, In Dostojewskijs Werk* (3rd ed. Munich: Hegner Bucherei, Bei Josef Kösel, 1947).

people blessing, healing, and raising from the dead, is far less the Jesus of the Gospels than the traditional symbolic Christ of the ikon: "He moves silently in their midst with a gentle smile of infinite compassion. The sun of love burns in His heart, light and power shine from His eyes, and their radiance, shed on the people, stirs their hearts with responsive love." The Grand Inquisitor, who has the day before burnt a hundred heretics at the stake *ad majorem gloriam Dei,* sees and arrests him, and so great is the Inquisitor's power over the people that they obediently make way even though they recognize who it is that has come. The Inquisitor throws Christ in a prison cell and tells him that the next day he will burn him at the stake like a heretic. And then he speaks to him in a long monologue which becomes a dialogue only in the final response of the silent Christ.

In the figure of the Grand Inquisitor, Dostoievsky has combined the Catholic potentate who has betrayed for earthly power the gospel of love, the socialist who desires to force men into a compulsory, collective, and impersonal social harmony, and the man-god who arrogates to himself a superior humanity and a higher law that entitles him to rule over the herd. As such, the Grand Inquisitor is a résumé of Raskolnikov's and Ivan's theory of the exceptional individual to whom all things are lawful, Kirilov's teaching of the man-god, and Shigalyov's teaching in *The Devils* of the collective herd, ruled over by a small minority, headed by the Pope. At the same time and by the same token, the Grand Inquisitor presages the dictator of the totalitarian state as does no other work of the nineteenth century. In the light of the events of our day, one is tempted to accept the judgment that Dostoievsky puts into the mouth of the Inquisitor, namely, that in the three temptations of Christ, as the Inquisitor interprets them for us, " 'the whole subsequent history of mankind is, as it were, brought together into one whole, and foretold, and in them are united all the unsolved historical contradictions of human nature.' "

We have corrected your work, the Grand Inquisitor says to Christ. In order to make men happy we have taken from them that unendurable freedom to choose between good and evil which you gave them. We have accepted in your name the three temptations which you rejected in the wilderness and have founded the new order upon "miracle, mystery, and authority." And we have done all this for the sake of mankind whom we love as you do not.

The Inquisitor builds his argument upon two paradoxes. First, Christ has no right to add a word to what he said of old. This would be tantamount to a miracle which would deprive men of the freedom of faith which he exalted above all else. What is more, Christ has given the power "to bind and unbind" to the Inquisitors, and this power is irrevocable —so irrevocable, indeed, that they are able, for the happiness of man, to use it to undo Christ's work, to take from man the freedom that he gave him. Thus there can be no present revelation for the opposite reasons that it would deprive men of freedom and give them freedom. The second paradox, one that links this legend with Ivan's declaration of rebellion, is the Inquisitor's recognition that " 'Man was created a rebel' " and is " 'rebellious by nature' " and therefore incapable of being happy, coupled with the assertion that through miracle, mystery, and authority the Inquisitors have conquered and held " 'captive for ever the conscience of these impotent rebels for their happiness.' " In the handwritten sketches, there appears over the words "Man was created a rebel" a sentence which links these two paradoxes in a reproach of Christ for offering freedom to rebellious man: "You have rejected the kingdom, we have been forced to accept it and even if it costs blood and whole generations, it is you, solely and uniquely, who are guilty for it. One sings of you as the one man sinless, and I say to you that you are the only one who is guilty." This sentence points to a third paradox which emerges still more clearly in the course of the Inquisitor's argument, namely, that in the name of justice and love for humanity, the Inquisitor is ready to destroy any number of individuals and to reduce all men to means to the end of an abstract ideal of general happiness. This is the paradox that Berdyaev singles out as central to Dostoievsky's social thought.

In the name of his Magnificence the Superman, in the name of the future happiness of some far-away humanity, in the name of the world-revolution, in the name of unlimited freedom for one or unlimited equality for all, for any or all of these reasons it is henceforth lawful to torture and to kill a man or any number of men, to transform all being into a means in the service of some exalted object or grand ideal.[9]

By pursuing his position to its logical consequences, the Inquisitor reveals its paradoxes—and this is obviously the intention of Ivan, the creator of the Legend, and Dostoievsky, the creator of Ivan. But this does not make the paradoxes any the less real. The first temptation that " 'the wise and dread spirit, the spirit of self-destruction and non-existence'" offered Christ in the wilderness was to turn stones into bread. Christ rejected this, saying, "Man does not live by bread alone." But for the sake of earthly bread man will build again the "terrible tower of Babel," Shigalyov's collective. " 'Humanity will proclaim by the lips of their sages that there is no crime, and therefore no sin; there is only hunger.'" They will lay their freedom at the feet of the Inquisitors, " 'for they will understand themselves, at last, that freedom and bread enough for all are inconceivable.'" In our day we have again and again been placed before an apparent choice between a freedom which leaves the mass of mankind in misery and an equality which leaves them slaves. Freedom tends to become the freedom of the few to exploit the many, equality the enslavement of the many under the dictatorship of the few. No one who has ever cared and fought for social justice has failed to run head on into the Inquisitor's paradox.

The Inquisitor grounds his conception of justice on his understanding of human nature. He declares men " 'weak, vicious, worthless and rebellious,'" " 'ever sinful and ignoble,'" yet justice is for him not Thrasymachus' "interest of the stronger" but the interest of just these weak and sinful men. There is an echo of Ivan's concern for the suffering of helpless children when the Inquisitor asks Christ, " 'What is to become

[9] Berdyaev, *op. cit.*, p. 100.

of the millions and tens of thousands of millions of creatures who will not have the strength to forego the earthly bread for the sake of the heavenly?'"

"'Or dost Thou care only for the tens of thousands of the great and strong, while the millions, numerous as the sands of the sea, who are weak but love Thee, must exist only for the sake of the great and strong? No, we care for the weak too. They are sinful and rebellious, but in the end they too will become obedient.'" (301)

At this point a fourth paradox emerges, namely, that the Inquisitor and his fellows constitute a signal exception to human nature as the Inquisitor has characterized it—so signal as to constitute a qualitatively different race of supermen. "'They will marvel at us and look on us as gods, because we are ready to endure the freedom which they have found so dreadful and to rule over them.'" The Grand Inquisitor is not Nietzsche's higher man who is ready to subordinate the will of the herd to his own will in order that man may move to the Superman. He is the Superman himself acting in the name of the collective—in short, the modern dictator of the totalitarian state.

By refusing the first temptation, the Inquisitor points out, Christ has failed to provide men with what they most need—someone to worship. Instead of giving man a stable conception of life, which he needs more than bread, Christ has aggravated his anxiety and his suffering by giving him complete freedom in the choice between good and evil.

"'Thou didst desire man's free love, that he should follow Thee freely, enticed and taken captive by Thee. In place of the rigid ancient law, man must hereafter with free heart decide for himself what is good and what is evil, having only Thy image before him as his guide. But didst Thou not know he would at last reject even Thy image and Thy truth, if he is weighed down with the fearful burden of free choice?'" (302)

Christ as the image of man to whom man freely responds and through that response finds the direction to authentic existence is set in opposition to an order which abolishes not only freedom and choice but the image of man and man's response to that image. This opposition is constructed in such a way as to offer an impossible choice between the extremes of unstructured freedom and iron law. Here again we have a Gnostic overtone. "Law" is not, as in the Torah of the Hebrew Bible, the instruction and direction that God gives to the heart of man just because he is free to choose good or evil, life or death. It is instead an inexorable realm of strict justice divorced from mercy. Freedom, correspondingly, is not the freedom of man in community but a "spiritual" freedom divorced from the demands that justice places upon men in their life with one another.

The Inquisitor also reproaches Christ for rejecting the second temptation—to make manifest his special relationship with God by casting himself down from the pinnacles of the Temple. He would not "tempt God"; he wanted man to cling to God and not ask for a miracle. " 'But Thou didst not know that when man rejects miracle he rejects God too; for man seeks not so much God as the miraculous.' " If man's first great need is for someone to worship, his second is for someone to keep his conscience. Respecting man less, Christ would have loved him more, says the Inquisitor, for he would have placed a lighter burden on him. Like Ivan, the Inquisitor too has a "Euclidian mind": " 'Canst Thou have simply come to the elect and for the elect? But if so, it is a mystery and we cannot understand it.' "

The Inquisitor has his own mystery, however, which he reveals to his listener—the secret that for eight centuries the Church has not been working for Christ but for Satan, the dread spirit who tempted him in the wilderness. " 'The third and last anguish of man' " is the craving for community of worship, for universal unity. The Church has accepted the kingdoms of Caesar which Christ rejected and is working to create with it the original paradise of Shigalyov's obedient herd, the paradise of the " 'unanimous and harmonious antheap.' " The Inquisitor, like Shigalyov, is concerned to " 'plan the universal happiness of man,' " and to do so he will persuade men that " 'they will only become free when they renounce their freedom to us and submit to us.' " In a remarkable anticipation of the Nazis, the Grand Inquisitor unfolds a picture of a totalitarian society which restores men to the Garden of Eden by making the borders of the social world coincide with the total reality that men know and experience. The Inquisitors are thus able to take from men the fearful knowledge of good and evil that came with man's fall and his exile from paradise. Since the mass of men are really no better than children, justice demands that they should be rescued from their miserable freedom and their impotent rebellion and restored to the state of happy children whose leisure will be planned for them and whose sins will be condoned.

> " 'We shall set them to work, but in their leisure hours we shall make their life like a child's game, with children's songs and innocent dance. Oh, we shall allow them even sin, they are weak and helpless, and they will love us like children because we allow them to sin. We shall tell them that every sin will be expiated, if it is done with our permission. . . . We shall allow or forbid them to live with their wives and mistresses, to have or not to have children—according to whether they have been obedient or disobedient—and they will submit to us gladly and cheerfully.' " (307 f.)

The Inquisitor will exclude from the new society not only Prometheus and Job, the Greek rebel and the Biblical one, but even Adam himself who left the state of the child and became the prototype of historical man precisely through the sin of disobedience. Nor will there be any room for an Oedipus who oversteps the limits of the order and who, like Cain, must pay the penalty of exile. In the Inquisitor's "unanimous ant-heap" there will be neither rebel nor exile, history nor man. And yet the Inquisitor's plan for the universal happiness of mankind is itself an expression and consequence of Ivan's rebellion—his rebellion against the injustice of suffering. This might imply a suicidal drive on the part of the rebel to abolish himself in the name of his rebellion were it not for the fourth paradox to which we have pointed: the existence of two human natures, with the higher one of which Ivan obviously identifies himself. Although men in general cannot bear the knowledge that there is no God and no immortality, the

Inquisitors can. Like Plato's philosopher king, they govern men by means of a royal myth while they alone know the truth. For the sake of the happiness of the millions, the hundred thousand who rule over them take on the unhappiness and suffering of the knowledge of good and evil, the knowledge that there is no God. " 'Judge us if Thou canst and darest,' " the Inquisitor will say to Christ when he comes again in victory. Once the Inquisitor too was the rebel who prized freedom, the exile who lived in the wilderness on roots and locusts, but now " 'I have turned back and joined the ranks of those *who have corrected Thy work*. I left the proud and went back to the humble, for the happiness of the humble.' " Like Fyodor with Zossima, the proud Inquisitor, creation of the proud Ivan, identifies the god-man with the proud and himself with the humble!

It is pride, nonetheless, which is the key to the Inquisitor. Plato's philosopher king is the fantasy guise in which the philosopher who rejects society as it is is able to imagine himself ruling over an ideal one. Ivan's Inquisitor, similarly, is the guise in which the metaphysical rebel who rejects the order of the universe is able to imagine himself creating a new one. In the chapter "Rebellion," in fact, Ivan has invited Alyosha to imagine himself the creator of the "fabric of human destiny." But the paradox is heightened when we recall the terms on which Ivan and Alyosha agreed that they would *not* consent to build human destiny, namely, the sacrifice of an innocent child for the sake of the universal happiness of man. Ivan's Inquisitor is ready to sacrifice any number of children, if they are disobedient, and to put to the stake all rebels and heretics who stand in the way of his harmonious ant-heap.

Although he claims that he loves man more than Christ does, the Inquisitor has nothing but contempt for the mass of mankind and wishes to establish his unqualified superiority and his unconditional power over them. He pictures himself as a noble humanitarian, suffering for the masses, yet we are at a loss to understand what motive he could possibly have for taking on himself this suffering other than this strengthening of his power and heightening of his sense of superiority. It is not love of men, certainly, for he cannot really love those for whom he has such contempt. Neither is it humanitarianism. Since he knows that there is neither God nor immortality and that the higher men, like him, are a law unto themselves, he also knows, as Ivan said in his lecture, that there is no heavenly *or* earthly reason why he should love his neighbor or care about his happiness. The Inquisitor is like a "suffering servant of the Lord" when there is no longer a Lord. His concern for humanity presupposes the very values which he himself has denied—the basic equality of men, despite all differences, as persons each of whom is of unique value in himself, the dignity and worth of the individual, the brotherhood of men with one another. When Thrasymachus said to Plato's Socrates that "justice is the interest of the stronger" and challenged him to disprove this thesis, he was far more consistent than the Inquisitor, whose moral nihilism is no less absolute than that of the Sophist yet who claims, nonetheless, that he acts out of moral motives. We have seen this same paradox before in Ivan's "Gnostic" doctrine of the higher men whose knowledge that all things are lawful leads not to a "value-free" existence but to an inversion of the old moral values into their exact opposite in the name of morality itself.[10]

[10] Although "The Legend of the Grand Inquisitor" can and does stand as a masterpiece of modern thought apart from its relationship to Ivan, we must not forget that it is Ivan who tells this legend and that it is an integral part of his dramatic development. This does not mean that Ivan is simply to be identified with his Inquisitor any more than Dostoievsky is to be simply identified with Ivan. In a letter to Lyubimov of June 11, 1879, Dostoievsky draws a sharp distinction between his upright socialist Ivan and the nihilistic socialist of contemporary Russia and yet poses to the latter the very question of respect for man that we have posed to the Inquisitor: "To our Russian, idiotic, but dreadful socialism (dreadful because the youth adhere to it) it shall be an indication, and I believe an energetic one, that the bread, the Tower of Babel (namely, the future kingdom of socialism) and the complete subjugation of the freedom of conscience are just that goal to which the desperate deniers of God and atheists strive. A difference exists only in that our socialists (to whom, as you know, not only the miserable, illegal nihilists belong) are conscious Jesuits and liars who do not confess that their ideal is the violation of the human conscience and the degradation of mankind to the level of animality, while my socialist (Ivan Karamazov) is an upright man, although clearly in agreement with the view of the 'Grand Inquisitor' about mankind. He has accorded to man's faith in Christ a far higher position than it in fact has. The question is sharply posed:

When the Inquisitor is through with speaking, Christ makes no reply to him, even though the old man longs "for Him to say something, however bitter and terrible." Instead, Christ suddenly approaches the old man in silence and softly kisses him "on his bloodless aged lips." The old man shudders and turns Christ out, telling him to go and come no more. "The kiss glows in his heart," Ivan tells Alyosha, "but the old man adheres to his idea." This silent kiss is enough to balance the whole weight of the Inquisitor's dialectic. It is a great symbol of compassion and forgiveness—compassion for the suffering of the aged Inquisitor and forgiveness for his betrayal and his apostasy.

Yet, as Romano Guardini has observed, Ivan's all-forgiving Christ has no connection either with the creation or the creator.[11] He is the Son without the Father—an extension, therefore, of the Christ whom Shatov believes in even though he does not yet believe in God, of Kirilov's non-divine Christ who is the only possible meaning and purpose of a meaningless and purposeless creation. Neither Shatov, Kirilov, nor Ivan connect their image of Christ with the power underlying the universe. Ivan's Christ is the proper complement of his Inquisitor: the latter embodies the evil demigod who rules over creation with blind and inexorable law, while the former embodies the redeemer God of the Gnostic heresies, the loving and merciful Christ of the Marcionites whose transcendent existence is utterly separate from the Father and creator of the Old Testament.

Ivan's Christ thus represents his "turning the ticket in" just as much as his Inquisitor, since both mean a rejection of creation—the one for a hermetically sealed order which abolishes man's freedom, the other for a pure spiritual freedom which abolishes the situation within which man exercises his freedom, namely, his position as a creature within creation. If the Inquisitor's "love of man" has no room for mercy, his Christ's mercy has no room for the love that places on the beloved a

---

'Do you despise the human race or do you esteem it, you, its future saviors?'" (*Die Urgestalt der Brüder Karamasoff* [Munich: Piper & Co., 1928] pp. 562 f. My translation from the German.)
[11] Guardini, *Religiöse Gestalten*, Chap. V, pp. 121-128.

demand in the name of the relationship itself. Ivan's Christ differs from the Jesus of the Gospels who asked *both* justice and love of those who followed him and who demanded decision *for* him or *against* him. Ivan abandons creation as unredeemable and takes refuge in an upper world of spirit and love. As a result, the impossible opposites of perfect order and perfect freedom are as much present in the silent dialogue between his Inquisitor and his Christ as in the Inquisitor's preceding statement of their two positions.

It is the merciless "justice" of the Inquisitor that makes necessary the unconditional "mercy" of his Christ. The severity of Ivan's own judgments of himself and others and his correspondingly strong sense of guilt make any judgment coming from without unbearable for him. They make it necessary for him to imagine a realm of pure consolation—the image of Christ as isolated compassion divorced from that loving demand which points the way to real existence. When Alyosha cries out in dismay, "But the little sticky leaves . . . and the blue sky" and asks how Ivan can live with such a hell in his heart and his head, Ivan replies that the "Karamazov baseness" gives strength to endure everything. "Everything is lawful, is that it?" Alyosha challenges him, at which Ivan scowls and turns strangely pale, but will not deny his formula. At the same time, he reveals how much Alyosha's love means to him, how much he too, like the Inquisitor, needs a kiss to glow in the coldness of his heart.

> "I thought that going away from here I have you at least," Ivan pronounced suddenly, with unexpected feeling; "but now I see that there is no place for me in your heart, my dear hermit. The formula, 'all is lawful,' I won't renounce—will you renounce me for that, yes?"
>
> Alyosha got up, went to him and softly kissed him on the lips.
>
> "That's plagiarism," cried Ivan, highly delighted. (312 f.)

Ivan's devil is a great comedown from his noble Inquisitor, but he is like him in his fondness for dialectic. There is nothing he would rather do than shout "Hosannah" with the other angels, but he realizes that the whole order of the universe depends upon his everlasting negation, so he magnanimously abstains. He would like nothing better than to go to church and offer a candle in simple-hearted faith. But he is the "indispensable minus," the eternal negative without which everything would disappear, "even magazines and newspapers." Like Goethe's Mephistopheles he knows that evil is the necessary corollary of creation—not a reality in itself, but mere negation and absence of unity. The effect of his words is to make evil seem an unreal, intellectual, and paltry thing, and heaven drab and uninteresting—if not Svidrigailov's bath-house with spiders, still a place where nothing happens. He intensifies this sense of everlasting futility by a perfect, if undoubtedly unconscious take-off on Nietzsche's "eternal return":

> "Our present earth may have been repeated a billion times. Why, it's become extinct, been frozen; cracked, broken to bits, disintegrated into its elements, again 'the water above the firmament,' then again a comet, again a sun, again from the sun it becomes earth—and the same sequence may have been repeated endlessly and exactly the same to every detail, most unseemly and insufferably tedious . . ." (783)

Ivan's devil has a Euclidian mind, just like Ivan and the Grand Inquisitor. He too cannot understand the secret behind the eternal harmony. But he does understand Ivan who, for all his boredom and disgust, has an intensity to which his devil cannot lay claim. Ivan is secretly longing, says his devil, "to enter the ranks of 'the hermits in the wilderness and the saintly women,'" to dine on locusts and wander in the wilderness to save his soul. But it is precisely this strain of noble longing that his devil mocks and in so doing exposes the motivation underlying the humanitarian pretensions of both Ivan and his noble Inquisitor. "No, I was never such a flunkey!" Ivan wails, "How then could my soul beget a flunkey like you?" To which his devil responds:

> "My dear fellow, I know a most charming and attractive young Russian gentleman, a young thinker and a

great lover of literature and art, the author of a promising poem entitled 'The Grand Inquisitor.' I was only thinking of him!"

"I forbid you to speak of 'The Grand Inquisitor,'" cried Ivan, crimson with shame. (788)

Ivan regards his devil, like his other double, Smerdyakov, as a "flunkey." But now he is forced to face that there is a flunkey within himself as well. To put the lofty legend of the Inquisitor into this context where everything is decadent and disgusting means to strip off all the moral and romantic coloration from Ivan's most cherished theories. It is a process of disillusionment exactly comparable to the way in which Raskolnikov's lofty sentiments are deflated by the confrontation with Svidrigailov, the prototype of both Ivan's lascivious father and his ironic devil. It is as if Ivan's devil were present all along, listening to Ivan's high soundings and biding his time. Now he steps forth, a full-bodied figure from the realm of the unconscious, and turns Ivan's dialectical monologue into an unendurable dialogue in which the philosophy that "all things are allowable" is devastatingly caricatured and the Gnostic teaching of the man-god unmasked for what it is.

> " 'There are new men,' you decided last spring . . . 'they propose to destroy everything and begin with cannibalism. Stupid fellows! . . . I maintain that nothing need be destroyed, that we only need to destroy the idea of God in man. . . . As soon as men have all of them denied God . . . the old conception of the universe will fall of itself . . . and what's more the old morality, and everything will begin anew. Men will unite to take from life all it can give, but only for joy and happiness in the present world. Man will be lifted up with a spirit of divine Titanic pride and the man-god will appear.' " (788 f.)

The devil's caricature of the Promethean "man-god" is only a caricature by virtue of its ironic context. In its details it is accurate enough, and the shattered Ivan presses his hands over his ears and begins trembling all over. Even as it recounts, the broad irony questions the notion that this ephemeral happiness will be enough to make the new man "accept death proudly and serenely like a god" and "love his brother without need of reward." If the modern Titan denies not only the realm of the gods, like Aeschylus' Prometheus, but also the very order and immortality that sustained the latter in his opposition to Zeus, what will be the new morality that will replace the old? The answer is not the realm of brotherly love and of noble stoics that Versilov and Ivan foretell but the self-deification of the "clever man" who knows that all things are lawful, the unlimited tyranny of the man-god, the modern Gnostic elite, who acts, like Raskolnikov, Shigalyov, and the Grand Inquisitor, out of a consciousness of his superiority to the herd.

> "Every one who recognises the truth even now may legitimately order his life as he pleases, on the new principles. In that sense, 'all things are lawful' for him. What's more, even if this period never comes to pass, since there is anyway no God and no immortality, the new man may well become the man-god, even if he is the only one in the whole world, and promoted to his new position, he may lightheartedly overstep all the barriers of the old morality of the old slave-man, if necessary. There is no law for God. Where God stands, the place is holy. Where I stand will be at once the foremost place . . . 'all things are lawful' and that's the end of it!" (789)

The Nietzschean contrast between the master morality and the slave morality does not lead merely to social tyranny but also to absolute, metaphysical self-affirmation. The place of the holy is not left empty. For Ivan as for Kirilov the vacuum is too dreadful. If there *is* no God, then, rather than have *no* God, I myself become God. "Who is over me," cries Ahab. "The truth hath no confines!" And yet, strangely enough, this very man who arrogates to himself not only divinity but superiority to every moral law is convinced that now for the first time man will become really moral, moral out of love and not out of hope of heaven and fear of hell. This is not the "active love" that Zossima counsels to Madame Hohlakov as the way to become convinced of God and immortality. Rather, it is the abstract love of humanity of the man who tolerates the particular and concrete person as little as Zossima's doctor and Ivan.

> The other love, which is directed to man apart from God, . . . is impersonal and collective, it drives people to huddle together so that they may not be so frightened of living . . . That sort of love is the final term of self-will and self-affirmation . . . The last refuge for man's "idealism" is in the pity he feels for his fellows as feeble creatures who are the plaything of blind necessity. . . . If there be no God, to love man means to deify him, to revere him as an absolute . . .[12]

Berdyaev's conclusion is not the only one that may be drawn from the dialectic of Dostoievsky. One may also draw the conclusion of Sartre, that since there *is* no God, we must accept the consequences and recognize that there is no longer any basis for values, that values are something we ourselves invent, the name for the meaning that we give to an otherwise meaningless life. What one *cannot* do, however, is the very thing which Dostoievsky's "man-god" has repeatedly tried to do, namely, to construct a new and higher morality on the foundation of a nihilism which has destroyed all possible basis for morality. Ivan's devil need only add one light thrust to bring the whole romantic, pseudo-Gnostic structure tumbling to the ground: "That's all very charming; but if you want to swindle why do you want a moral sanction for doing it?" If there is no morality, why cannot Ivan accept this fact with the courage of his ruthless nihilism and not dress up his conclusions as something lofty, noble, romantic, and idealistic?

But Ivan does not have the courage of his convictions, as Smerdyakov already observed to him. When Alyosha breaks Ivan out of his hallucination and tells him that Smerdyakov has hanged himself, Ivan not only insists that his devil has already told him this fact, but adds, "It was all he did talk about, if you come to that." Actually Ivan's devil has not said a word about Smerdyakov, unless it be by implication when he tells him that it is his brother Alyosha knocking "with the most interesting and surprising news." Yet what Ivan says is

[12] Berdyaev, *op. cit.*, pp. 131 f.

nonetheless true. Ivan's devil lays bare the motivation of Ivan's noble Inquisitor whose love for humanity is basically an affirmation of himself and a contempt for those for whom he supposedly suffers. But he exposes still more cruelly, even if only by implication, Ivan's relation to Smerdyakov and his father's murder. It is no accident that this hallucination comes to Ivan just when it does, after his third interview with Smerdyakov and before his brother's trial at which he has asserted he will testify.

What Ivan now tells Alyosha is not about the devil's dialectic but about the implications of what he said for Ivan's own situation. Although Ivan characterizes him as "a paltry, trivial devil" who brought out only what was base, mean, and contemptible in him, he confesses that he told him a great deal that was true about himself that he should not otherwise have owned to. What his devil has been teasing him about, according to his report to Alyosha, is his outmoded conscience, his intention of confessing that the valet murdered his father at his instigation when Smerdyakov has already hung himself and no one will believe him. "He was unfair to me . . . about lots of things. He told lies about me to my face. . . . 'You are going from pride,' he says . . . 'for the sake of principle. But you are a little pig like Fyodor Pavlovitch and what do you want with virtue? Why do you want to go meddling if your sacrifice is of no use to any one? . . .' He called me a coward, Alyosha! . . . 'It is not for such eagles to soar above the earth.' . . . And Smerdyakov said the same. He must be killed!" Ivan's devil puts his finger precisely on the center of Ivan's conflict:

> " 'You are going to perform an act of heroic virtue, and you don't believe in virtue; that's what tortures you and makes you angry, that's why you are so vindictive.' He said that to me about me and he knows what he says."
> (794)

Alyosha sees *two* possibilities that lie before Ivan, whereas Ivan's devil sees only one:

He began to understand Ivan's illness. "The anguish of a proud determination. An earnest conscience!" God, in

Whom he disbelieved, and His truth were gaining mastery over his heart, which still refused to submit . . . "Yes, if Smerdyakov is dead, no one will believe Ivan's evidence; but he will go and give it." Alyosha smiled softly. "God will conquer!" he thought. "He will either rise up in the light of truth, or . . . he'll perish in hate, revenging on himself and on every one his having served the cause he does not believe in," Alyosha added bitterly. (796)

Until the end of the book we do not know if Ivan will recover from the "brain fever" in which he lies unconscious.[13] Still less can we answer the more important question of whether Ivan will set aside his Modern Promethean rebellion in submission to the higher truth of God or will perish revenging on himself and on everyone else the fact that he has felt compelled to an act of heroic virtue when he does not believe in virtue. But what evidence does exist is all on the side of the latter alternative and not of the former. Ivan's last statement to Alyosha suggests that his confession will take place precisely in the spirit of hatred and superior pride that Father Tikhon detected in the confession of Stavrogin:

"Katya despises me. I've seen that for a month past. Even Lise will begin to despise me! 'You are going in order to be praised.' That's a brutal lie! And you despise me too, Alyosha. Now I am going to hate you again! And I hate the monster, too! I hate the monster! I don't want to save the monster. Let him rot in Siberia! . . . Oh, to-morrow I'll go, stand before them, and spit in their faces!" (795 f.)

Ivan does testify, as Alyosha thought, but not in the way Alyosha expected, and if anyone conquers in his soul, it is not God nor his devil, but the divided man himself![14]

---

[13] Unless we are to go on the dubious evidence offered by Dostoievsky's statement about Ivan's love for Katya in Book XI, Chap. IV: "This is not the time to begin to speak of this new passion of Ivan's, which left its mark on all the rest of his life: this would furnish the subject for another novel, which I may perhaps never write."

[14] In his penetrating study of Dostoievsky, Berdyaev suggests that the divided man who goes the way of self-will and revolt may end in self-

Ivan combines the noble rebellion and defiance of the romantic hero with the exile and alienation of the Underground Man, but in such a way as to reveal the latter looking out from within the former. It is not Ivan's Inquisitor but his devil who has the last word. Ivan's history is in no small part a tragic progress from Raskolnikov to Svidrigailov. Yet his rebellion is for all that real, far more real than anything that can be ascribed to the Underground Man and far more convincingly conceived and carried through than that of Raskolnikov. Ivan is a Prometheus without the order that supports Prometheus in his struggle with Zeus, a Job without the trust that enables Job to contend with God and still remain in dialogue with him, a dialectical Faust with a cynical relationship to his own knowledge and the sure intuition that even the direct experience of life—the "sticky little leaves"—will soon sour on him. Although Ivan's "man-god" is not able to withstand the test of reality, Ivan remains, even in his illness and defeat, Dostoievsky's finest embodiment of the Problematic Rebel.

---

deification and self-annihilation or he may, through wildest license and evil, find his way to the higher freedom "in the heart of the good." "Dostoievsky attributed to man the ability to tread the road of truth which would lead him through the darkness and horrors of division and catastrophe to a definite freedom." Tempting as this dialectical view of freedom and evil is, the evidence in Dostoievsky's novels does not bear out this central thesis on which Berdyaev's whole systematic interpretation rests. The Underground Man remains rotting in his underground. Raskolnikov undergoes only a dubious conversion that might be the road back to some humanity but not to any "definite freedom" in "the heart of the good." Myshkin, Rogozhin, Ippolit, Kirilov, and Stavrogin end in self-destruction. And Ivan, Dostoievsky's divided man par excellence, ends in a draw.

10

PERSONAL FREEDOM,
PSYCHOLOGICAL COMPULSION,
AND GUILT

THE UNDERGROUND MAN AND RASKOLNIKOV

The series of problematic characters that Dostoievsky presents to us in his great novels embody the points of greatest tension between forces of destruction and forces of integration, between compulsion and freedom, between alienation and rebellion. Behind these points of tension, in every case, stands the figure of the Underground Man. He is the divided man who in probing to the depths finds antinomy and conflict rather than any single united self. He is the man who lives out the full tension of psychological compulsion and personal freedom. He is the exile whose rebellion only condemns him to still greater exile.

In the story the Underground Man tells, suffering is so mixed with masochism and sadism that is is impossible to affirm suffering as a human good, much less as the chief human good that he has made it. The Underground Man glorifies this suffering not because it purifies and exalts, for it does neither, but because it offers the relief that comes from having reached the bottom: he is only happy when he has made himself so utterly miserable that he can exchange the shameful and complex misery of being a "rat" for the ecstasy of complete degradation. Yet in *Notes from the Underground* we find all the elements of Dostoievsky's own later philosophy in which humility and suffering are exalted to the very image of the god-man—Sonia in *Crime and Punishment*, Prince Myshkin in *The Idiot*, the pilgrim Makar in *The Raw Youth*, Father Zossima in *The Brothers Karamazov*. If these cannot be reduced to their origins in the Underground Man, neither can they quite deny this origin, and as a result we are left with the problem of the profoundly ambivalent nature of Dostoievsky's affirmation of suffering and consciousness.

It is this very ambivalence which is the key to the connection between the two parts of *Notes from the Underground*. The Underground Man is the man whose subjective existence is more threatened than the "gentlemen" to whom he speaks with such lofty irony. They may have founded their scale of values on logarithms and logical exercises but, unlike him, they have a hold on and a ground in real existence. The abortive contact with Lisa is as close as he can come to actual existence, and this ends in stupid cruelty and bathos. The Underground Man wants to be left in peace in his "funk hole," to be left to his fantasy life, through which he can continually rectify the unrectifiable abjectness of his real position in regard to men. "I could not even imagine any place of secondary importance for myself, and for that very reason I quite contentedly occupied the most insignificant one in real life. Either a hero or dirt—there was no middle way." Wallowing in dirt, he consoles himself with being a hero, suffering attacks of the "sublime and beautiful" precisely during his spells of odious dissipation when he is touching bottom.

It is not, indeed, that others necessarily treat him like dirt, but since he feels like dirt, and since he acts in relation to others in such a way as to force them to maltreat him, he is repeatedly confirmed in the view that he has of himself, and this in turn reinforces the grandiloquence of his fantasy life. This fantasy life feeds itself on ready-made romantic forms, "snatched forcibly from the poets and novelists"—the final *reductio ad absurdum* of the romantic man who has managed to substitute literature for life. "For instance, I triumphed over everything; all of course lay in the dust at my feet, compelled of their own free will to acknowledge all my perfections, and I forgave them all." Thus the other side of his wishing everyone to hell is his readiness to forgive everyone when everything is established on his terms.

An either-or of this nature precludes authentic existence in the most effective way imaginable. Since the only relation to life he can accept is one of complete dominance, he can have no real connection with existence but must content himself with his fantasies in which his omnipotence reigns unchecked. This fantasy and detachment, this suppression of all interhuman life in favor of an existence "underground," is precisely what makes necessary his rejection of the mathematical abstractions of those who see men in terms of enlightened self-interest. So far from being expressions of free will, his actions are of a compulsiveness that destroys all spontaneity; his every act originates in his fear of the way others regard him. All that is left of his humanity, his personhood, is his subjective consciousness, and this he feels constantly threatened by the crushing weight of the social and the objective. He is perhaps as close to the border as one can get, and still remain in touch. For the sake of his very existence, therefore, he must strike out at what would deny his humanity and transform him into an "organ-stop."

This does not mean that our "anti-hero" and his philosophy with him are to be dismissed as merely neurotic. On the contrary, in him a process has worked itself out that is equally present, if hidden, in the "gentlemen" to whom he speaks— the consequences of having no direction toward authentic existence. The Underground Man has carried consciousness and subjectivity to the absurd extreme where they have no real reference to anything outside themselves; the "gentlemen" have objective social structures and objective social values without any real subjective existence. Neither have any share in real life. "We have all lost touch with life," asserts the Underground Man, "we are all cripples, every one of us—more or less." We are angry when people remind us of real life, for we are disgusted with it and find it a burden compared to which "life" as we find it in books is far preferable. We have lost our birthright as men: "We even find it hard to be men, men of real flesh and blood, our own flesh and blood. We are ashamed of it. We think it a disgrace." We are ashamed that we cannot subsume our existence under beautiful ideas and universal ideals, that we have to make our way through the mud and grime, the blood and slime of our private hells. "We do our best to be some theoretical 'average' men. We are stillborn." The empty society and the exiled neurotic are two sides of the same coin: "I knew no real life." The rebellion of the Underground Man forces those who are not exiled to discover the alienation from authentic existence that lies at the very heart of their situation. We cannot accept his philosophy at its face value, for he *is* neurotic: he has taken freedom and subjectivity to the point where they destroy all possible human existence. Yet his protest is a valid one, and his philosophy is a meaningful part of that protest.

Raskolnikov continues both the protest and the problematic of the Underground Man. Raskolnikov feels intense disgust for Svidrigailov and is convinced that he is "the most worthless scoundrel on the face of the earth." Why then is he so drawn to Svidrigailov and fascinated by him? There is a part of Raskolnikov that is like Svidrigailov, and his high-minded overstepping of the barriers has opened the way for this low-minded part to work itself out without hindrance. But Raskolnikov still clings to the illusion that he has acted morally, and the self that he recognizes and identifies with actually is moral. What Svidrigailov represents is that part of his personality that Raskolnikov cannot allow into his awareness—the part which is so dissociated from his image of himself that, as Harry Stack Sullivan might say, the confrontation with it produces horror and revulsion.

By forcing Raskolnikov to face that he has got himself into a "coil" that leaves no way out except suicide, Svidrigailov plays an important part in Raskolnikov's confession and his eventual breakthrough to a relationship with Sonia. When Raskolnikov finally comes to confess, he learns about Svidrigailov's suicide and is unable to go through with the confession. He turns pale and feels "as though something had fallen on him and was stifling him." There is an obvious identification here that works both ways: he feels as if he were committing suicide by giving himself up, yet he also has to recognize that the only alternative to giving himself up is a hopeless isolation and cynical despair which can only end in actual suicide. Thus his fear of following in Svidrigailov's footsteps in the end becomes greater than his fear of giving himself into the hands of the authority which will punish him for his rebellion.

STAVROGIN AND VERSILOV

Stavrogin also has his devil-doubles that reveal his inner division. The question that haunts us throughout *The Devils*, however, is whether Stavrogin's enigmatic character and antisocial actions are to be explained as madness or as attitudes for which he is responsible. After six months in the society of the town where the story takes place, Stavrogin suddenly breaks loose and pulls a gentleman by the nose at his club, kisses the wife of another man at a party in the latter's house, and bites the ear of the Governor, who is trying to help him in a fatherly way. These actions offend local society all the more because they seem a tangible expression of the insufferable pride and contempt that people sense in him. When it is discovered that he has "brain fever" and these incidents are retroactively attributed to his "not being himself," people receive his apologies sympathetically but are still embarrassed, and some remain "convinced that the blackguard was merely having a good laugh at us all and that his illness had nothing to do with it."

Stavrogin, like Ivan, has a lackey devil with whom he talks, though almost all indications of this have been omitted from the finished version. Stavrogin assures Dasha in a deleted passage that he does not believe in the existence of this devil, that his devil is himself in different form; that, in fact, he splits himself and talks with himself.[1] But in his conversation with Tikhon, which Dostoievsky also omitted, he not only tells him that he has had hallucinations of the devil for a year, but suggests that even though he speaks of it as aspects of himself, he wonders whether it is not really the devil. In fact, he declares categorically, "I do believe in the devil, I believe canonically, in a personal, not allegorical devil," and raises the same question as his lackey devil: whether one can believe in the devil without believing in God. These hallucinations again pose the problem of the extent to which Stavrogin's actions are to be attributed to madness, and Stavrogin himself says that he should see a doctor, to which Father Tikhon immediately assents. The form of the hallucination is even more important than the fact—the heightening of the "double" that reveals not only the extent of Stavrogin's inner split but also the demonic and even diabolical character of that ignoble and not at all heroic part of himself that confronts him in Peter and still more in his lackey devil.

In his last letter to Dasha, Stavrogin seems to equate losing one's reason with an uncompromising belief in an idea. He does not see that a personality split into opposing extremes, like his own, might also mean madness, though in a different way from the monomania of Kirilov. When he apologizes for the supposedly irresistible impulses that led him to pull Gaganov by the nose and bite the Governor's ear, he says he was "not himself," and when Liputin implies he was, he turns pale and cries, "Good Lord . . . do you really think that I'm capable of attacking people while in the full possession of my senses?" Stavrogin turns pale every time someone scores a direct hit. It is easier for him to face that he acted on impulse, under the influence of "brain fever," than that it is his very self that is split so that one part of him acts out these impulses while the other fully knows what it does.

[1] *Der unbekannte Dostojewski*, pp. 355-57, 371-73.

In the St. Petersburg version of the Confession Stavrogin says, "I suspect that this is all a sickness," and the narrator himself says, "This document is, in my opinion, a product of sickness, a work of the devil that has gained mastery over this gentleman." [2] In the finished Moscow version of the Tikhon chapter, Stavrogin opines that his hallucination of the devil is a product of his inner split. But he repeatedly insists that his actions in relation to Matryosha and Mary were *not* the products of madness. And his evidence for this is always of the same nature, namely, that no idea ever took full hold of him, that he could always control himself "if he wanted to," that he was always completely aware of what he was doing.

> "I tell all this in order that every one may know that the feeling never absorbed the whole of me absolutely, but there always remained the most perfect consciousness (on that consciousness indeed it was all based). And although it would take hold of me to the pitch of madness, . . . it would never reach the point of making me forget myself . . . I could at the same time overcome it completely, even stop it at its climax, only I never wished to stop it." [3]

While he waits for Matryosha to hang herself, Stavrogin's breathing stops and his heart beats violently but, at the same time, he looks at his watch and notes the time "with perfect accuracy" and has a heightened awareness of every detail around him. When he sits by the window and looks at the little red spider, he thinks of how he will "stand on tiptoe and peer through this very chink" to see if Matryosha has hanged herself. "I mention this detail because I wish to prove fully to what an extent I was obviously in possession of my mental faculties and I hold myself responsible for everything." A more sophisticated awareness of mental illness would have led Stavrogin not to dismiss so conclusively the possibility that the reputation of being mad that he had in his town was right. His heightened awareness of every-

2 *Der unbekannte Dostojewski,* pp. 403, 409.
3 *Stavrogin's Confession,* pp. 44 f.

thing and his complete consciousness of what he is doing and sense of perfect control might as easily be the mark of some type of schizophrenia, or even of paranoid schizophrenia, as of being responsible and in his right mind. Like the Underground Man, he makes the mistake of equating consciousness and will and of thinking that because he knows what is happening, he is free to stop it.

> "I know I can dismiss the thought of Matryosha even now whenever I want to. I am as completely master of my will as ever. But the whole point is that I never wanted to do it; I myself do not want to, and never shall. So it will go on until I go mad." [4]

The fact that he never *wants* to stop what is happening, even though it leads to madness, may cause us to suspect that his perfect mastery of his will is an illusion.

Stavrogin's split is nowhere more clearly manifested, in fact, than in these scenes in which one part of him acts out to the last extreme his tormented impulses while the other looks on with clinical detachment. In addition to this, his constant insistence that his statements prove that he is "of sound mind" are in themselves enough to raise the question of whether he is. That this is a question that Dostoievsky also wants to leave in our minds we have already seen, and it is significant that the final comment of the book, after "the citizen of the canton of Uri" is found "hanging there behind the door," is again on just this matter of Stavrogin's sanity:

> On the table lay a scrap of paper with the words: "No one is to blame, I did it myself." Beside it on the table lay a hammer, a piece of soap, and a large nail, evidently prepared in case of need. The strong silk cord with which Stavrogin had hanged himself had evidently also been prepared and chosen beforehand. It was thickly smeared with soap. All this was evidence of premeditation and consciousness to the last minute.

The verdict of our doctors after the post-mortem was

[4] *Ibid.*, pp. 56-58, 62 f., 67, 69.

that it was most definitely not a case of insanity. (668 f.)

What does Dostoievsky want us to believe—that Stavrogin was insane or that he was not insane? Neither the one nor the other. He wants us to understand Stavrogin as precisely that compound of freedom and compulsion, personal responsibility and impersonal determinism that we have described in the Underground Man and that we find later in Ivan Karamazov. Like the Underground Man, Stavrogin confronts us not only with his sickness but with the fact that he is aware of it himself, and this means that there is always more to Stavrogin than the psychological categories that he himself offers us. Dostoievsky has created in Stavrogin a truly independent character who has the right to give us his own conclusions about himself and to demand of us that we meet him as a person—an existential subject—and not just as the object of his or our analyses. We have the right to draw our own conclusions about Stavrogin and in so doing to make use of all the material that Stavrogin and his author offer us, but we do not have the right to substitute our own conclusions for the wholeness and uniqueness of the person who is before us. Stavrogin is not a real person, to be sure, but neither is he a "case." He is a literary creation *and* an image of man created by an author who has succeeded, as few others, in using literature as a medium for bringing us man in his wholeness. Both Stavrogin's despair and his self-awareness show that there is something more to him than any psychological categories can explain—that, in contrast to Peter Verkhovensky, he is a real human being. Dostoievsky clearly wants us to consider the possibility of Stavrogin's madness, or he would not revert so often to this theme, but he does not want us to conclude that he is mad, for this would mean dismissing him as a person and diminishing his stature as an image of man. What he wishes us to understand, rather, is the *problematic* of Stavrogin, which cannot be resolved into the easy either-or's of sane and insane, free or compulsive, responsible or irresponsible.

Versilov, the paradoxical central figure of *The Raw Youth*, illuminates Dostoievsky's attitude toward Stavrogin still further, for Versilov inherits many of Stavrogin's traits, including his pride and his uncontrollable impulses, and his personality is as clearly split and subject to extremes as Stavrogin's. When Versilov breaks in two the ikon that the saintly pilgrim Makar Ivanovitch has left to him and his wife, he explains his action in advance, as an almost irresistible impulse brought about by the presence in him of a "second self." Versilov does not mean by his "two selves" merely two opposing tendencies, such as Faust's "two souls," one of which pulls him up to heaven while the other drags him down to earth, but one self that is rational and another that is definitely irrational. His description of this state is similar to Stavrogin's self-analyses with one significant difference: Versilov does not believe that his rational self can control his irrational one.

"I am really split in two mentally, and I'm horribly afraid of it. It's just as though one's second self were standing beside one. One is sensible and rational oneself, but the other self is impelled to do something perfectly senseless, and sometimes very funny, and suddenly you notice that you are longing to do that amusing thing, goodness knows why. That is, you want to, as it were, against your will: though you fight against it with all your might, you want to." (552 f.) [5]

When Versilov breaks the ikon, his pale face suddenly flushes red, almost purple, and every feature in his face quivers and works. Versilov's bastard son Arkady Dolgoruky interprets this event at the time as a symbolic way of showing that Versilov is putting an end to everything. Yet he adds, "But that second self was unmistakably beside him, too, of that there could be no doubt." In the last chapter Arkady, who is also the narrator, dismisses the notion of "actual madness" on Versilov's part but accepts the theory of "the second self" as "the first stage of serious mental derangement, which may lead to something very bad." His conclusion is again

[5] Page references are to the Dial Press edition of Fyodor Dostoievsky's *A Raw Youth*, trans. Constance Garnett, Introd. by Alfred Kazin (New York: 1947).

precisely that mixed state of freedom and compulsion, responsibility and sickness that we have seen in Stavrogin and that we have pointed to as the place in which the image of man and psychotherapy meet:

> Though that scene at Mother's and that broken ikon were undoubtedly partly due to the influence of a real "second self," yet I have ever since been haunted by the fancy that there was in it an element of a sort of vindictive symbolism, a sort of resentment against the expectations of those women, a sort of angry revolt against their rights and their criticism. And so hand in hand with the "second self" he broke the ikon, as though to say, "That's how your expectations will be shattered!" In fact, even though the "second self" did come in, it was partly simply a whim. . . . But all this is only my theory, it would be hard to decide for certain. (602 f.)

It *would* be hard to decide for certain, but what appears clear is that it is not a question of an either-or; that in Versilov, as in Stavrogin, we see the sick self and the whimsical person together, inextricably mixed. If we contrast Versilov's analysis of his "second self" with Arkady's, we can see not only what Dostoievsky thinks about the problematic of Versilov and Stavrogin, but also his understanding of man as such. Versilov assumes that the sane and free self is the sensible and rational one and that the "senseless," "funny," and "amusing" things that he feels impelled to do are the product of a sick and unfree self. Thus he equates the rational with the sane, the irrational with the sick. Arkady, in contrast, sees the "whim" as a product not of the sick "second self" but of the free person. Like the Underground Man, he knows that the self of man is just as much irrational as it is rational and that the very essence of that self is the freedom to do the arbitrary and whimsical, what is *not* sensible and rational. Hence, in a perfectly clear and precise formulation, Arkady states, "And so hand in hand with the 'second self' he broke the ikon," in which sentence the "he" refers to the free and responsible self in contrast to the unfree "second self." In the same way, when he says, "Even though the 'second self' did come in, it was partly simply a whim," he is contrasting the lack of freedom of the "second self" with the freedom of the self that acts on whims, whereas Versilov identifies acting on a whim with being compelled by impulses dissociated from his real self. There can be no question that Dostoievsky's view of man in general—and of Versilov and Stavrogin in particular—coincides with Arkady's analysis and not with Versilov's.

PRINCE MYSHKIN

The problematic of Prince Myshkin, the hero of Dostoievsky's novel *The Idiot*, takes us even deeper than that of Stavrogin and Ivan into the inextricable intermixture of personal freedom and psychological compulsion. Dostoievsky, according to his letters, intended to create in Myshkin a Christlike figure and a "positively good man," somewhat after the model of Don Quixote, whom Dostoievsky regarded as the only such figure in literature.[6] One must see Prince Myshkin not in terms of Dostoievsky's stated intention, however, but of his actual achievement, and in actuality Myshkin is a complex figure—at once epileptic and saint, wiser than other men and far more naïve, intellectually unaware of evil and intuitively attuned to the deepest horror, meek, forgiving, and loving, yet careless of the one he loves while fascinated by the demonic beauty and suffering of her rival.

The plot of *The Idiot* is circular rather than linear: the progress from an abyss back into an abyss. Prince Myshkin is not an idiot, but he is a severe epileptic, and this epilepsy has affected both his character and his understanding. Sent to Dr. Schneider's clinic in Switzerland, he is patiently taught by the doctor until he emerges into sufficient independence to venture on a new life in Russia. The specific reason for returning is to receive an inheritance that has been left him by his benefactor, but the return to his homeland is charged for him with high idealistic purpose and lofty abstractions that really do make him something of a Don Quixote. On his very first evening in Russia he offers his hand to Nastasya Filip-

---

[6] Letter of Dostoievsky to his niece Sofiya Ivanovna, quoted in Simmons, *op. cit.*, pp. 166 f.

povna, a beautiful but desperately unhappy young woman who had been the unwilling mistress of an older protector and is now throwing herself into the arms of Rogozhin to escape a mercenary fiancé. In all this he plays the part of the "poor knight" in Pushkin's poem, marked out for ridicule and disaster but cherishing his ideal untainted. As Yevgeny Pavlovitch later analyzes it to Myshkin himself:

> "What's at the bottom of all that's happened is your innate inexperience (mark that word, 'innate,' prince), and your extraordinary simple-heartedness, and then the phenomenal lack of all feeling for proportion in you . . . and finally the huge mass of intellectual convictions which you, with your extraordinary honesty, have hitherto taken for real, innate, intuitive convictions! You arrived in the first glow of eagerness to be of service, so to say; you rushed, you flew headlong to be of service. And on the very day of your arrival, a sad and heartrending story of an injured woman is told you, you a virginal knight—and about a woman! . . . you were bewitched by her beauty, her fantastic, demoniacal beauty." (563) [7]

The motif of the idealistic, abstracted, and romantic Don Quixote only takes us a little way into Myshkin's character, however. We are still left with the dilemma of why a man who is so ridiculous and arhythmic in his social behavior as constantly to cover himself with shame—for which he always blames himself even before others do—is nonetheless sought after by others and loved by them. And, conversely, why a man who astounds all who deal with him by the depth and sureness of his insights into people is constantly referred to by them as "an idiot." This is a problem that his fiancée Aglaia Ivanovna Epanchin puzzles over and solves for herself by a theory of "two minds":

> "I consider you the most honest and truthful of men, more honest and truthful than anyone; and if they do say . . . that you're sometimes afflicted in your mind, it's unjust . . . though you really are mentally afflicted

[7] All page references are to the Bantam Classic edition of *The Idiot*, trans. Constance Garnett (New York: 1958).

. . . yet the mind that matters is better in you than in
any of them. It's something, in fact, they have never
dreamed of. For there are two sorts of mind: one that
matters, and one that doesn't matter." (415)

What Myshkin says of modern men is true of himself: that
they are broader than they were in the old days and "this
prevents their being so all-of-a-piece as they were in those
days." And yet he is at the same time, as people constantly
say, "a perfect child." He is in the ancient tradition of "the
fool of God" and of the idiot whom, as Dostoievsky tells us
in *The Brothers Karamazov,* the Russian people hold to be
"specially dear to God." Yet he is what one might expect if
one set out, as Dostoievsky clearly did, to create a modern
saint, a man of unusual moral and spiritual qualities who,
nonetheless, bears within himself the tensions and contradictions of modern existence. "At last I have seen a man," says
Nastasya Filippovna after she has met Myshkin and, for all
his social awkwardness, he is indeed more simply man than
anyone in the book. Yet he combines the complex modern
man with the pure-hearted saint in such an incongruous way
that he is basically neither saint, nor modern, nor image of
man.

Myshkin is best understood not in himself but in his relationships, and particularly those with Nastasya Filippovna
and Rogozhin—a fatal triangle which dominates the story
from beginning to end. Myshkin cannot understand how Nastasya can again mean to marry Rogozhin and adds that if
she thinks as badly of Rogozhin as the latter believes, "it
would be as good as deliberately going to be drowned or
murdered to marry you." There is a split between the intuitive and the fully conscious intellectual part of Myshkin, for
in his next statement he completely denies what he has so
surely intuited: "Who would deliberately go to be drowned
or murdered?" to which Rogozhin responds, "Why, that's just
why she is marrying me, because she expects to be murdered!
Do you mean to say, prince, you've never yet had a notion of
what's at the root of it all?" "I don't understand you," says
Myshkin, yet one part of him understands all to well, and

the dread that he feels is all the greater because he cannot admit his intuition to his conscious mind.

The same split shows itself in the weird series of incidents that follow: the garden knife in Rogozhin's book that Myshkin examines repeatedly; the interchange between Rogozhin and Myshkin about a copy of Holbein's picture of Christ just taken down from the Cross that hangs in Rogozhin's house ("Why that picture might make some people lose their faith," says Myshkin intuiting its effect on Rogozhin but not accepting it consciously. " 'That's what it is doing,' Rogozhin assented unexpectedly"); the exchange of crosses in which Myshkin insists on embracing the reluctant Rogozhin; the attempt afterward to recall something he had been looking for while feeling an epileptic fit coming on; going back and finding a shop window and an object in it costing sixty kopecks that he had been looking at earlier and only much later realizing that this was the knife Rogozhin had bought; and finally, as his intuitions gain dominance and dread seizes his soul, the reversion to periods of abstract intellectuality in which he tries to shame himself because he has felt Rogozhin's eyes repeatedly looking at him, because he expects Rogozhin to follow him, because he knows Rogozhin will try to murder him.

Myshkin's intuitions are right in every case, his merely conscious mind wrong: they are Rogozhin's eyes he has seen staring at him, Rogozhin does follow him when he goes to try to find Nastasya and when he returns to the hotel, and it is Rogozhin who, with the same burning eyes, stands hidden in the niche and raises the knife to murder him as Myshkin pulls him out toward the light "to see his face more clearly." Myshkin is saved at that moment by an epileptic fit, the one that he has felt coming on all through this series of incidents.

Myshkin's relation to Rogozhin obviously exists on a deeper level than his conscious mind. His intuitions are right because he is attuned to a depth of horror that his conscious mind cannot admit. Why then does Myshkin feel such shame and inner loathing because of his prescience as to Rogozhin's actions? One reason is that consciously he has to believe in the goodness of men—one part of his saintliness and "Christ-likeness" is the idealism of a Don Quixote who cannot accept reality as it is. A second is his feeling that "in his own soul there was darkness, since he could imagine such horrors!"— a conviction which is no less true for his imagination proving right.

Here, indeed, is the crux of Myshkin's problematic: something in him draws him to horror, darkness, gloominess, destruction and that something is a kindred darkness at the center of his own being. Not that he himself has murderous impulses, as some psychoanalytically oriented critics have said, but there is some deep dread and tension in his soul which is drawn to the very murderous impulses in Rogozhin that he fears. After telling Rogozhin he will not try to see Nastasya, he goes to seek her, *knowing that Rogozhin will follow him.* Seeing Rogozhin standing across the street looking at him and making no attempt to conceal himself, Myshkin pretends that he does not see him and goes away —an action for which he later reproaches himself. In a curious way, he is doing the same thing that Rogozhin said of Nastasya: in coming to Rogozhin, talking to him of their relation to Nastasya, being open with him in the house and playing a sinister psychodrama with him once he has left, he is inviting Rogozhin to murder him.

This fact touches in turn on a further reason for his shame, which brings us equally deeply into his problematic: for all his protestations, he does have passion for Nastasya, albeit in the only form he can recognize it and allow it to become conscious. "For him, Myshkin, to love that woman with passion was almost unthinkable, would have been almost cruelty, inhumanity" he thinks, meditating on his private conviction —which he constantly repeats throughout the book—that she is mad. With equal unreality, he tells himself that Rogozhin's mind will be awakened to forgiveness by compassion, "when he realised what a piteous creature that broken, insane woman was." Even more remarkable from this standpoint, and deeply moving because it expresses at the same time a genuine brotherly feeling, is Myshkin's cry at the moment when Rogozhin raises his knife: "Parfyon, I don't believe it!"

In the scenes with Rogozhin we sense, flowing underneath

Myshkin's strange presentiments like an underground stream, his approaching epileptic fit. As he feels increasingly unwell, his intuitive mind is able to gain more and more the ascendancy so that in reacting against the illness he also tends to reject his intuitions as merely a product of that illness. Merely that they are not, as we have seen, but they are an integral part of his illness, all the same, and the classic description of Myshkin's epilepsy that Dostoievsky inserts in the middle of this sequence of events is in no way arbitrary or out of place. The crux of this description is a feeling of intense consciousness and aliveness which seems worth a lifetime of suffering and remains real for Myshkin even after the final, terrible stage of the fit has reduced him to "stupefaction, spiritual darkness, idiocy."

> The sense of life, the consciousness of self, were multiplied ten times at these moments which passed like a flash of lightning. His mind and his heart were flooded with extraordinary light; all his uneasiness, all his doubts, all his anxieties were relieved at once; they were all merged in a lofty calm, full of serene, harmonious joy and hope. . . . Since . . . at the very last conscious moment before the fit, he had time to say to himself clearly and consciously, "Yes, for this moment one might give one's whole life!" then without doubt that moment was really worth the whole of life. (218 f.)

Actually Myshkin's thoughts follow a dialectical pattern in his reflections on this experience. Since these "gleams and flashes" are "nothing but disease," then these moments are not the highest but the lowest, he thinks. But then he thinks, "What if it is disease? . . . and an abnormal intensity, if . . . the minute of sensation, remembered and analysed afterwards in health, turns out to be the acme of harmony and beauty, and gives a feeling . . . of completeness, of proportion, of reconciliation, and of ecstatic devotional merging in the highest synthesis of life?" Despite Myshkin's propensity for abstract philosophizing, it is clear that he has in these moments a mystic experience which justifies his quotation of the sentence in Revelations, "There shall be no more time," and his comparison of his moment of ecstasy with that of "the epileptic prophet" Mohammed.

It is, nonetheless, a mysticism born of disease, and Myshkin knows himself that "there was undoubtedly a mistake . . . in his estimate of that minute," while at the same time "the reality of the sensation somewhat perplexed him." We can no more separate Myshkin's mysticism from his epilepsy than his "saintliness." His ambivalent reaction to these moments of ecstasy betrays the shame of a man who is tempted to substitute the intensity of inner feeling for the reality of life lived in the everyday and who, just because of that shame, cannot let himself believe in the promptings of an "inner voice" that is so inextricably bound up with this heightened inwardness. That this inwardness is not all bliss, harmony, and reconciliation is shown not only by the unendurable second that follows the moment of ecstasy and the subsequent physical and mental stupor but by the horror and self-destruction which his inner voice not only informs him of but leads him to.

Whether Myshkin's epilepsy is organic or a pseudo-epilepsy born of hysteria, as Freud judged Dostoievsky's own, Dostoievsky's portrayal of Myshkin is amazingly successful in capturing the unity of the psychic and the physical—or rather their coexistence as aspects of some underlying reality. As a result, we can neither reduce the psychic aspect of Myshkin to the physical nor consider it without the latter. Myshkin's progress from the abyss back into the abyss lies outside the dichotomy between freedom and necessity. His whole person is involved; just that person, throughout its being, is sick. But his sickness, in its turn, is inseparable from that rare compassion for and intuitive understanding of other men in their depths that make him "a man" as no other figure in the book is. Myshkin's epilepsy, seen as a spiritual as well as a physical state of being, represents an unbearable inner tension that he carries like a tight knot at the center of his being, shut away from his intellectual convictions and his gentle nonjudging nature. His suffering is so great that he seeks out the sufferings of others, not just out of identification, but in desperate release of a tension which he cannot bear. This undirected release of energy necessarily results in self-destruction.

This pattern of passive identification with the sufferings of the demonic and tormented is clearest in the final interaction between Nastasya, Myshkin, and Rogozhin. Literally on the way to the church, Nastasya sees Rogozhin in the crowd, leaps out of the carriage, and begs him to "save her," just as she had run to Myshkin in the past to save her from Rogozhin. Myshkin sets out to St. Petersburg to search for her, and there Rogozhin takes him to his room, where he discovers the body of Nastasya, whom Rogozhin has murdered with the same knife with which he tried to kill Myshkin. Myshkin's reaction is a violent trembling that will not stop even after his terror has abated. Yet so far from judging Rogozhin or turning against him, he agrees that they will stay hidden with Nastasya's body, and he lies beside Rogozhin all night, as the latter requests. Rogozhin lapses into madness, and the terrified Myshkin, overcome with hopeless sadness and infinite anguish, declines into idiocy. Yet when people at last break in and find them, Myshkin is sitting beside the raving man, passing a trembling hand over his hair and cheeks every time he breaks into a scream or babble, "as though caressing and soothing him." The mad Rogozhin is also, to the terrified Myshkin, a child who must be comforted—a feeling so deeply rooted within him that it persists even when his own reason has deserted him.

The problematic nature of suffering in Dostoievsky that we have already encountered in *Notes from the Underground* is intensified rather than resolved in *The Idiot*. Myshkin's attraction to suffering is not only temptation; it is also demonic and absurd. It is an irresistible fascination with those interactions that will release the unbearable inner tension. It is also real compassion, but even this compassion is of a problematic nature. It is the hopeless attempt of the man who is himself unconfirmed to supply an absolute confirmation to others. It is his own lack of confirmation, in fact, that may, in part at least, impel him to confirm others. When Myshkin comforts first Nastasya and then later Rogozhin as if each were a little child, is he not comforting at the same time the "little child" at the center of his own being? The Underground Man's praise of suffering is questionable because of the masochism underlying it. Myshkin's suffering is questionable because, Christlike though it may at first appear, it means, in fact, not crucifixion of the body but the death of the self—something which Jesus never experienced even in his moments of temptation or agony or forsakenness. Myshkin has not denied his self: he has destroyed it. There is something genuinely terrifying about the ending of *The Idiot* that cannot be resolved or alleviated. Myshkin's suffering points us, in fact, to the dreadful question of whether a man can find the highest meaning in a lonely suffering in which he is not only abandoned but unconfirmed; whether he can continue *as a person* to follow a path in "fear and trembling" without the grace received from others that enables him to be human. Myshkin is not able to descend into the abyss of horror into which he is drawn without succumbing to the terror himself and experiencing, as a result, the most dreadful engulfment of his spiritual and physical self. "If Schneider himself had come from Switzerland to look at his former pupil and patient, . . . he would have flung up his hands in despair and would have said, . . . 'An idiot!' "

RASKOLNIKOV AND FATHER ZOSSIMA: THE PROBLEM OF GUILT

The relationship between alienation, inner division, and the problematic of guilt has already been starkly dramatized for us by Raskolnikov, Stavrogin, and Ivan. Raskolnikov gives us a special insight into the problematic of guilt, namely, the relationship between guilt as a feeling and guilt as a reality in the relations between men. Raskolnikov's crime is a perfect one. He leaves no clue, and if it were not for his inner compulsion and the clever cat-and-mouse game of Porfiry he might have gone scot-free. It is only his own attitude toward his crime which he cannot sustain. Although he remains convinced of his theory, he feels guilty, and this guilt is reinforced by his conviction that if he really were a Napoleon he would feel no guilt at all. When ordinary people confuse themselves with extraordinary ones and let their fancies run away with them, Raskolnikov tells Porfiry, they later chastise themselves with their own hands and "impose various public acts of penitence upon themselves" for "they are very conscientious." Seen from this standpoint, Raskolnikov's kissing the earth and begging its forgiveness and his later public confession are simply the product of psychological guilt. The crime of transgressing the taboo, whether understood in Freudian terms or otherwise, has been followed by the punishment of conscience, or the "super-ego." "It's a law of nature," says Raskolnikov.

Psychological guilt is a very poor basis for repentance, however, since it is all too often a neurotic guilt-feeling and may have less to do with the actual crime than with a longstanding psychological complex—the guilt felt because of desires that the child knows will be severely punished if expressed, desires that it has repressed but not extirpated. The crime itself, in fact, may have been committed to relieve an overwhelming feeling of guilt by doing something that one can actually recognize as wrong and receiving punishment for it. Put in another way, the tension between the two parts of Raskolnikov's character may have been so unbearable that he sought relief by giving the rebellious side full sway *in order that* the submissive side might then be able to take over in just retribution for the open transgression. Seen in these terms, the split between theoretical mind and ambivalent emotions takes on new meaning.

However, if we stop here, the preposterous possibility opens of a purely psychological cure which would remove Raskolnikov's neurotic guilt-feelings without entailing any acknowledgment on his part of the real guilt he has incurred in murdering Alyona and Lizaveta. In fact, such emotional repentance as Raskolnikov displays from time to time is not too far from just that—an emotional catharsis that has to do only with his own inner cycle of psychic states and not with the interhuman realm that he has violated.

Dostoievsky's attitude toward guilt moves closer to the interhuman in the teaching of Father Zossima that "each is responsible for all." " 'No one can judge a criminal, until he recognizes that he is just such a criminal as the man standing before him, and that he perhaps is more than all men to blame for that crime." If he had been righteous himself, there might have been no criminal. Instead of saying, "Evil environment is mighty, and we are lonely and helpless," one should make oneself responsible for all men's sins. "Each has the power to forgive all in the name of all," Dostoievsky has Zossima add in the sketches for the novel.[8] To remove a man's responsibility for his actions because of the conditioning influence of his environment is to deny his existence as a person. To place all the responsibility on the individual criminal is to deny the equally real responsibility that other persons and society have for what he has become. Neither the one nor the other affords a realistic understanding of guilt. To affirm that each is responsible for what he does and at the same time that each is responsible for all is not mere excess of humility but the most realistic way of describing personal responsibility.

[8] *Die Urgestalt,* pp. 310 f.

11

FATHERS AND SONS

THE RAW YOUTH AND THE BROTHERS KARAMAZOV

The theme of fathers and sons is central to *The Raw Youth* and *The Brothers Karamazov,* but it is also present in *Crime and Punishment* and *The Devils.* When Dostoievsky's father was murdered by serfs, Dostoievsky, who knew, like Ivan Karamazov, that he had wished for his father's death, was left with a burden of guilt. Hence his relationship was less to the absent father whom he longed for and sought, like Melville, or the present father whom he both loved and hated, like Kafka, than to the absent father toward whom he felt hatred and guilt—and also, no doubt, resentment that he was not the father whom he would have wished.

The result is a recurrent bifurcation of the father figure into a hated figure and a respected one, an image that repels and an image that attracts, or a problematic image and a clear one. Raskolnikov relates to both Porfiry and Svidrigailov as father figures; Stavrogin, who also lost his father when he was a child, to both Stepan Trofimovitch and Father Tikhon. In *The Raw Youth*, Arkady Dolgoruky is the bastard son of the nobleman Versilov while legally the son of his former serf Makar Ivanovitch. During the time that he grew up Arkady had almost no contact with the aloof and enigmatic Versilov. The plot of the novel is largely centered on his coming to live near Versilov and his attempts to penetrate the mystery and solve the riddle of this fascinating, divided man. His need to do this is the need to provide himself with a sense of patrimony. But it is even more clearly the search by an intense and troubled young man for an image of the father that will give him some guidance and sense of direction. Yet the deeper he enters into relationship with Versilov, the more baffled and put off he is by the contradictions in Versilov's character and in his relationship to the other members of the family. As a result, Arkady not only finds himself reacting against Versilov and periodically breaking with him "forever," but he also becomes aware of a very different quest in his soul: the quest for "seemliness."

This quest is answered by the man who is legally his father—Makar Ivanovitch. After relinquishing his wife to his master Versilov, Makar has spent twenty years as a pilgrim and now comes home to the family to die. Like his desire to become rich through self-control, Arkady's conversations with Makar Ivanovitch derive directly from Dostoievsky's plan for "The Life of a Great Sinner." This same discussion between Tikhon and the boy, Dostoievsky portrayed three times, in fact: in the meeting of Stavrogin and Father Tikhon, in the conversations of Arkady and the pilgrim Makar, and in the relationship of Alyosha to Father Zossima in *The Brothers Karamazov*. In the original drafts of this last novel, moreover, Dostoievsky even planned a meeting between the learned brother, Ivan, and the *staretz*, or holy man. Father Tikhon, the pilgrim Makar, and Father Zossima are successive attempts by Dostoievsky to represent the god-man, and in each case this god-man serves as father and image of man for a young man in the process of becoming.

The relation of father to sons is as central to *The Brothers Karamazov* as it is to *The Raw Youth*. Here too the father figure is bifurcated—into the depraved sensualist Fyodor Karamazov and the god-man Father Zossima, with the Grand Inquisitor as something of an ideal father figure to Ivan. Fyodor Karamazov, the father of Ivan, Dmitri, and Alyosha, characterizes himself aptly as "the old buffoon." He is sly, greedy, rapacious, sensual, dishonest, masochistic. It is significant that we are introduced to Fyodor at the same time as to the other father who dominates the book, the *staretz* Zossima, and that we meet them both at a gathering in the latter's cell in which all three sons are present and in which all the main, interrelated themes of the novel are brought out: Dmitri and the desire to murder the father, Ivan and the death of God, Alyosha and his holy Zossima. The two worlds of *The Brothers Karamazov* are the village and the monastery. These are the natural worlds of Russian rural life of that time, but, at the same time, they are also the symbolic worlds in which the drama unfolds. Fyodor Karamazov is the father of the village world and Father Zossima of the world of the monastery. In the confrontation of these two men in Father Zossima's cell these two worlds are also brought into confrontation. This meeting takes place in unadulterated fashion, not as that of the sacred and the secular, but as that of the sacred and the profane. Fyodor Karamazov plays out his buffoonery to the full and shows that he is able to bring a challenge of equal force, not in the traditional sense of evil opposing good, but in the much more dreadful sense of meaninglessness opposing meaning, directionlessness opposing direction, a mask opposing a person.

For fifty years past, we are told, no visitors have entered the cell of the present or former elders "without feelings of the profoundest veneration." Fyodor, in contrast, has no trace of respect or awe and obviously acts all the more shamefully and scandalously just because of where he is. When Father Zossima says to him, "Make yourself quite at home. And, above all, do not be so ashamed of yourself, for that is at the root of it all," Fyodor responds, "Quite at home? To be my natural self? Oh that is much too much . . . you'd better not invite me to be my natural self. Don't risk it. . . . I will not go so far as that myself." He manages at one and the same time to fling back into Father Zossima's face his kindness and yet to say the truth about himself. Father Zossima may be right in supposing that shame is at the root of Fyodor's buffoonery, but there is no evidence that he is right in assuming that Fyodor has a self to which he might appeal *through* the buffoonery. Fyodor cannot "be himself." All he has to present to other persons are his masks. What is behind them he cannot reveal, for it is not so much a self as a horrible vacuum. Every time he is caught out in some stupid lie, he makes a flourish of admitting it and telling the truth, only, of course, to invent a still more stupid lie. Lying has become so habitual to him that he no longer has any clear notion of the difference between honesty and dishonesty.

"Do you think I always lie and play the fool like this?" Fyodor asks Father Zossima when the latter leaves:

> "Believe me, I have been acting like this all the time on purpose to try you. I have been testing you all the time to see whether I could get on with you. *Is there room for my humility beside your pride?* " (50. Italics mine) [1]

Again Fyodor is lying, and again he is lying in order to exasperate—by contrasting himself with Zossima to the latter's disfavor, by scandalously inverting the ordinary conceptions of Christian humility, by flagrantly flouting the reverence in which Zossima and the disrepute in which he himself is held. But there is also truth in what he says. Zossima is not a proud man, but he is a man who has a self, who stands his ground, who, in claiming to live for some other purpose than women, brandy, and money, is claiming a great deal more from existence than Fyodor. Father Zossima is humble, but he is not, like the shameless Fyodor, fundamentally ashamed of himself. Here too the extremes meet. No writer has succeeded, as

---

[1] Dostoievsky, *The Brothers Karamazov.*

has Dostoievsky, in holding in tension the opposites, keeping them fully opposite yet never allowing them to separate entirely, confronting them in such a way as to suggest both their antagonism and their interpenetration.

Terrible as he is—and he is one of the most terrible and fully unsympathetic figures in literature—Fyodor Karamazov has a stature in some sense greater than anyone in the book. He is elemental passion, the base Karamazov energy and will to live. Out of him come all three of the sons, even Alyosha, and the cold, inhuman, emasculate bastard Smerdyakov, son of the idiot girl Stinking Lizaveta, whom Fyodor raped as the last stage of depraved sensuality. Fyodor has an energy which exceeds that of any of his sons, but in him it lies formless, stagnant, and corrupt. Although he neither rears his sons nor provides for them and even cheats them out of what is rightfully theirs, he bequeathes this elemental Karamazov passion to each of them and with it the abyss of shame and the sordid depths of existence. This heritage can either be overcome, as in Alyosha, through going the way of Father Zossima and the god-man, or affirmed, as in Ivan, through throwing off every demand that is placed on him and becoming himself the higher law, or acted out, as in Dmitri, by one minute following out a lofty impulse and the next minute a base one.

"Why is such a man alive? . . . Tell me, can he be allowed to go on defiling the earth?" cries Dmitri at the meeting at the monastery in which his father, instead of accepting the reconciliation with Dmitri that was to have been the purpose of the meeting, shamelessly baits him. "Listen, monks, to the parricide," Fyodor cries in response to Dmitri's words. Parricide, the murder of the father, is indeed the primary motif of the novel—a motif which involves in the closest possible way not only Dmitri, who almost murders his father, but Ivan, who wishes his father dead and half knowingly encourages the murder, and the bastard son Smerdyakov, who actually commits the murder.

Ivan, as Smerdyakov says, is more like the father than either of the other two brothers. On his intellectual side he remains grand and noble, bold and courageous, with only the loftiest passions admitted to his self-image. But the other side of him remains nasty and mean. One part of him identifies with his father and, for that reason, passionately hates him, while the other part of him is simply detached or at best emotional only in a lofty and abstract manner. While he likes to think that his whole being is placed at the service of his ideals, the truth is that the other, baser part of him uses both his ideals and his detachment in its own service.

The superior Ivan, who is above conventional morality, regards his brother Dmitri not merely as a "reptile," but as a "scoundrel," a "murderer," a "parricide," and a "monster" and constantly refers to him as such. When Katya says to Ivan, "It was you, you who persuaded me that he murdered his father. It's only you I believed!" and informs him she has been to see Smerdyakov, Ivan is unable to bear it and rushes off to see Smerdyakov to force him to tell what transpired between him and Katya. Ivan's irrational hatred of Dmitri is as much connected with his own feeling of guilt for desiring his father's death as his jealousy of his rival for Katya's love. At one point Alyosha says to Ivan that he has been sent by God to tell him that it was not he Ivan who killed his father even though he has several times told himself that he and no one else is the murderer. Trembling all over, Ivan accuses Alyosha of having been in his room and having seen his "visitor." Once earlier, when troubled by doubts, Ivan asks whether Alyosha had thought that he desired his father's death. When Alyosha softly answers, "I did think so," Ivan says, "It was so, too; it was not a matter of guessing." Yet when he goes to see Smerdyakov and the latter also says that Ivan desired his father's death, Ivan jumps up and strikes the sick man on the shoulder with all his might. After Alyosha confesses that he thought that Ivan wished Dmitri to kill their father and was even prepared to help bring it about, Ivan takes a dislike to Alyosha and avoids seeing him. Ivan is too honest to rationalize his actions altogether, but he is too shaky in his own self-image to bear the truth. A large part of Ivan's thought, in fact, from his saying that "all is lawful" to his sin-carrying and sinless Grand Inquisitor and his all-forgiving Christ, can be seen as arising from his inability to accept guilt and his need to sublimate his guilt-feeling into the semblance of noble motives which will satisfy his conscious mind.

In his relationship with Smerdyakov, Ivan's rationalizations gradually break up and he is left helpless before the onrush of negative and suppressed emotions which he cannot accept as part of his self-image. The sight of Smerdyakov, the very thought of him, arouses gloom, loathing, and a responsive anger in Ivan's heart as well as the question of how a contemptible creature like that could worry him so much. Smerdyakov puts premeditated questions to Ivan and acts as if there were some secret compact and understanding between them, and Ivan, in fact, is driven to fury by the way in which one part of him responds to Smerdyakov in a manner directly contrary to what he consciously intends and expects. At one moment he speaks softly and meekly, "realizing, with disgust, that he was feeling intense curiosity," while the next moment he passes from meekness to violence—a violence which is even more anger at himself than at Smerdyakov. Smerdyakov suggests that Ivan should go to Tchermashnya and not Moscow because Smerdyakov may have an epileptic fit, Dmitri may then kill Fyodor, and Ivan would have to return. Ivan is fully aware that his brother may kill his father and that he is leaving at the very point when he might stay to prevent it. He even accuses Smerdyakov of planning to fake an epileptic fit and of arranging the situation so that Dmitri can get in to kill Fyodor. Yet he turns back and announces to Smerdyakov that he is going away the next morning, and leaves laughing, "not from lightness of heart," but "as though in a nervous frenzy."

The dialectical and intellectual Ivan is so divided from that part of himself which has acted in response to Smerdyakov that he cannot, even now, admit to his conscious mind what has gone on. He keeps that part of himself which he does not care to recognize in a separate compartment, and he uses his hysteria as a relief from the nervous tension that comes from his inner division and from the fact that he is choosing to let things happen rather than make a real decision. Only in this murky, half-conscious world can he persist in this decisionless state of not taking responsibility and at the same time giving a negative "go ahead" to what one part of him, at least, must know is going on. That night he is fretted by all sorts of strange and surprising desires, including the impulse to go to the lodge and beat Smerdyakov, and is overcome at times by an "inexplicable humiliating terror, which he felt positively paralysed his physical powers." He goes out on the staircase twice, listening, not with hatred but with intense curiosity, to Fyodor Pavlovitch stirring below. "That 'action' all his life afterwards he called 'infamous,' and at the bottom of his heart, he thought of it as the basest action of his life."

As Ivan takes leave of Smerdyakov, the words "You see . . . I am going to Tchermashnya" break from him as if of themselves, followed by "a peculiar nervous laugh," to which Smerdyakov significantly responds, "It's always worth while speaking to a clever man." Ivan sets out feeling very happy, only to be gripped later by the memory of his final interchange with Smerdyakov. When he gets into the train for Moscow, he says to himself, "Away with the past. I've done with the old world forever, and may I have no news, no echo, from it," as if he had, in fact, succeeded in raising himself from the morass in which his petty emotions were involved and lifting himself to the grand level on which he might look forward to new life and new adventures. But this time he cannot even feel happy for a moment. "Instead of delight his soul was filled with such gloom, and his heart ached with such anguish, as he had never known in his life before." He thinks all night and in the morning rouses himself from his meditation with the exclamation, "I am a scoundrel."

After his father's murder, Ivan is three times impelled to visit Smerdyakov and question him. When he leaves Smerdyakov after the first interview, he says to him, "I shan't say anything of your being able to sham a fit, and I don't advise you to, either," to which Smerdyakov responds, "And if you don't speak of that, I shall say nothing of that conversation of ours at the gate." Yet Ivan is able to dismiss the insulting inference he senses in these words because of his relief at Smerdyakov's statement that Dmitri is the murderer. When he goes to see Smerdyakov a second time, he tells him, "I swear I did expect some wickedness from you . . . at the time," and Smerdyakov replies, "If you had a foreboding about me and yet went away, you as good as said to me, 'You can murder my parent, I won't hinder you!'" Nonetheless, after arriving at the obvious conclusion that Smerdyakov murdered Fyodor, Ivan accepts Smerdyakov's statement that he is innocent! He knows, as he later tells Katya, that "if it's not Dmitri, but Smerdyakov who's the murderer, I share his guilt, for I put him up to it." Still, no doubt for this very reason, he once more convinces himself of Dmitri's absolute guilt when Katya produces a letter from Dmitri declaring that he will murder his father if necessary in order to get the three thousand roubles that he owes her. He hates Dmitri as the murderer of his father, but he is impelled to plan his escape because of the burning and rankling sensation that he is "as much a murderer at heart."

When Ivan goes to visit Smerdyakov for the third time, prompted by Katya's statement, Smerdyakov greets him with open contempt and frenzied hatred and asserts with all explicitness, "*You* murdered him; you are the real murderer, I was only your instrument, your faithful servant, and it was following your words I did it." Something now gives way in Ivan's brain, he shudders all over, and gazes at Smerdyakov in a paroxysm of insane terror. He jumps up and stands stiff and straight against the wall. The trembling Ivan is forced to hear all the facts, including the part his silence played in indicating eagerness and consent. Yet even in this brutal form, the facts cannot altogether penetrate the consciousness of the man who has resisted looking at them for so long.

"God sees," Ivan raised his hand, "perhaps I, too, was guilty; perhaps I really had a secret desire for my father's . . . death, but I swear I was not as guilty as you think and perhaps I didn't urge you on at all. No, no, I didn't urge you on!" (767)

Ivan insists that he will testify at the trial the next day, both against Smerdyakov and himself, but Smerdyakov confidently retorts that he will be too ashamed to do so, that he is too "clever"—too fond of money, prestige, women, and, above all, his own freedom and comfort: "You are like Fyodor Pavlovitch, you are more like him than any of his children; you've the same soul as he had." Smerdyakov has followed out Ivan's dictum that "all things are lawful," only to discover that Ivan is no "higher man" himself, that he does not have the courage of his convictions, that he is cowardly and irresolute in action, no matter how bold he is in theory. In Raskolnikov the theory and the action are combined in one figure. Raskolnikov, as a result, is not so painfully and irrevocably divided as Ivan: he has more chance of regeneration if he faces the consequences of his actions and accepts responsibility for them. But Smerdyakov is a double for Ivan who carries out his ideas and desires and allows him to escape responsibility for them. When Smerdyakov realizes that Ivan, "who used to be so bold" "won't dare to do anything," he is completely disillusioned and no longer even desires the new life he has planned for himself in Paris with the three thousand roubles he has stolen from Fyodor. He gives the money to Ivan and, unable to live without his idol, hangs himself.

Despite his resolve to make an end of the wavering that has so tortured him of late, Ivan is destined to keep on wavering unto the end. Why, we may ask, cannot Ivan either accept Alyosha's assurances that he is *not* the murderer or accept Smerdyakov's assertion that he is? The answer is twofold and both parts are an expression of his wavering. Because of his ambivalent attitude to the crime before it was committed, he is neither simply innocent nor simply guilty. He recognizes that he wanted his father's murder and, if he were able to be more honest still, he would recognize how one part of him tacitly encouraged Smerdyakov. Yet what Smerdyakov cannot grasp until the end is that Ivan is not a whole person and does not act as one. He is guilty, but not in the clear-cut way of an intentional murderer.

Ivan is unable to cast off his guilt by identifying his self with his *conscious* self only or to accept his guilt by identifying himself with that other, surprising self that emerges into thought and action before his eyes. Ivan cannot bear to look into the foul pit of his own inner life and neither can he turn away from it. Versilov's theory of the second self applies equally to Ivan and with it the ambiguities of responsible freedom and impersonal compulsion that Versilov does not see but his son Dolgoruky does. On the way to Smerdyakov's, Ivan knocks down a drunken peasant and leaves him in the snow with the reflection that he will freeze to death. On the way back, he runs into the peasant still lying there and gets him to a doctor. "If I had not taken my decision so firmly for to-morrow," he reflects with satisfaction, "I should not have stayed a whole hour to look after the peasant." He thinks at the same time, and with still greater satisfaction, that he is quite capable of watching himself, though the doctors have decided that he is going out of his mind. As he reaches his house he stops short and asks himself whether he ought not to go at once to the prosecutor and tell him everything, but instead he goes into his house, whispering to himself, "Everything together to-morrow!" "And strange to say," his author reports, "almost all his gladness and self-satisfaction passed in one instant." This is the last moment in which it is really possible for Ivan to act, and one part of him knows this all too well. Whatever he may say about his firm resolution and his clear mind, when he decides to go into the house again, one part of him knows that the old rationalizations have again won out, that Smerdyakov is right, that he is too self-entangled and self-preoccupied to use what Smerdyakov has told him in any other context than that of his own inner dialogue.

Torn apart by his inner conflict he is gradually and inexorably submerged in hallucination and delirium. Unable to use the shock of Smerdyakov's revelation to break out of his isolation and save his innocent brother, Ivan finds himself in dialogue with his own "second self," which has become independent and personified as his devil. Ivan's devil is a "poor relation" bearing "every appearance of gentility on straitened means"—the fashions of a few years back, an ingratiating desire to please, the spacious dignity of a hanger-on who is received in the best society but never honored.

The hell into which Ivan now finds himself plunged is that of the mirrored images of the self—a mirrored self which he at once recognizes and denies, for even as it speaks to him in his own outworn thoughts and stories, it shatters the ideal self-image that had protected him from facing the malignant reality which it covered over. Ivan is desperately anxious to prove that his devil is but a projection of his own imagination. He wants above all to prove to himself that he is still sane, that he retains some shred of detached perspective to which to cling while the dark and fearful torrents of his inner world rush over him. Yet, like Stavrogin, his pride is wounded because his devil has appeared to him in such a shabby, uninteresting form. He would like to think of his own evil as something grand and romantic, and instead he finds it merely disgusting and mediocre.

"Moderate your expectations, don't demand of me 'everything great and noble' and you'll see how well we shall get on," said the gentleman impressively. "You are really angry with me for not having appeared to you in a red glow, with thunder and lightning, with scorched wings, but have shown myself in such a modest form. You are wounded, in the first place, in your aesthetic feelings, and secondly, in your pride. How could such a vulgar devil visit such a great man as you!" (786)

Ivan complains that his devil chooses only his worst and most stupid thoughts to repeat back to him as if they were something new and splendid. "You are the incarnation of myself," Ivan says, "but only of one side of me . . . of my thoughts and feelings, but only the nastiest and stupidest of them." "Scolding you, I scold myself," he goes on, yet adds, "You are stupid and vulgar . . . No, I can't put up with you!" Ivan's devil forces him to see and smell the rotting organs beneath the fair exterior, the ugly emotions and the stupid, petty vanity beneath the fine phrases and the noble sentiments. This is a new and horrible image of man: "*Satan sum et nihil humanum a me alienum puto.*"

As little as Ivan can identify this devil with his "I," even less can he push him aside. The more he tries to deny his existence, the more he falls into the contradiction of speaking to him as a "Thou." Ivan's devil claims that one can believe in devils without believing in God. Ivan's devil is, in fact, the obverse of the God Ivan denies. His inability to say "Thou" not only to God, but in the end to any being outside him, condemns him all the more helplessly to say it to the devil within him. The dialectical, intellectual Ivan has reached the point of actual as well as philosophical solipsism—of an absolutization of consciousness and the self—and his devil is as much of a solipsist as himself.

"Is there a God or not?" Ivan cried with the same savage intensity.

". . . My dear fellow, upon my word I don't know. There! I've said it now!"

". . . No, you are not some one apart, you are myself . . ."

"Well, if you like, I have the same philosophy as you, . . . *Je pense, donc je suis,* I know that for a fact, all the rest, all these worlds, God and even Satan—all that is not proved, to my mind. Does all that exist of itself, or is it only an emanation of myself, a logical development of my ego which alone has existence for ever." (781)

Here the emphasis on pure consciousness of the Underground Man has reached its final term, its ultimate Pyrrhic victory, and with it that modern philosophy from Descartes to Kant which thought to build the new world of science and man on the triumph of rational subjectivity freed from any but a secondary and nonmutual knowledge of the reality of "other" persons. So far from preserving the self, as the Underground Man hopes, pure consciousness destroys the self by abandoning it to a hopeless inner division—the "dialogue" between the "selves" of the divided man.

From this inner division there lies no way forward for Ivan. Even his testimony at the trial is nothing but the final, futile gesture of the divided man. He is so far gone in his mental illness that his action is in no sense the product of a real decision or the action of a whole man. It has no redeeming force through which we could claim that Ivan has found personal integrity. When he first goes up to testify, he declares he has nothing to say and asks to be excused. Then as he leaves the court, he turns back, but only to combine an exaggerated statement of his own guilt—"I am not mad. I am only a murderer"—with a diatribe against the audience:

> "It was he, not my brother, killed our father. He murdered him and I incited him to do it . . . Who doesn't desire his father's death?"
>
> "Are you in your right mind?" broke involuntarily from the President.
>
> "I should think I am in my right mind . . . in the same nasty mind as all of you . . . as all these . . . ugly faces." He turned suddenly to the audience. "My father has been murdered and they pretend they are horrified," he snarled, with furious contempt. "They keep up the sham with one another. Liars! They all desire the death of their fathers. One reptile devours another." (834)

We have heard these accents before, in Raskolnikov's anger at society shortly before he gives himself up. Though they may suggest a tormented honesty—an honesty much tarnished by Ivan's failure to go to the prosecutor while still in his right mind and by his almost not testifying at all—they hardly indicate any real decision to take on himself the suffering that one part of him feels he deserves. Ivan is not Smerdyakov, able to act without conscience and without guilt, but neither is he Dmitri, ready to receive the suffering that comes to him as a way of working out of dividedness and guilt to some sort of personal wholeness. After the conflict within him between man-god and lackey devil has wreaked its havoc, Ivan is left less rebel than simply divided man. The bifurcation of the father figure means the bifurcation of the son.

At first glance, the problematic aspects of Dmitri are identical with those of Ivan: his divided nature, his relationship to his father Fyodor, his relationship to Katya, and his attempts to overcome his inner division and become a new man. Yet in its essence the problematic of Dmitri is as different from that of Ivan as the passionate and Dionysian nature of the one is from the intellectual and dialectical nature of the other.

Dostoievsky describes Dmitri as a young man of twenty-eight, "of medium height and agreeable countenance," who looks older than his years. Despite physical strength, his cheeks are hollow and unhealthily sallow. His pensive and sullen eyes are combined with a mirthful and light-hearted laugh, all of which add up to a contradictory and irascible nature, "an unstable and unbalanced mind." Dmitri himself describes his contradictory nature to Alyosha in the chapter "Confession of a Passionate Heart—in Verse." Dmitri starts like Ivan from the fact of man's suffering, but unlike Ivan he remains aware of his own suffering and sees his personal degradation as inseparable from that of man:

> "Don't think I'm only a brute in an officer's uniform, wallowing in dirt and drink. I hardly think of anything but of that degraded man—if only I'm not lying. I pray God I'm not lying and showing off. I think about that man because I am that man myself." (126)

Dmitri's suffering is neither purely masochistic nor purely ennobling, but both at once, divided and problematic like himself. He asks Alyosha not to identify him with how he appears and how he acts. At the same time he knows that he cannot identify himself simply with what he would like to be. In this sense Dmitri's inner division is very different from Ivan's. Ivan identifies what he is with his ideal of himself and tries to push the other, considerably less than ideal part of himself out of his awareness. Dmitri is all too conscious that what he is contrasts greatly with his ideal, yet he cannot give up the ideal and with it the feeling that one part of himself belongs to that ideal through this very refusal to abandon it. At the same time, he knows that his devotion to the ideal is not altogether an honest one, that it is sometimes sentimental and insincere—"if only I'm not lying . . . and showing off."

Here is the fruit of Fyodor, the "father of lies." Fyodor is never sincere. His lie is a lie which knows itself as a lie. Dmitri is always sincere—at the moment of his feeling and acting. But since the next moment he will feel or act in a completely different and even contradictory way, he is forced to doubt his own sincerity. We must distinguish here, in fact, between two very different meanings of sincerity, one of which has to do with the relationship of the person to his feelings and actions at any given moment, the other to the relationship of the person to his feelings and actions over a period of time. Fyodor's relationship to his thoughts and feelings at any moment is a distorted and twisted one, and his communications to others are never direct and whole-hearted. In this sense too, perhaps, the dialectical Ivan is closer to Fyodor than the other brothers. Dmitri's relationship to his thoughts and feelings is direct and his communications whole-hearted. He is not a liar or a hypocrite. Yet if we mean by sincerity any sort of personal continuity and consistency— what enables a man to stand behind his promise and enables someone else to put faith in him—Dmitri is not sincere. His "I," his self, is in danger of deteriorating into a succession of feeling-states rather than being a true person who is the *subject* of his experiences not their sum.

This type of insincerity would be no problem for Dmitri if he did not cling to the ideal and with it the never quite extinguished hope that he will reform and begin a new life. He does not reform, however, and at the same time he does not give up the tension between the real and the ideal. Unlike Ivan, he does not set before himself the choice between two images of himself, one ideal and one real, but proudly constructs out of this very tension his own image, and the image of the Karamazovs.

"Has it reformed me? Never! For I'm a Karamazov. For when I do leap into the pit, I go headlong with my heels up, and am pleased to be falling in that degrading attitude and pride myself upon it. And in the very depths of that degradation I begin a hymn of praise. Let me be accursed. Let me be vile and base, only let me kiss the hem of the veil in which my God is shrouded. Though I may be following the devil, I am Thy son, O Lord, and

I love Thee, and I feel the joy without which the world cannot stand." (126)

It is not necessary, apparently, to be moving toward God to be God's son. On the contrary, one may be following the devil with abandon and still be clinging to the love of God. The further one falls downward, in fact, the more one may love God upward. This is a disclaimer of the ordinary conception of personality and of integrity which judges a man by what he does—"By their fruits ye shall know them"—in favor of one which sees the personality not as a direction but as a totality encompassing the opposites.

Dmitri's "confession" is a Dionysian affirmation of the earth, of wine, of joy, of emotional extremes, abundantly illustrated with quotes from Schiller's "Ode to Joy." But more than this, it is an affirmation of what both the prosecutor and the defense attorney at Dmitri's trial later call the two-sided Karamazov nature, "fluctuating between two extremes"—the same combination of filth and degradation with a thirst for "the sublime and the beautiful" that we have already seen in the Underground Man. In the Karamazovs this degradation is connected with sensual lust—the true heritage of Father Fyodor. " 'To angels—visions of God's throne, to insects —sensual lust,' " Dmitri quotes, and he applies the latter not only to himself, but to Alyosha: "We Karamazovs are such insects, and, angel as you are, that insect lives in you, too, and will stir up a tempest in your blood." What Dmitri finds in himself and in man is the simultaneous and conscious coexistence of opposites in which "the boundaries meet and all contradictions exist side by side." "I cannot bear the thought that a man begins with the ideal of the Madonna and ends with the ideal of Sodom," says Dmitri. Yet in contrast to Melville, who sees man's innocence as an "insular Tahiti" to which one can never return once one has pushed off from it, Dmitri sees man as preserving unsullied, in the midst of the fire of passion, the "ideal of the Madonna" in his soul, "and his heart may be on fire with that ideal, genuinely on fire, just as in his days of youth and innocence."

Beauty does not dwell simply with the pure ideal of the

Madonna, but with the profane. At the heart of the Dostoievskian man, says Berdyaev, is not a unity but an antinomy.
To Dmitri the Karamazovs are man, the contradictory attitude toward beauty the antinomy at the heart of man.

> "Man is broad, too broad, indeed. I'd have him nar-
> rower. . . . What to the mind is shameful is beauty and
> nothing else to the heart. Is there beauty in Sodom? Be-
> lieve me, that for the immense mass of mankind beauty is
> found in Sodom. . . . The awful thing is that beauty is
> mysterious as well as terrible. God and the devil are
> fighting there and the battlefield is the heart of man."
> (127)

Dmitri's image of man is not a dialectical one, like Ivan's, an
alternation between extremes. It is, rather, a *coincidentia
oppositorum,* and this *coincidentia oppositorum,* as Dmitri
has portrayed it, is perhaps the broadest and most adequate
statement of Dostoievsky's own image of man in all his contradictory totality.

In the next chapter, "The Confession of a Passionate Heart
—in Anecdote," Dmitri reveals himself to Alyosha as "a bug,"
"a noxious insect," given over to lust and sadism in a manner
not unlike Stavrogin. In the original sketches of the novel, in
fact, Dmitri was to have committed Stavrogin's crime of the
rape of a young girl. In Dmitri, however, these traits are presented as past minor incidents and present major possibilities
rather than as central actualities. We begin with Dmitri as a
divided man, but not as one burdened with a weight of guilt
comparable to that of Raskolnikov or of Stavrogin.

What he is burdened with, however, is a hatred of his father that stops just short of murder. The crux of Dmitri's conflict with his father is his passion for Grushenka. Dmitri's
rivalry with his father seems to be almost as much cause as
effect of this passion and in any case something stronger than
any mere jealousy of a rival. Dmitri himself is aware that at
the root of his hatred of his father is not their rivalry for
Grushenka nor even the money that Dmitri feels is rightfully
his. "Perhaps I shan't kill him, and perhaps I shall," he says
to Alyosha. "I'm afraid that he will suddenly become so loath-

some to me with his face at that moment. I hate his ugly throat, his nose, his eyes, his shameless snigger. I feel a physical repulsion. That's what I'm afraid of. That's what may be too much for me." Dmitri's outcry at the monastery, "Can he be allowed to go on defiling the earth?" has almost the same tone of physical repulsion. When Grushenka tells that her first lover, the Pole, has returned and may send for her, Dmitri is so preoccupied by "all the hideous horror of his struggle with his own father for this woman" that he is not even jealous of the Pole and never gives the matter any thought. When Grushenka gives him the slip in order to go meet her Pole, Dmitri assumes without further inquiry that she must have gone to his father and rushes there. In answer to the secret signal that Smerdyakov has told Dmitri, the old man comes to the window and calls Grushenka, thus proving that Grushenka is not there. Yet at this point Dmitri comes close to killing his father, out of sheer repulsion, divorced from any feeling about Grushenka.

> The old man's profile that he loathed so, his pendant Adam's apple, his hooked nose, his lips that smiled in greedy expectation were all brightly lighted up by the slanting lamplight . . . A horrible fury of hatred suddenly surged up in Mitya's heart, "There he was, his rival, the man who had tormented him, had ruined his life!" (476)

Dmitri's bitterness against his father is clearly not just a matter of his present rivalry for Grushenka. Like Ivan, Dmitri desires his father's death, and he desires it not because of what his father *is* doing to him or may do to him but because of what he has done to him—"the man who had tormented him, had ruined his life."

Why is this sense of physical repulsion so strong and so unbearable for Dmitri? We can partly guess the answer from the fact that he so often refers to himself as a "noxious insect" and that he contrasts this idea of himself with the ideal he would like to attain. His problem is not simply an Oedipus complex, but the relation of his self-image to the image of the father who should have, but has not provided him with an image of man. This problem is shared by Ivan too, who constructs in his Inquisitor a noble father image to replace his actual father whom he detests but knows he is like. For both Dmitri and Ivan, Fyodor is himself the embodiment of the devil, the negative image of man. Fyodor has accepted and affirmed the "noxious insect," the Karamazov baseness, and has become this insect entirely, whereas Dmitri and Ivan, each in his own way, remains in desperate conflict with it. Even Alyosha, who alone seems to have no feeling of repulsion for his father, has transferred his father image and image of man almost entirely to Father Zossima. From all that we can see, Alyosha appears as unmoved by the death of his own father as he is moved by the death of his beloved *staretz*.

Dmitri himself makes explicit this link between his ideal self-image and the hated image presented him by his father. During the preliminary investigation before the trial he stresses repeatedly his feeling that he is "a man of the highest honour" who "has always been, and still is, honourable at bottom, in his inner being" even though all his life he has "been doing filthy things." The man of honor is Dmitri's image of man, and, no matter how he acts, he cannot see himself as less than a man of honor so long as he clings to his image. It is no accident that immediately following this statement about himself he thinks of his father—his negative image of man.

> His brows contracted with pain. "You see, gentlemen, I couldn't bear the look of him, there was something in him ignoble, impudent, trampling on everything sacred, something sneering and irreverent, loathsome, loathsome." (561)

Unlike Ivan, however, Dmitri actually accepts the fact that what he hated was the threat to his own self-image that arose from the part of him which was like his father.

> "Now that he's dead I feel differently . . . I wish I hadn't hated him so. . . . I'm not much good myself, I'm not very beautiful, so I had no right to consider him repulsive. . . ." Saying this Mitya became very mournful. (561 f.)

Although Dmitri has done far worse things than Ivan and has come close to murdering his father, he is not only a more sympathetic character than Ivan but is actually less responsible for his father's death. All four brothers have a share in Fyodor's death: Smerdyakov has committed the murder, Ivan has half-consciously permitted and incited him to do it, Alyosha has forgotten about his brother Dmitri at the very time when Father Zossima has sent him to be near him, and Dmitri has provided the opportunity for Smerdyakov to murder Fyodor by coming himself with almost the same intent. Dmitri actually might have killed his father in a moment of rage, and Ivan would never have done so. Yet Dmitri is "spared by God" from murdering Fyodor, while Ivan has acted half-knowingly as an essential link in the chain of events.

Dmitri's honesty does not preclude a childlike naïveté which amounts, at times, to an incredible capacity for self-deception. He expects "a new life to begin at once" if only Grushenka will say to him, "Take me, I'm yours for ever." Once they are married, thinks this "very simple-hearted man," "it would mean the beginning of a new Grushenka and a new Dmitri, free from every vice. They would forgive one another and would begin their lives afresh." A more serious possibility of a new life arises for Dmitri after his father's murder. Dmitri confesses to Alyosha that since a remarkable dream in which his heart was flooded by pity for a suffering "babe," a hymn has been born in his heart, and it is for this "hymn" that he is going to accept twenty years in the Siberian mines. He will be a new "Underground Man" who will not seek to escape from the underground, like Raskolnikov, but to redeem it.

> "A new man has risen up in me. He was hidden in me, but would never have come to the surface, if it hadn't been for this blow from heaven. I am afraid! . . . afraid that that new man may leave me. Even there, in the mines, underground, I may find a human heart in another convict and murderer by my side . . . and at last bring up from the dark depths . . . a feeling, suffering crea-

ture . . . It's for the babe I'm going. Because we are all responsible for all. For all the 'babes,' for there are big children as well as little children. All are 'babes.' I go for all, because some one must go for all." (719 f.)

"If they drive God from the earth, we shall shelter Him underground," says Dmitri. His "new man" is thus the opposite of Ivan's—the man-god for whom "all things are lawful." "They have this social justification for every nasty thing they do," says Dmitri of the "clever" man who substitutes chemistry for God and whom he calls Claude Bernard after the famous nineteenth-century scientist. When it comes to the question of whether he will escape, Dmitri is not only afraid that *his* new man may leave him, but also that the *other* "new man" may get the upper hand. "After the trial . . . you'll find that new man in yourself and he will decide," says Alyosha. "A new man, or a Bernard who'll decide *à la* Bernard," replies Dmitri with a bitter grin, "for I believe I'm a contemptible Bernard myself."

To what extent, in fact, does Dmitri's "new man" mean a real change, to what extent only an apocalyptic emotion at a moment of extreme crisis? When Dmitri's former fiancée Katya comes to see Alyosha after the trial to arrange Dmitri's escape, Alyosha tells her that Dmitri will be unhappy all his life if she does not go to see him. Dmitri's desperate need for the woman who has so hated and betrayed him and because of whom he has been condemned must cause us to wonder whether he has liberated himself from the inner conflict that held him to her in the past. Alyosha assures the jealous Grushenka that Dmitri loves only her. But Dmitri says of himself, "I want Katya! Do I understand what I want? It's the headstrong, evil Karamazov spirit! No, I am not fit for suffering. I am a scoundrel." The interchange between Dmitri and Katya when she does come makes us wonder still more. Katya says that she has come to him " 'to tell you again that you are my god, my joy, to tell you that I love you madly. . . . Love me, love me all your life,' she cried with a quiver almost of menace in her voice." Dmitri replies to this hysterical, hostile profession of love in kind. He tells Katya that he loved her even

when she betrayed him at the trial and that "I shall love you
. . . All my life!" The author himself provides the fitting
commentary: "So they murmured to one another frantic
words, almost meaningless, perhaps not even true, but at that
moment it was all true, and they both believed what they said
implicitly."

This final picture of Dmitri is a dismaying one which might
well lead us to conclude that the "old Mitya" has reasserted
himself entirely. The ambivalent relationship with Katya and
the emotional "sincerity" of the moment that practically
amounts to a constitutional insincerity are compelling evidence that even intense suffering and an overwhelming emotional crisis have not effected a permanent transformation in
Dmitri's contradictory Karamazov nature.

A tempered, but by no means a contrary conclusion is offered us by Dmitri's conversation with Alyosha about his escape. Already before his trial Dmitri's "hymn" is coupled with
the "secret" that Ivan is arranging his escape. "I can't live without Grusha!" he cries. "And without Grusha what should I do
there underground . . . I should only smash my skull with
the hammer!" But if I go to America, Dmitri asks himself,
"what becomes of our hymn from underground? . . . I should
have run away from suffering. . . . I have a way of salvation
and I turn my back on it." Even with Grushenka, Dmitri is
not ready for suffering. "If they beat me on the way out there,
I won't submit to it," he tells Alyosha after his condemnation.
"I shall kill some one and shall be shot for it. And this will be
going on for twenty years!" With Grusha "I would bear anything," he adds, only to qualify even this statement by "anything except blows." "I shall escape, that was settled apart
from you. . . . Could Mitya Karamazov do anything but run
away? . . . But I shall condemn myself and will pray for my
sin for ever," he adds. "That's how the Jesuits talk, isn't it?" he
asks, and Alyosha gently smiles, "Yes." Dmitri is no "Jesuit,"
any more than he is a "Bernard," but neither is he the "new
man" who will sing a hymn from the underground!

In the end it is not Dmitri but Alyosha who has the more
realistic view of what Dmitri is and of what he can become.
Both Dmitri's strength and his weakness lie in his passion, for

while this passion lifts him to moments of greatness, he is incapable of directing it into the ordinary work of life. He does not rebel on principle, like Ivan, but from his nature itself, and he cannot overcome this nature even when he wholeheartedly wants to become a new man. He wants an apocalyptic transformation of reality from suffering into joy, but human suffering is an obdurate and resistant reality that cannot be overcome by emotion alone. He wants a once-and-for-all conversion from his "old man" to his "new man," but his "old man," too, is stubborn and will not yield even in the face of the most sincere and intense feeling. The real choice for Dmitri is not between the old man and the new but between losing sight of his "new man" once his crisis is over and clinging to it as an image of man that will help him to grow like it. It is this choice that Alyosha puts before him:

"You are not ready . . . you are innocent, and such a cross is too much for you. You wanted to make yourself another man by suffering. I say, only remember that other man always, all your life and wherever you go; and that will be enough for you. Your refusal of that great cross will only serve to make you feel all your life an even greater duty, and that constant feeling will do more to make you a new man, perhaps, than if you went there. For there you would not endure it and would repine, and perhaps at last would say: 'I am quits.' . . . Such heavy burdens are not for all men." (925)

Dmitri's refusal of the cross of Siberia will not in itself keep his image of the new man before him, any more than that image will in itself enable him to become a new man. All we can say with assurance is that there has been some change in Dmitri, that he has been tempered and chastened, and that he has the possibility of a new life with Grushenka in America. We cannot say that the coincidence of opposites has been transformed into a way, the tension between extremes into a directed passion.

Dostoievsky describes Alyosha, the youngest of the three legitimate sons of Fyodor Karamazov, as habitually silent through inner preoccupation, yet so fond of people that throughout his life he puts implicit trust in them. He is "an early lover of humanity" who adopts the monastic life "as the ideal escape for his soul struggling from the darkness of worldly wickedness to the light of love." The main attraction of the monastery is the presence of Father Zossima, yet Alyosha's relation to his father, according to the author, is "without the slightest sign of contempt or condemnation" and Fyodor himself "felt a real and deep affection" for Alyosha, "such as he had never been capable of feeling for any one before." In contrast not only to his brothers but to most other human beings, "Alyosha was certain that no one in the whole world ever would want to hurt him, and, what is more, he knew that no one could hurt him." Nor is this remarkable trust disappointed. From his earliest childhood everyone loved Alyosha wherever he went, and in the course of the book, no one, with the exception of the opportunist Rakitin, wishes to hurt him. "No one ever looked on him as a simpleton or a naïve person." Rather, they sensed that he never judges and condemns others or is ever surprised or frightened by them, no matter how much they may grieve him. "Here is perhaps the one man in the world," Miusov says of Alyosha, "whom you might leave with a penny, in the centre of an unknown town of a million inhabitants, and he would not come to harm." People would take him in and shelter him and would consider it a pleasure to do so.

In Alyosha, Dostoievsky seems to have created the good man whom he had long had in mind—the "god-man," loving, forgiving, courageous, simple, and vitally real. Yet in Alyosha too there is something problematic, hints of which are strewn throughout the book. Although we are twice told that Alyosha never judges or blames his father, in the scene in the monastery where Fyodor plays the buffoon, Alyosha is ashamed that his family appears so in the presence of his beloved elder, and the blood rushes to his cheeks. His father, in fact, undoubtedly has much to do with his seeking a refuge from "worldly wickedness" and with his search for an ideal image of man in Father Zossima. An equally important element in his problematic heritage is his mother. Although she died when he was four, he remembers her all of his life, her face "frenzied but beautiful," sobbing hysterically and snatching him up to hold him before the ikon of the Mother of God, to whom she prayed "as though to put him under the Mother's protection." When Fyodor recounts how he spat on her holy image of the Mother and how his meek Sonia "wrung her hands, hid her face in them, began trembling all over and fell on the floor," Alyosha has the precise reaction that Fyodor describes in "the crazy woman": "He jumped up from his seat . . . wrung his hands, hid his face in them, and fell back in his chair, shaking all over in an hysterical paroxysm of sudden violent, silent weeping."

It is evident that Alyosha has inherited a certain contradiction from the strange relationship between his lascivious father and his crazy, saintly mother. This contradiction expresses itself in his desire to flee from the evil of the world to the monastery and in the "wild fanatical modesty and chastity" which in his childhood made him put his fingers in his ears and try to hide when the other boys used "dirty" expressions and talked of sex. If Alyosha relives the sufferings of his pure mother and her violation by his lewd father, he has also inherited something of his father's crude sensual nature, the "insect lust" of which Dmitri speaks, and this is what he is trying to flee from. "You're a Karamazov too, you know!" Rakitin says to Alyosha. "In your family sensuality is carried to a disease."

> "Oh, you virgin soul! You're a quiet one, Alyosha, you're a saint, I know, but the devil only knows what you've thought about, and what you know already! You are pure, but you've been down into the depths. . . . You're a sensualist from your father, a crazy saint from your mother." (91)

Alyosha himself acknowledges the insect lust in his own blood: "The ladder's the same," he tells Dmitri. "I'm at the bottom step, and you're above, somewhere about the thirteenth. . . . Any one on the bottom step is bound to go up to the top one." To little Lise, the sixteen-year-old cripple to whom he becomes temporarily engaged, Alyosha says that he has "a sordid soul" and that when he leaves the monastery for the world, as Father Zossima has bid him, he wants to marry her because she is more light-hearted and innocent than he.

> "My brothers are destroying themselves, . . . my father, too. And they are destroying others with them. It's 'the primitive force of the Karamazovs,' as Father Paissy said the other day, a crude, unbridled, earthly force. Does the spirit of God move above that force? Even that I don't know. I only know that I, too, am a Karamazov. . . . Me a monk, a monk!" (262)

In this speech Alyosha makes manifest the dualism within his soul, the dualism represented by his father and his mother or, equally clearly, by his two fathers—the physical one who represents the "crude, unbridled, earthly force" and the spiritual one who stands as his opposite. And because he does not know whether there is any real connection between these two antagonistic elements, whether the spirit of God moves above this earthly sensuality, he even observes to Lise that perhaps he does not believe in God. "There was something too mysterious, too subjective in these last words of his, perhaps obscure to himself, but yet torturing him." Later, when Lise recounts to Alyosha a dream in which she drives away a host of devils by crossing herself, brings them down upon her by reviling God aloud, and escapes once more through crossing herself, Alyosha tells her that he has had the same dream. In the crisis that Alyosha goes through after the death of Zossima, his fear of sensual lust and his wavering trust in God are again closely intertwined.

To understand this crisis we must look more closely at the role that Father Zossima plays as the image of man for Alyosha. Alyosha's image of Zossima includes some of the traits of Ivan's Grand Inquisitor and of his Christ. He is the one person who is holy and exalted, the exception to the "sin, injustice, and temptation" that otherwise prevail.

> "Oh! he understood that for the humble soul of the Russian peasant, worn out by grief and toil, and still more by the everlasting injustice and everlasting sin, his own and the world's, it was the greatest need and comfort to

find some one or something holy to fall down before and worship." (30)

Thus, although Zossima is the exception for Alyosha, the man who compensates others for their misery and provides them with someone to worship, he also is an example for all men, if a solitary one. "He is holy. He carries in his heart the secret of renewal for all: that power which will, at last, establish truth on the earth, and all men will be holy and love one another." With the possible exception of Alyosha's mother, Father Zossima constitutes the greatest single influence in Alyosha's life. It is through him that Alyosha's natural grace is given the strength and resiliency of religious insight and is consciously directed to a life of service in the world. It is only at Zossima's express command, indeed, that Alyosha returns to the world, and his life in the world is founded upon Zossima's teachings.

At the point of his greatest despair over Father Zossima's death Alyosha allows himself to be taken off by Rakitin to Grushenka, who has promised Rakitin twenty-five roubles if he will bring Alyosha to see her. In the touching and humorous scene that follows, Alyosha expects to abandon himself entirely to the devil, and Grushenka, in fact, confesses that she had wanted to seduce him. Yet when they actually meet, she neither wants to corrupt him nor does he feel anything but brotherly love for her, even when she sits on his lap. Although Alyosha's temptation thus turns out to be an unreal one, the form that it takes is nonetheless significant. In going to face Grushenka he turns away, symbolically, from his own fanatical chastity to the profanation of sex, from the purity of his saintly mother to woman as prostitute. Grushenka, the fallen woman, here stands in contrast to Sonia, the meek woman, whereas in *Crime and Punishment* the two are bound together in the figure of Sonia. It is unchastity, impurity, which has symbolized more than anything the corrupt and evil world from which Alyosha has fled, and it is the "insect lust" in his own blood which has stood at the heart of his problematic and led him to doubt whether he believes in God.

Alyosha's great grief, says his author, provides him with

"the strongest armour to protect him from every lust and temptation" while not shutting out "a feeling of the intensest and purest interest" which is aroused in him by the formerly dreaded woman sitting on his lap. In the original sketches, however, the temptation is much more real: "Lust for Grushenka had gnawed at him for days before!" Dostoievsky notes in his draft for Book VI, originally entitled "Grushenka" rather than "Alyosha." [2] The problem of lust arises only symbolically for Alyosha, and its resolution in his meeting with Grushenka and his vision of Cana of Galilee is also only symbolical. In the unfinished narrative which this novel offers us, the character of Alyosha not only lacks the problematic of *modern* man but that of man.

[2] *Die Urgestalt,* p. 322.

12

DMITRI, IVAN, AND ALYOSHA:
THE THREE FACES OF JOB

In Dmitri Karamazov the human suffering of Job emerges more clearly than in either Ivan or Zossima-Alyosha. Until he is accused of the murder of his father, Dmitri's suffering is like that of so many of Dostoievsky's characters—a familiar state of being that he prolongs and enjoys. At the gathering at the monastery, however, Father Zossima prostrates himself before Dmitri because of the new and more terrible suffering that he senses to be in store for him. The "ordeals of the soul" that Dmitri goes through in the course of the investigations, imprisonment, and trial are indeed terrible—too terrible and enveloping to be *enjoyed.* Only this heavy hammer that falls on the anvil of Dmitri's soul is able to temper his metal. As Dostoievsky himself says in a letter, Dmitri is like the Russian peasant who so long as the thunder does not roll does not cross himself. In contrast to Raskolnikov and Stavrogin, however, what is in question for Dmitri, as Dostoievsky also points out, is purification through suffering for a crime that he has *not* committed. [1]

At the end of the third bout of questioning during the preliminary interrogation, Mitya has a "strange dream, utterly out of keeping with the place and the time." Driving somewhere on the steppes, he passes through a poverty-stricken village, half of whose huts were burnt down, and sees a woman holding a baby that is crying with hunger and blue with cold. "Why are they crying?" he asks the driver as they dash gaily by. " 'It's the babe,' answered the driver, 'the babe weeping.' . . . 'But why is it? Why?' foolish Mitya still persisted. 'Why, they're poor people, burnt out. They've no bread.' " But Mitya still cannot understand or accept, for what he wants to know is not the immediate cause, but why people are poor at all, why the steppe is barren, why they do not hug each other, kiss, and sing songs of joy instead of being "so dark from black misery?"

> And he felt that a passion of pity such as he never known before, was rising in his heart, and he wanted to cry, that he wanted to do something for them all, so that the babe should weep no more, so that the dark-faced, dried-up mother should not weep, that no one should shed tears again from that moment, and he wanted to do it at once, at once, regardless of all obstacles, with all the recklessness of the Karamazovs. (616)

Like Ivan, Dmitri proceeds from the suffering little child within him to the suffering of others, particularly of children. His manner of doing so, however, is not intellectual but stubborn and irrational: "He felt that though his questions were unreasonable and senseless, yet he wanted to ask just that, and he had to ask it just in that way." The pity that he feels

[1] Letter to Nikola Alexeyevitch Lyubimov, November 16, 1879, quoted in *Die Urgestalt*, pp. 580 f.

for the babe so floods his heart that it is as if someone had taken pity on him. In contrast to Ivan who says, "All I know is that there is suffering and that there are none guilty," Dmitri concludes from the fact of universal suffering that *all* are to blame. Ivan's Euclidian mind sees only the problem of whether the suffering of the individual corresponds to his individual guilt. Dmitri discovers through his dream that all men are bound to one another and that there is no way to draw exact demarcations between the responsibility of one man and that of another. This does not mean a guilt so general that it erases the distinctions between those who do wrong and those who do not. The guilt that Dmitri accepts is real guilt and not a general abasement. Like Job, he continues to witness to the fact of his own innocence even while recognizing and affirming the reality that limits him.

> "Gentlemen, we're all cruel, we're all monsters, we all make men weep, and mothers, and babes at the breast, but of all, let it be settled here, now, of all I am the lowest reptile! I've sworn to amend, and every day I've done the same filthy things. I understand now that such men as I need a blow, a blow of destiny to catch them as with a noose, and bind them by a force from without. Never, never should I have risen of myself! But the thunderbolt has fallen, I accept the torture of accusation, and my public shame, I want to suffer and by suffering I shall be purified. . . . But . . . *I am not guilty of my father's blood.*" (617 f., italics mine.)

In Ivan Karamazov the rebellion of the Modern Promethean is fused with the rebellion of the Modern Job. In the chapter on "Rebellion" Ivan recounts the descriptions of inhuman cruelty to children that he—and his author before him[2]—has collected from newspapers and books, and he uses the suffering of innocent children who have not eaten of the "apple" as the basis for an indictment of a universe whose

---

[2] In a letter to Lyubimov of May 10, 1879, quoted in *Die Urgestalt,* pp. 554-56, Dostoievsky writes: "All that my hero says in that part . . . is founded on reality. All the ancedotes of children have really taken place, have appeared printed in the newspapers—I can show where—and I have invented nothing."

"universal harmony" demands the sacrifice of these little ones. Although Ivan tells Alyosha that cruel, rapacious, even violent people are often fond of children, his tales of sadistic, sensual brutality (such as that of the general who had his dogs tear a serf boy to pieces before the eyes of his mother because the boy had thrown a stone that injured the paw of a favorite dog) illustrate just the opposite and lead him to conclude that underlying man is irrational violence.

> "In every man, of course, a demon lies hidden—the demon of rage, the demon of lustful heat at the screams of the tortured victim, the demon of lawlessness let off the chain, the demon of diseases that follow on vice, gout, kidney disease." (287)

But the injured image of man also means an injured image of God. "I think if the devil doesn't exist, but man has created him, he has created him in his own image and likeness," says Ivan, at which Alyosha observes, "Just as he did God, then?" "Yours must be a fine God," laughs Ivan, "if man created Him in His image and likeness." The God who created man must be a devil, Ivan implies, stating in his own way the conclusion of Melville's Confidence Man that the loss of trust in man means a loss of trust in man's creator.

If even Alyosha agrees that the general should be shot "for the satisfaction of our moral feelings," then it proves, says Ivan, that "the world stands on absurdities, and perhaps nothing would have come to pass in it without them." In his emphasis on the absurd and on the irreducible particular, Ivan clearly anticipates the modern existentialist. "If I try to understand anything, I shall be false to the fact," declares Ivan, "and I have determined to stick to the fact." Ivan's "fact" is the unique existing person whose life and happiness he refuses to subsume under any general plan, no matter how beneficently conceived. Why should the little child who has been shut in a privy all night and whose mother has rubbed its face with faeces and put them in its mouth "beat her little aching heart with her tiny fist in the dark and the cold, and weep her meek unresentful tears to dear, kind God to protect her?"

Like Kierkegaard, Ivan refuses to see the Single One *sub specie aeternitatis*. Seen from the standpoint of the universal, the individual person has meaning only in terms of that universal. Seen from his own standpoint, however, a knowledge of good and evil which reveals itself to be diabolical is not worth the cost.

Ivan sees man as himself to blame for his exile from paradise since, like Prometheus, he stole fire from heaven. But Ivan's "pitiful, earthly, Euclidian understanding" cannot accept the daily suffering, as does Prometheus, who has foreknowledge of some future rectification of the order in his favor. Rather, like the other, Biblical, rebel Job, Ivan cries out that he, that all men, are suffering and that they are innocent. Like Job, he demands justice and cannot accept an impersonal order of cause and effect in which justice has no place.

"I must have justice, or I will destroy myself. And not justice in some remote infinite time and space, but here on earth, and that I could see myself. . . . Surely I haven't suffered, simply that I, my crimes and my sufferings, may manure the soil of the future harmony for somebody else." (289)

Ivan's rebellion is not the rejection of the transcendent for the sake of the immanent, like that of Nietzsche and Sartre. It is the much more terrible rebellion of Job, who curses the day of his birth and questions the very meaning of his existence. Like Captain Ahab, Ivan has nothing of Job's answer, even though he starts with Job's question. Yet in his demand that God be real for this world, the atheist Ivan is far closer to Job than those who have forgotten the present world for the promise of a future harmony, religious or secular, or have "adjusted" themselves to the world and ceased to care about its evil and suffering. Ivan says that he accepts God, but he cannot accept his world and the eternal harmony in which, in some indefinite future, the sufferings of all the generations of mankind will somehow be reconciled and redeemed. He knows that no meaning attained in the future can make up for the lack of meaning in the present. This is a voice that we have heard before in Kirilov, who kills himself because he wants the new era for mankind to begin *now*. Like Kirilov, Ivan protests in the name of humanity; like Job, he demands that he himself see: "I want to see with my own eyes the hind lie down with the lion and the victim rise up and embrace his murderer." If he cannot see it, if his Euclidian, three-dimensional mind cannot understand such mysteries, then he rejects this harmony and hastens to return to God the "entrance ticket" for which He has asked too high a price. "From love for humanity I don't want it. . . . I would rather remain with my unavenged suffering and unsatisfied indignation, *even if I were wrong*." [3]

If Ivan embodies Job's contending, Father Zossima embodies Job's trust. If Ivan is haunted by the sense of God's distance, like the Job of Chapters 3 to 31, Zossima is filled with the sense of God's nearness, like the Job of the Prologue and the Epilogue. In Father Zossima's teaching that each is responsible for all, Dostoievsky contrasts the isolation and individualism which marks modern man, exemplified in Ivan, with that social solidarity which alone gives men true security. The basis for Zossima's teaching that each is responsible for all is

[3] Dostoievsky indicates the contemporary significance of Ivan's position in this same letter of May 10, 1879: "This conviction marks just that which I hold to be the synthesis of contemporary Russian anarchism, namely, the denial, not of God but of the meaning in His creation. The whole of Socialism has proceeded from there and begun with this, that it denies the meaning of historical reality and has finally descended to a program of destruction and anarchy." In a letter to R. P. Pobyedonovstev of May 19, 1879, Dostoievsky expands this theme: "I describe the blasphemy of God . . . as it prevails with us (in almost the whole higher layer of society, before all in the youth); that is, the scientific and philosophical refutation of the existence of God has already been thrown overboard, the 'active' socialists today no longer concern themselves with it at all as they did in the whole of the past and the first half of the present century; they deny with all their forces the divine creation, the world of God and its meaning." (*Die Urgestalt*, pp. 560 f.) The resemblance we have noted to Kirilov is made clearer still in a passage of the handwritten sketches not included in the finished novel: "Such conceptions as the return of the entrance ticket and the Grand Inquisitor smell of epilepsy, of tormented nights"—presumably a statement of Alyosha's since it is followed by "—Ah, is it called, do you yourself concede that it is epilepsy?" (*Ibid.*, p. 321. My translations from the German.)

his belief in the power of active love and in the reciprocal interrelationship of all things. In contrast to the Augustinian emphasis on the original sin that cuts man off from God and makes him dependent upon transcendent grace, Zossima rehearses the Eastern Orthodox emphasis upon the immanence of the Holy Spirit and upon *sobornost,* the community of man created through the Holy Spirit.

> "Brothers, have no fear of men's sin. Love a man even in his sin, for that is the semblance of Divine Love and is the highest love on earth. Love all God's creation, the whole and every grain of sand in it. Love every leaf, every ray of God's light. Love the animals, love the plants, love everything." (382)

We have here almost a nature mysticism, were it not for the stress on the transforming power of man's love. The secret of active love, as Zossima says to Madame Hohlakov, is that it teaches one the real mystery that binds everything together. "If you love everything, you will perceive the divine mystery in things. . . . And you will come at last to love the whole world with an all-embracing love."

We have "a precious mystic sense of our living bond . . . with the higher heavenly world, and the roots of our thoughts and feelings are not here but in other worlds." Everything lives only through this mystic contact, and through this contact too each thing is in touch with each other thing. "My brother asked the birds to forgive him; that sounds senseless, but it is right; for all is like an ocean, all is flowing and blending; a touch in one place sets up movement at the other end of the earth." "Everything touches reciprocally," Zossima adds in the sketches as Dostoievsky notes further, " 'From the individual organism to the universal organism' in the words of the *staretz*" [4] and links the love of all creation and even of sin with the teaching, already present in *The Devils,* that life is a paradise to which we have the key.[5]

---

[4] For the influence of the Russian philosopher Fyodorov on Dostoievsky's belief in the organic interrelation of man and nature, cf. *Die Urgestalt,* pp. 8-49.

[5] *Ibid.,* pp. 293-299.

We are not, as Ivan thinks, isolated individuals to be judged by Euclidian standards. We live in a constant, invisible interchange with each other in such a way that each is, in fact, responsible for all. This is a mysticism of active love. It does not posit an absolute unity of divine reality nor does it retreat within the soul to find reality. Rather, it finds the divine love in the reciprocal relationship of all being, in the "ocean, flowing and blending." This mysticism is not a denial of immediacy but its strongest affirmation, not a rejection of the material world but its transformation, not a turning away from the social world but its transfiguration. "If two of you are gathered together—then there is a whole world, a world of living love." This is the answer which Zossima offers to the problem of evil that is raised by Ivan and his Inquisitor. For it is the "ocean, flowing and blending" which makes humble, active love a transforming and redeeming force.

> "At some thoughts one stands perplexed, especially at the sight of men's sin, and wonders whether one should use force or humble love. Always decide to use humble love. If you resolve on that once for all, you may subdue the whole world. Loving humility is marvellously strong, the strongest of all things . . ." (383)

Starting with the Cartesian assumption of the isolated individual, Ivan can find no compelling reason for loving one's neighbor, and his Inquisitor sees Jesus' teaching of love as a mockery of human nature. Father Zossima, in contrast, starts with the recognition of the reciprocal contact of all things and sees the love taught by the Sermon on the Mount not as an unattainable ideal but as a basic reality, a reality to be taken seriously not merely in the inner world of the spirit but in the life between men. Here is the real conflict between the Inquisitor and Father Zossima and the reason Dostoievsky saw this sixth book of his novel as an answer to the fifth. The divergence between the two is not that of reality and ideal but of two different understandings of reality, two different images of man—the isolated individual whose real life is found in his consciousness and the person who stands in living relation to all things.

The Euclidian mind calculates the results of its actions and understands the problem of evil and of justice in terms of the external rewards and punishments which these actions produce. It is a way of thinking which sees only the abstract surfaces of reality and divides even these surfaces into a means here and an end there. This is the calculation of the isolated thinker who begins with the fact of his individual consciousness, "*cogito ergo sum,*" and never gets beyond it. Zossima, in contrast, understands that even though one cannot see the effect one's active love enters into the living flow and enriches it while the love one withholds impoverishes this flow and obscures its reality. "Try to determine where your personality ends and another personality begins," writes Dostoievsky in his *Diary of a Writer.*[6] Because such reciprocal contact is the basic reality, active love needs no extrinsic motivation in the hope of heavenly reward or the fear of the punishments of hell: "Seek no reward, for great is your reward on this earth: the spiritual joy which is only vouchsafed to the righteous man." Hence the problem of evil and the problem of justice do not turn on the question of whether an individual's suffering is greater than his crimes but of whether or not he attains authentic existence. Man can find meaning and spiritual joy even in the midst of suffering if he is moving toward a whole and genuine way of life, a reciprocally confirming relationship with other men and with nature.

Even in hell, according to Zossima, the real torment is not external, but the "flaming thirst for responsive, active and grateful love which is now impossible." Even in hell, moreover, the active love of the righteous for the sinners may have a redeeming effect and lead them to humility and a semblance of active love. The compassionate Zossima prays even for suicides, for he cannot bear to see anyone cut off from the love of God. Yet he acknowledges that there are men who cut themselves off for all eternity from the love of God. These are the vindictive souls "who remain proud and fierce even in hell, in spite of their certain knowledge and contemplation of

[6] Quoted in Vyacheslav Ivanov, *Freedom and the Tragic Life: A Study of Dostoevsky* (New York: Noonday Press, 1957), p. 55.

the absolute truth . . . For such, hell is voluntary and ever consuming . . . they have cursed themselves, cursing God and life." Thus evil and suffering remain, but the responsibility for them rests with man in his irrevocable freedom and not with God.

Dostoievsky's god-man both is and is not an answer to his man-god. Zossima's teaching poses Ivan and the man-god with the question of the very meaning of freedom. Freedom for self-indulgence and self-gratification leads to anarchy, tyranny, and mutual annihilation, for it inevitably entails the affirmation of one's own freedom at the expense of the freedom of others. The man who is free from attachments is really free, because he is able to dedicate and devote himself, to find authentic existence and real spiritual happiness. Freedom, therefore, is not a mechanical concept, something *added* to the self, but a reality of personal existence that is intertwined with the self at every stage. Conversely, the self itself cannot be taken for granted as it is at any given moment but must be understood in terms of stages of the movement toward personal freedom or the fall away from it. Despite the profundity of its insights, Zossima's teaching falls short of true personal freedom, however. The dualism he establishes between the freedom which gratifies the desires and the spiritual freedom founded on denying them leaves us without a freedom for the whole man in his body-soul, individual-social reality. It recalls, indeed, the dualism between Ivan's rebellious Job and Zossima's submissive one, whose suffering existence is ordained in order that his praise may serve the whole of creation.

A similar dualism between the material and the spiritual and between the social and the individual characterizes Zossima's teaching on equality. The Russian peasant proves his dignity as a man by the fact that he respects the rich without envy. Only in Russia, in fact, will it be understood that "equality is to be found only in the spiritual dignity of man." We are not, indeed, equal in any objective, measurable sense, whether in intelligence, talent, strength, or comeliness. The only equality is that with which the Bible begins—the unique value and dignity of each individual as a being created in the image of God. But for Zossima, unlike the Bible, the spiritual equality of man has no social consequences. While he teaches that without the brotherhood founded on spiritual dignity all attempts at dividing the wealth and creating justice will only end in flooding the earth with blood, he does not suggest that with this brotherhood men will realize the demands for social justice and community set forth by the Hebrew prophets. What he foresees, rather, is a brotherhood in Christ which leads to individual deeds of kindness but in no way alters the social hierarchy. One will still have servants as before, but one can be a servant to one's servants. "Can it be a dream, that in the end man will find his joy only in deeds of light and mercy, and not in cruel pleasures as now, in gluttony, fornication, ostentation, boasting and envious rivalry of one with the other?" Though he is concerned about child labor, Zossima couples his teaching of spiritual freedom and equality with a virtual acceptance of the economic misery and social inequality of the Russian people.

If Ivan's "Euclidian mind" loses sight of the interconnections of human existence, Zossima's mystic mind fails to take note of its contradictions and tragic cleavages. Father Zossima's "exhortations" are just that: they have power to inspire and uplift—they belong, indeed, to the great classics of devotional literature—but they cannot give even their author the resources to live by them. One cannot "always use humble love." Even the saint is not always able to follow this counsel of perfection in the interhuman situations in which he finds himself, for to exist as a person means at times to have to stand one's ground, to resist and oppose. It is in this realm of the personal and the interhuman, too, that the tragic contradictions which give rise to Ivan's "rebellion" take shape. Although Zossima's mysticism is based upon love and reciprocity, it is significant that the ecstasy he promises is as readily available to the man who is alone as to the man who is with his fellow men. The "active love" of which Zossima talks appears often as more of an emotion *within* the person than a concrete reality *between* persons. That Job's question is a real one Dostoievsky knew all too well in creating Ivan and the Grand Inquisitor. But when he wrote the Exhortations which were to answer Ivan, he did not recognize that this question is too deeply grounded in human existence itself to be resolved by any mere change of perspective, however penetrating and all-encompassing.

The common concern of Ivan and Father Zossima with Job —and the very different relation that each of them has to this figure—provides us with an insight concerning the basic Dostoievskian dichotomy of the man-god and the god-man. Each of them—the man-god and the god-man—represents one half of Job, as it were, and nowhere is there a figure who brings these halves together. Ivan has Job's question, his contending, without his trust, whereas Father Zossima, when he speaks of Job, speaks only of the Job of the Prologue and Epilogue, the Job of unquestioning faith and complete submission. Neither knows *both* the contending and the trust that mark Job and enable him to enter into dialogue with God while standing his own ground and retaining his independence.

Alyosha comes closest to bringing the two Jobs together in one figure while retaining the separate meaning of each. Through his crisis after Father Zossima's death, the terrible God of Ivan and the merciful God of Zossima are united for him in a vision which affirms the whole of reality despite sin and death. The immediate occasion for the crisis is that, contrary to the confident expectation of Alyosha and the many others who regard Zossima as a saint, the monk's body decays and, what is more, decays even more quickly than is usual. This "breath of corruption" gives great support to Father Zossima's envious detractors, led by the ascetic Father Ferapont, while it throws his followers into confusion. Alyosha has fled to the monastery from the world only to discover the corruption of the world within the monastery itself. Zossima's injunction to return to the world shows that Alyosha's task is not to escape from evil but to withstand a reality in which sacred and profane are inextricably mixed—to bring the sacred into the profane and transform the profane through contact with the sacred. Or, if his dread of evil is too great, he may succumb to the horror of the realization that there is nowhere that evil is not to be found! He may lose both his instinctive trust in life and the faith which his contact with

Zossima has given him.

Alyosha's faith itself is not pure and unmixed. Alongside his trust in God is an element of faith in "miracle, mystery, and authority." Not that his faith is based on miracles, but he unquestioningly expects a miracle as a confirmation of his faith, and his faith is shaken when it does not occur. He takes it for granted that the natural order will follow the moral and spiritual, and when it does not, he is torn loose from the unquestioning Job of Father Zossima to the questioning Job of Ivan. What bothers Alyosha in particular is that which troubles the psalmist in Psalm 73 who comes close to losing his faith when he sees the prosperity of the wicked. How can one believe in the reality of Zossima's teachings when his spiritual attainments remain unconfirmed not only by the natural order but also by the social? What is outraged in Alyosha is not his desire for a miracle *per se*, but his sense of "the higher justice" which had led him to expect such a miracle.

> And now the man who should, he believed, have been exalted above every one in the whole world, that man, instead of receiving the glory that was his due, was suddenly degraded and dishonoured! . . . He could not endure without mortification, without resentment even, that the holiest of holy men should have been exposed to the jeering and spiteful mockery of the frivolous crowd so inferior to him. (408)

Alyosha even experiences that same sense of the powerlessness of the holy before the inexorable order of nature that Rogozhin and Kirilov feel in relation to the crucified Christ: "Why did Providence hide its face 'at the most critical moment' . . . as though voluntarily submitting to the blind, dumb, pitiless laws of nature?" For Alyosha, however, the "eclipse of God" does not mean the "death of God," as it does for Kirilov, but rather Ivan's Gnostic division between the world and God. Rakitin comes on Alyosha sitting with his back against a tree, with "a look of suffering and irritability in his face" and none of his "famous mildness to be seen in it," as the envious Rakitin gleefully points out. "So now you are in a temper with your God, you are rebelling against Him," cries Rakitin. "He hasn't given promotion. He hasn't bestowed the order of merit!" "I am not rebelling against my God," Alyosha replies with a forced smile; "I simply 'don't accept His world.'"

Later, after he has visited Grushenka and returned to the monastery and is kneeling before Zossima's body, Alyosha falls asleep and has a vision of the marriage of Cana in Galilee in which Zossima comes and calls him to the feast. "I am called, too, called and bidden," Zossima says to him, and tells him of "the bride and bridegroom" and of the many guests at the feast, all of whom are rejoicing and drinking "the wine of new, great gladness." "He is expecting new guests, He is calling new ones unceasingly for ever and ever . . . There they are bringing new wine."

"Our age goes beyond the miracle of turning water into wine," writes Kierkegaard in *Fear and Trembling*. "It turns wine into water." It reduces everything meaningful to a lowest common denominator of banality and insignificance. For Alyosha, in contrast, Jesus' joyful miracle is still real. His vision of the sacrament which transforms the profane into holy reality comes as the culmination of what has already taken place symbolically in his meeting with Grushenka—the transmutation of his lust and her wantonness into spiritual love and joy, the transfiguration of profane and lawless sex into pure, sexless marriage. Both in his meeting with Grushenka and in his vision, the marriage feast is based upon the "onion," the little acts of compassion that men have had for one another. The Zossima of his vision says to him:

"I gave an onion to a beggar, so I, too, am here. And many here have given only an onion each—only one little onion. . . . What are all our deeds? And you, my gentle one, you, my kind boy, you too have known how to give a famished woman an onion today. Begin your work, dear one, begin it, gentle one!" (435)

Alyosha understands now that instead of there being two worlds—the world of the holy Zossima and the world of the profane Grushenka—there is only one world—the world of common humanity and of compassion, the world where one can go forth and meet another human being in love and create thereby a whole world, a world of living love." Alyosha understands too what Job grasped but Ivan could not, that in the heart of suffering is to be found joy, in the heart of terror, love. Behind the creator of sex and death is not Satan but God; there are not two Gods—one of mercy and one of wrath —but one God, who is terrible and merciful at once.

> "I am afraid . . . I dare not look," whispered Alyosha.
> "Do not fear Him. He is terrible in His greatness, aw-ful in His sublimity, but infinitely merciful. He has made Himself like unto us from love and rejoices with us. He is changing the water into wine." (435)

After he awakens from his vision, Alyosha goes out into the night, his soul overflowing with rapture and throws himself on the ground, kissing it and watering it with tears of joy and love, the words of Zossima echoing in his soul. In his ecstasy he experiences the union of the mystery of the earth with that of heaven; he glimpses the threads linking his soul to other worlds. He falls to the earth "a weak boy" and rises up "a resolute champion," ready to carry Zossima's teachings into the world.

Alyosha faces the problem of death and loss in his crisis over Father Zossima, and the strength which comes to him through this crisis is undoubtedly real and lasting. On the other hand, we can hardly say that he has looked into Job's abyss or that he wrestles and contends like Job for the mean-ing which he finds. His "rebellion" is expressed in the words of Ivan, his reconciliation in those of Zossima. He is not a man who has really faced meaninglessness and fought through to a meaning on his own. He stands as a comfort and an inspira-tion in his natural grace, and he directs us through his crisis to the image of man that he has found in Zossima. But he has not realized that image in the world of contradictions from which he originally fled. Alyosha's temptation remains sym-bolic, his rebellion a short-lived imitation of Ivan's.

--- --- --- ---

PART FOUR

FRANZ KAFKA

13

_____

KAFKA AS
HUNGER ARTIST

-What is at stake in the question of the image of modern man is nothing less than the very meaning of human existence face to face with the absurd. No one puts this question before us so compellingly as Franz Kafka. In every line that he has written, whether in finished stories, unfinished novels, notations in his diary, or letters, this is his central concern. To say this is not to dismiss the wealth of aspects and levels in Kafka's writings which have received so much attention from his interpreters. Rather, it is to indicate the wholeness that gives his work its central significance and to designate that sphere within Kafka's manifold meanings upon which we shall concentrate.

Despite his numerous depictions of animal and insect life —in fact, just through them—Kafka is essentially a philosophical anthropologist, if we extend this term to include those whose main interest is the problem of man. Again, if concern for human existence in its concrete reality makes one an "existentialist," then Kafka is more of an existentialist than most of those who today are called by this name. He does not start with any absolute or with the assumption of the death of God, but with human existence itself. Those who seek to understand and interpret Kafka through some allegorical key, whether religious, psychoanalytic, or sociological, miss the simple fact that, paradoxical as it is,–Kafka's world is not a transparent one through which we can glimpse some other, more familiar reality. It is just what it is in its irreducible opaqueness and absurdity. "The only really difficult and insoluble problems are those which we cannot formulate," writes Kafka, "because they have the difficulties of life itself as their content." Kafka, however, is not a philosopher but an artist. His writing cannot be reduced to abstract philosophical concepts any more than it can be reduced to religious or political allegories, mystical symbols, or psychoanalytic case histories.–Yet his stories and novels have a curiously abstract quality, for all that—too abstract for us to speak of Kafka as offering us a concrete image of man in the same sense as do either Melville or Dostoievsky. Kafka's heroes are never full-dimensional, concrete human beings, and his stories never have the ring of everyday reality, no matter how detailed and circumstantial they may be. It is this that tempts us to see his stories as parables pointing to universal truths through thinly concretized abstractions. Yet this view is as illicit as that which would find in Kafka concrete images of man.[1]

[1] In the case of "A Report to an Academy" and "Jackals and Arabs" Kafka explicitly rejected the designation "parable" in favor of "animal stories" (Kafka's letter to Martin Buber, May 12, 1917). Martin Buber was the editor of *Der Jude*, the periodical in which these stories were first published. In this letter Kafka wrote Buber: "So komme ich also doch in den 'Juden' und habe es immer für unmöglich gehalten. Gleich-

The key to Kafka, perhaps, is that sense of caricature which is borne in on us again and again.-If one feels that one recognizes reality in Kafka, one always feels at the same time that it is a reality that is somehow caricatured. Though this caricature is of the nature of an abstraction from concrete reality, it does not point outward to some still more abstract concept but back to an altogether concrete way of seeing—a perception of reality that again and again lays bare the absurdity inherent in Kafka's particular relationship to it, if not in reality itself. The variety of Kafka's stories represents aspects of this way of seeing. They do not suggest a really open response to the unique reality of person and situation such as we find again and again in Dostoievsky. Dostoievsky's political and religious views colored his presentation of certain characters and situations, such as Peter Verkhovensky and the conspiracy that forms the central plot in *The Devils,* but they did not distort his portrayal of the nihilist Stavrogin or the outmoded liberal Stepan Trofimovitch. In Kafka, on the other hand, the distortion lies in his way of seeing itself. Kafka is a more honest and consistent writer than Dostoievsky, for he never substitutes general views for his concrete perception of existence. Yet his mode of seeing is too strong and individual to enable him to communicate the real otherness and uniqueness of situations and people as does Dostoievsky. In Kafka, as a result, the romantic grandeur of Melville and the profound realism of Dostoievsky is replaced by an almost ascetic restriction in subject matter and perspective that makes his creations more thoroughly unromantic, unheroic, and nonpathetic than even the most "realistic" and sordid of portrayals. One is sometimes tempted to feel, indeed, that so far from offering us an image of man, Kafka's writings are highly personalized documents whose significance is more autobiographical than it is human or even

---

nisse bitte ich die Stücke nicht zu nennen, es sind nicht eigentlich Gleichnisse; wenn sie einen Gesamttitel haben sollen, denn am besten vielleicht 'Zwei Tiergeschichten'." Quoted in a letter from Martin Buber to the author, Aug. 17, 1959. The stories appeared under the title that Kafka requested, "Two Animal Stories," in Vol. II of *Der Jude* (Oct. and Nov. 1917), pp. 488, 559-65.

modern. Yet it is precisely this autobiographical quality that joins Kafka's individualized mode of seeing with the concrete uniqueness of human existence. Our feeling that each of the central figures, no matter how fantastic, is in some sense Kafka himself, combined with the vividness and power with which Kafka forces us into the heart of this character's personal existence, makes his characters, thus caricatured, at once Kafka, modern man, and simply man.

In Kafka, more than in Melville, Dostoievsky, or even Camus, the Modern Exile comes to his full stature, and the forlornness of his situation is portrayed with a poignancy unweakened by sentimentality. "I am no protestant," Kafka said to Janouch. "I wish to accept everything and bear it patiently." [2] In the fact that he is not a rebel, Kafka is perhaps more modern than either Melville or Dostoievsky. In Kafka there is no trace of romanticism. In him the alienation of modern man has worked itself out to the farthest reaches. Kafka, as few before or since, is the Modern Exile.

Kafka saw himself as by his "essential nature, a reserved, silent, unsocial dissatisfied person," lacking "all aptitude for family life except, at best, as an observer," a position in relation to family life which Kafka himself described as "acrobatics of the everyday." Kafka did not see this unsocial nature as a misfortune, however, but as "the reflection of my goal." "In me, by myself, without human relationship, there are no visible lies," he naïvely asserted. "The limited circle is pure." [3] Kafka's friends relieved the seriousness of his lonely crucifixion, as in the parable of the crusader's sword: a man discovers with horror a large knight's sword sheathed in his back, but his faithful friends come in and laughingly draw it out. In general, however, he felt more deserted with a second person than by himself. With another he felt attacked or "helplessly delivered into his hand," whereas "if he is alone, all mankind reaches out for him—but the innumer-

---

[2] Gustav Janouch, *Conversations with Kafka*, trans. Goronwy Rees (New York: Frederick A. Praeger, 1953), p. 50.

[3] Janouch, *Conversations*, pp. 105 f.; *The Diaries of Franz Kafka, 1910-1913*, ed. Max Brod, trans. Joseph Kresh (New York: Schocken Books, 1948), Aug. 21, 30, 1913, pp. 298-300.

able outstretched arms become entangled with one another
and no one reaches to him." When marriage means the join-
ing of loneliness to loneliness or even loneliness to security,
"it never leads to a being-at-home, but to a *Katorga*"—the
Russian long-term imprisonment followed by exile.[4]

Yet Kafka by no means saw his exile as simply voluntary.
Chief among the symbols of his inescapable loneliness was
that very bachelorhood which he so often seemed to choose
as necessary for his goal. "Without forebears, without marriage, without heirs, with a fierce longing for forebears, marriage and heirs," Kafka described himself in his diary. "They
all of them stretch out their hands to me . . . but too far
away for me." [5] Kafka's description of "the bachelor" in an
early diary entry is an archetype which he himself grew
into, as he recognized years later when he wrote of his uncle
Rudolf, the model for his bachelor, "In single details he was
my caricature, in essentials I am his."

> The bachelor . . . has nothing before him and there-
> fore nothing behind him . . . he went astray at that time
> when he felt his depth lastingly . . . the man stands
> once and for all outside our people, outside our humanity,
> he is continually starved, . . . he has only one thing
> always: his pain; . . . he has only as much ground as
> his two feet take up, only as much of a hold as his two
> hands encompass.[6]

The bachelor experiences a progressive shrinking of the space
that is given him to exist in:

> The farther he moves away from the living . . . so much
> the smaller a space is considered sufficient for him . . .
> this bachelor, still in the midst of life, apparently of his

[4] *The Diaries of Franz Kafka, 1914-1923*, ed. Max Brod, trans. Martin
Greenberg in co-operation with Hannah Arendt (New York: Schocken
Books, 1949), Jan. 19, 1915, pp. 109 f.; May 19, 1922, p. 229; Franz
Kafka, *Letters to Milena*, ed. Willi Haas, trans. Tania and James Stern
(London: Secker & Warburg, 1953), p. 234.

[5] *Diaries, 1914-1923*, Jan. 21, 1922, p. 207.

[6] *Ibid.*, Jan. 22, 1922, pp. 207 f.; *Diaries, 1910-1913*, Jul. 19, 1910, pp.
25 f.

own free will resigns himself to an ever smaller space, and when he dies the coffin is exactly right for him.[7]

"I am divided from all things by a hollow space and I don't even push myself to the limits of it," Kafka adds two weeks later. A year later he complains "My life has dwindled dreadfully, nor will it cease to dwindle," and three years later he writes, "I awoke to find myself imprisoned in a fenced enclosure which allowed no room for more than a step in either direction."[8] "My life is a hesitation before birth," says Kafka of himself, and in the fragment "He" he exclaims, "He has the feeling that merely by being alive he is blocking his own way."[9]

Kafka not only saw himself as a lonely exile. He saw himself as essentially lonelier and more in exile than anyone else. After describing himself as turning to stone, he adds, "I shun people not because I want to live quietly but because I want to die quietly." Other people also waver, he admits, "but in lower regions, with greater strength" and supported by "the kinsman who walks beside them for that very purpose." Kafka, in contrast, wavered "on the heights; it is not death, alas, but the eternal torments of dying." Although he knew himself as representative of the problematic of modern man—"an end or a beginning"—Kafka did not believe that there existed others whose "inner plight" resembled his. He could, for all that, imagine such people, "but that the secret raven forever flaps about their heads as it does about mine, even to imagine that is impossible." "The secret raven" accompanied Kafka on his lonely journey through life as an ever-present accentuation of his loneliness and reminder of his exile. When Janouch told Kafka how the Jews in the Ghetto ran out to pay homage to his mother who had helped to save their lives during pogroms, Kafka made the astonishing reply, "I should like to run to those poor Jews of the

[7] *Diaries, 1910–1913*, Dec. 3, 1911, pp. 168 f.
[8] *Ibid.*, Dec. 16, 1911, p. 180; *Diaries, 1914–1923*, Aug. 6, 1914, p. 77; Jul. 4, 1916, p. 157.
[9] *Diaries, 1914–1923*, Jan. 24, 1922, p. 210; Franz Kafka, *The Great Wall of China, Stories and Reflections*, trans. Willa & Edwin Muir (New York: Schocken Books, 1946), "He," p. 240.

Ghetto, kiss the hem of their coats, and say not a word. I should be completely happy if only they would endure my presence in silence." When Kafka nodded affirmatively to Janouch's question whether he was then so lonely, Janouch added, "Like Kaspar Hauser?"—referring to the traditional German orphan. At this Kafka laughed and replied, "Much worse than Kaspar Hauser. I am as lonely as—as Franz Kafka." [10] To be as lonely as Franz Kafka is indeed more terrible than any traditional embodiment of exile that one can imagine!

Your will is free, says a Kafka aphorism, in having wanted the desert and in choosing the path and the pace across the desert, "but it is also unfree since you must go through the desert, unfree since every path in labyrinthine manner touches every foot of the desert's surface." The Jews of old may have wandered across the wilderness to the Promised Land. Kafka, in contrast, is the Wandering Jew, or as he once described himself, "the eternal Jew . . . wandering senselessly through a senselessly obscene world." [11] Like the Biblical Ishmael and even more like Melville's Ishmael, he is a citizen of the wilderness rather than of the cultivated land: "I have been forty years wandering *from* Canaan," wrote Kafka.

It is indeed a kind of Wandering in the Wilderness in reverse that I am undergoing: I think that I am continually skirting the wilderness and am full of childish hopes (particularly as regards women) that "perhaps I shall keep in Canaan after all"—when all the while I have been decades in the wilderness and these hopes are merely mirages born of despair, especially at those times when I am the wretchedest of creatures in the desert too, and Canaan is perforce my only Promised Land, for no third place exists for mankind.[12]

[10] *Diaries, 1914-1923*, Jul. 28, 1914, p. 68; Aug. 6, 1914, p. 77; Oct. 17, 1921, pp. 194 f.; Janouch, *op. cit.*, p. 43.
[11] *Dearest Father, Stories and Other Writings*, ed. Max Brod, trans. Ernst Kaiser and Eithne Wilkins (New York: Schocken Books, 1954), "The Eight Octavo Notebooks," pp. 97 f.; *Letters to Milena*, pp. 163 f.
[12] *Diaries, 1914-1923*, Jan. 28, 1922, pp. 213 f.

There are four exiles that Kafka knew and described: the exile from Paradise, which Kafka shared with all men; the exile of the Jews from the land and the community of Israel (both ancient Canaan and modern Palestine to which Kafka dreamed of going as a farm laborer[13]); the exile of the unconfirmed son and the confirmed bachelor from marriage and family life; and the alienation of modern man from the world in which he finds himself.

"A REPORT TO AN ACADEMY"

Kafka's heroes move from self-sufficiency to ever more anxious isolation and exile. The self in its complacent self-sufficiency is nowhere better portrayed than in "A Report to an Academy," the story of the "free ape" who, essentially alone and by "an effort which up till now has never been repeated," "managed to reach the cultural level of an average European." Whether or not this progress, which could never have been achieved "had I been stubbornly set on clinging to my origins, to the remembrances of my youth," is a satire on the assimilation of the Jew into Western European culture,[14] it is still more of a satire on the image of man of the average European and of modern man in general. In a tone of detached, scientific observation, the ape reports to the

---

[13] Janouch, *op. cit.*, p. 27.

[14] Cf. William C. Rubinstein, "A Report to an Academy" in *Franz Kafka Today*, eds. Angel Flores and Homer Swander (Madison: University of Wisconsin Press, 1958), pp. 59 f. After pointing out that "A Report to an Academy" was first published in *Der Jude*, Rubinstein writes: "*Der Jude* was conceived and published by Martin Buber, a leading Zionist. In the opening number (Apr. 1916), there was a declaration of purpose: to spread and promote knowledge of Judaism. Throughout the eight years of the magazine's history, it dealt exclusively with Jewish problems, usually from a Zionist viewpoint. While there is not the slightest reason to suppose that Buber would not have published a story by a friend of his friend Brod, unless it explicitly furthered the views of the magazine, the appearance of 'A Report to an Academy' in *Der Jude* does add, however little, to the probability that the story dealt with the problems of European Jewry." In reply to a question of mine on this point, Martin Buber wrote me in a letter of Aug. 17, 1959: "I have published Kafka's story as such, as I did with some poetry of Werfel's, simply as representative Jewish authors. I have of course thought of the interpretation you mention (Rubinstein's), but not as the only possible one."

gentlemen of the Academy how he "fought through the thick of things," knowingly renouncing freedom in order to become man, until he reached his present unassailable "position on all the great variety stages of the civilized world." In a tone which belies his claim that he is not complacent, he reports that he has achieved what he has set out to achieve—"a success which could hardly be increased"—plus the comforts of a bottle of wine and a half-trained little chimpanzee when he comes home late at night from banquets, scientific receptions, or social gatherings. His self-satisfaction demands no approval or confirmation; his personal disclosures are made only for the sake of science.

> Do not tell me that it was not worth the trouble. In any case, I am not appealing for any man's verdict, I am only imparting knowledge. I am only making a report. To you also, honored Members of the Academy, I have only made a report. (180)[15]

This contribution to "philosophical anthropoidology" is thoroughly depressing in its portrayal of the utter banality of the image of man of the average cultured European, the meaninglessness and triviality of the ideal goals that he sets for himself. But it is also a rare picture of the complacent self before the world breaks in on it. As such, it offers us a backdrop for the various stages of anxiety and guilt that this self must undergo.

"THE BURROW"

"The Burrow," in contrast, shows the self striving for complete self-sufficiency but experiencing ever greater anxiety because of the impossibility of the complete attainment of this goal. If it did not recapitulate so many motifs familiar from our own lives, we should be tempted to describe as paranoiac this story of an animal who has spent his life perfecting a marvelously complex burrow to protect him against every possibility of attack. Like the ape in "A Report to an

---

[15] All page references to Kafka's stories, unless otherwise stated, are to *Selected Short Stories of Franz Kafka*, trans. Willa & Edwin Muir, Introd. by Philip Rahv (New York: Modern Library, 1952).

Academy," he begins with the report of his success—in this case the successful completion of his burrow. Yet he confesses that he can scarcely pass an hour in complete tranquillity. Even in theory he cannot eliminate all risk, for "prudence itself demands, as alas! so often, the element of risk in life." What is more, he knows that he is not so strong as many others and his enemies are countless: "There have been happy periods in which I could almost assure myself that the enmity of the world towards me had ceased or been assuaged, or that the strength of the burrow had raised me above the destructive struggle of former times." But these are succeeded by periods in which he realizes all the more acutely that he can discover no way to exist without exposing his self to the world. His system would be airtight only if he could trust someone else during the times when he enters or leaves his burrow. But it is impossible "completely to trust some one outside the burrow when you are inside . . . that is, in a different world." "I can only trust myself and my burrow." He is, moreover, too realistic not to recognize that, even though his burrow gives him new strength and a considerable degree of security, he is never free from anxieties inside it.

> These anxieties are different from ordinary ones, prouder, richer in content, often long repressed, but in their destructive effect they are perhaps much the same as the anxieties that existence in the outer world gives rise to. (276)

Despite this deficiency in his burrow, he has an almost personal relationship with it which seems to take the place of whatever relations might have been possible with those outside it. When he finally takes the plunge and returns to his burrow after keeping watch on it from above, he cries, "It is for your sake, ye passages and rooms, and you, Castle Keep, above all, that I have come back, counting my own life as nothing in the balance. . . . What do I care for danger now that I am with you? You belong to me, I to you, we are united; what can harm us?"

Every man's desire, says Cecil Connolly, is for "a womb

with a view." Kafka's "mole," in contrast, desires only the womb. He is quite willing to give up all knowledge of the outer world in exchange for the peace of his burrow, "the murmurous silence of the Castle Keep." He even acknowledges to himself that "the danger of an attack, and consequently the need to organize the place for defense, seemed . . . infinitely less important than the need to put it in a state where one could live peacefully." But the very need for complete peace and perfect protection against the world makes it impossible that the burrow can bring either peace or a sense of security. From beneath this compulsive mastery of one's surroundings ever fresh anxiety must inevitably break forth. It is a losing battle, moreover, for the danger continues to threaten, while one's own resources must eventually diminish. "The great burrow stands defenseless, and I am no longer a young apprentice, but an old architect and the powers I still have fail me when the decisive hour comes." He has even reached the stage where he no longer wishes to have certainty. His existence has degenerated into a permanent, unredeemable dualism—a vision of timeless peace and a reality of restless anxiety. "Up there under the moss no change touches one, there one is at peace, uplifted above time; but here every instant frets and gnaws at the listener." Even his surroundings reflect his agitation, looking at him to read from his expression the saving solution that he has not found and cannot find.

The compulsiveness with which the "mole" builds his burrow is matched by the endless patience with which Kafka spins out the details and implications of his situation. The conclusion that such an attempt to attain complete self-sufficiency in face of the world is doomed to failure is coupled with the depressing fact that the mole himself knows this, yet cannot cease from his labors.[16]

[16] The ambiguity in the point of view of this story is anticipated in a striking passage in one of Kafka's earliest letters: " 'To live like a hermit is repulsive, one lays one's egg proudly before all the world, the sun will hatch it; one prefers to bite into the world instead of into one's tongue; one honors the mole and his kind, but one does not make them into one's saints.' Then someone who is no longer behind the tree says to me: 'Is that really true or is it an illusion of summer?' " Franz Kafka,

"THE METAMORPHOSIS"

If Kafka's "mole" remains in the stage of unsuccessful defensiveness, Gregor Samsa in "The Metamorphosis" suffers an involuntary transformation from the self that he has built up and the life that he has successfully constructed to the monstrous reality that he discovers he has become. Gregor Samsa is a commonplace traveling salesman, who awakes one morning to find himself metamorphosed into a gigantic insect. In Kafka, man no longer compares himself with vermin, as in Dostoievsky. He becomes vermin! Gregor is a hardworking, conscientious young man, devoted to his family, whom he supports, and concentrated on his work. In order to pay back his parents' debts to his chief, he has taken on this irregular life and irritating work rather than the pleasanter and less remunerative work that he could have had in the office. His parents and sister now take his support for granted, and he himself asks nothing better out of life than to continue this support and, if possible, even to extend it by sending his sister to a conservatory to study the violin.

The metamorphosis itself is not so significant in the story as the transformation of Gregor's situation that results. The first effect, of course, is that he does not appear for work that morning and is no longer able to play the role of a duti-

---

Briefe, 1902-1924, ed. Max Brod (New York: Schocken Books, 1958), to Oskar Pollak, Nov. 6, (1903?), pp. 18 f., my translation. The following year, in a letter to the same friend, the young Kafka compares himself to a man who in jest rolled a boulder before the entrance of his cave, "but then when the boulder made the cave dark and cut it off from the air, became frightened and tried to push the stone away. But it has now grown ten times heavier and the terrified man must exert all his forces before light and air return." The defensiveness which at first seems to protect the self from what threatens it finally cuts it off from existence itself. But it is not always possible for the self which has walled itself in its cave to free itself. The world must break in on the self before it can again find light and air, as Kafka himself suggests in the same letter: "We need, however, books which work on us like a misfortune, that grieve us very much, as the death of one whom we love more than ourselves, as if we were banished into the forests, away from all men, as a suicide; a book must be the axe for the frozen sea within us." (*Ibid.*, to Oskar Pollak, Jan. 27, 1904, pp. 27 f., my translation.) "The axe for the frozen sea within us"—in Kafka's works this axe is the world that breaks through the walls of the self.

ful son supporting his parents. The chief clerk who comes to see Gregor and finds him barricaded behind the door says to him, "I thought you were a quiet, dependable person, and now all at once you seem bent on making a disgraceful exhibition of yourself." "Oh, sir, do spare my parents!" cries Gregor, but to no avail. Gregor's pride in providing a fine life for his parents and sister now turns into hot shame and grief that he can no longer protect them from catastrophe. But his family shows unexpected resources. His sister goes to work, and his father proves quite capable of holding down a job.

> Truly, this was not the father he had imagined to himself. . . . The man who used to lie wearily sunk in bed whenever Gregor set out on a business journey, who welcomed him back of an evening lying in a long chair in a dressing gown, who could not really rise to his feet . . . was standing there in fine shape, dressed in a smart blue uniform with gold buttons. (62 f.)

In a Beauty-and-the-Beast fantasy, Gregor imagines forcing his sister to remain with him forever in his room. Eventually she will stay of her own free will, bursting into tears when she learns what he had meant to do for her while he kisses her on her bare neck. What actually happens is quite different. She becomes indifferent to the fact that he hardly eats and ends by refusing to identify this gigantic insect with her brother's memory. By a curious double logic she insists that they must get rid of the creature since they have put up with it as far as is humanly possible, and that it is not really Gregor anyway since, if it were, "he would have realized long ago that human beings can't live with such a creature, and he'd have gone away on his own accord," enabling them to "keep his memory in honor" while ridding them of his embarrassing presence.

Gregor starves to death because he cannot find any food that he can eat. His death itself, however, comes immediately after, and to some extent because of, his family's rebuff of his last attempt to appear in their midst. He has heard his sister's statement, and he holds even more strongly than she to the decision that he must disappear. As he lies dying with the apple rotting in his inflamed back, covered with dust from the uncleaned room and surrounded by all kinds of furniture that has been shoved into his room for storage, he thinks "of his family with tenderness and love." At last, his body completely flat and dry from not having eaten, he expires. A short time later, to the relief of the family, the charwoman announces that she has already got rid of "the thing next door."

While Gregor is thus excluded from the life of his family and reduced from a person to a thing, the family basks in the warm sunshine of the new future that lies before them. Their prospects are not at all bad, and the daughter has now "bloomed into a pretty girl with a good figure" who will soon be ready for a husband. As once the family had battened off Gregor's devotion and support, so now they batten off his voluntary self-removal. There was room for Gregor only in his role as breadwinner. As an insect, he could not communicate any longer with his family, and they regarded him increasingly as an object, not a person. But for Gregor too, it was this way. Before his metamorphosis he had thought of nothing but his work, never going out in the evening and having no other amusement than doing fretwork. After it, when the *raison d'être* that his work gave him was removed from him, he became, even for himself, a creature who had no justification for existence.

Though there is a curious note of self-pity throughout the story, this note is not sounded by Gregor but by the author, who presents us simultaneously with the growing callousness of the family and the all-too-exemplary filial piety of Gregor. Gregor himself seems to fade out of the picture without protest. If Gregor's former existence seems a relatively meaningless and inauthentic one, this does not mean that any new existence opens out for him when the world breaks in on him. There is only the acceptance of his own nonexistence as the best "solution" to the new situation in which he and his family find themselves. Thus the "metamorphosis" turns someone who stands on a very narrow plot of ground into someone who has no ground at all!

There are three senses in which one may speak of "The Metamorphosis" as the world breaking in on the self. The first is that of "judgment": the routine and inauthentic existence of Gregor Samsa leads, in some way incomprehensible to us, to the quasi-existence of the gigantic insect and from there to nonexistence. This is the "judgment" that his own existence makes on itself—without being aware of it, he finds the life that he has taken on too much for him and retires into the shape of an insect *or* his existence has imperceptibly lost its humanity so that he wakes up one morning to find himself an insect. The second sense in which the world breaks in on the self is the experience of something entirely unexpected coming along and tearing the self out of the social role and the accustomed routine that it has built up for itself. The third, and most important sense, however, is the loss of all confirmation from others as soon as Gregor ceases to play the role of breadwinner.

This third sense grows out of the second, in so far as Gregor's loss of his social role results in the loss of his family's confirmation. Yet if Gregor's family had really loved him, it might have continued to confirm him even after he no longer supported them, just as it might have continued to hold on to the fact that this was Gregor even after he had suffered his monstrous metamorphosis. Instead, his father and sister not only cease to confirm Gregor but even actively reject him: they neglect him and shut him away; they assume that because he cannot speak he cannot understand; soon they refuse even to identify him any longer with their son and brother; they come to regard the very existence of this "creature" as intolerable; and they actively contribute to his death by bombarding him with apples, by allowing him to starve for want of proper food, and by rejecting him as if he were no longer human. Although it is *because* he has become an insect that he cannot play his former family role, we might also say that when he ceases to play it, his family is no longer able to regard him as anything but an insect. In other words, even *before* his metamorphosis he was confirmed only as dutiful son and family support but not as a person. When this confirmation is withdrawn, then he cannot continue to exist; for he too sees himself, divested of his social role, not as a person, a genuine self, but as an insect!

"THE HUNTER GRACCHUS" AND "A COUNTRY DOCTOR"

One of the forms in which Kafka never tired of reflecting on the exile of modern man and of man in general is the Fall. The Fall means that we no longer hear the call that can lead us to true existence: "What is sin? . . . We know the word and the practice, but the sense and the knowledge of sin have been lost. Perhaps that is itself damnation, God-forsakenness, meaninglessness." [17] This is why the Bible, the word of revelation, "is a sanctum," but the world, that to which the word is addressed, "is a sputum." [18] This does not imply, as the Gnostics think, that we are *entirely* cut off and abandoned to evil. Kafka took strong exception to Leon Bloy's notion that the tragic guilt of the Jews is that they did not recognize the Messiah.

"Perhaps that is really so," said Kafka. "Perhaps they really did not recognize him. But what a cruel God it is who makes it possible for his creatures not to recognize him. After all, a father always makes himself known to his children, when they cannot think or speak properly." [19]

The problematic situation in which the exile finds himself after the Fall is aptly set forth in Kafka's little story "The Hunter Gracchus." Gracchus, a hunter in the Black Forest many centuries ago, fell to his death from a precipice. As a result of a wrong turning of his death ship, for which he himself bears no blame, he is condemned to travel after his death through all the lands of the earth. He lives neither in one world nor the other, therefore, but at the midpoint between the two.

"And you have no part in the other world?" asked the Burgomaster, knitting his brow.
"I am forever," replied the hunter, "on the great stair

[17] Janouch, *op. cit.*, p. 73.
[18] *Dearest Father*, "The Eight Octavo Notebooks," p. 80.
[19] Janouch, *op. cit.*, p. 70.

that leads up to it. On that infinitely wide and spacious stair I clamber about, sometimes up, sometimes down, sometimes on the right, sometimes on the left, always in motion. The hunter has been turned into a butterfly." (185)

The Hunter Gracchus' world, as a result, like that of fallen man, is a continual going astray. The Hunter Gracchus concludes his description of his existence with an image that recalls that circle of Dante's Inferno in which men are continually blown about by the wind—the circle of Francesca da Rimini and Paolo: "My ship has no rudder, and it is driven by the wind that blows in the undermost regions of death."

A still deeper level is plumbed by "A Country Doctor" in which the going astray is seen as the direct result of answering a call. The call is the sort of call for help that has given the vocation of the country doctor its reputation of unselfish response to the needs of his patients no matter how great the hardships that he must bear. One expects, too, a warm, personal relationship between the country doctor and his patients. The country doctor, in short, is the very symbol of help—a fact which makes the doctor's inability to help in Kafka's story all the more tragic and grotesque.

While the doctor in this story is trying in vain to borrow a horse so that he can make an urgent journey, a groom comes up with a pair of enormous horses and yokes them up for him. Despite the protests of the doctor, the groom sets the horses going before he can do anything to rescue his servant girl Rose, whom the groom is about to attack. As the groom breaks down the door of the house in which Rose has locked herself, the helpless doctor is whirled off in the gig at an unbelievable speed and finds himself without interval at the house of his patient. The patient, a young boy, puts his arm around the doctor's neck and whispers in his ear, "Doctor, let me die." The doctor wants to die too. He always makes great efforts to do his duty throughout the district and, though badly paid, is generous and helpful to the poor. This time, he feels his efforts exact too high a price: "That I should have to sacrifice Rose this time as well, the pretty girl who

had lived in my house for years almost without my noticing her—that sacrifice was too much to ask." What is more,
he had come to help, but the boy is not really ill and should
best be "turned out of bed with one shove." "I am no world
reformer," the doctor adds, "and so I let him lie."

Now, however, the doctor discovers a rose of a very different nature from the Rose he has lost—a terrible wound in
the side of the boy. Looked at from a distance, the wound
appears almost like a flower:

> Rose-red, in many variations of shade, dark in the hol-
> lows, lighter at the edges, softly granulated, with irreg-
> ular clots of blood, open as a surface mine to the day-
> light. . . . I could not help a low whistle of surprise.
> Worms, as thick and as long as my little finger, them-
> selves rose-red and blood-spotted as well, were wriggling
> from their fastness in the interior of the wound towards
> the light, with small white heads and many little legs.
> Poor boy, you were past helping. I had discovered your
> great wound; this blossom in your side was destroying
> you. (153)

If the doctor could not help before because he thought the
boy was not really ill, now he cannot help because the boy
is "past helping." Either way, this visit is a mockery of his vocation as a country doctor. The boy sobs a plea for the doctor to save him, and the doctor complains to himself that people are "always expecting the impossible from a doctor,"
who has now replaced the parson as the omnipotent helper
"with his merciful surgeon's hands."

The doctor is resigned to being misused "for sacred ends":
"What better do I want, old country doctor that I am, bereft
of my servant girl!" He is resigned, too, when the people, so
far from respecting him, come and strip his clothes off him
while singing

> Strip his clothes off, then he'll heal us,
> If he doesn't, kill him dead!
> Only a doctor, only a doctor. (154)

He even reports himself as "altogether composed and equal
to the situation" as he is helplessly laid into bed next to the

patient, on the side of the wound. The boy, too, turns on the doctor: " 'Do you know,' said a voice in my ear, 'I have very little confidence in you. . . . Instead of helping me, you're cramping me on my deathbed. What I'd like best is to scratch your eyes out!' " The doctor weakly responds, " 'Right, it is a shame. And yet I am a doctor. What am I to do? Believe me, it is not too easy for me either.' " When the boy reveals that his wound is an original evil that he brought into the world with him as his only endowment, the doctor's response seems still less helpful: " 'My young friend,' said I, 'your mistake is: you have not a wide enough view. I have been in all the sickrooms, far and wide, and I tell you: your wound is not so bad.' " One wonders what view is wide enough to make this wound, which the doctor himself said was destroying the boy, seem "not so bad"!

The doctor's mind is actually not on helping the boy any longer but on "escaping," as he puts it. When he does set off, the horses prove unbearably slow contrary to their lightning speed on the way there: "Slowly, like old men, we crawled through the snowy wastes." In striking contrast to his advice to his patient, the doctor shows no inclination to minimize his own misfortunes in the light of some general perspective —quite the reverse, in fact. His own going astray becomes in his eyes a general cataclysm, his own answer to a false call a wrong direction taken by a whole age.

> Never shall I reach home at this rate; my flourishing practice is done for; my successor is robbing me, but in vain, for he cannot take my place; in my house the disgusting groom is raging; Rose is his victim; . . . Naked, exposed to the frost of this most unhappy of ages, . . . old man that I am, I wander astray. . . . Betrayed! Betrayed! A false alarm on the night bell once answered— it cannot be made good, not ever. (156)

"A Country Doctor" confronts us with an evil not of man's making—the boy's wound already existed when he was born —an evil which it is not in man's power to remove and which is not going to be removed by any extra-human power or grace. Here is an almost Gnostic view of an abyss between man and God which abandons man to the evil of the universe without hope or appeal. It would not be difficult to discover sexual overtones linking the violation of Rose with the violation of the rose-wound by the worms, particularly if we play on traditional associations of original sin with sex. If so, these only add to the existential immediacy of there being no resources to bridge the abyss and to heal the wound.

> The true way goes over a rope which is not stretched at any great height but just above the ground. It seems more designed to make people stumble than to be walked upon.

> Leopards break into the temple and drink the sacrificial chalices dry; this occurs repeatedly, again and again: finally it can be reckoned upon beforehand and becomes a part of the ceremony.[20]

"THE NEW ADVOCATE" AND "A HUNGER ARTIST"

In "The New Advocate," answering a false call is replaced by calmly accepting the fact that we no longer hear a call or know a way and by settling down into tradition as the only sensible thing. The new advocate in this tiny story is Dr. Bucephalus, who was once Alexander the Great's battle charger. Nowadays there is no Alexander the Great, says the commentator. Many know how to reach over a banquet table and pink a friend with a lance,

> and for many Macedonia is too confining, so that they curse Philip, the father—but no one, no one at all, can blaze a trail to India. Even in his day the gates of India were beyond reach, yet the King's sword pointed the way to them. Today the gates have receded to remoter and loftier places; no one points the way; many carry swords, but only to brandish them, and the eye that tries to follow them is confused. (159 f.)

In the face of this general situation, "it is really best to do as Bucephalus has done and absorb oneself in law books." In a

---

[20] *The Great Wall of China*, "Reflections upon Sin, Pain, Hope, Suffering, and the True Way," Nos. 1, 17, pp. 253, 258.

time when men no longer hear a call, one might as well spend one's life in quietly reading about the times when people did hear a call. "Free and far from the clamor of battle, he reads and turns the pages of our ancient tomes." It is significant that Dr. Bucephalus settles down in the Law Courts, the very place that one might have thought most depended upon still hearing the call. But the Law Courts, as we know from *The Trial,* can exist and function without connection with the higher courts, like those men who spend their lives studying theology or the Talmud even though they believe that in our age it would be unthinkable to hear the voice of God.

Kafka's hunger artist cannot sensibly settle down in tradition, like Dr. Bucephalus, for his very existence is at stake. "A Hunger Artist" is the story of a man whose self-imposed fasts are of such spectacular length that an impresario is able to exploit this talent to draw huge crowds into a coliseum to watch as, against his will, he breaks his fast after forty days. The hunger artist, too, is concerned about the public, but in a quite different sense. He would like to find some way to convince those who take up watch all night before his cage that he does not nibble something on the sly.

> No one could possibly watch the hunger artist continuously, day and night, and so no one could produce first-hand evidence that the fast had really been rigorous and continuous; only the artist himself could know that; he was therefore bound to be the sole completely satisfied spectator of his own fast. (190 f.)

He is dissatisfied with himself, too, because "he alone knew, what no other initiate knew, how easy it was to fast. It was the easiest thing in the world." He has never yet left his cage voluntarily after a fast, and he cannot understand why his public, which pretends to admire him so much, should not have the patience to endure his fasting still longer. The people even take the exhaustion that comes as the result of the premature breaking-off of his fast as the cause of his ceasing to fast! "To fight against . . . a whole world of non-understanding was impossible." As a result the hunger artist lives for years "in visible glory, honored by the world, yet in spite of that troubled in spirit, and all the more troubled because no one would take his trouble seriously." Yet when he ceases to attract great crowds and is sold to a circus as a minor side show, he cannot be happy just fasting but wishes the admiration of the world.

> When once in a time some leisurely passer-by stopped, made merry over the old figure on the board and spoke of swindling, that was in its way the stupidest lie ever invented by indifference and inborn malice, since it was not the hunger artist who was cheating; he was working honestly, but the world was cheating him of his reward. (199 f.)

The hunger artist is caught in a still more basic paradox than that of his relation to his public, however, and that is his relation to his fasting itself. When at last he is entirely forgotten and an overseer discovers him dying in the straw of his cage, the hunger artist whispers, "Forgive me everybody." He confesses that although he has always wanted everybody to admire his fasting, actually they should not admire him since his fasting is at bottom not an art but an inescapable necessity.

> "I have to fast, I can't help it," said the hunger artist. "What a fellow you are," said the overseer, "and why can't you help it?" "Because . . . I couldn't find the food I liked. If I had found it, believe me, I should have made no fuss and stuffed myself like you or anyone else." (200)

With these words he dies and is buried, straw and all, while the cage is now used to hold a wild young panther that leaps around it and eats with relish the food that is brought him. As new life bursts forth in the bloom of young womanhood when Gregor Samsa's starved and dried-out body is forgotten by his parents in their admiration of his sister, so now, when the skeleton-thin corpse of the hunger artist is cleared away, his life-denial is succeeded by a "joy of life" that streams "with such ardent passion" from the panther that it is hard for the onlookers to stand the shock of it. "But they braced themselves, crowded round the cage, and did not want ever to move away."

The striking similarity between the deaths of Gregor Samsa and the hunger artist makes all the more significant the fact that in "The Metamorphosis" an invisible tone of self-pity seems to characterize the point of view of the commentator, whereas in "A Hunger Artist" the commentator seems to share the feeling of the spectators that it is "refreshing to see this wild creature leaping around the cage that had so long been dreary." Nonetheless, the basic irony remains the same: that of the man whose fading out of existence seems all the more pitiful because of the joyful stream of life that succeeds him. Although Gregor Samsa and the hunger artist die ostensibly for the same reason, namely, that neither can find food he likes to eat, the underlying causes of their deaths are actually quite different. Gregor first experiences a metamorphosis and only then finds that he no longer has any ground on which to stand. The hunger artist experiences no metamorphosis. He dies as he has always lived, with "the firm though no longer proud persuasion that he was still continuing to fast." If the overseer's order, "Well, clear this out now!" suggests that, like Gregor Samsa, the artist too at his death is regarded not as a person but as a thing, this "thingification" represents no gradually developing condition, as with Gregor, but only a continuation of the utter isolation that has always been his fate. Most important, while Gregor has obviously lost the will to live quite apart from his not liking the food that his sister brings, the hunger artist would have "stuffed" himself had he only found "food" he could eat—had he found some way open to a meaningful existence.

"INVESTIGATIONS OF A DOG" AND "THE GREAT WALL OF CHINA"

The "philosophical caninology" of Kafka's story, "Investigations of a Dog," stands as a companion piece to the "philosophical anthropoidology" of "A Report to an Academy." The dog in question lives "solitary and withdrawn," with nothing to occupy him save his hopeless but indispensable little investigations. Yet in contrast to the hunger artist, the canine recluse sees his questions as understandable only with the assistance of the whole dog world: "I do not possess that key except in common with others; I cannot grasp it without their help." What is more, he does not see his situation as unique, as the hunger artist does, but, with an almost ludicrous single-mindedness subsumes all questions, his own or others, under the heading of "dog" (or, as we would translate it, "man").

> All that I cared for was the race of dogs, that and nothing else. For what is there actually except our own species? To whom but it can one appeal in the wide and empty world? All knowledge, the totality of all questions and all answers, is contained in the dog. (218)

Although he sees both the method and the subject of his investigations as necessarily social, his ceaseless labors progressively cut him off from communication with anyone else and entomb him "deeper and deeper in silence, it seems, so deep that one can never be dragged out of it again by anybody." One reason for this growing silence is his awareness, in contrast to other dogs, of the meaninglessness of an accelerating progress of knowledge which only leaves the canine race more burdened than before. The modern dog is problematic as the ancient dog was not, and the very heart of his problematic is that he no longer hears the Word, he no longer hears a call. It was easier to get the dogs of old times to speak out, or at least they had the possibility. It is this that moves the dogs of the present so deeply when they listen "to those old and strangely simple stories": "Here and there we catch a curiously significant phrase and we would almost like to leap to our feet, if we did not feel the weight of centuries upon us." Thus the ancient tomes which Dr. Bucephalus ponders can lead us to the recognition that people of the past heard a call even if we no longer hear one ourselves.

Although his concern is the dog, our hero sees the advantages of the dogs of old as lying in the fact that they had not yet become so "doggish" and were therefore open to hearing the Word as later dogs are not.

The edifice of dogdom was still loosely put together, the true Word could still have intervened, planning or re-planning the structure, changing it at will, transforming it into its opposite; and the Word was there, was very near at least, on the tip of everybody's tongue, any one might have hit upon it. (232)

When dogs began to enjoy a dog's life, when the sole ambition of young dogs was to become old dogs, then the Word disappeared. "What had become of it today? Today one may pluck out one's very heart and not find it." When men became "human, all too human," in Nietzsche's phrase, they closed off their existence from the hearing of the call. But our hero does not blame the new generation for the problematic situation in which it finds itself: "Our generation is lost, it may be, but it is more blameless than those earlier ones."

> Well for us that it was not we who had to take the guilt upon us, that instead we can hasten in almost guiltless silence towards death in a world darkened by others. When our first fathers strayed they had doubtless scarcely any notion that their aberration was to be an endless one, they could still literally see the cross-roads, it seemed an easy matter to turn back whenever they pleased, and if they hesitated to turn back it was merely because they wanted to enjoy a dog's life for a little while longer. (232 f.)

Here we have no original evil such as is darkly hinted at in the wound of the boy in "A Country Doctor," nor any "original sin" that might account once and for all for the Fall. Instead, a social evil is pictured that gradually and imperceptibly changes man's situation from one in which he has freedom to hear the Word and to respond to one in which he no longer has that freedom and is cut off from true existence by his social heritage.

"The Great Wall of China" is also a scholarly inquiry and report, and it too concerns a call that comes from a remote distance. The Great Wall of China was built as a protection against the invasion of the barbarian tribes from the north. Since it was to be a protection for centuries, "the most scru-

pulous care in the building, the application of the architec-
tural wisdom of all known ages and peoples, an unremitting
sense of personal responsibility in the builders, were indispensable prerequisites for the work." The wall was constructed piecemeal, however, with the result that even now,
it is said, "there are gaps which have never been filled in at
all." The commentator dismisses this assertion as one of the
many legends to which the building of the wall gave rise
and points out that it "cannot be verified, at least by any
single man with his own eyes and judgment, on account of
the extent of the structure." This ambiguous situation anticipates *The Trial*, in which the succession of the courts is too
vast for any court official to be able to know the whole, and
The Castle, in which each castle official knows only the workings of his own department. The work on the wall is so ardu-
ous and slow that it took five years to accomplish five hundred yards, by which time "the supervisors were as a rule
quite exhausted and had lost all faith in themselves, in the
wall, in the world."

The land itself is so vast "that no fable could do justice to
its vastness, the heavens can scarcely span it." Pekin, the
capital of the Empire, is a mere dot in this vastness and is so
far removed from the native place of the commentator that
there is no actual contact with it. When the people think
about the Emperor, they cannot know whether they are thinking of the present one or some long dead one, for they know
neither who the present Emperor is nor anything definite
about him. Moreover, while the Empire itself is immortal,
the Emperor and even whole dynasties of Emperors totter
and fall from their thrones because of the "brilliant and yet
ambiguous throng of nobles and courtiers—malice and enmity in the guise of servants and friends" who always sur-
round the Emperor. These courtiers "form a counterweight
to the Imperial power and perpetually labor to unseat the
ruler from his place with poisoned arrows."

If it is almost impossible for the people to know the Emperor, it is still less possible for the Emperor to reach the people directly. "The Emperor from his death-bed has sent a
message to you alone," so runs the famous parable that Kafka

inserts here, "a message to you, the humble subject, . . . cowering in the remotest distance before the imperial sun." He has sent the message before all the spectators assembled to witness his death, and he has commanded the messenger to whisper it back to be sure that it is right. The messenger, a powerful and indefatigable man, sets out immediately on his journey, and his way is made easier for him by the symbol of the imperial sun that glitters on his breast. But the multitudes are so vast that he wears out his strength just making his way through the chambers of the innermost palace. He will never get to the end of them, much less fight his way down the stairs, cross the courts and the second outer palace, a second set of stairs and courts, another palace, and so on for thousands of years.

> And if at last he should burst through the outermost gate—but never, never can that happen—the imperial capital would lie before him, the center of the world, crammed to bursting with its own refuse. Nobody could fight his way through here even with a message from a dead man. (142)

Although the message of the Emperor never reaches you, you dream it to yourself, we are told. The conclusion of the story into which Kafka inserts this parable is very different. The effect of the distance between people and Emperor is such that in reality they have no Emperor. "There is perhaps no people more faithful to the Emperor than ours in the south, but the Emperor derives no advantage from our fidelity." Pekin and the Emperor seem to the people of the south so strange and remote that they lead "a life on the whole free and unconstrained" by any imperial edict or law. It is not that they are immoral: "Hardly ever have I found in my travels such pure morals as in my native village." But their life "is subject to no contemporary law, and attends only to the exhortations and warnings which come to us from olden times." There is revelation and there is law, but as with Dr. Bucephalus and the scholar dog, the call is heard only through what has come down from far earlier generations.

The "feebleness of faith and imaginative power on the part

of the people" prevents them from clasping the "palpable living reality" of the Empire to their breasts. What is more, their very weakness of imagination and faith is one of the greatest unifying forces among them—"the very ground on which we live." For this reason, our commentator declines to inquire any further into these matters, valuing existing society above any meaning that society might find through contact with an "above" or response to a call. "To set about establishing a fundamental defect here would mean undermining not only our consciences, but, what is far worse, our feet." The community of men has now become an end in itself.

That this view of the commentator is not that of Kafka is suggested by Kafka's parable of the Tower of Babel. Beginning with the goal of reaching heaven, hesitating to lay the foundations of the Tower for fear that a future generation with greater knowledge might destroy them and start all over, taking for granted that such a goal, once grasped by man, cannot be lost, the people spend their time in beautifying the sections of the city in which they live. They fall into such competitive rivalry that within two or three generations the heaven-storming venture is abandoned as nonsensical, while all their time is spent in fighting one another. They are too closely bound to one another to leave the city, but all the sayings and songs of the city are "filled with the longing for a prophesied day in which the city will be smashed to pieces by a gigantic fist." [21]

THE CASTLE

The contrast between the individual who dreams the message of the Emperor and the community whose very ground is their lack of faith that any such message exists points us, like so much else in this story, toward Kafka's last and greatest novel, *The Castle*. This novel is the story of the attempt of K., "a disreputable-looking man in his thirties," to get some foothold in the village which he has just entered as a total

[21] Franz Kafka, *Parables and Paradoxes*, ed. Nahum N. Glatzer (New York: Schocken Books, paperback, 1961), "The City Coat of Arms," pp. 37, 39.

stranger and to make some contact with the Castle which stands above the village. Though K. at first glance seems to be the lone exile in a community of secure and settled villagers, it becomes clear that the villagers too are in exile at the very place where it seems most unthinkable, namely, in their relation to the Castle. The mutual distrust which exists between the villagers and the Castle officials belies the assertion that there is no gulf between them and nothing to be bridged. Anyone in the village may be in the Castle as well, in the sense that the village belongs to the Castle, but "when anything really important crops up," says Olga to K., there is "grim evidence" that a gulf actually exists. Fear of the authorities is born in the villagers, says Olga, and is suggested to them by everyone, including themselves. When Olga's sister Amalia refuses to go to the official Sortini, tears up his insulting letter, and throws it in the messenger's face, her whole family becomes "taboo." What is more, definite relations between the Castle and the village seem to be impossible by their very nature.

Despite all this, practically everyone in the village has a childlike trust or dogmatic faith in the officials that rules out categorically all possibility of error and evil on their part. "The very possibility of error must be ruled out of account," the Mayor tells K. "Errors don't happen, and even when once in a while an error does happen, as in your case, who can say finally that it's an error?" "The supreme control is absolutely efficient." "Nothing here is done without taking thought." Like the man in Kafka's aphorism who is fettered to both earth and heaven in such a way that he can reach neither, the Mayor refuses to account for any discrepancy "by an error in the original fettering." He does not even suggest that beyond a certain point one stop thinking about the problem of error and of evil, as does the commentator in "The Great Wall of China." There are no such problems. The whole village shares this view, including the Barnabas family, the very people who suffer the most from an act on the part of an official which, according to any ordinary moral standards, could only be condemned as evil.

The "girl from the Castle," whom K. sees in one of the village homes with her baby at her breast, has often suggested to Kafka interpreters a picture of the Madonna and her child. Amalia, however, recalls quite a different tradition from that of the virgin who begets a child through immaculate conception, namely, the mythical Greek maidens like Leda and Europa who were raped by Zeus or some other god! But Amalia will not let herself be raped; she insists on preserving her personal dignity in the face of an overriding power that no other girl from the village could have resisted. "Her not going was heroic," says Olga, but this heroic action only serves to sink her whole family beneath a burden of guilt that they cannot handle. It is not that the Castle took action against them, but precisely that they did not—that no word came from them to assuage this guilt—which made the situation unbearable. No one accused them or made any charge against them, but so far from this leaving them free from guilt, it meant that they had to prove their guilt before they could be forgiven. Even if they could do that, no single official could pardon them, and apparently even the whole authority "can only condemn and not pardon." Their fear was the child's fear of silence, of being cut off, the adult's fear of the "eclipse of God": "While we couldn't help noticing the ostracism of the village," Olga says to K., "the Castle gave us no sign. . . . This blankness was the worst of all."

What is most terrible about the silence is that in the situation of no communication that exists between the Castle and the village, the Castle official is presumed to be right, even when he seems wrong, while the villager must presume himself wrong even when he seems right. The punishment for Amalia's "offense," as a result, is actually self-inflicted: "We weren't afraid of anything in the future," says Olga, "we were suffering under the immediate present, we were actually enduring our punishment." Even if the family had merely come out in the open and picked up its old connections without saying a word about the affair, it would have been enough. But when the villagers saw that the family had not the strength to stand up to the situation and shake itself clear of the scandal, "they turned what had only been a temporary measure into a final resolve, and cut us off from the community forever." As a result of this situation, the father, like K., spends all his time in desperate and hopeless attempts to get personal interviews with the Castle officials until the exhaustion of the family's money and the complete ruin of his health force him to his bed. Barnabas becomes an unofficial messenger in the hope of contact with the Castle that may help his family; Olga spends all of her time working with the Castle servants at the inn in the childlike hope and trust that someday some official must notice what she is trying to do for her family; and Amalia walls herself off in the silence of utter hopelessness.

K. looks on the Castle as happy and free in itself but as threatening and cruel in its relations with him. When he sees the Castle a second time, it lies before him silent and lifeless, like someone who gazes quietly in front of him "free and untroubled." The Castle seems to him so elevated that even the man who sits in the most worthless of all the antechambers is incomparably higher than he is in the village. When he turns back from attempting to reach the Castle, a Castle bell rings merrily after him "as if to give him a parting sign till their next encounter." But "its tone was menacing too as if it threatened him with the fulfillment of his vague desire." When he calls the Castle and, pretending to be one of his own assistants, asks when K. may come to the Castle, the answer is, Never. "Neither tomorrow nor at any other time." By the end of the book, K. comes to see the Castle's relation to him, as to Olga and Amalia, as "simply one single game, a game that is amazingly all of one piece."

K.'s relation to particular officials tends to follow a pattern of hope followed by disappointment ending finally in indifference. When Barnabas gives him the first letter from Klamm, "the expression in his eyes, his smile, his bearing, seemed also to convey a message." But when K. accompanies Barnabas and discovers that he is going home and not to the Castle, his "smile seemed less brilliant, and his person more insignificant." Although K. shocks the landlady of the Bridge Inn by insisting on seeing Klamm, he soon concludes himself, to quote a deleted fragment, "that anyone who believed he could, say, reach Klamm by taking a leap in the dark was after all seriously underestimating the distance separating him from Klamm." When he gets a second letter from Klamm expressing appreciation for the surveying work that he has done so far, his reaction is not pleasure at how well-disposed Klamm is to him, but "humiliation and despair" that Klamm is not aware of "the fact that till now he has not carried out any surveying at all." In the thirteenth chapter Frieda opines that K. has even stopped trying to reach Klamm, and he does indeed seem to give up his direct assaults out of exhaustion and despair. In the eighteenth chapter, when he has come to the Inn to answer a summons from Erlanger, one of Klamm's secretaries, he stumbles by chance into the room of another secretary, Bürgel, who explains to him in endless circumlocutions that his unannounced entrance has created a rare opportunity for K. and that he, Bürgel, is willing and able to help him. K. by this time is too sleepy to stay awake and too indifferent to care any more about anything closely concerning himself. The projected ending that Kafka once related to Max Brod is equally ironic: as he dies, worn out by his struggle, word comes from the Castle "that though K.'s legal claim to live in the village was not valid, yet, taking certain auxiliary circumstances into account, he was to be permitted to live and work there." [22]

K.'s relations with women at first seem more hopeful than his relations with the officials. But they are still more confused and complex, and they end with no more hope. The dominant fact about these relationships is that K. quite simply and shamelessly uses the women he relates to as means to reach the Castle. As they lie in each other's arms in the beer puddles on the floor of the bar, Klamm's mistress, Frieda, says to K. that she is never going to Klamm again. K. is dismayed and tries to fasten her disordered blouse so that she may go to answer Klamm's call. "What could he expect from Frieda now that she had betrayed everything?" He agrees to marry Frieda, but says that before he does so he must have a talk with Klamm. "It was the nearness to Klamm that had made her so irrationally seductive," he later thinks to himself as he sees her withering in his arms. He even admits to himself on another occasion that if the plump little chambermaid Pepi had been in the bar instead of Frieda and he had supposed her to have some connection with the Castle, "he would have tried to clutch the secret to himself with the same embraces by means of which he had had to do it with Frieda." The way in which K. abandons Olga, with whom he has come to the Inn, because he sees more advantage in Frieda; the way in which he works on little Hans, the son of the woman from the Castle, in order to try to get an interview with his mother; the way in which he later neglects Frieda while working to create an alliance with Olga "with the Castle in mind"—all bear out the accusation that K. exploits his affairs with women as a means to the end of reaching the Castle and that he does so "out of calculation of the lowest sort."

It is not so simple as all that, however, for at times K.'s relationship with Frieda clearly seems to be a value in itself and not just a means to an end. The first time he makes love to Frieda, on the barroom floor, K. feels that he is "losing himself or wandering into a strange country, farther than ever man had wandered before," and even as he wants to protest about her not going to Klamm, he is too happy to have her in his arms to speak and too troubled about losing her to want to send her away. When Frieda accuses him later of simply using her, as he is planning to use the woman from the Castle, he truthfully replies, "You came to meet me, just as I went to meet you, and we found each other without a thought for ourselves." Even before he knows that Frieda is Klamm's mistress, K. is struck by a vague sense of meaning that her glance conveys to him: "As soon as her eye met K.'s, it seemed to him that her look decided something concerning himself." When they are having sexual relations for the second time, their ecstasy is described as an "urgency of seeking something, and their embraces and their tossing limbs did not avail to make them forget, but only reminded them of what they sought."

What constitutes the tragic paradox for K. is the fact that

even when he sees his relationship with Frieda as his goal he sacrifices this relationship for "will o' the wisps" that he hopes will promote it.

> The conversation with Hans had raised new hopes in him, improbable, he admitted, completely groundless even, but all the same not to be put out of his mind . . . If he gave himself up to them—and there was no choice—then he must husband all his strength, trouble about nothing else—food, shelter, the village authorities, no, not even about Frieda—and in reality the whole thing turned only on Frieda, for everything else gave him anxiety only in relation to her. (199)[23]

When Frieda has left him for Jeremiah, K. seems to have some illusions that she may return to him, but he has no illusion about how he himself would act if she did. "I should be happy if she was to come back to me," he says to Pepi, "but I should immediately begin to neglect her all over again."

If K. thinks of Frieda as a means of reaching Klamm and through Klamm the Castle, he also thinks of Frieda as his entrance into a community in which he would otherwise have no foothold. Through marriage with Frieda he would cease to be a stranger and would become a member of the community with rights and duties. Without Frieda he is "a nonentity, staggering along after silkily shining will-o'-the-wisps." To Amalia he declares that all of the power he now feels at his back, all his prospects he owes to Frieda. K. wants Frieda for herself and he also wants her as a key to reaching Klamm and to belonging to the community. If he keeps her to himself, then these precious connections are lost; if he lets her go to Klamm or to the community, then he fears that he will lose her. It is, in fact, the very ties with Klamm and the community which attracted him to her that later take her from him. She cannot bear the ambiguous position that K. has taken up between belonging and not

---

[23] All page references are to the definitive edition of *The Castle*, trans. Willa and Edwin Muir with additional materials trans. by Eithne Wilkins and Ernst Kaiser (New York: Alfred A. Knopf, 1956).

belonging, conforming and not conforming. As a result, K.'s negative relationship with the assistants, of whom she approves, and his positive relationship with the Barnabas family, of whom she disapproves, become the rocks on which their own relationship runs aground.

It is K.'s going again to see Olga after Frieda has begged him not to that is the immediate occasion for Frieda's leaving him. Frieda cannot bear that the man who is her lover and future husband should have anything to do with the pariah family. It is Frieda who spread the word about Amalia's incident with Sortini's messenger so that everyone in the community could know what was afoot, and once the community has ostracized them, it is unthinkable to her that K. or anyone else could have an independent relationship with them. Frieda is, in fact, a complete and thoroughgoing social conformist. When little Hans seems to reflect some of the community scorn of the Barnabases, Frieda is so delighted that she runs over and gives Hans a kiss. Even Amalia does not see Frieda's attitude toward them as hostility but "only a parrot repetition of what she hears everywhere."

K. seems to be incapable of taking into consideration Frieda's predicament as a conformist who has put herself in an exposed position for love of him. Even though he knows it will be difficult for him to keep his visit to Olga concealed from Frieda or to justify it to her, he feels free to occupy himself with the Barnabases exhaustively as long as this furthers his relations with the Castle, and he does so "without grave qualms," even if not without grave consequences. K. comes to identify his own lonely struggle to reach the Castle with the Barnabas family's efforts to attain a Castle connection which will restore their place in the community: "He regarded it as a great consolation to find other people who were at least externally much in the same situation as himself, with whom he could join forces and whom he could touch at many points, not merely at a few points as with Frieda." Amalia has a strength that none of the other members of her family possess and that K. himself does not have— the strength to live without asking anything from the Castle or the community, the strength to resist the authorities and bear the consequences, the strength to live without illusion and without hope. "Amalia not only suffered but had the understanding to see her suffering clearly," says Olga to K. "She stood face to face with the truth and went on living and endured her life then as now."

Although *The Castle* is unfinished, it does not so much break off as taper off, leaving us with the question of whether K. continues to strive or gives up his striving. In the eighteenth, nineteenth and twentieth chapters there are a number of indications that he is abandoning his efforts. When he fails to take advantage of the unexpected grace that Bürgel offers him, it is not only because of sleepiness and fatigue but also because of indifference: he no longer cares enough or has energy enough to try to advance himself and make himself his own end. "K. . . . did certainly realize that what Bürgel was talking about probably concerned him closely, but he now felt a great dislike of everything that concerned him." This attitude is all the more interesting in the light of the fact that, so far from representing the bureaucratic red tape which has always frustrated K., Bürgel offers him a direct approach which by-passes the ordinary official channels and promises him unheard-of personal attention for his case. When K. leaves Bürgel's room, at the behest of Erlanger, who bangs on the wall and asks if the Land-Surveyor is there, he would have walked past Erlanger's room without stopping if the latter had not been standing in the open door beckoning him. When Erlanger orders him in peremptory fashion to see that Frieda is back at her job at the bar, so that Klamm may not be disturbed by even the most trivial alteration, the order sounds to K. like "scornful laughter" that confronts him with "the futility of all his endeavors.'

> The orders, the unfavorable and the favorable, disregarded him, and even the most favorable probably had an ultimate unfavorable core, but in any case they all disregarded him, and he was in much too lowly a position to be able to intervene or, far less, to silence them and to gain a hearing for his own voice. (355)

After Erlanger leaves, K. remains standing in the hall, no longer caring, watching the servant distributing the files to the rooms of the gentlemen and feeling at once detached and sympathetic. He is only mildly curious as to whether the last scrap of paper which the servant still holds is his own case, and when the servant departs from the rules and tears this paper up, K. is not particularly concerned. In the twentieth chapter, K. seems about ready to accept Pepi's invitation to come live in secret in her room at the inn with her and the two other chambermaids who are held together by "the fact that the future was barred to all three of us in the same way." There they will be safe from the winter, and spring and summer will be only a memory, "as though outside the room nothing could really happen, it's warm and snug and tight there, and we press together still more tightly." After all his strivings and all his conflict, K. seems ready to regress to a situation from where he will no longer have to go out to face the world!

In order to judge K.'s efforts properly, we have to ask whether K. is, in fact, simply defeated or whether his striving is rewarded with some confirming answer. In the interview with Bürgel, Bürgel tells K. that he must not let himself be frightened off by disappointments, and in a kindly and even eager manner unfolds at length to him the "opportunities that are almost not in accord with the general situation, opportunities in which by means of a word, a glance, a sign of trust, more can be achieved than by means of lifelong exhausting efforts." He even explains his own function to K.:

"With the loquacity of those who are happy, one has to explain everything to him . . . how extraordinarily rare and how uniquely great the opportunity is, one must show how the applicant, though he has stumbled into this opportunity in utter helplessness . . . can however, now, if he wants to, Land-Surveyor, dominate everything and to that end has to do nothing but in some way or other put forward his pleas, for which fulfillment is already waiting, which indeed it is already coming to meet. . . . But when one has done even that, then,

Land-Surveyor . . . one must resign oneself and wait."
(349 f.)

Bürgel waits in vain, however, for K. to put forward the plea
the fulfillment of which is already coming to meet him, for
"K. was asleep, impervious to all that was happening." It is
clear that a confirming grace of some kind has come K.'s
way, but it is equally clear that without a personal response on
his part, without his going out to meet what is coming to
meet him, this "fulfillment" cannot be his. Bürgel himself pro-
nounces the post-mortem on this meeting that did not come
off, and with it, perhaps, on *The Castle* itself:

> "You don't need to apologize for being sleepy, why
> should you? One's physical energies last only to a certain
> limit . . . this limit is significant in other ways too . . .
> That is how the world itself corrects the deviations in
> its course and maintains the balance. This is indeed an
> excellent . . . arrangement, even if in other respects
> dismal and cheerless. . . . There are . . . opportunities
> that are, in a manner of speaking, too great to be made
> use of, there are things that are wrecked on nothing but
> themselves." (351)

Like the Lurian Kabbala's vessels of divine grace that
burst because of a fullness which is too great for them to bear
and thus bring about the fall of the world and of man, so K.'s
sudden grace is more than he can rise to meet and is ship-
wrecked on itself. For once the endless Gnostic hierarchies
are suspended and the possibility of a direct answer to a
clearly apprehended call is present, but K. is impervious
to the call and is left with the sorry comfort that through
his limitations the order of the world is established even
though his own prospects remain "dismal and cheerless."
It reminds one of Kafka's answer to Max Brod's question
whether he could promise any hope in the view of reality
presented by *The Castle*. "Much hope for God—infinite
hope," replied Kafka, "but none for ourselves." [24] Now it is
neither the obstructions put in the way by the Castle hierar-

[24] Max Brod, *Franz Kafka. An Autobiography,* trans. G. Humphreys
Roberts (New York: Schocken Books, 1947), p. 95.

chy nor his own impatient striving but the sheer inability to respond which stands in K.'s way. "His weariness had today done him more harm than all the unfavorableness of circumstances." Or perhaps one might say that he alternates between fighting against life and retreating and has no margin left for a meeting which is not a battle with officials—an ironic comment on the man who wants to meet Klamm as a private person and meet him face to face! [25]

K.'s call is not a call to life in relation to people. It is a call to a unique and lonely relation to the Castle, the call of the artist Kafka who preferred solitude and writing to marriage and the community. K.'s fear of losing his freedom and being deflected from his goal is very similar to Kafka's own fear of losing his writing—"not that, not that!"—when he debates the pros and cons of his marriage to Felice Bauer. It is the fear of losing meaning on the part of a man who already feels that his life can offer no ordinary meaning, a man who cannot take seriously his own aping of those roles—marriage, member of the community—that give meaning to others. In other

[25] Despite all the anxious impatience of his striving, K. has always trusted that there is an overall basic meaning to the Castle and his relations to it, and his trust has been justified to the extent that through Bürgel he has received a call that offers him the confirmation of his calling that he has sought. This grace comes to him even as grace does, unexpectedly, without his having sought for it or even known of its existence. One cannot say, however, that because K. has stopped striving he has found the Tao, or the true way, nor, with Ronald Gray, that his interview with Bürgel and his detached sympathy with the distribution of the files shows that he is a man who has found grace. One cannot even say, with Emrich, that K. has risen above the tragic antinomies of his existence. Equally unsatisfactory, on the other hand, is Nahum Glatzer's contention that K. is simply a negative illustration of the error of striving while Kafka's positive message is reserved for his aphorisms: "Seeking is of no avail; but there is salvation in not-seeking: 'He who seeks will not find; he who seeks not—will not be found.' . . . This *vita contemplativa* of creative passivity, is the true home to which the exiled may return. . . . Kafka, who let his fictional characters—mediocre creatures—struggle in the sphere of impatient, impersonal, routinized, aimless activity, has transcended this sphere in his non-fiction notations." (Nahum N. Glatzer, "Franz Kafka and the Tree of Knowledge" in *Between East and West. Essays in Memory of Bela Horovitz* [Oxford: East and West Library, 1958], pp. 56-58.) *The Castle,* the crown of Kafka's work, is neither a religious allegory of a man who finds grace and fulfillment nor a nihilistic statement of hopelessness and despair.

words, the estrangement from the community is *not* a voluntary one. K. wishes to use the village as a means to the goal of reaching the Castle, but his contact with the Castle is also a means for him and not his goal. K. wants to reach the Castle in order to find a confirmation for his calling that will enable him to attain the immediacy that his life has denied him. This immediacy is not simply membership in the community and social confirmation—all of the villagers have that, and few of them seem to have what K. is seeking. But neither is it some mystic or transcendental immediacy that can be attained apart from the concrete and the everyday. It is nothing less than living in the present, a direct relation to the concrete reality of one's existence which does not have to resort to calculations and devices. Seen in these terms, K.'s tragic irony is that he uses every present moment as a means to the end of someday arriving at an immediacy which his every action prevents and denies. The result, of course, is that his striving takes him further and further away from this immediacy. Immediacy never exists in the future but only in the present; it is never reached indirectly by any sort of means but only directly when all means are put aside. It is just this direct meeting with the concrete which K. is unable to make real when he falls asleep in Bürgel's room, and the reason he cannot do so is that he is too worn out with striving for the future to be able to respond directly in the present. This is a vicious circle because it is K.'s position as an exile—one who is cut off from immediacy—that leads him in the first place to turn the whole of his existence into a means to an end and thus cut himself off still further from any possibility of direct living.

The problematic of K.'s striving is thus the problematic of the "true way": Does his failure to reach his goal mean only that he has taken the wrong way to his goal? Does it mean that "the true way . . . seems more designed to make people stumble than to be walked upon?" Or does it mean that "there is a goal, but no way: what we call the way is only a wavering" (or "hesitation"—*Zögern*)? [26]

[26] *The Great Wall of China*, "Reflections" No. 23. Cf. the German

K.'s ceaseless striving has not a few resemblances to the tireless activities of Kafka's compulsive mole. One of the reasons that K. can never cease striving is that, unlike Amalia, he is not able to face reality without hope but instead, like her father, keeps deluging himself with the hope that "this very day" he will "receive decisive news." The speaker in the fragment written from another point of view says of K., "When it comes to applying his knowledge, he somehow gets moving in a wrong way, he revolves as though in a kaleidoscope." "He makes use of every opportunity to increase his knowledge," but his knowledge "mocks him." It is not only K.'s knowledge that mocks him but all of his relationships and all of his activities. He is a man who in using everything as a means to his end loses both the means and the end. "When one begins at the bottom," says K., defending himself against Frieda's charge that he was betraying the woman from the Castle even before he had won her, "one must take advantage of everything that offers any hope whatever." So far from putting K. ahead of things, however, this "taking advantage" of everything constantly puts him behind. Thus the unknown commentator says of him:

> He has more connections here than families that have been living here for centuries, all these connections are meant solely to serve this Land-Surveyor affair of his, and because they are the result of hard fighting and have to be fought for over and over again, an eye must be kept on them all the time. (424)

K. is guilty, in fact, of impatience—the primal sin, says Kafka, which drove men out of paradise and prevents their return.[27] In the final chapter he himself recognizes that it is

original in *Gesammelte Werke*, ed. Max Brod (Berlin: S. Fischer Verlag; New York: Schocken Books), *Hochzeitsvorbereitungen auf dem Lande* (1953), p. 42.

[27] Cf. The interesting comparison of K.'s impatience with idolatry in *Franz Kafka Today*, Maurice Blanchot, "The Diaries: The Exigency of the Work of Art," trans. Lyall H. Peters, pp. 212-14. By setting out to reach the limit at once, says Blanchot, K. engenders an image, or idol, that takes the place of that limit—the imageless reality which lies behind the Biblical injunction against graven images, one that Kafka took

precisely his anxiety to attain his goal that has stood in the way of his attaining it. Speaking to Pepi and likening her situation to his own, he says:

"It is as if we had both striven too intensely, too noisily, too childishly, with too little experience, to get something that for instance with Frieda's calm and Frieda's matter-of-factness can be got easily and without much ado. We have tried to get it by crying, by scratching, by tugging—just as a child tugs at the tablecloth, gaining nothing, but only bringing all the splendid things down on the floor and putting them out of its reach forever." (404 f.)

K.'s impatience is the result of his anxiety, however—the anxiety of the exile and the stranger who has no sure ground on which to stand. Even if there were such a thing as a "true way," K. could not find it, or if he found it, he could not follow it. He does not have any access to immediate existence that would make it possible for him to live the moment for itself or relate to another person for the sake of the relationship alone. He is an exile, and none of his attempts to make contact with the community essentially changes this fact. K. himself sums up his situation when he says to the schoolteacher in the first chapter, "I am to be staying here for some time and already I feel a little lonely. I don't fit in with the peasants, nor, I imagine, with the Castle." Gardena is equally forthright: "You are not from the Castle, you are not from the village, you aren't anything. Or rather, unfortunately, you are something, a stranger, a man who isn't wanted and is in everybody's way, a man who's always causing trouble." This situation in no wise changes later on, as the unknown commentator points out:

He's been living here among us in the village long enough, after all, but he's as strange here as though he'd only arrived yesterday . . . he makes a strenuous effort

---

quite seriously. "It is impatience that makes the limit inaccessible by substituting for it the nearness of an intermediate figure. It is impatience that destroys the approach to the limit by preventing us from recognizing in the intermediate the figure of the immediate."

to be very observant, and he follows up his own affairs like a hound on the trail, but he hasn't the knack of making himself at home here . . . Finally, I suppose, it can all be reduced to the fact that he doesn't belong here. That's probably why he doesn't make any progress in his cause either. (422 f.)

K.'s not belonging is the reason for his not making any progress in his cause.

14

PSYCHOLOGICAL MIRROR-WRITING

PERSONAL FREEDOM AND PSYCHOLOGICAL COMPULSION

In Kafka the interpenetration of personal freedom and psychological compulsion is basic not only to his characters but to the relation between his writings and his life. If in his "Letter to His Father" Kafka "raised his conflict to the level of literature," he also left in that literature a content of neurotic conflict that is inseparable from it.[1] If Kafka's "Letter" and his diaries are as much literature as his novels and

---

[1] In his essay on the "Letter to His Father," (*Franz Kafka Today*, pp. 235 f.) Heinz Politzer offers us a healthy corrective to earlier Freudian analyses of this work. Kafka's "Letter" is "a literary rather than a personal document," Politzer claims, taking the very reference to the ending

stories, his novels and stories are as much autobiographical revelations as his "Letter" and his diaries. We are mistaken if we see them *either* as merely literature *or* as a psychoanalytic case history: we must see them as a total artistic and personal expression of which the literary and the psychoanalytic are both aspects.

Although Kafka's literature was nourished by his powerful inner fantasy life, it was not identical with it. On the contrary, it was, in a very special sense, a world of literary communion and dialogue which protected him as much from the insanity that threatened him from within as from the alien social world that threatened him from without. Even his diaries served Kafka as such a double protection as is illustrated, for example, in the difference between *having* and *describing* the fantasy which he relates in the entry of May 4, 1913:

---

of *The Trial* to which we have pointed as evidence of how Kafka uses "the biographical data of his life to comment upon his writings and his writings to comment upon his life." "The Oedipus situation which the letter described so eloquently had served Kafka as a literary symbol: beyond the father stands a father image upon which Kafka had bestowed enough semblance with Kafka Senior to prevent it from ever becoming God . . . a passage like this is apt to question the father-son relationship to a degree where there is nothing left but two masks grinning at each other in utter despair: a Kafka commentary on the alienation that governed his life. . . . Tongue in cheek, Kafka used both the biographical material and the therapeutic intention of the letter to perform one of the strangest and most daring games a writer ever had played with the very substance of his life. By telling his life as a fable and commenting upon it in his peculiar way, he raised his conflict to the level of literature." As soon as Kafka's "imagery is interpreted as a vehicle of messages—psychological, theological, moral or otherwise—" concludes Politzer, "the unity of his style is broken asunder, its ambiguity is spoiled, and the only wisdom to be gained is that the incompatible is incompatible."

To agree with this conclusion does not dispel the problematic aspect that Kafka's neurosis adds to his literature: it deepens it. If Politzer's principle of ambiguity bars us from following the Freudians in finding the "meaning" of Kafka's writing in its psychoanalytic implications, it bars us equally from the conclusion to which Politzer himself seems to tend, namely, that Kafka is to be regarded solely as "a writer in his own right, a litterateur if there ever was one." It is true that Kafka's poetic images are untranslatable, but that does not mean that their meaning is solely that of art.

Always the image of a pork butcher's broad knife that quickly and with mechanical regularity chops into me from the side and cuts off very thin slices which fly off almost like shavings because of the speed of the action. [2]

"I myself have torn myself to shreds," wrote Kafka. "The world—F. is its representative—and my ego are tearing my body apart in a conflict that there is no resolving." [3] Kafka managed to resolve—negatively—his specific conflict about whether he should marry Felice Bauer, but the basic conflict that underlay it he never resolved, and it did tear him apart. This conflict is at the root of the savage cruelty of stories like "The Penal Colony" as of aphorisms such as that of the animal who "snatches the whip from its master and whips itself so as to become master, and does not know that all this is only a fantasy caused by a new knot in the latter's whip lash." [4] Kafka himself underscored the autobiographical character of this aphorism when he referred to it, in a letter to Milena Jisenska, as an expression of the stupidity inherent in the fact that "torturing is extremely important to me. I'm preoccupied with nothing but being tortured and torturing." [5] This preoccupation expresses itself again and again in the fantasies that Kafka recorded in his diaries, such as standing in front of a butcher shop and imagining a huge pork sausage being inserted into his mouth and pulled out of him at the other end, or "to be pulled in through the ground-floor window of a house by a rope tied around one's neck and to be yanked up, bloody and ragged, through all the ceilings, furniture, walls and attics; the empty noose, dropping the last fragments of me when it breaks through the roof tiles, is seen on the roof." [6]

Kafka's diaries are full of references to women and sex that cast light on his heroes' relations to women, such as the following comment in which he links Felice Bauer, "The

[2] *Diaries, 1910-1913*, May 4, 1913, pp. 286 f.
[3] *Dearest Father*, "The Eight Octavo Notebooks," p. 109.
[4] *The Great Wall of China*, "Reflections," No. 26 (2nd), p. 260.
[5] *Letters to Milena*, p. 216.
[6] *Diaries, 1910-1913*, Jul. 21, 1913, pp. 290 f.

Judgment," and his fear of sex:

> I love her as far as I am capable of it, but the love lies buried to the point of suffocation under fear and self-reproaches. Conclusion for my case from The Judgment. I am indirectly in her debt for the story. But Georg goes to pieces because of his fiancée. Coitus as punishment for the happiness of being together. Live as ascetically as possible, more ascetically than a bachelor, that is the only possible way for me to endure marriage.[7]

The vague sense of meaning and promise that women hold out for K. in *The Castle* brings to mind Kafka's own relations with women, not only with Milena Jisenska, which may have been the immediate stimulus for *The Castle*, but also with his fiancées Felice Bauer and J. W., and with Dora Dymant, the girl who was with him during the last years of his life. Kafka's relations with women constituted the only middle ground between the two alternatives that tore his life apart—solitude and writing, on the one hand, and marriage and the community, on the other. As such they held a meaning for him that transcended their tempting, threatening function as doors to membership in the community. If this vague promise of meaning again and again proved itself illusory, as it does with Joseph K. and with K., it was nonetheless irresistible. Though Kafka often compared himself with Kierkegaard, he could not, like the latter, renounce women once and for all and take up his stand in isolation. This promise of meaning does not mean that women are to be regarded as phases of Kafka's or K.'s self-realization or simply as neurotic attempts to compete with the father or escape from him. All efforts to render this most opaque part of *The Castle* lucid must necessarily fail, for it is precisely here that K.'s striving to answer a call is probed to the core and its essentially ambiguous and problematic nature is exposed.

Kafka's analysis of his own temptation by sex recalls the world of *The Trial*, with its never-ending law trial and no unconditional acquittal; it also brings to mind the heroes of

[7] *Ibid.*, Jul. 23, 1913, p. 294; Aug. 14, 1913, pp. 295 f.

The Trial and *The Castle,* both of whom in their relations with women "wanted to snatch at the world with twenty hands and not for a very laudable motive either."

I am certain that I should at once take advantage, with no feeling of fear or sorrow or shame, of the first opportunity to present itself quickly, close at hand, and willingly. . . . It is true that there is a middle ground between "doing" and the "opportunity to do," namely this, to make, to tempt one's "opportunities" to one, a practice I have unfortunately followed not only in this but everything. As far as the "law" is concerned, there is hardly anything to be said against this, though this "tempting" of opportunities, especially when it makes use of ineffectual expedients, bears a considerable resemblance to "dallying with the idea of conquest," and there is no trace in it of calm open-eyed fearlessness. Despite the fact that it satisfies the "letter" of the "law," there is something detestable in it which should be unconditionally shunned. To be sure, one would have to force oneself to shun it—and so I shall never have done with the matter.[8]

Kafka knew that his endless self-analyses contributed to his illness:

This past week I suffered something very like a breakdown; the only one to match it was on that night two years ago . . . impossible to sleep, impossible to stay awake, impossible to endure life, or, more exactly, the course of life. The clocks are not in unison; the inner one runs crazily on at a devilish or demoniac or in any case inhuman pace, the outer one limps along at its usual speed. What else can happen but that the two worlds split apart . . . or at least clash in a fearful manner. There are doubtless several reasons for the wild tempo of the inner process; the most obvious one is introspection, which will suffer no idea to sink tranquilly to rest but must pursue each one into consciousness, only itself to become an idea, in turn to be pursued by renewed introspection. . . . This pursuit, originating in the midst of men, carries one in a direction away from

[8] *Diaries, 1914-1923,* Jan. 18, 1922, pp. 203 f.

them . . . it may lead to madness . . . the pursuit goes right through me and rends me asunder.[9]

Yet this very instrospection which brought Kafka so near to madness gives a unique character to his writings. If Kafka's letters to Milena Jisenska throw light on a tormented relationship that provided invaluable background for *The Castle*, as Max Brod suggests,[10] they also show Kafka as himself fully aware of the way in which his relationship with Milena was linked with his inner fantasy world, on the one hand, and his memories of childhood helplessness, on the other.[11]

Kafka found in his writing a way to listen to "the terrible voice from within" and still remain sane, a "new secret doctrine" which enabled him

> to keep my feet somewhat and be carried along in the wild pursuit . . . I can also say "assault on the last earthly frontier," an assault, moreover, launched from below, from mankind, and since this too is a metaphor, I can replace it by the metaphor of an assault from above aimed at me from above.
>
> All such writing is an assault on the frontiers; if Zionism had not intervened, it might easily have developed into a new secret doctrine, a Kabbalah. There are intimations of this. Though of course it would require genius of an unimaginable kind to strike root again in the old centuries, or create the old centuries anew and not spend itself withal but only then begin to flower faith.[12]

If Kafka's writing was his nearest approach to "striking root again in the old centuries" and creating them anew, this is in part because he recognized that his "illness" was not just an individual neurosis but the result of an uprooting—the dissolution of the community of faith in which the individual formerly lived.

You say, Milena, that you don't understand it. Try to

[9] *Diaries, 1914-1923*, Jan. 16, 1922, pp. 201-203.
[10] Janouch, *op. cit.*, Introd. by Max Brod, pp. xvi-xix; Brod, *Franz Kafka*, 3rd ed., "Neue Züge," pp. 264-294.
[11] Cf. *Letters to Milena*, pp. 63 f., 66.
[12] *Diaries, 1914-1923*, Jan. 16, 1922, pp. 201-203.

understand it by calling it illness. It's one of the many manifestations of illness which psychoanalysis believes it has uncovered. I don't call it illness and I consider the therapeutic part of the psychoanalysis to be a hopeless error. All these so-called illnesses, sad as they may appear, are matters of faith, efforts of souls in distress to find moorings in some maternal soil; thus psychoanalysis also considers the origin of religions to be nothing but what (in its opinion) causes the "illnesses" of the individual. Nowadays, of course, we generally lack a sense of religious community; the sects are countless and confined to single individuals.[13]

Kafka thus understood his "illness" as only an aspect of his existence as an Exile—his own exile and that of modern man. Kafka's works, in fact, again and again show us modern man both as problematic and as in exile.

In pointing to his exile, Kafka displayed an understanding of his "illness" that his Freudian and psychoanalytic interpreters in general do not. His sickness was an existential one: it grew not merely out of a pattern of instincts and repressions but out of a unique existential situation which is, at the same time, representative of the situation of modern man. This does not mean, however, that the various psychoanalytic interpretations of Kafka are to be dismissed out of hand. On the contrary, one of the things that makes Kafka so significant for the problematic of modern man is precisely the fact that he stands at the meeting point of psychotherapy and the image of man. We can neither ignore the neurotic aspects of Kafka's life and writings, like his religious interpreters, nor make them the clue to the meaning of his writings, like his psychoanalytically oriented interpreters. We must see them, rather, as an inseparable aspect of one whole. Kafka himself commented on Max Brod's objection that Dostoievsky allowed too many mentally ill persons to enter his novels:

Completely wrong. They aren't ill. Their illness is merely a way to characterize them and moreover a very delicate and fruitful one. One need only stubbornly keep repeat-

13 *Letters to Milena*, pp. 212-220.

ing of a person that he is simple-minded and idiotic, and he will, if he has the Dostoievskian core inside him, be spurred on, as it were, to do his very best.[14]

KAFKA'S "ESCAPE FROM FATHER"

For Kafka the search for the father was a lifelong affair and his novels and short stories are almost exclusively occupied with or dominated by this theme. In his "Letter to His Father" Kafka refers to the last words of *The Trial* in the context of his own relationship to his father: "I had lost my self-confidence where you were concerned, and in its place had developed a boundless sense of guilt. (In recollection of this boundlessness I once wrote of someone, accurately: 'He is afraid the shame will outlive him, even.)' "[15] In an earlier passage in this same "letter" Kafka leaves no doubt that it is his relationship with his father that was the origin of his whole sense of life as a trial. Referring to himself and his sister Ottla,

[14] *Ibid.*, Dec. 20, 1914, pp. 104 f. Wilhelm Emrich in *Franz Kafka* (Bonn: Athenäum Verlag, 1958) pp. 298-410, offers still another approach to the meeting of psychotherapy and the image of man in Kafka. To him, *The Castle* represents a total allegory in which K., through a face-to-face interview with Klamm, attempts to transform impersonal Eros into personal love and find thereby a synthesis of freedom and binding. Frieda is the natural woman who cannot understand why K. must go to the Barnabas family for the conscious fulfillment of his quest. Nothing would be gained, says Emrich, if K. returned to Frieda at the end, because she cannot resolve the conflict between her allegiance to impersonal Eros—Klamm—and personal love—K. Taken as an interpretation of *The Castle*, Emrich's scheme is open to serious objections, including the fact that if K.'s goal really is to make love personal through meeting Klamm face to face, the actual effect of these efforts is just the opposite, namely, to neglect Frieda constantly, to use his relationship with her as a means to an end, and to turn away from direct, personal relationship to indirect, impersonal machinations. K.'s conflict is not between personal and impersonal love but between his individual freedom, on the one hand, and marriage and the community, on the other, with his relationship to women as an uneasy middle point between the two. In linking K.'s attempt to reach the Castle with his relationship to women, Emrich indicates, nonetheless, the problematic that K. embodies. In concentrating, moreover, on the merging of personal and impersonal love, freedom and binding, he makes that problematic more specific and points us in particular to the area where the image of man and psychotherapy meet, namely, that of freedom and conditioning inextricably mixed.
[15] *Dearest Father*, pp. 170 f.

he writes:

> It is not in order to plot something against you that we
> sit together but in order to discuss—with all our might
> and main, jokingly and seriously, in affection, defiance,
> anger, revulsion, submission, consciousness of guilt . . .
> this terrible trial that is pending between us and you, to
> discuss it in all its details from all sides, on all occasions
> . . . a trial in which you keep on claiming to be the
> judge, whereas, at least in the main (here I leave a mar-
> gin for all the mistakes I may naturally make) you are a
> party too, just as weak and deluded as we are.[16]

"For me you took on the enigmatic quality that all tyrants
have whose rights are based on their person and not on reason," writes Kafka in the "Letter." His father's very speech was
marked by "that frightful hoarse undertone of anger and utter
condemnation that only makes me tremble less today than in
my childhood because the child's exclusive sense of guilt has
been partly replaced by insight into our helplessness, yours
and mine." If the child remained alive after the father chased
it around the table with threats to kill it, it was only through
his father's undeserved mercy. The mistrust that Kafka's father tried to instill in him toward other people was converted
"into mistrust of myself and into perpetual anxiety in relation
to everything else."[17] Other people belonged to that third,

---

[16] *Ibid.*, pp. 167 f.

[17] "At one time he had thought of collecting all his writings under the
title *The Attempt to Escape from Father*. Kafka saw in his father the
model of an authority which ought not be questioned—which *can* not
be questioned, without serious damage to the questioner. . . . Authority
often overrules the question of human dignity; at no time does it permit
the subject to escape without some scar, in memory of the unequal conflict. . . . Kafka's life, then, is an ever-shifting law-court scene, in
which the son is always the defendant, the father both the prosecutor
and the judge. In the course of this lifelong trial, the weight of argument brought forth by the defendant is intelligible and intelligent . . .
The Judgment and accusation, on the other hand, are frequently mysterious and vague. One is not always sure, either, that this accusation
comes from the prosecutor. It appears at times to come from the defendant—a psychological ventriloquism which is essentially a self-accusation.
Two important points stand out from the mass of court proceedings: the
deeply certain and authoritative pronouncement of the judge, which
must be accepted, though it is not entirely understood; and the vacillat-

neutral world that did not come under his father's jurisdiction
—the world outside the "penal colony."

"In the Penal Colony," is illuminated, in fact, at the very
point where it differs from Kafka's other writings by a passage
from "A Letter to His Father":

> The world was divided for me into three parts: into one
> in which I, the slave, lived under laws that had been in-
> vented only for me and which I could, I did not know
> why, never completely comply with; then into a second
> world, which was infinitely remote from mine, in which
> you lived, concerned with government, with the issuing
> of orders and with annoyance about their not being
> obeyed; and finally into a third world where everybody
> else lived happily and free from orders and from having
> to obey. [18]

If we renounce the attempt to find detailed analogies, and
with it the fruitless endeavor to discover the meaning of a
Kafka story through demonstrating its roots in his personal
life, we are left with the broad outline of three worlds. In the
first of these the accused—a figure already familiar to us—
stands under the judgment of incomprehensible laws whose
multifarious demands on him he knows he cannot possibly
obey. In the second is the judge and lawgiver—also already
familiar to us, at least twice in the shape of the father that
Kafka here gives it. In most of Kafka's writings these two
worlds confront each other, unrelieved by any third. In "In
the Penal Colony," however, we see the third world of which
Kafka speaks, a broader, happier world that lies outside the
opposition of accuser and accused—the world of the explorer.
If for a moment we think of the officer as Kafka's father, we
might look on this story as an elaborate childhood fantasy. In
this fantasy the oppressed child imagines the impossible situation of some benevolent and powerful outsider intervening to
protect him from the tyranny of his father, judging him by

ing querulousness of the defendant, as though he did not entirely trust
the reasonableness of his own argument." (Frederick J. Hoffman, "Escape from Father," in *The Kafka Problem*, ed. Angel Flores [New
York: New Directions, 1946], pp. 214-216, 245 f.
[18]*Dearest Father*, pp. 148 f.

higher standards which show up the arbitrariness and injustice of the "laws" and so-called "justice" that the father administers.

Even though his father's mistrust was directed at others, Kafka applied it only to himself, for "the world consisted only of me and you, a notion I was much inclined to have." "My writing was all about you; all I did there, after all, was to bemoan what I could not bemoan upon your breast. It was an intentionally long-drawn-out leave-taking from you." Seen from this perspective, Kafka's inability to marry was not caused by his need to write but by his fear of his father. Through marriage Kafka would become the equal of his father, a possibility which disturbed him so profoundly that "from the moment when I make up my mind to marry I can no longer sleep, my head burns day and night, life can no longer be called Life, I stagger about in despair." He analyzed this himself as "the general pressure of anxiety, of weakness, of self-contempt." The very fact that Kafka saw marriage and the family as the highest thing a man can achieve permanently barred him from it. This seems to be as much from his desire to cling to the relationship that he had with his father as from fear of his father's "castrating anger," as the Freudians would say: to attain the liberty and independence of marriage "it would be necessary to make all that has happened be as though it had never happened, which means, we ourselves should have to be cancelled out." More than this, however, marriage was his father's exclusive prerogative and private possession—"your most intimate domain."

> Sometimes I imagine the map of the world spread out flat and you stretched out diagonally across it. And what I feel then is that only those territories come into question for my life that either are not covered by you or are not within your reach. And, in keeping with the conception that I have of your magnitude, these are not many and not very comforting territories, and above all marriage is not among them.[19]

---

[19] *Dearest Father,* "Letter to His Father," pp. 190 f.

"The Metamorphosis," "The Judgment," and *The Trial* are identical in that the central theme is a "judgment" that suddenly or progressively removes the hero from the world of business and successful activity to a situation in which he no longer has any ground on which to stand. In the two stories the father makes or participates in this "judgment," and Kafka himself, as we have seen, links the judgment in *The Trial* to his relationship with his father. When Gregor Samsa's father first sees Gregor after the metamorphosis, his instant reaction is one of anger and only then of grief: "His father knotted his fist with a fierce expression on his face as if he meant to knock Gregor back to his room, covered his eyes with his hands and wept till his great chest heaved." Gregor can expect from his father even less sympathy or understanding for his plight than from his sister and mother. From the very first day of his new life Gregor is aware that his father believes only the severest measures suitable for dealing with him. To Gregor's single venture out into the living room, which his sister exaggerates to his father as "Gregor's broken loose," his father's reaction is one of triumph. "Just what I expected," says his father, rushing to the conclusion that Gregor has been guilty of some violent action. While Gregor is painfully turning round to go back to his room, his father cries out in a tone at once angry and exultant, chases him around the room, and bombards him with apples. He injures Gregor so seriously, indeed, that he is disabled for a month and his power of movement is permanently impaired. One apple remains sticking in Gregor's body, causing a festering wound that probably helps bring on his death.

Georg Bendemann, the hero of "The Judgment," seems to lead a successful, extroverted life, yet it is precisely on this man that the "judgment" falls, and in a way that implies a dualism between the self that acts and succeeds and the self that keeps to itself, like the mole, and fails. This dualism is represented in "The Judgment" by the contrast between Georg Bendemann and the friend who had "run away to Russia some years before, being dissatisfied with his prospects at home." While Georg's business is flourishing, his friend's has gone steadily downhill. In his personal life his friend has neither regular connections with the colony of his fellow countrymen nor social intercourse with Russian families. While Georg is preparing to get married, his friend has resigned himself to becoming a permanent bachelor—a theme with which Kafka was much occupied in his diaries. Georg is ashamed to write of his success and his engagement to a friend who has so "obviously run off the rails." His fiancée Frieda Brandenfeld complains that she has a right to know all his friends and significantly adds, "Since your friends are like that, Georg, you shouldn't ever have got engaged at all," thus confirming our understanding of the dualism within the self that is here implied.[20]

Georg's relation to his father also turns on his relation to his friend. When he finally writes a letter telling the news of his engagement to his friend in St. Petersburg, instead of proceeding to mail the letter he makes a special trip to his father's room, which he has not visited for months, to tell his father of his action. The scene that follows is reminiscent of Gregor Samsa's relation to his father even as it anticipates Kafka's own "Letter to His Father." "My father is still a giant of a man," Georg says to himself. His father greets his announcement with the question, "Do you really have this friend in St. Petersburg?" to which Gregor replies in embarrassment, "Never mind my friends. A thousand friends wouldn't make up to me for my father." His guilt before his father leads him mentally to revise his intention of leaving the old man living alone after he marries to "a quick, firm decision to take him into his own future establishment." He carries his senile father to bed and snugly tucks him in, but his father suddenly springs up and demonstrates that, like the father of Gregor Samsa, he has by no means lost all his strength. So far from wishing Georg to choose between his father and his friend, moreover, his father identifies himself with the interests of the friend and sees himself as protecting him from Georg's betrayal. "Of course I know your friend," he cries.

[20] For an illuminating exposition of this dualism and its relation to Kafka's own life, cf. Kate Flores, "The Judgment," in *Franz Kafka Today*, pp. 9-23.

"He would have been a son after my own heart. That's why you've been playing him false all these years." What follows is perhaps only comprehensible if we see the friend as another part of Georg's self. Georg's father describes the engagement as something that takes place only after Georg imagines he has got his friend so far down that he can set his "bottom on him and sit on him and he wouldn't move." The real reason for the engagement is a vulgarly sexual one—"she lifted her skirts like this and this"—yet "in order to make free with her undisturbed, you have disgraced your mother's memory, betrayed your friend and stuck your father into bed so that he can't move." But Georg's father has been representing his friend: "He knows everything a hundred times better than you do yourself, in his left hand he crumples your letters unopened while in his right hand he holds up my letters to read through!"

"You comedian!" Georg retorts at one time and at another, "So you've been lying in wait for me!" But his father proves on the spot his contention that, due to the strength given him by Georg's dead mother, he is still much the stronger of the two. To his claim that he has "established a fine connection with your friend" and that he has Georg's "customers here in my pocket," he adds the threat, "Just take your bride on your arm and try getting in my way! I'll sweep her from your very side, you don't know how!" It is not in any future trial of strength, however, but in the present confrontation that his father's strength proves decisive. His father's last words to Georg combine the recognition that this confrontation is already a revelation to Georg about himself—the world breaking in on the self in the most explicit sense of the term—with the judgment that seems inevitably to follow from the confrontation:

"So now you know what else there was in the world besides yourself, till now you've known only about yourself! An innocent child, yes, that you were, truly, but still more truly have you been a devilish human being!—And therefore take note: I sentence you now to death by drowning!" (17 f.)

Georg's guilt is twofold, as his father expounds it. On the one hand, it is the guilt of a man who has remained a child; who has allowed the world to center in himself; who has not been aware of the real otherness of the people with whom he has lived. On the other, so far from being able to plead the innocence of his prolonged childhood as any sort of excuse, he is described at the same time as a "devilish human being." Hence in his own person Georg combines the two principal kinds of evil—that which is committed out of ignorance and that which is committed out of an evil will or an evil nature.

Although it is difficult for us to take Georg's guilt seriously on the basis of anything that is told us in the story, he accepts it unquestioningly. Like Gregor Samsa, he has no comeback or protest to make in the face of this judgment on his existence, and like him he too accepts the cessation of his existence as inevitable. Only Georg's life does not gradually fade away, like Gregor's, but hurtles to its destruction. Georg feels himself urged from the room by his father's "sentence" and rushes to put it into execution. As he releases his hold on the railings of the bridge and lets himself drop into the water, he calls in a low voice, "Dear parents, I have always loved you, all the same." This filial piety again calls to mind Gregor Samsa, and the "unending stream of traffic" that is "just going over the bridge" as Georg falls reminds us of the continuation of their normal life by Gregor's family after his death. In "The Judgment," however, the theme of judgment and guilt is quite overt whereas in "The Metamorphosis" it is at best implied.

Why is Georg impelled to carry out his father's seemingly arbitrary and unjust sentence? In part, at least, because it is a judgment on his existence, a judgment which his guilt before his friend and before his father shows that he has already made on himself. Georg's external success is clearly of the mushroom variety—substantial to all outward appearances but crumpling at the first resistance it encounters. Although this encounter takes the form of the world breaking in on the self, the inability to withstand it seems to have something to do with the split between the external, social self that is "successful" and the internal, isolated self that has "run off the rails." Like Gregor Samsa, Georg Bendemann cannot stand his ground before his father's judgment because in reality he has no ground on which to stand. This situation, which becomes literally true at the end of the story when Georg hangs over the water, is in itself the basic existential fact of this story, alongside which the questions of whether the father's sentence is justified and whether Georg's guilt is real or neurotic are secondary.

Kafka's own commentary on "The Judgment" in his diaries throws light on the split between the two selves that helped to produce it. "The story came out of me like a real birth," writes Kafka, "covered with filth and slime, and only I have the hand that can reach to the body itself and the strength of desire to do so."

> The friend is the link between father and son, he is their strongest common bond. . . . In the course of the story the father . . . uses the common bond of the friend to set himself up as Georg's antagonist. Georg is left with nothing; the bride, who lives in the story only in relation to the friend, that is, to what father and son have in common, is easily driven away by the father since no marriage has yet taken place, and so she cannot penetrate the circle of blood relationship that is drawn around father and son. What they have in common is built up entirely around the father, Georg can feel it only as something foreign, something that has become independent, that he has never given enough protection, that is exposed to Russian revolutions, and only because he himself has lost everything except his awareness of the father does the judgment, which closes off his father from him completely, have so strong an effect on him.[21]

Kafka thus explains Georg's having no ground to stand on by the fact that he has, in the end, no access to existence except through the relationship to his father. The cutting off of this access is explained, in turn, as the result of the split between that part of Georg's self with which Kafka identifies himself and that part, increasingly alien to him, which he

[21] *Diaries, 1910-1913,* Feb. 11, 1913.

identifies with Georg's friend.

In this same entry Kafka expressly identifies himself with Georg by pointing out that Benda has the same number of letters as Kafka, and Georg's fiancée, Frieda Brandenfeld, the same initials as Kafka's own fiancée, Felice Bauer. In an entry six months later, moreover, he makes quite clear the link between his ambivalent attitude to his own engagement and the split between the two selves, one of which he identifies with his social self, the other with himself as writer. Thus, in a rather pedantic summary of the arguments for and against his marriage, he writes:

1. Inability to endure life alone, . . . of bearing the assault of my own life, the demands of my own person, . . . the nearness of insanity. . . . The connection with F. will give my existence more strength to resist. . . .
3. I must be alone a great deal. What I accomplished was only the result of being alone.
4. . . . Conversations bore me (even if they relate to literature). . . . Conversations take the importance, the seriousness, the truth out of everything I think.
5. The fear of the connection, of passing into the other. Then I'll never be alone again.
6. In the past, especially, the person I am in the company of my sisters has been entirely different from the person I am in the company of other people. Fearless, powerful, surprising, moved as I otherwise am only when I write. If through the intermediation of my wife I could be like that in the presence of everyone! But then would it not be at the expense of my writing? Not that, not that! [22]

If this list leaves little doubt as to the outcome of Kafka's internal debate, the sixth item raises a question about the nature of Kafka's aloneness that is important both for our understanding of the split between the two selves and for our understanding of the relation of Kafka's heroes to women, especially in *The Trial* and *The Castle*. Although Kafka feared that being able to become with others the person he was with his sisters might get in the way of his writing, the differ-

[22] *Ibid.*, Jul. 21, 1913, pp. 292 f.

ence between his personality with his sisters and his personality with others suggests that it was not just his aloneness but a special sort of family communion that enabled him to write. Originally, perhaps, this was the closeness of children banded together against the father, building a special world of their own in which they could move and breathe with a freedom they could not in the world of Kafka's tyrannical father. It is only one step from this fantasy world of childhood to the fantasy world that Kafka constructs and dwells in in one story and novel after another.

15

"THE TRIAL":
THE PROBLEMATIC OF GUILT

Our fullest insight into guilt as an interhuman reality and
into the problematic of guilt that grows out of it comes to
us from the works of Franz Kafka. Kafka's treatment of guilt
unquestionably includes a strong neurotic component, as the
relation of son to father in Kafka's writings strongly suggests.[1] Yet it is equally clear that Kafka is not only con-

[1] "Nowhere in twentieth-century letters is there a better case for the
Freudian," writes Frederick J. Hoffman. "The writings of Franz Kafka
are . . . persistent demonstrations of an anxiety neurosis—a constant
flight from anticipated affective danger." Hoffman links this anxiety
with the guilt arising from Kafka's Oedipus complex. ("Escape from
Father," in *The Kafka Problem*, pp. 214, 246.)

cerned with neurotic guilt but also with real guilt that arises as a corollary of one's personal situation and one's personal responsibility. "Existential guilt," writes Martin Buber, is "guilt that a person has taken on himself as a person and in a personal situation." As such, it cannot be comprehended adequately through such psychoanalytic categories as "taboos," "conventions," and "repression." It is not merely guilt-feelings but an objective reality: "Existential guilt occurs when someone injures an order of the human world whose foundations he knows and recognizes as those of his own existence and of all common human existence." [2]

"Although he imagines that he knows more about himself than did the man of any earlier time," writes Buber, "it has become more difficult for the man of our age than any earlier one to venture self-illumination with awake and unafraid spirit." Buber sees this modern problem of guilt illustrated in two of the figures whom we have seen as representative of the problematic of modern man—Stavrogin and Joseph K. Stavrogin, "the man on the outermost rim of the age," " 'commits' the confession as he commits his crimes: as an attempt to snatch the genuine existence which he does not possess." Joseph K. is not able to make a confession at all. "Not merely before the world, but also before himself, he refuses to concern himself with an ostensible state of guilt. . . . Indeed, it now passes as proved, in this his generation, that no real guilt exists; only guilt-feeling and guilt convention." [3] Each man in so doing is faithful to the stage that the problematic of modern man had reached in his author's lifetime:

> *The Possessed* was written in 1870, Kafka's *Trial* in 1915. The two books represent two basically different but closely connected situations of human history from which their authors suffered: the one the uncanny negative certainty, "Human values are beginning to shatter," and the other the still more uncanny uncertainty, "Do world-meaning and world-order still have any connection at all with this nonsense and this disorder of the human

[2] Martin Buber, *The Knowledge of Man*, "Guilt and Guilt Feelings," trans. Maurie Friedman.
[3] *Ibid.*

world?"—an uncertainty that appears to have arisen out of that negative certainty.[4]

Although the Court that K. is confronted by is "wild, crude, and senselessly disordered through and through," writes Buber, "Joseph K. is himself, in all his actions, of hardly less indefiniteness . . . as charged with guilt, he confusedly carries on day after day a life as directionless as before." He refuses to confess, not because he is proud, like Stavrogin, but because he does not distinguish himself from other men. His statement, "And, if it comes to that, how can any man be called guilty? We are all simply men here, one as much as the other," is his way of denying the existence of personal guilt and escaping "the demand to bear into his inner darkness (of which Kafka speaks in his diaries) the cruel and salutary light." In denying "the ontic character of guilt, the depth of existential guilt beyond all mere violations of taboos," writes Buber, Joseph K. is doing just what Freud wished to do "when he undertook to relativize guilt-feeling genetically."[5]

Guilt, to Kafka, must be understood within the context of two discernible stages in Kafka's thought: the world breaking in on the self, and the self seeking to answer a call. To say

[4] *Ibid.*

[5] Buber answers the question, "how the absurd confusion that rules in the court is to be reconciled with the justice of the accusation and the demand," by the assertion that Kafka lets "the just accusation of an inaccessible highest judgment be conveyed by a disorderly and cruel court." For Kafka the meaning that reaches man and demands response from him comes to him only through the absurd. Buber's conclusion, nonetheless, has to do not with man's encounter with the absurd but with the man himself and his illumination of his personal guilt: "Only that man can escape the arm of this court who, out of his own knowledge, fulfills the demand for confession of guilt according to its truth through executing the primal confession, the self-illumination. Only he enters the interior of the Law." (*Ibid.*) Buber's discussion of existential guilt includes an emphasis upon concrete and specific acts of guilt that seems quite foreign to *The Trial*, where no specific action is ever in question. By the same token, Buber's emphasis upon illumination and confession of one's personal guilt has a far more particular ring than anything in Kafka. Even when Kafka speaks of confession in his diaries, it is doubtful that he means confession of particular acts. Kafka was a man who lived all his life in a shadow world of guilt in which "the profound ambiguity between good and evil," to use Tillich's phrase, far outweighed any specific sense of sin.

that guilt originates with the world breaking into the self is to say that the world in some sense calls a man to become himself through fulfilling his "calling," that to which he is called, and that it calls him to account when he does not do so. Kafka understands this calling to account, however, in a thoroughly problematic way.

We have already seen two striking examples of Kafka's first stage in "The Judgment" and "The Metamorphosis." But the fullest and most significant treatment of the world breaking in on the self with which Kafka provides us in his novel *The Trial*. In this novel the focus up to a certain point is on the hero, Joseph K., after which it is on the Court that "tries" him and finally on how he meets the accusation of the Court. The central problem of *The Trial*, that of guilt, cannot be referred simply to K.'s subjectivity, nor to the frighteningly irregular and corrupt bureaucracy that has him in its "clutches," but to the encounter between the two. The world of Joseph K. gradually changes from the everyday business world that he takes for granted into a mysterious Gnostic hierarchy that, like some gigantic octopus, wraps its tentacles around the whole of reality until it finally crushes him to death—and most startling of all, does so with his compliance!

"Someone must have traduced Joseph K., for without having done anything wrong he was arrested one fine morning." Thus begins a book which, while it never brings to light even the most trivial offense for which K. might be arrested and punished, increasingly places in question the unambiguous insistence of the hero that he is simply the innocent victim of injustice. K. is arrested on his thirtieth birthday, executed on his thirty-first, biographical coincidences which suggest already that his "trial" is not a judgment on what he has specifically done or left undone but on his life itself. When he is told that the Law does not hunt for crime but is drawn to the guilty, K. says, "I don't know this Law," to which the warder who has arrested him replies, "All the worse for you." When K. then says, "And it probably exists nowhere but in your own head," the warder responds, "You'll come up against it yet," while the other warder comments,

"See, Willem, he admits that he doesn't know the Law and yet he claims he's innocent." K.'s very guilt, we may surmise, lies in the fact that he does not know the Law, that his life is closed to the *hearing* of the Law.

Joseph K. has successfully constructed, in fact, a life which excludes "hearing." Between the meaningless routine of his work at the Bank, where he is the chief clerk, and the meaningless routine of his "bachelor pleasures," there is no room for any kind of self-examination. This is the case with his life before his arrest:

> That spring K. had been accustomed to pass his evenings in this way: after work whenever possible—he was usually in his office until nine—he would take a short walk, alone or with some of his colleagues, and then go to a beer hall, where until eleven he sat at a table patronised mostly by elderly men. But there were exceptions to this routine, when, for instance, the Manager of the Bank, who highly valued his diligence and reliability, invited him for a drive or for dinner at his villa. And once a week K. visited a girl called Elsa, who was on duty all night till early morning as a waitress in a cabaret and during the day received her visitors in bed. (23) [6]

It is also the case after his "arrest" when he cannot bring himself to take the time needed for recalling his past life in detail.

> It would do well enough, perhaps, as an occupation for one's second childhood in years of retirement, when the long days needed filling up. But now, when K. should be devoting his mind entirely to work, when every hour was hurried and crowded—for he was still in full career and rapidly becoming a rival even to the Assistant Manager—when his evenings and nights were all too short for the pleasures of a bachelor life, this was the time when he must sit down to such a task! (161)

Since after his arrest as before it K. is allowed to carry on

---

[6] All page references to *The Trial* are from the definitive edition, trans. Willa and Edwin Muir, revised, and with additional materials trans. by E. M. Butler (New York: Alfred A. Knopf, 1957).

his business as usual and since he "cannot recall the slightest offense that might be charged against" him, he begins by dismissing his arrest as an affair of no great importance. The warders cannot say that he is charged with any offense, but they advise him: "Think less about us and of what is going to happen to you, think more about yourself instead." This advice directs us away from any specific guilt on K.'s part to his existence as such. In striking contrast to Kafka himself, however, K. acknowledges no guilt whatsoever and persists in regarding his trial as real only if he recognizes it as such. When he goes to his first interrogation, he makes a point of arriving late and does not listen at all to anything anyone else might have to say. He speaks with an arrogant tone of sure superiority that presumes a knowledge of the Court that he cannot have:

> "Behind all the actions of this court of justice . . . there is a great organization at work . . . And the significance of this great organization, gentlemen? It consists in this, that innocent persons are accused of guilt, and senseless proceedings are put in motion against them, mostly without effect, it is true, as in my own case." (57)

The significance of K.'s ignorance of the law—of his having no time for hearing and for self-examination—is indicated not merely by the routine character of his work and his pleasures but still more by his attempt, reminiscent of Georg Bendemann, to turn his whole existence into one of professional smoothness and efficiency and exclude any part of him that might "run off the rails" and become introverted or antisocial, like Georg's friend in Russia. K. must always "be prepared," he must always be in control. What makes his arrest a special nightmare to him is that it comes to him when he is unprepared, at home, in bed, not ready to master the situation with smooth professional skill without involving himself personally.

> "In the Bank . . . I am always prepared, nothing of that kind could possibly happen to me there, I have my own attendant, the general telephone and the office telephone stand before me on my desk, people keep coming in to see

me, clients and clerks, and above all, my mind is always on my work and so kept on the alert, it would be an actual pleasure to me if a situation like that cropped up in the Bank." (26 f.)

Throughout the opening stages of the trial, K. preserves the demeanor of the detached observer who is somehow not really involved in his own case. Other people seem to him mad and incomprehensible; he is always sane and cool. By the same token, he is constantly impelled to contrast the orderly nature of his own life and the disorderly character of the Court. He has no respect for the Court because its warders are "degenerate ruffians" who eat his breakfast and try to get him to give them his clothes, because its offices are in the attic of a tenement house, because the offices are dirty, the lawbooks pornographic volumes with obscene pictures, the proceedings themselves subject to interruption by a law student carrying off the wife of the usher.

> How well-off K. was compared with the Magistrate, who had to sit in a garret, while K. had a large room in the Bank with a waiting-room attached to it and could watch the busy life of the city through his enormous plate-glass window. (75)

In the course of his trial, however, K. meets other businessmen who at first thought they could conduct their cases in the same way they conducted their businesses. When he sees a roomful of defendants in the Law Court offices, he is struck by the contrast between the professional sureness of these men before the outer world and their deep unsureness before this court. He asks the man nearest him what he is waiting for, and this man immediately becomes confused and undone,

> which was the more deeply embarrassing as he was obviously a man of the world who would have known how to comport himself anywhere else and would not lightly have renounced his natural superiority. (79)

Yet neither this experience nor the warning of the Examining Magistrate that by his behavior at the first interrogation he has "flung away with your own hand all the advantages which an interrogation invariably confers on an accused man" serve to change his determination to meet his problem only with professional competence and as if it were a mere business problem, not one involving, as it so clearly does, his very existence as a human being.

> There was no need for exaggerated anxiety at the moment. In a relatively short time he had managed to work himself up to his present high position in the Bank and to maintain himself in that position and win recognition from everybody; surely if the abilities which had made this possible were to be applied to the unraveling of his own case, there was no doubt that it would go well. Above all, if he were to achieve anything, it was essential that he should banish from his mind once and for all the idea of possible guilt. There was no such guilt. This legal action was nothing more than a businesss deal such as he had often concluded to the advantage of the Bank. (158 f.)

The conclusion that he draws from this is that what is needed is the sort of strengthening of self-confidence through autosuggestion which is regularly preached to the modern businessman as the gospel of success: "The right tactics were to avoid letting one's thoughts stray to one's own possible shortcomings, and to cling as firmly as one could to the thought of one's advantage." The Court would encounter in him a formidable opponent, a man with "know-how": "These tactics must be pursued unremittingly, everything must be organized and supervised; the Court would encounter for once an accused man who knew how to stick up for his rights."

K. desires to know the people in the proximity of the Court only to "make them dance to his piping," as a deleted fragment says. If he seeks to know the inner workings of the Court, it is not that he wishes a real contact with what is higher but only information for purposes of self-defense. He persists in holding himself "completely innocent" and predicts that "in the end, *out of nothing at all,* an enormous fabric of guilt will be conjured up." (Italics mine.) He is not only "stiffnecked," as Leni, the nurse whom he takes up with, says, but also displays in general an attitude of vengeful freedom. He regards it as a good sign "that he could snatch a letter away from an official who actually had some connection with the Court and tear it up without any kind of apology and without reprisals."

In his unsuccessful competition with the law student for the wife of the usher, he consoles himself with the thought that he has been defeated only because he has insisted on giving battle. "While he stayed quietly at home and went about his ordinary vocations he remained superior to all these people and could kick any of them out of his path."

K.'s attitude is rooted in part in a distrust of other people that makes him feel that he must be completely self-reliant. In a passage reminiscent of Freud's statement in *Civilization and Its Discontents* that the more helpless one man is the more surely will another attack him even though he get no advantage out of it, a deleted fragment states, obviously as K.'s own point of view:

> No, K. had nothing whatsoever to hope for if his trial became common knowledge. Anyone who did not rise up as a judge to condemn him out of hand would certainly try to humiliate him at the very least, that being now such an easy thing to do. (322)

A more important clue to the attitude which leads K. to try to master his trial as a business deal and completely deny any guilt is the written defense that he thinks of drawing up when he finally does turn his attention to his case:

> He had often considered whether it would not be better to draw up a written defense and hand it in to the Court. In this defense he would give a short account of his life, and when he came to an event of any importance explain for what reasons he had acted as he did, intimate whether he approved or condemned his way of action in retrospect, and adduce grounds for the condemnation or approval. (142)

It is clear from this passage that K. wishes to reduce the question of his guilt to a sum of external actions, that he wishes to see himself, in fact, as accountable only in his actions and not as a person. But everything in *The Trial* suggests that it is not his detached actions but precisely his existence which is on trial and that his insistence on regarding his life as no more than the sum of his actions is itself, perhaps, his chief guilt.

K.'s guilt, in other words, so far as we can glimpse it, is neither legal nor social, but existential. By this we do not mean, as so many existentialists do, that his guilt is only or even primarily in relation to himself, for his existence is inseparable from his relations to others. But we do mean that he is accountable as a person and not just as someone who fulfills a social role. When the novel opens, he knows his existence only as that of the chief clerk of the Bank. By drawing him forth from the social confirmation that such a role gives him to the solitude in which he has to face his trial just as the person he is, with no help from others, his "arrest" has forced him to become aware of a personal dimension of existence that he would never have noticed of his own free will. He learns the hard way that "combined action against the Court is impossible. Each case is judged on its own merits." He not only speaks in the name of the general public, but at the first interrogation tries to aid his cause through winning over a significant part of the audience to his side. When he discovers that both the parties of the Right and of the Left have identical badges, he sees this as a conspiracy against him.

> "So!" cried K., flinging his arms in the air, his sudden enlightenment had to break out, "every man jack of you is an official, I see, you are yourselves the corrupt agents of whom I have been speaking, you've all come rushing here to listen and nose out what you can about me, making a pretense of party divisions, and half of you applauded merely to lead me on, you wanted some practice in fooling an innocent man." (59 f.)

This situation can be interpreted in quite a different way,

however, namely, that the men with whom K. comes in contact cannot be his allies since he has built his life on the exclusion of the reality of other people and wants to relate to them only in so far as he has mastered them. Every person who meets him is a potential judge, for that person has a reality quite alien to his own existence that confronts it and calls it in question.

To understand the full significance of the fact that even after his arrest and during his trial, K. is still unwilling to relate to others or himself in a way essentially different from before, we must seek to know more fully the nature of what he is confronted with—the court and its officials and the procedure of the trial. Our questions concerning K. by no means imply that he is faced with a system of law which is, in fact, rational, orderly, and just. All the evidence implies the contrary, or rather, it implies that most of the workings of the Law are far removed from sight and understanding, while what can be seen offers us a spectacle of disgusting disorder, as in the dirt and confusion that greet K. at the entrance to the flat of the Court painter Titorelli. Like the *deus absconditus* of the Gnostics, "the higher officials keep themselves well hidden." [7] Their remoteness keeps them from be-

[7] According to Martin Buber, Kafka was very much concerned about the Gnostic conception of powers that rule over the world in God's stead: "In an important note in his diary, from the time of the genesis of *The Trial* Kafka speaks 'of being occupied with the Biblical figure of the unjust judges. . . .' The Eighty-second Psalm, of which he is clearly speaking here, has as its subject God's judgment over those 'sons of God,' or angels, to whom He had entrusted the regimen over the human world and who had vilely misused their office and 'judged falsely.' The content of this late psalm is connected with that of the Oriental myth, elaborated by the Gnostics, of the astral spirits who fatefully determine the destiny of the world, but from whose power that man may become free who dedicates himself to the concealed highest light and enters into rebirth. I have reason to assume that Kafka also knew this myth at that time." In a footnote Buber adds, "I refer to a question concerning this myth that Kafka put to me at the time of his visit to my house in Berlin in 1911 or 1912." (Martin Buber, "Guilt and Guilt Feelings," *op. cit.*)

If in most of Kafka's writings, the world seems given over without recourse to unjust rulers, in "In the Penal Colony" a higher reality enters for once to establish a higher justice. Kafka's world ordinarily resembles that of the Gnostics, who removed God to an unreachable distance and

ing in touch with the populace, with the result that they have no understanding of human relations and are often utterly at a loss in difficult or even quite simple cases. What is more, they do not even understand the workings of their

---

set a demiurge, or evil creator God, in unrestricted dominion over the world. "In the Penal Colony," however, resembles Psalm 82 in which the psalmist calls on God to awaken and judge the judges who do evil in his name. If the result of the Explorer's intervention is a seemingly permanent modification of the more inhuman aspects of this tyranny (assuming, as we cannot really do, that the old Commandment does not return to power as the prophecy predicts), we are nonetheless left with the fact that the intervention is only temporary, that in the end the world of the colony remains sealed off from the rest of the world, and that this world is a *penal* colony whose inmates must be punished by one method or another. In other words, if we put too much emphasis either on the abolition of the Harrow or on the intervention of the Explorer, we lose sight of the basic fact that dominates the story from the beginning to the end, namely, that human existence is seen as essentially that of a penal colony from which there is no possibility of escape. In the face of this gruesome and omnipresent fact, the horrors of the Harrow fade into mere sensationalism.

A remarkable link between "In the Penal Colony" and *The Trial* is the sketch, "A Singular Judicial Procedure," which we find in Kafka's diaries. This sketch combines all the horror of "In the Penal Colony" with the arbitrariness of "The Judgment" and the sense of inexorability and impossibility of appeal of *The Trial*. The condemned man is stabbed to death in his cell by the executioner without any other person being permitted to be present. When the executioner asks him if he is ready, he screams: " 'You're not going to kill me, not going to put me down on a cot and stab me to death, you're a human being after all, you can execute someone on a scaffold, with assistants and in the presence of magistrates, but not here in this cell, one man killing another! . . . You will take me to another jail; . . . they will not execute me!'

"The executioner loosens a new dagger . . . and says: 'You are probably thinking of those fairy tales in which a servant is commanded to expose a child but does not do so and instead binds him over as apprentice to a shoemaker . . . this, though, is not a fairy tale.' " (*Diaries, 1914-1923,* Jul. 22, 1916, pp. 162 f.) Only in the world of fairy tales can the self hope for either justice or mercy in the face of the world. The Gnostic conception to which we referred above—that of being cut off from the higher powers of mercy and love even while being delivered inexorably to the lower powers of cruel justice and evil—is brought out explicitly in the first version of "A Singular Judicial Procedure," which occurs in Kafka's diaries three days before the one we have quoted. In this version, at the time when the condemned man is stabbed to death in his room without witnesses, he is seated at his table finishing a letter in which he writes: "O loved ones, O angels, at what height do you hover, unknowing, beyond the reach of my earthly hand."

own vast, complex, and secretive system which, again like the system of the Gnostics, is divided into gradations of higher and lower.

> The ranks of officials in this judiciary system mounted endlessly, so that not even the initiated could survey the hierarchy as a whole. And the proceedings of the Courts were generally kept secret from subordinate officials, consequently they could hardly ever quite follow in their further progress the cases on which they had worked. (149)

As a result of this situation "all the officials were in a state of constant irritation," and it is much better not to bring oneself to the attention of the "ever-vengeful officials" by suggesting reforms lest the machinery of justice become "still more rigid, more vigilant, severer, and more ruthless." If there ever is any grace on the part of the officials, it is not predictable, for one can lay down no fixed principles for dealing with them. When Titorelli sets out to paint the goddess of Justice for an official of the Court, he is instructed to paint it as the goddesses of Justice and Victory in one. The picture that results ominously resembles neither the goddess of Justice, nor even the goddess of Victory, "but looked exactly like a goddess of the Hunt in full cry." At the same time, K. is told by Titorelli that "everything belongs to the Court."

As under totalitarianism, which Kafka himself never experienced but perhaps foresaw, the loss of his case means not only the absolute ruin of the accused but the ruin of all his relatives along with him. The methods of justice, too, are typical of totalitarianism. Defending counsel is eliminated as much as possible in order to lay the whole onus of defense on the accused. The proceedings are not only kept secret from the general public, but from the accused as well. The accused has no access to the Court records, and finally the case reaches the stage where it is "conducted in remote, inaccessible Courts, where even the accused was beyond the reach of a lawyer." The only way to get out of "the clutches" of the Court is to confess one's guilt at the first possible moment, Leni tells K., and even then one cannot manage it without outside help. And the tradesman Block tells K., "People under suspicion are better moving than at rest, since at rest they may be sitting in the balance without knowing it, being weighed together with their sins." This principle, which recalls the story of Kafka's mole, throws an ironic light on the statement that the friend of a typist he is pursuing makes to K.: "The slightest uncertainty even in the most trifling matter is always a worry."

That anxiety, uncertainty, and ceaseless movement are the very principle of the Law as well as the best course for the accused is depressingly illustrated by the choices which Titorelli outlines to K. when he comes to visit him. "Since you're innocent," he says to him, "of course it would be possible for you to ground your case on your innocence alone. But then you would require neither my help nor help from anyone." In the light of what follows, this sounds very much like irony. Titorelli has never encountered one case of definite acquittal, and though the majority of legends of former times are about such acquittals, "they can be believed, but they cannot be proved." In any case, Titorelli knows of only two actual possibilities: "ostensible acquittal" and "indefinite postponement." The power to grant a final acquittal "is reserved for the highest Court of all, which is quite inaccessible to you, to me, and to all of us." All that the Judges of the lower Courts can do is to take the burden of the charge off the accused man's shoulders for the time being, with the possibility that he will be arrested again as soon as he gets home, when his best hope will once again be ostensible acquittal. "The great privilege . . . of absolving from guilt our Judges do not possess." Postponement, on the other hand, necessitates remaining continuously in personal touch with the Court. It "does not demand such intense concentration of one's energies as an ostensible acquittal, yet on the other hand it does require far greater vigilance."

"Both methods have this in common, that they prevent the accused from coming up for sentence." "But they also prevent an actual acquittal," said K. in a low voice, as if embarrassed by his own perspicacity. "You have grasped the kernel of the matter," said the painter quickly. (202)

If the contrast between the lower and the higher Judges and the impossibility of real salvation for those to whom the higher Court is inaccessible reminds us once again of the Gnostics, it can also be translated into terms of our own existence. The situation of K., who is torn out of the security of his social role into the anxiety of personal accountability, is to some extent the situation of every man who at one time or another in his life suddenly finds himself standing alone without those supports of family, position, and name that are so familiar to him that he has come to take them for granted. So, too, every man stands, whether he knows it or not, in a continuous personal accountability so long as he lives. No man achieves a plane where he may not only approve of all he has been but may take for granted his responses to the new, unforeseen situation that awaits him. Our existence in time is characterized above all else by just this necessity of meeting the new face that the moment wears. In other words, the possibility of a final decision that is true of an ordinary trial is not true of our existence itself. "Only our concept of time makes it possible for us to speak of the Day of Judgment by that name," says Kafka in one of his aphorisms; "in reality it is a summary court in perpetual session." [8] If one thinks of guilt not in legal but in personal and existential terms, then it becomes impossible to say, as K. says, that one is completely innocent. The question of whether one's existence is authentic or inauthentic cannot be answered by the sum of one's actions, as K. wishes, nor by any objective standard that detaches guilt from one's personal existence itself. Neither is it merely a subjective or arbitrary matter, but the responsibility of the self in relation to the world. This responsibility cannot be judged from the standpoint of the world alone or of the self alone nor of any third party looking at the world and the self, but only within the relationship itself. "Only he who is a party can really judge," reads an-

[8] *The Great Wall of China,* "Reflections on Sin, Pain, Hope and the True Way," No. 38, p. 263.

other Kafka aphorism, "but as a party he cannot judge. Hence it follows that there is no possibility of judgment in the world, only a glimmer of it." [9] This means too that man is accountable for his existence and is accountable alone, without any possibility of a "joint defense." "You are the problem. No scholar to be found far and wide," says Kafka in a remarkably Zen-like aphorism. [10]

In the course of the book K. experiences a growing anxiety about his case arising from the failure of his attempts to master the situation. His trial works on K. as an ever greater distraction so that he is no longer able to concentrate on his business or be really present to the external world which was his life. Speaking psychologically, one might say that Kafka describes a man whose unconscious impulses or anxieties block his conscious drive for success, a man whose life is more and more preoccupied with and distracted by a guilt that he cannot face. Although he feels that he cannot afford the time, when he leaves the office to visit Titorelli, he is "almost elated at the thought of being able to devote himself entirely to his case for a while." This, in turn, produces growing anxiety about his work, fear lest his rival the Assistant Manager will take over all his clients, fear lest some time when he leaves he will not be allowed to return. This anxiety results in self-delusions, such as attacking the Assistant Manager's peace of mind so that he "be made to realize as often as possible that K. was still alive, and that like all living things he might yet one day astonish the world with new potentialities."

This is not, however, the chief delusion of the man who claims that he is completely innocent and who regards Leni's advice that he must make a confession of his guilt as merely a further proof of the corruption of the Court. As he waits in the Cathedral to show around a visiting Italian businessman, he hears a priest call out his name in words that "were unambiguous and inescapable." The priest ascends the pulpit and addresses his one-man audience, "Do you know that your

[9] *Dearest Father,* "The Eight Octavo Notebooks," p. 76.
[10] *The Great Wall of China,* "Reflections," No. 19, p. 258.

case is going badly? . . . Your guilt is supposed, for the present, at least, to have been proved." In his response K. shows that even now he has not succeeded in understanding the two essential points which he might have learned from his trial, namely, that his guilt is not a question of specific external acts measured on some objective scale and that he is being called to account as the unique person he is and not as a social being who may sidestep his personal responsibility through comparison with other men.

> "But I am not guilty," said K.; "it's a mistake. And, if it comes to that, how can any man be called guilty? We are all simply men here, one as much as the other." "That is true," said the priest, "but that's how all guilty men talk." (264)

Then the priest tells K. that the verdict is not suddenly arrived at like the usual legal decision: "The proceedings only gradually merge into the verdict." The proceedings and the verdict have an organic continuity with each other since what is in question here is no single crime but a line of inauthentic existence that gradually crystallizes into its own judgment on itself.

K.'s reaction to all this is to think once again in terms of extrinsic actions and external rearrangements: "There are several possibilities I haven't explored yet." But like the warders who advised K. to think about himself, the priest says to him disapprovingly, "You cast about too much for outside help, especially from women. Don't you see that it isn't the right kind of help?" When even now K. cannot understand what is in question, the priest, in a desperate attempt to get through to him, shrieks from the pulpit, "Can't you see one pace before you?" and the author himself comments, "It was an angry cry, but at the same time sounded like the unwary shriek of one who sees another fall and is startled out of his senses." All that K. can sense, however, is the priest's good intentions, and his only thought is how he can use the priest to "obtain decisive and acceptable counsel" which may help circumvent his case, "a breaking away from it altogether, a mode of living completely outside the jurisdiction of the

Court." In short, either through the fact that one man is no different from another or through some clever manipulation of circumstances, K. still hopes to escape from personal accountability back into the routine, professional existence which he led before his arrest.

"I have more trust in you than in any of the others," K. confides to the priest, to which the priest replies, "You are deluding yourself about the Court," and tells him Kafka's famous parable of the Law. In this parable the man from the country who demands admission to the Law is told by the doorkeeper that, although it is possible that he may be admitted later, he cannot be admitted at the moment. The man from the country thinks that the Law "should be accessible to every man and at all times," but he is too frightened of the succession of doorkeepers to try to force his way in. Instead he waits for years before the door of the Law, wearying the doorkeeper with his importunity. Finally, when his eyes grow dim, he perceives in the darkness "a radiance that streams inextinguishably from the door of the Law." Before he dies he calls the doorkeeper over to him and says, "Everyone strives to attain the Law, how does it come about, then, that in all these years no one has come seeking admittance but me?" "No one but you could gain admittance through this door," answers the doorkeeper, "since this door was intended for you. I am now going to shut it."

All K. can see in this parable is that the doorkeeper deceived the man and that he "gave the message of salvation to the man only when it could no longer help him." The priest points out that the doorkeeper was not asked the question any earlier and that his two statements—that he cannot admit the man at the moment and that this door was only intended for him—do not necessarily contradict each other. The essential meaning of the parable of the Law is clearly that of the existential character of K.'s guilt and the uniqueness of his personal responsibility for that guilt. The Law is not available to every man at every moment for the simple reason that in the reality of one's personal existence one is not approached at every moment and one is not always ready to go forth to meet what comes. Something is required of one before a decisive meeting can take place, something that K. is unwilling to do, namely involving one's whole person in one's actions in such a way that one becomes genuinely responsible for them. This in no way contradicts the statement that the door is intended just for this man, for what is in question here is not some universal law that applies to men in general, but a unique relationship to reality that is available to no one else. The door is shut at the time of the man's death because with the end of his existence the possibility of the realization of this unique relationship also disappears.

Although K. himself insists on leaving, he complains to the priest, "You were so friendly to me for a time, . . . and now you let me go as if you cared nothing about me." The priest's reply once more points K. back to himself: "The Court wants nothing from you. It receives you when you come and it dismisses you when you go." All that K. seems to have learned from his whole trial, in the end, however, is not to rebel. "There would be nothing heroic in it were he to resist, to make difficulties for his companions, to snatch at the last appearance of life by struggling." Even at the moment of his own death he wishes to keep up his role as a detached observer: "The only thing for me to go on doing is to keep my intelligence calm and analytical to the end." Now that he has lost his case and is about to be executed he incomprehensibly becomes concerned with showing other people that he has learned something from his year's trial: "Are people to say of me after I am gone that at the beginning of my case I wanted to finish it, and at the end of it I wanted to begin it again?"

K. actually has learned something from his trial—"I have been left to say to myself all that is needed"—and something about the real nature of his guilt—"I always wanted to snatch at the world with twenty hands, and not for a very laudable motive, either." Although the gaps in the novel leave us with no explanation for this change in his point of view, it is clear that K. now accepts his guilt and complies with his own execution. When, on the way to the place where he is executed, he sees a girl in front of him who reminds him of the typist, he keeps her in sight "only that he might not forget the lesson she had brought into his mind"—presumably his folly in seeking help from women instead of from himself. But when a window opens above him as he lies on the ground waiting for the partners to kill him and someone leans forward and stretches out his arms toward him, he cannot resist a moment of protest and a moment of hope:

> Who was it? A friend? A good man? Someone who sympathized? Someone who wanted to help? Was it one person only? Or was it mankind? Was help at hand? Were there arguments in his favor that had been overlooked? Of course there must be. Logic is doubtless unshakable, but it cannot withstand a man who wants to go on living. Where was the Judge whom he had never seen? Where was the High Court, to which he had never penetrated? He raised his hands and spread out all his fingers. (286)

K.'s reaching out does not save him from a grotesque and cruel death. As he lies dying, after the knife is plunged into his heart, he exclaims, "Like a dog!" to which the author adds, in the last words of the novel, "it was as if the shame of it must outlive him." If Kafka, as we have seen, identified this ending with a sense of guilt inculcated in him since childhood, it is also equally clearly a moment of judgment and self-judgment. "I really do envy youth,' Kafka told his young friend Gustav Janouch in a statement remarkably like the ending of *The Trial:* "The older one grows, the larger one's horizon. But the possibilities of life grow smaller and smaller. In the end, one can give one one look upwards, give one breath outwards. At that moment a man probably surveys his whole life. For the first time—and the last time." [11]

In the story of Amalia and her family, dimensions of the problem of guilt are reached that do not appear in *The Trial.* In *The Trial*, K. is guilty without any specific act ever being charged against him. In Amalia's case there is a specific act, but one which, on the face of it, would seem in no way to involve guilt. In *The Trial*, K. is arrested—"the world breaks

[11] Janouch, *op. cit.,* p. 91.

in on the self." In *The Castle* there is nothing but withdrawal —withdrawal of the official Sortini into impregnable silence, withdrawal of the villagers from association with the taboo family, and withdrawal of the family themselves. Guilt, then, becomes the state of being in which the relation of the self to the world is broken, the obstacle which must be overcome before this relation can be resumed. The more guilty one is, the more one is thrown back on oneself; the more one is thrown back on oneself, the more guilty one is likely to feel.

This vicious circle of isolation is experienced by the members of the Barnabas family. The father, Olga, and Barnabas tend to handle the "family burden of guilt" by ceaseless, senseless acts of propitiation. Amalia reacts to this burden by withdrawal into silence. Both attitudes have the same effect of intensifying and making irrevocable the isolation from other people and the world. Amalia's proud reserve bears much resemblance to the "demonic shut-inness" of the Kierkegaardian genius whose suffering cuts him off from the universal. It is as much a recognition of guilt as her father's frantic efforts to obtain forgiveness, and, like the latter, has the curious effect of making real a guilt which before was only a possibility. By failing to stand up to this situation they not only accept their guilt and encourage everyone else to do so, they actually become guilty for cutting themselves off from life. Hence K.'s feeling of revulsion when he first encounters the family, and his uncertainty, after his initial indignation with the authorities and sympathy with Amalia, as to whether Amalia's action "was noble or petty, clever or foolish, heroic or cowardly."

The problem of evil enters all over again, however, as soon as we ask whether they can be expected to have the strength to stand up to the situation when its primal presupposition is the removal of that connection with life which had formerly sustained them. Their ostracism by the village is less the result of the taboo that attaches to the transgressor than it is the result of that which attaches to the man who innocently suffers and whose suffering is somehow shameful in its very helplessness. "They didn't underestimate our difficulties . . ." says Olga, "and they knew that probably they wouldn't have stood up to them any better themselves, but that made it only all the more needful to keep clear of us. . . . We were no longer spoken of as ordinary human beings. . . . Whatever we did, whatever we had, it was all despicable."

In *The Trial,* Kafka is clearly as concerned about the grotesque absurdity of the world that K. encounters as about K.'s existential guilt. But he is concerned most of all about the confrontation of these two, about what happens when the world breaks in on the self as it does on K. Although the world that confronts the self is absurd, it places a real demand on the self that the latter must meet. The self can find meaning in its existence neither through rationalizing away the absurdity of the world nor through rejecting the world's demand because of this absurdity, but through answering with its existence the demand that comes to it through the absurd and that can reach it in no other way. This is the ultimate meaning of the self breaking in on the world, as Kafka develops the theme.

In the light of this meaning many of Kafka's paradoxical aphorisms become clear, even as they serve to illuminate our understanding of Kafka's treatment of judgment and guilt. "In the fight between you and the world back the world," says Kafka and adds, "One must not cheat anybody, not even the world of its triumph." One may back the world because, frightening and grotesque as it is, it is only through letting the world break in on oneself and answering its demands that one can attain true existence. Therefore, one cannot, indeed, make the "mole" and his endless efforts for self-defense one's model, nor Eduard Raban who in a Kafka fragment stays home in the form of an insect while he sends his poor body forth. "From a real antagonist boundless courage flows into you," writes Kafka, in a spirit exactly the contrary of his peace-seeking mole. The choice is not between the self and the world; the self becomes itself in the meeting with the world. "Test yourself on humanity. It makes the doubter doubt, the believer believe." One ought not retreat into oneself in order to avoid suffering, but bear suffering as an inescapable part of one's meeting with the world: "You can hold back from the suffering of the world, you have free permission to do so and it is in accordance with your nature, but perhaps this very holding back is the one suffering that you could have avoided." The way in which the world breaks in on the self and the judgment and demand that the world makes on the self vary, accordingly, with the way in which the self goes forth to meet the world: "In a light that is fierce and strong one can see the world dissolve. To weak eyes it becomes solid, to weaker eyes it shows fists, before still weaker eyes it feels ashamed and smites down him who dares to look at it." [12]

This does not mean that the key to real existence lies in sociality. On the contrary, it is necessary for the self to know how to stand alone in meeting the demand of the world that is placed on it. "Truth is what every man needs in order to live but can obtain or purchase from no one. Each man must reproduce it for himself from within. Otherwise he must perish." [13] "Evil is anything that distracts" from one's essential task, and "one means that Evil has is the dialogue." [14] One must stand one's own ground and not be drawn off into distracting relationships, but not in the sense of Joseph K., whose concern for self-protection leaves him without a real self: "Two tasks on the threshold of life: To narrow your circle more and more, and constantly to make certain that you have not hidden yourself somewhere outside it." [15] In the end, the demand that the world makes on us cannot be separated from the demand that we, by our very existence, make on it: "We hold the world fast and complain that it is holding us." [16]

Kafka emphatically denies that his view of life as a judgment was merely a psychological matter. On the contrary, he sees life itself as erected upon inner justification, and the

[12] *The Great Wall of China,* "Reflections," Nos. 50, 51, 20, 71, 99, 52 (2nd), pp. 266, 258, 273, 283, 267.
[13] Janouch, *op. cit.,* p. 94.
[14] *Dearest Father,* "The Eight Octavo Notebooks," p. 72.
[15] *The Great Wall,* "Reflections," No. 90, p. 280.
[16] *Dearest Father,* "The Eight Octavo Notebooks," p. 94.

task of such a justification as essential to human existence:

> It seems as though he were underpinning his existence with retrospective justifications, but that is only psychological mirror-writing;—in actual fact he is erecting his life on his justifications. Admittedly, every human being must be able to justify his life (or his death, which amounts to the same); he cannot escape this task. . . . We see every human being living his life (or dying his death). This achievement would not be possible without an inner justification: no human being can live an unjustified life.[17]

By "inner justification" Kafka in no sense means an act of arbitrary self-confirmation or the self's free choice of its own image of man in responsibility only to itself. On the contrary, he holds that time itself, and our own existence in time, must be justified before eternity: "Eternity is not temporality at a standstill. What is oppressive about the concept of the eternal is the justification, incomprehensible to us, that time must undergo in eternity and the logical conclusion of that, the justification of ourselves as we are."[18]

Eternity, to Kafka, is not a mystic absolute which we contemplate but a reality beyond space and time which *calls* us, and our existence in space and time is our answer or our failure to answer this call. "Every human being is here asked two questions of creed: first as to the credibility of this life, secondly as to the credibility of his goal."[19] The very fact of being asked about one's life and having to answer—of being called and responding to the call—is the inner meaning of the justification which Kafka sees as the underpinning of human existence. We may even say that this call is at the same time a "calling to account," in the sense that it makes us accountable for our lives. Moreover, when we have tried to avoid this accountability, like Joseph K., then the judgment that follows is a calling to account for our failure to answer the call. "Sin is turning away from one's own vocation, mis-

[17] *Ibid.*, p. 100.
[18] *Ibid.*, p. 94.
[19] *Ibid.*, p. 101.

understanding, impatience, and sloth—that is sin." [20] Impatience and sloth, therefore, are failure to follow one's vocation—to answer one's call—or the attempt to follow it in the wrong way. Because of this failure we have gone astray, and because of it "this world" continues to be "our going astray." [21]

> There are two cardinal sins from which all others spring: impatience and laziness. Because of impatience we were driven out of Paradise, because of laziness we cannot return. Perhaps, however, there is only one cardinal sin· impatience. Because of impatience we were driven out, because of impatience we cannot return. [22]

Our sin is not that we know good and evil but that, knowing it, we have no share in true existence: "We are sinful not merely because we have eaten of the Tree of Knowledge, but also because we have not yet eaten of the Tree of Life. The state in which we find ourselves is sinful, quite independent of guilt." [23] This does not mean that some "original sin" has deprived us of moral freedom. "The root of men's guilt," said Kafka to Janouch, is

> "that they prefer the evil which lies so temptingly close at hand to the moral values which seem so difficult to attain." "Perhaps they cannot act otherwise," I said. Kafka shook his head vigorously. "No. Men can act otherwise. The Fall is the proof of their freedom." [24]

We hear the call only in a confused and ambiguous way. Perhaps, like the man in Kafka's "He," we do not so much hear the call as feel its effect upon us: "He has no anxiety of any kind about himself. There exists, however, a Someone completely unknown to him, who has a great and continuous anxiety for him—for him alone . . . the consciousness of this anxiety sometimes causes him torturing headaches in his

[20] Janouch, *op. cit.*, pp. 96 f.
[21] *Dearest Father*, "The Eight Octavo Notebooks," p. 90.
[22] *Great Wall*, "Reflections," No. 3, pp. 253 f.
[23] *Parables and Paradoxes*, "Paradise," p. 29.
[24] Janouch, *op. cit.*, p. 65.

quieter hours." [25] Or, like Kafka himself, we may hear the call of eternity and feel ourselves commanded by it, and at the same time hear an opposite call which makes the call of eternity seem only a dream.

> I should welcome eternity, and when I do find it I am sad. I should feel myself perfect by virtue of eternity—and feel myself depressed? . . . In saying this do you express a commandment that is within yourself? That is what I mean. . . . I believe . . . it is a continual commandment, but that I hear it only occasionally. . . . I hear it, as it were, even when I do not hear it, in such a way that, although it is not audible itself, it muffles or embitters the voice bidding me do the other thing: that is to say, the voice that makes me ill at ease with eternity.
>
> And do you hear the other voice in a similar way when the commandment of eternity is speaking?
>
> Yes, then too, indeed sometimes I believe I hear nothing but the other voice and everything else seems to be only a dream and it is as though I were just letting the dream go on talking at random. [26]

The problematic of our existence can be defined as our standing at a mid-point between what Kafka calls the "sanctum" and the "sputum."

> He is a free and secure citizen of the world, for he is fettered to a chain which is long enough to give him the freedom of all earthly space, and yet only so long that nothing can drag him past the frontiers of the world. But simultaneously he is a free and secure citizen of Heaven as well, for he is also fettered by a similarly designed heavenly chain. So that if he heads, say, for the earth, his heavenly collar throttles him, and if he heads for Heaven, his earthly one does the same. And yet all the possibilities are his, and he feels it; more, he actually refuses to account for the deadlock by an error in the original fettering. [27]

[25] *The Great Wall,* "He," p. 251.
[26] *Dearest Father,* "The Eight Octavo Notebooks," p. 92.
[27] *Parables,* "Paradise," pp. 25 ff.

At this mid-point we hear the Law but can no longer hear it with clarity or know just what it asks of us. Man knows himself as called but he does not know who calls nor the direction from which the call comes nor the way in which he must answer it. This is the problematic of modern man. Speaking of a Franciscan monastery, Kafka said to Janouch:

> "Man voluntarily limits his own self, surrenders his highest and most real property, his own person, in order to find salvation. By outward restraint he tries to achieve inner freedom. That is the meaning of self-submission to the Law." "But if a man does not know the Law," I said, "how will he achieve freedom?" "He will have the Law beaten into him. If he does not know the Law, he will be harried and whipped into knowledge." "So you mean that sooner or later every man must arrive at true knowledge." "I did not quite say that. I did not speak of knowledge, but of freedom as a goal. The knowledge is only a way." "To fulfillment? Then life is only a task, a commission." Kafka made a helpless gesture. "That is just it. Man cannot see beyond himself. He is in the dark." [28]

We are left, therefore, with the paradox which is at the center of *The Trial*. The man who does not know the Law has the Law beaten into him: he is harried and whipped into knowledge. Yet acquisition of this knowledge never means that he penetrates to the High Court or that he even knows in what his guilt lies or what it is that is asked of him. It is possible, therefore, to say, at one and the same time that life is a commission and a task, as Janouch suggests, and that man does not know who commissions or what his task is. The conclusion from this is not, as Joseph K. thinks, that we are all absolved from guilt, but that we are accountable for our existence in a way that eludes our rational grasp of guilt and innocence. We are guilty for not answering or answering in the wrong way the call that we could never clearly hear. "Only those fear to be put to the proof who have a bad conscience," said Kafka to Janouch. "They are the ones who do not fulfill the tasks of the present.

[28] Janouch, *op. cit.*, p. 95.

Yet who knows precisely what his task is? No one. So that every one of us has a bad conscience." [29]

16

THE PARADOX OF THE PERSON
IN THE MODERN WORLD

For Kafka, guilt, sin, and judgment are linked, as we have seen, with a call which we hear only indistinctly and ambiguously and to a response which is at worst a failure to answer at all, at best a striving to fulfill a task one barely understands by following a way one cannot clearly see. Here we have the link between the one stage in which the world breaks in on the self and the other in which the self seeks to answer a call. The problematic of modern man that Kafka has revealed to us in the first stage deepens in the second. The going astray of Kafka's "country doctor" is the going astray of modern man. His experience of helplessness and of being unable to help reminds us of our repeated experience of being in a situation in which there are not enough resources, a situation in which the help that one man gives another cannot bear fruit. His experience of the irreparable consequences of answering a false call is not unlike our experience of answering a siren-call that we think is the call of life and finding ourselves, as a result, on a path that we know leads nowhere yet we cannot reverse.

"A HUNGER ARTIST"

The problematic of the calling becomes clear still in Kafka's "A Hunger Artist." We are confronted in "A Hunger Artist" with the tragic paradox of an artist who needs and wants the confirmation of the public but wants it as true appreciation of an accomplishment that only he himself is able to understand. Like every true artist, the hunger artist wants to be valued not for impresario tricks but for the fineness of his art, and like every true artist he is caught in the lonely tension of needing confirmation from others yet needing it on a level that others cannot meet him on. He lives not solely as an artist concentrated on his art but also as a person in relation to other persons—a person who desires no direct relations with others, indeed, but who nonetheless wants to relate to others through his art. Yet only he himself has standards for his art that he can respect, only he knows how easy and difficult it is. As a result, he can neither accept the confirmation of the public nor live without it.

More than any other of Kafka's stories, perhaps, "A Hunger Artist" is a poignant and moving commentary on Kafka's own life. This commentary helps, in turn, to illuminate the basic meaning of "A Hunger Artist" and its significance for the problematic of modern man. In an age in which the inability of the artist to adjust to society has often become a pose and Kafka himself a fad, it is sometimes hard to remember that Kafka's suffering was not simply material for his literature but that his literature was the necessary expression of his suffering. "The poet is always much smaller and weaker than the social average," said Kafka to Janouch:

"Therefore he feels the burden of earthly existence much

more intensely and strongly than other men. For him personally his song is only a scream. Art for the artist is only suffering, through which he releases himself for further suffering. He is not a giant, but only a more or less brightly plumaged bird in the cage of his existence." [1]

Kafka did not lead an existence as an artist separate from his existence as a human being. "Art is always a matter of the entire personality," he told Janouch. "For that reason it is fundamentally tragic." [2] Kafka put his life in the service of literature, but he did so because to him literature was the only way to life. Although he was too great an artist to be merely subjective in his writings, his art is limited in its scope by an obsession with themes that are autobiographical in the deepest sense of the term. Although Flaubert could say, "Madame Bovary, c'est moi," as artist he attained an artistic and even ironic detachment from her that made possible a beauty and perfection of style in uttermost contrast to the sordidness of the story itself. Kafka was not inferior to Flaubert in artistic integrity, but he could tolerate no such split. Although he used his life for his art, he never turned it into mere material for detached artistic observation. "A 'Tribuna' reader told me recently he thought I must have made extensive studies in a lunatic asylum," Kafka wrote to his friend Milena. "'Only in my own,' I said, whereupon he continued trying to pay me compliments on my 'own lunatic asylum.'" [3] To understand the profound irony of this incident is to understand the tension between objectivity and identification that bound Kafka's art to his life.

The fact that Kafka left so many of his works unfinished and that he asked his friend Max Brod to burn the largest part of what had not yet been published, including *The Trial* and *The Castle*, reveals his similarity to his ever-dissatisfied hunger artist. Kafka, too, wanted the confirmation that every artist wants, yet his own standards were so pure that he preferred to destroy his work rather than publish it

[1] Janouch, *op. cit.*, p. 28.
[2] Janouch, p. 38.
[3] *Letters to Milena*, p. 149.

as less than he wanted. Kafka's art was not for him a separate realm where he could take refuge from existence, but the special form of his existence itself. People who can find no access to direct, joyful life play the major roles in his writings not because of some literary pose on his part but because their "fasting" was his own. He, too, would have stuffed himself had he found food that he liked. He, too, would have lived spontaneously and fully had he found a way to do so. His own desire for confirmation from his readers must have seemed to him a fraud since "fasting"—substituting writing for the joyful living that was inaccessible to him—was for him, too, not an "art" but a necessity. Kafka's art, too, was a world of indirect dialogue that floundered on the paradox of a communication which became ever more doubtful on the side of the reader as it became ever more perfect on the side of the author. We know that Kafka is a "great artist," but he himself did not know this. Only the call to be a writer gave his life meaning, yet he could appeal to no objective scheme or design that proved that he was destined to be an artist nor simply affirm himself as an artist by a Nietzschean "will to power" or a Sartrian invention of values. He could not be satisfied with the confirmation that he received from his friends or his public, for he was not satisfied with himself, yet he had no choice but to live as an artist, taking the risk that he had no genuine call or that, if he did, he had neither the means nor resources to answer it.

Kafka's scholar dog is perhaps as isolated as the hunger artist, but he has the conviction, which the latter does not have, that all his fellow beings share in the problematic that concerns him, that he is not just a lonely misfit, a neurotic and insignificant exception to "the happy breed" of dogkind. This is a conviction which his author too may have shared, despite the poignant isolation of Gregor Samsa and the hunger artist. If so, the sense of meaning in Kafka's existence—of hearing and answering a call—may have been greater than "A Hunger Artist" would lead us to believe. On the other hand, there is no doubt that Kafka, too, shared the dog's growing sense of entombment in a silence "so deep that one can never be dragged out of it again by anybody." The desire of the dog, so reminiscent of the hunger artist, that everybody should know his work and be his audience, the impetus which he experienced when he "still expected to produce some effect or other" and that left him when he became solitary, may correspond to Kafka's own experience.

THE CASTLE

As in "A Hunger Artist," it is Kafka's own calling as the unique artist and person that he was that helps more than anything else to illuminate the existential meaning of *The Castle*. What is implicit in "A Hunger Artist," moreover, is explicit in *The Castle*. In the former, the artist endures the paradoxical tension of needing a confirmation of his uniqueness that can never be derived from any objective scheme or general standards—a confirmation that he cannot give himself and that others are reluctant to give him. What is true of the artist and of Kafka is true, we have suggested, of every man: every man needs the confirmation which comes when he knows his life as a "calling"—an answer to a call. But in *The Castle* the situation of the artist and that of man in general are even more closely allied. No man can be confirmed in his calling until he has gone through that transitional stage in which the burden of proof is laid on him to assert that he is called, that he has a vocation, and to make that assertion stick.

This transitional state provides the central dynamic of *The Castle*: K. is in it at the beginning of the novel and he remains in it throughout, while trying in vain to leave it by every means possible. K. is constantly assured from all sides that he was not called and not needed and that his "calling" is no real "calling." He is left to establish his calling himself, yet this is exactly what he cannot do. Before he can be accepted in the village, and still more important, before he can begin his work as Land-Surveyor, he needs the confirmation of the Castle—a confirmation which he never receives in any unequivocal or really effective way. What we have here, therefore, is a sort of "inverted calling"—the need to be called coupled with the impossibility of proving that one is called and the improbability that anyone else will prove it for one.

At the beginning of *The Trial* we find Joseph K. firmly established in a social role from which he is only later extracted by the "arrest" which gradually forces him to move from a purely social to a personal existence. In *The Castle* it is the other way around. K. arrives in the village like a newborn child, bringing nothing with him from where he was before, starting a completely new life without either position or connections that might help him make his way. He is not a child, of course, but a grown man—"a disreputable-looking man in his thirties," as he is described by Schwarzer, the son of an under-castellan, who officiously tells him that he cannot spend the night in the village without a permit from the Castle. To this K. replies, "I am the Land-Surveyor whom the Count is expecting. My assistants are coming on tomorrow in a carriage with the apparatus." Like the young man or woman who enters on a vocation, K. begins his stay in the village with the assertion that he has a calling and that he has a call, and like him too his problem is to "make good"—to make his assertion stick.

In another less frightening, less absurd, or perhaps even less "modern" world than that of the Castle, K.'s problems would soon be over. Either he would be courteously received from then on or an official check would establish that he was an impostor and he would have been dealt with accordingly. In the world of the Castle, however, the problem of K.'s social role and of its recognition by others is never resolved and apparently never can be resolved. The phone call of inquiry to the Castle produces the answer that there is no record of a Land-Surveyor having been summoned, from which Schwarzer concludes that K. is not only an impostor but, what is worse, a man without status in society—"a common, lying tramp." The phone rings again, however, and announces that the first call was a mistake. K.'s answer to this shows that he is quite clear that it is up to him to establish his calling and his call in the teeth of the very organization that supposedly called him:

So the Castle had recognized him as the Land-Surveyor. That was unpropitious for him, on the one hand, for it meant that the Castle was well informed about him, had estimated all the probable chances, and was taking up the challenge with a smile. On the other hand, however, it was quite propitious, for if his interpretation was right they had underestimated his strength, and he would have more freedom of action than he had dared to hope. And if they expected to cow him by their lofty superiority in recognizing him as Land-Surveyor, they were mistaken; it made his skin prickle a little, that was all. (7 f.)

This freedom and necessity to establish his own calling seems implicit to K. in the first letter that he receives from Klamm, the Castle official to whom he is responsible. Since by this time K. is aware of how very difficult, if not impossible, it will be for him to obtain a personal interview with Klamm, he is all the more concerned about analyzing the contents of the letter. On the one hand, he feels that it deals "with him as a free man whose independence was recognized"; on the other, "as a minor employee, hardly visible to the heads of departments." K. sees in these inconsistencies "a frankly offered choice," which leaves it to him to make what he likes out of the letter—to decide whether he prefers to become an actual village worker with a merely apparent connection with the Castle or an ostensible village worker with a real connection with the Castle. The village Mayor too interprets the letter as leaving it up to K. to establish his calling himself: "There isn't a single word in it showing that you've been taken on as Land-Surveyor; on the contrary, it's all about state service in general, and even that is not absolutely guaranteed, . . . that is, *the task of proving that you are taken on is laid on you.*" (Italics mine.)

How difficult this task is, even in relation to the village, is symbolically indicated by the little interchange at the very end of the book between K. and the landlady of the Herrenhof Inn: "'What actually is it you are?' 'Land-Surveyor.' 'What *is* that?' K. explained, the explanation made her yawn." The withholding of confirmation of K.'s calling does not stop at mere neutrality, moreover. The schoolteacher, who has reluctantly accepted K. in the position of school janitor, says, "Our need for a janitor is just about as urgent as our need for a land-surveyor. Janitor, land-surveyor, both are a burden on our shoulders." And what the teacher thinks concerning the attitude of the village, K. himself thinks concerning the Castle: "I came here of my own accord, and of my own accord I have settled here . . . True, I was engaged to come here as Land-Surveyor, yet that was only a pretext, they were playing with me."

One of the startling things about K. is that though he spends most of his time trying to get confirmation of his position as Land-Surveyor, he often leaves his position entirely out of account when thinking of his relation to the village. "What, after all, was he without Frieda?" he says to himself in a deleted fragment. "A nonentity." Again, when he is reflecting on his arrival in the village, he tells himself that if it had not been for Schwarzer's drawing the attention of the authorities to him, he might have been accepted "for one day as a stray wanderer, his handiness and trustworthiness would have been recognized and spoken of in the neighborhood, and probably he would have soon found accommodation somewhere as a servant." There is no suggestion in all this that he was called as Land-Surveyor or that his proclaiming himself one was anything but a bluff to enable him to spend the night and try to get a foothold. Even when he imagines reporting to the Mayor the next day, it is as a wandering stranger "who would probably be leaving the place tomorrow unless the unlikely were to happen and he found some work in the village, only for a day or two, of course, since he did not mean to stay longer."

From this we must conclude that K.'s engagement as Land-Surveyor is "only a pretext" for K. as well as for the Castle, *or* that he is trying to find official confirmation of work which by its nature is not and cannot be official work. At one point K. speaks of his fiancée-mistress Frieda as taking "her share of my professional duties when I have other business," a phrase which, if it refers to anything, can refer only to the aid she gives him in his job as school janitor, for K. has carried out no professional land-surveying at all. "Another person would have surveyed ten countries in this time," says the sole fragment in which the story is told from a point of view other than that of K. "*He* is still here in the village dangling to and fro between the secretaries." In another fragment K. speaks of the job that he has taken at the school as only a temporary one: "I'm only staying on there till I get the certificate of my appointment as Land-Surveyor." He even adds that "it may come at any moment." Yet nothing gives him the slightest hope of ever receiving such a certificate, and many of his own actions raise the question of whether this is his chief aim. The only thing that is certain is that now he is in the village he intends to remain. At one point he enumerates for the benefit of the Mayor all the things that keep him there: "The sacrifice I made in leaving my home, the long and difficult journey, the well-grounded hopes I built on my engagement here, my complete lack of means, the impossibility after this of finding some other suitable job at home, and last but not least my fiancée, who lives here." But to Frieda, his fiancée, he drops all pretense that he came because of "well-grounded hopes" that he built on his "engagement," and says simply, "What could have enticed me to this desolate country except the wish to stay here?"

THE CALL

If K. needs a call to confirm his calling, he also uses his "calling" as a way of answering whatever it is in this "desolate country" that has called him and that makes him want to stay. Whatever this call is, it does not come from other people, no matter how much K. gets himself involved with them in the course of the novel. He sees people as a means to the end of contacting the Castle or as a trap to sidetrack him and prevent his reaching it. He hardly ever sees his relationship to others as a value in itself. Kafka's first sketch of *The Castle*, in fact, is significantly entitled, "Temptation in the Village." [4] It is to the Castle, then, that we must look for the call which K. is striving to answer, as is strikingly prefigured in an entry in Kafka's diaries:

Our King made no display of pomp; anyone who did not know him from his pictures would never have recognized

⁴ *Diaries, 1914-1923*, Jun. 11, 1914, pp. 48-58.

him as the King. His clothes were badly made, not in our shop, however, of a skimpy material, his coat forever unbuttoned, flapping and wrinkled, his hat crumpled, clumsy, heavy boots, broad, careless movements of his arms, a strong face with a large straight masculine nose, a short moustache, dark, somewhat too sharp eyes, a powerful, well-shaped neck. Once he stopped in passing in the doorway of our shop, put his right hand up against the lintel of the door and asked, "Is Franz here?" He knew everyone by name. I came out of my dark corner and ‚made my way through the journeymen. "Come along," he said, after briefly glancing at me. "He's moving into the castle," he said to the master.[5]

K. himself never receives any such clear-cut call, nor does Klamm—despite the two letters he sends K.—seem to know him by name, that is, as a person. The King in Kafka's diary who knows all his workmen by name is like the Father in Jesus' teaching who sees the sparrows fall. But the Castle, K. is told, is concerned only with the common welfare and cannot "simply interfere with the natural course of events for the sole purpose of serving the interest of one man." Nonetheless, there remains the common factor of a call. K.'s first impression of the Castle seen from the village even bears a resemblance in an unpleasant distorted way to the physical description of the King. The Castle has more of an unconventional and unkempt appearance than the King but it has nothing of that sense of solid reassurance that emanates from the King.

If K. had not known that it was a castle he might have taken it for a little town. . . . It was, after all, only a wretched-looking town, a huddle of village houses. . . . The tower . . . pierced by small windows that glittered in the sun—with a somewhat maniacal glitter—and topped by what looked like an attic, with battlements that were irregular, broken, fumbling, as if designed by the trembling or careless hand of a child. (11 f.)

K. contrasts the Castle in his mind with the church tower

[5] *Ibid.*, Jul. 29, 1917, pp. 170 f.

at home. The latter had "a loftier goal than the humble dwelling-houses, and a clearer meaning than the muddle of everyday life," while the former is like the madwoman in Charlotte Brontë's *Jane Eyre:* "It was as if a melancholy-mad tenant who ought to have been kept locked in the topmost chamber of his house had burst through the roof and lifted himself up to the gaze of the world." Max Brod sees the Castle as "heaven seen by human reason," the "relationship between man and God, running as it were along a distorted plane." It is distorted, says Brod, because of the gulf between human reason and divine grace, and the fact that this gulf is "seen from the wrong end of the perspective." [6] K. certainly does not see the Castle as heaven, however, and it is highly doubtful that Kafka did either. When K. sees the Castle, swarms of crows are circling around it, a fact that is in itself highly suggestive in the light of Kafka's aphorism about crows and the heavens: "The crows maintain that a single crow could destroy the heavens. Doubtless that is so, but it proves nothing against the heavens, for the heavens signify simply: The impossibility of crows." [7] In the case of the Castle, crows are not only possible but actual, and present in force. If the Castle resembles anything, it is Solomon's Temple in Kafka's parable where every stone is found permanently defaced by senseless scratchings made by the hands of children or by barbarian mountain-dwellers.[8]

The appearance of Klamm is even more puzzling than that of the Castle since it is constantly changing, apparently according to whoever looks at him and in whatever situation or mood that person finds himself at the time. Frieda, who was Klamm's mistress, feels that she has lost Klamm once she has denied his summons in order to stay with K. Yet she sees Klamm everywhere, even in the eyes of K.'s assistants, and she believes that it is Klamm's work that brought her and K. together and that they should, in consequence, "bless that hour and not curse it." K. insists on meeting Klamm face to face in order to talk with him about Frieda,

[6] Max Brod, "Additional Note," pp. 336 ff.

[7] *The Great Wall of China*, "Reflections," No. 29, p. 261.

[8] *Dearest Father*, "The Eight Octavo Notebooks," p. 105.

whom K. now plans to marry. The landlady of the Bridge Inn, in the strongest possible opposition, says that Klamm not only never *will* speak to K., but that he never *can* speak to him. K. is incapable "of seeing Klamm as he really is," she adds. Klamm will certainly not talk to K. when he has never yet spoken a word to anyone in the village, including Frieda. Even when he called Frieda's name it was not a personal address: "He simply mentioned the name Frieda—who can tell what he was thinking of?" What is more, she insists, "Anybody that he stops summoning he has forgotten completely, not only as far as the past is concerned, but literally for the future as well." Still more unthinkable than K.'s notion that he can force Klamm to see and talk with him, according to the landlady, is his intention of seeing him as a private person rather than as an official. No one has ever seen or even imagined him as a private person, she says in a deleted fragment: "He is always an official, to full capacity . . . I and Frieda are unanimous in this: we love no one but the official Klamm, the high, the exceedingly high, official." In another deleted passage the Village Secretary Momus tells K. that Klamm cannot endure the sight of him, and K. takes this not as a personal matter but as a phenomenon subject to rules and principles: "He only seemed to be closely scrutinizing the secretary's face, as though he were trying to discover a law according to which a face had to be formed so that Klamm could endure it."

When K. first arrives he peeps at Klamm through the keyhole in the barroom, and he thinks that he can easily bring about a face-to-face interview. Later the landlady's image of Klamm as an eagle and himself as a mouse no longer seems absurd to him.

> He thought of Klamm's remoteness, of his impregnable dwelling, of his silence, broken perhaps only by cries such as K. had never yet heard, of his downward-pressing gaze, which could never be proved or disproved, of his wheelings, which could never be disturbed by anything that K. did down below, which far above he followed at the behest of incomprehensible laws and which only for instants were visible—all these things

Klamm and the eagle had in common. (151)

The remoteness, anonymity, and chameleon-like appearance of Klamm give rise in some to blind faith and in others to a boundless skepticism such as leads Barnabas, the Castle messenger, to "doubt that the official who is referred to as Klamm is really Klamm." This skepticism extends to Klamm's letters to K., which both Barnabas and his sister Olga hold to be obviously worthless.

> "To estimate the just value of those letters is impossible, they themselves change in value perpetually, the reflections they give rise to are endless, and chance determines where one stops reflecting, and so even our estimate of them is a matter of chance." (297)

In Amalia, the fateful sister of Barnabas and Olga, this distrust becomes a general principle: The Castle officials are in the habit of saying pleasant things, she remarks, but "the words were hardly out of their mouths before they were forgotten, only of course people were always ready to be taken in again next time." Curiously, enough distrust is also a working principle with Sordini, one of the high Castle officials—a principle that the Mayor considers right, proper, and even necessary in an official.

> "He literally distrusts everyone; even if, for instance, he has come to know somebody, through countless circumstances, as the most reliable man in the world, he distrusts him as soon as fresh circumstances arise, . . . as if he wanted to know that he was a scoundrel." (82 f.)

Most of *The Castle* is devoted to the descriptions of K.'s attempts to answer the call and to confirm his calling. These attempts, oddly enough, focus as much or more on his relations with women than they do on his relations with the Castle and the Castle officials. Once his attempts to see Klamm directly are frustrated, K. finds women a more hopeful, even if less direct, way of achieving contact with the Castle than any of the official, masculine channels. Thus the movement of the book is along two separate, but inter-twining streams: that of K.'s changing relations with and attitudes toward the Castle officials and that of his relations with Frieda, the Bridge Inn landlady, Olga, Amalia, the woman from the Castle, Pepi, and the landlady of the Herren-hof Inn.

K. is in part drawn to Olga and Amalia because they represent two different commentaries on his own striving to answer the call. Olga has an openness and a readiness to give herself, Amalia a courage to face reality, that he does not possess. If he represents a happy combination of the two in the fact that he does not try to propitiate, like Olga, nor cut himself off, like Amalia, he also combines their less happy features—a tendency to never-ending hopeless efforts, like Olga, and toward stubborn isolation, like Amalia. In addition to all this, however, there is some sense in which K.'s relations with women are themselves a way in which he strives to answer a call; they have a promise of meaning quite apart from their usefulness as possible roads to the Castle.

THE LAND-SURVEYOR

The interlacing of vocation and life throws light on the possible meaning of land-surveying, nowhere explained in the book itself. The question of having a land-surveyor was apparently an issue long before K. arrived, an issue not entirely settled in the negative only because of a small dissident faction of peasants to whom it appealed. "They scented secret plots and injustices and what not, found a leader" and turned "a commonplace—namely, that a land-surveyor wasn't needed . . . into a doubtful matter at least." This tells us nothing of what land-surveying is, but it indicates that it may become associated with questions of social justice, not unlike the way in which Luther's Reformation, which he conceived of in purely religious terms, stimulated a peasant revolt. This analogy may be carried a step forward by the unequivocal assertion of the Mayor, representing the large majority of the Village Council: "We have no need of a land-surveyor. There wouldn't be the least use for one here. The frontiers of our little state are marked out and all officially recorded. So what should we do with a land-surveyor?" K.'s reaction is consistent with that of a religious reformer who claims that a reform—a new surveying of the land—is needed exactly where orthodoxy holds that all essential questions have been settled and defined: "Though he had not given the matter a moment's thought before, K. was convinced now at the bottom of his heart that he had expected some such response as this." One of the things K. discovers his first day in the village is that though one can see the Castle from the village, the roads that seem to lead there actually go around in a circle and take one back into the village itself. That a land-surveyor would in some way set himself up to clarify the relation of the village to the Castle through the drawing of boundaries and the mapping out of roads gives still more cogency to our religious analogy. Every reformer claims that the religion he is reforming has lost real contact with the divine, that its doctrines and ceremonies have become self-perpetuating obstructions to man's intercourse with God, and every reformer claims that his reform breaks through the mass of ossified tradition to a new, direct meeting with the divine.

An even more appropriate analogy is that of the writer. Kafka, as we have seen, could not divorce his art from his existence and establish it as a separate realm of meaning and value. Neither could he leave his life out of his art since "Art is always a matter of the entire personality." The artist, in Kafka's understanding of the term, is the man who expresses the inexpressible, who defines what cannot be defined, who sees and sets forth aspects and inner realities of our concrete existence that most people are not aware of or cannot express. For this reason a novelist like Kafka is doing more than creating a beautiful picture of existence or writing a commentary on it. He is disturbing the established order of things by redrawing the lines, by surveying the land anew. In this sense, the double meaning of *Vermesser* that Erich Heller points out—*vermessen,* measuring or surveying, and *sich vermessen,* presuming[9]—takes on new mean-

9 Erich Heller, *The Disinherited Mind* (New York: Meridian Books,

ing. The artist is both one who surveys existence and one who *necessarily* presumes by his claim that he creates a unique vision that fits neither into established categories of art nor established views of existence.

It does not follow that by Land-Surveyor Kafka "means" the artist or novelist any more than he means the religious reformer. Kafka's own relation to his writing is highly suggestive, nonetheless, and helps give essential content to what might otherwise seem an empty cipher at the center of this novel. Kafka could live only as a writer, not because he wished to escape from life but because in his writing alone could he find meaning in his existence and *understand* the meaning of his existence. Seen from this perspective, K.'s calling as Land-Surveyor makes him a man who seeks, in one way or another, to find, understand, and respond to meaning, and the meaning that he finds is not some essence of existence but concrete existence itself, the irreducible "given." Thus K.'s calling as Land-Surveyor is already in the deepest sense a seeking to answer a call—the call of existence itself. The confirmation that K. seeks for his role as Land-Surveyor goes beyond the confirmation desired by our hunger artist: K. wants not only appreciation of his "art" but also some assurance that he is not *merely* presuming, that he has the right to separate himself from the calling of ordinary men and take on the unique task of finding and defining meaning.

The second letter that K. receives from Klamm upsets him very much since it expresses approval for the land-surveying that K. has done so far while in fact he has done none. One might say, following the analogy with the artist, that actually everything that K. is doing belongs to his task of land-surveying; the very fact that he does not know this is an essential part of the task, since he must carry on his fight in a situation in which he has no ground on which to stand.[10] Establishing his calling is a task that K. must undertake, however, not a simple fact of his existence. Even being a Land-Surveyor does not change K.'s "heart-rending"

1959), p. 216.

[10] Cf. Emrich, *op. cit.*, pp. 302 f.

situation as a "nonentity," says Pepi, the chambermaid, for what counts is not what one is but what one does with what one is: "He was a Land-Surveyor, that was perhaps something, so he had learned something, but if one didn't know what to do with it, then again it was nothing after all."

K. AND THE AUTHORITIES

One of the best illustrations of this problematic is K.'s ambivalent attitude toward authority. "It's my most urgent wish, really my only wish," K. declares to Amalia, "to get my business with the authorities properly settled." Why, we may ask, is this K.'s chief goal? Is it because he needs permission from the authorities to lead his life as he wants to? Is it because he can reach the Castle and his goal only through the authorities? Or is it because his very stubbornness and his nonconformity grow out of a fear of authority and of the power it can have over him?

K.'s stubborn nonconformity is a constant theme on the lips of Gardena, the landlady from the Bridge Inn. Even if there were an exception to the rule, she remarks, "it certainly doesn't happen in the way you're trying to do it, simply by saying 'no, no,' and sticking to your own opinions and flouting the most well-meant advice." The landlord and landlady of the other Inn characterize K. as "someone who rode roughshod over everything, both over the law and over the most ordinary human consideration." There certainly is some justification for this view of K., as, for example, in his refusal to submit to any kind of examination by Momus, the Village Secretary. Yet there are also signs of growing submissiveness on his part, as in the studied politeness and diplomacy with which he responds to the indictment of the second landlady or the fact that, as a fragment puts it, "he no longer dares to approach the officials at all. . . . He contents himself with the secretaries." More significant still in this alternation between stubbornness and submissiveness is the fact that he thinks of Momus' examination as a "snare." Even when he wants to become a member of the community and sees taking Momus' statement as a way of doing so, he cannot help regarding this as a knuckling under and a submission. At the same time he is not secure about having refused to accede to the protocol and cannot tell whether he has thereby in "reality stood out or given in." Similarly, he sees Klamm's letter as treating him as a "free man whose independence was recognized," but also as "a minor employee," and he later recognizes in his qualms about being caught in the Inn by Klamm "the obvious effects of that degradation to an inferior status which he had feared."

The corollary of K.'s fear of being dominated by others is his readiness to dominate them. In many respects, indeed, he is what modern psychology would call "an authoritarian personality." When after trying unsuccessfully to fire K. the schoolteacher shouts at him, "Let your confounded assistants in!" K. shouts back, "I've dismissed them," and thinks to himself: "It had the incidental effect of showing the teacher what it was to be strong enough not merely to give notice, but to enforce it." This kind of strength that K. values is not that of Olga, who calmly holds her ground before the servants, but of Frieda who anxiously masters them with the whip. K. admires Frieda because "she saw . . . every individual person . . . and the glance that was left for each . . . was still intense enough to subdue him." Underneath this sort of strength is always weakness, and the very next moment, in fact, K. destroys the effects of his own firmness by going to the window and shouting at the assistants again that they are finally dismissed, with the result that they now recommence their din! When Jeremiah tells him that the assistants have left him, K., who has done everything in his power to get rid of them, is furious and crudely threatens him, promising that he will intervene to get them back and that then they will have reason to fear his switch. "Once I see that you haven't much joy in an assistant's work, it'll give me great satisfaction again . . . to keep you at it." In addition to dominating Frieda and the assistants, K. also wants to dominate Barnabas and Olga. His "alliance with the Castle in mind" means, in practice, that he alone is to make and direct the plans. It will be better, he suggests, "if Barnabas allied himself with me, let me think out the best ways and means here at my leisure, and then, trustfully, no longer relying only on himself, under constant observation, carried out everything himself." "Don't let yourself be deceived if what I say sounds domineering," he adds, as if aware of how domineering he actually is!

K.'s relations with the Castle officials are a combination of hostility and fear, rebellion and submission, which leads him to be careless about important matters and careful, to the point of superstition, about trivial ones.

> While a light and frivolous bearing, a certain deliberate carelessness, was sufficient when one came in direct contact with the authorities, one needed in everything else the greatest caution and had to look around on every side before one made a single step. (76)

He is, in fact, in the position of a man who feels it necessary to obey a law he does not know, to fulfill a code that he does not understand. The consequences of violating this invisible code are fatal, and as a result even seeming signs of benevolence can only operate for him as a trap.

> They let K. go anywhere he liked—of course only within the village—and thus pampered and enervated him, ruled out all possibility of conflict, and transposed him to an unofficial, totally unrecognized, troubled, and alien existence. In this life it might easily happen, if he was not always on his guard, that some day or other, in spite of the amiability of the authorities and the scrupulous fulfillment of all his exaggeratedly light duties, he might —deceived by the apparent favor shown him—conduct himself so imprudently as to get a fall; and the authorities, still ever mild and friendly, and as it were against their will, but in the name of some public regulation unknown to him, might have to come and clear him out of the way. (75)

The most revealing incident, however, and the one that makes K. himself question his insistence on freedom occurs at the Inn when K. tries to trap Klamm into an interview by waiting for him in the courtyard beside his coach. A gentleman, who turns out to be Momus, tells K. that he will miss

Klamm in any case, whether he goes or stays, and when K. still does not leave, he orders the coachman to unharness the horses. K. now sees himself deserted—by the sleigh in one direction and the gentleman in the other, both moving very slowly, however, "as if they wanted to show K. that it was still in his power to call them back." K. now holds the field, "but it was a victory that gave him no joy" since all he has gained by his stubborn insistence is hopeless, meaningless isolation. He has pushed his freedom from all social ties to its limit, and he discovers that at the limit this freedom negates itself:

> It seemed to K. as if at last those people had broken off all relations with him, and as if now in reality he were freer than he had ever been, and at liberty to wait here in this place, usually forbidden to him, as long as he desired, and had won a freedom such as hardly anybody else had ever succeeded in winning, and as if nobody could dare to touch him or drive him away, or even speak to him; but—this conviction was at least equally strong—as if at the same time there was nothing more senseless, nothing more hopeless, than this freedom, this waiting, this inviolability. (139)

KIERKEGAARD'S SINGLE ONE

K. is at times lacking in courage and at other times brazenly impudent, and he is far from "observing every rule of propriety with a glad and confident enthusiasm," like Kierkegaard's "knight of faith." But he does not exalt the Castle "meanly" and, unlike the villagers he dares "to enter those palaces where not merely the memory of the elect abides but . . . the elect themselves." He knows the *Angst* of Kierkegaard's "knight of faith" who is "born outside the universal" and walks "a solitary path, narrow and steep . . . without meeting a single traveller." Passage after passage in *The Castle*, indeed, shows K. as essentially a Single One, who has the courage to meet the officials face to face and who is willing to dispense with all the universal patterns and official procedures if he can do so. K. "had not come here simply to lead an honored and comfortable life." Like Kierkegaard's Single One, he involves himself with his whole person in his fight: "K. fought for something vitally near to him, for himself." In another version of the opening paragraphs K. says:

> "I have a difficult task ahead of me and have dedicated my whole life to it. I do it joyfully and ask for nobody's pity. But because it is all I have—the task, I mean—I ruthlessly suppress everything that might disturb me in carrying it out. I tell you, I can be mad in my ruthlessness." (419)

"Nobody can completely escape the influence of the world," says Olga to K., concerning his relation to her family, "but that you are capable of it to such an extent is a great deal." K. replies, "I am not interested in other people's opinions, and I am not curious to know their reasons. Perhaps—it would be a bad thing, but it is possible—perhaps that is a way in which I shall change when I marry and settle down here, but for the present I am free." K. realizes that if he goes through with his plans to marry Frieda and become part of the community, he may have to sacrifice his freedom and independence. For the time being, however, that is a sacrifice which he does not intend to make, one which, in fact, he cannot make.

K.'s resemblance to Kierkegaard's Single One comes out most clearly in the contrast between his notion of the way in which to reach the Castle and that of the villagers. "We have reverence enough for the authorities," Olga tells K., to which he responds, in a language very close to that of Kierkegaard, "But it's a mistaken reverence, a reverence in the wrong place, the kind of reverence that dishonors its object." If K.'s difficulties with Frieda arise in part from the fact that she is a social conformist and he is a nonconformist, the Bridge Inn Landlady confronts him as the veritable embodiment of tradition. Her advice to him is invariably based on the "common-sense" view of the general, the accepted, the proven-by-experience, whereas he holds out for the unique, the unaccepted, the yet-to-be-proved. K., the landlady complains, has been only a few days in the village and already acts as if he knows more than the people who have spent their lives there. She grants, to be sure, "that it's possible once in a while to achieve something in the teeth of every rule and tradition," but she has never experienced anything of that kind herself and is sure, even so, that K. is going about it in the wrong way. When she tells K. that Klamm forgets immediately, he asserts that this is nothing but an undemonstrable legend. "It's no legend," replies the landlady, "it's much rather the result of a general experience." K. at once rejects this wisdom of the general in the name of openness to the unique: "I see, a thing then to be refuted by further experience." When the landlady joins Momus in trying to force K. to submit to questioning, K. reflects on how little, despite all his efforts to get a glimpse of Klamm, he values "the post of a Momus who was permitted to live in Klamm's eye."

> It was not Klamm's environment in itself that seemed to him worth striving for, but rather that he, K., he only and no one else, should attain to Klamm, and should attain to him not to rest with him, but to go on beyond him, farther yet, into the Castle. (145)

The landlady, in contrast, as Klamm's former mistress, herself lives only on "the memory of the elect." She thinks that K. not only cannot, but need not, demand the actual presence of the elect since an indirect contact with them, "through channels," is good enough. "The only road that can lead you to Klamm is through this protocol here of Herr Momus," she asserts. Asked in what sense this protocol will lead him to Klamm, she answers that Klamm will undoubtedly not even read the protocol, yet that through the protocol K. has "a sort of connection, a sort of connection perhaps with Klamm." "Isn't that enough?" she adds. For K. it is not enough, and still less that name-magic that leads her to assert that whoever is appointed by Klamm is filled by Klamm's spirit.

> "Consider that Klamm appointed him, that he acts in Klamm's name, that what he does, even if it never

reaches Klamm, has yet Klamm's assent in advance. And how can anything have Klamm's assent that isn't filled by his spirit?" (150 f.)

THE VILLAGE AS MEANS OR OBSTACLE TO THE CASTLE

There is, of course, a negative side to K.'s resemblance to Kierkegaard's Single One, a side in which Kierkegaard's "knight of faith" also has some share. The "knight of faith" becomes one through the denial of the social—through Abraham's readiness to sacrifice "Isaac," or more exactly, Kierkegaard's actual sacrifice of his fiancée Regina for the sake of his own spiritual life. K.'s ruthlessness and his readiness to use others as means to his goal are closely connected with the fact that he is concerned only with his own task and not with anybody else. He rejects all demands from others that he cannot see as immediately useful for his own cause. When Olga tells him in a deleted fragment that her family has new hope through him, he finds the idea that he could be of help to someone else insupportable.

He had not come to bring luck to anyone; he was at liberty to help of his own free will, if things turned out that way, but nobody was to hail him as a bringer of luck; anyone who did that was confusing his paths, claiming him for matters for which he, being thus compelled, was never at their disposal; with the greatest good will on his part he could not do that. (470)

K. does not look on the Castle as the means to living in the village; the village, rather, is the means to reaching the Castle. Social reality is either a means or an obstacle for K. It is not a goal. Even when he thinks of becoming a common workman in the village and removing himself as far as possible from the sphere of the Castle, it is in the hope of achieving something in the Castle itself. "All kinds of paths would be thrown open to him, which would remain not only forever closed to him but quite invisible were he to depend merely on the favor of the gentlemen in the Castle." As soon as Barnabas brings him a message from the Castle, K. abandons the idea of becoming a workman in favor of a direct assault on the

Castle. With the conquest of Frieda, again, he believes he has "gained a means to power that might make the whole period of work in the village unnecessary." Even when he looks on marriage with Frieda as a means of "gaining another, better kind of security—member of the community—rights and duties—no longer a stranger," his aim is "to beware of the complacency of all these people, an easy matter with the Castle before his eyes," while his fear is of "knuckling under, humble work among humble people." He regards the people in the village who close their doors to him as much less dangerous than the Barnabas family, who want him to spend the night. All that the former "did was to throw him back on his own resources, helping him to concentrate his powers," while "ostensible helpers" such as the latter "deflected him from his goal." K. does not want to be at home in the village, and even his marriage to Frieda is not a sufficiently alluring goal compared with reaching the Castle: "When he pictured to himself in the fairest colors everything that he would find on his arrival home, he realized that today it would not suffice him." K.'s call is not a call to life in relation to people. It is a call to a unique and lonely relation to the Castle, the call of the artist Kafka who preferred solitude and writing to marriage and the community.[11]

[11] In what I have said in the above paragraph I am in agreement with Homer Swander who insists that life in the village is never K.'s goal but sees K., on the contrary, as a man who renounces all ties with the community for the sake of reaching the Castle. In the paragraphs that follow, however, I diverge sharply from Swander, who in stressing the distinction between the village's hostility to K. and K.'s voluntary estrangement from it, fails to consider the extent to which K. is making a virtue out of necessity, a choice out of fatality. Through concentrating on K.'s expressed intentions Swander misses his problematic. As a result his description of K. fits Kierkegaard's "knight of faith" much better than it does K. himself. This applies as much to the dualism that Swander sets up between "social integration" with the village and "metaphysical integration" with the Castle—"that unimaginable territory of the spirit"—as it does to his confusion of the unambiguous single-mindedness of Kierkegaard's renunciation of Regina with the ambiguous double-mindedness of K.'s relations with Frieda, Olga, and Pepi. (Cf. Homer Swander, *"The Castle:* K.'s Village," in *Franz Kafka Today,* pp. 190-92.) The same objection applies to Nahum Glatzer's thesis (see fn. 25 in Chap. VII above). In negating striving Glatzer negates man's part in answering the call and establishes a dualism that sees the ordinary hu-

But for all K.'s desire to by-pass the village and reach the Castle directly, he never does so and, in the nature of things, never can. This means that Kafka's world differs from Kierkegaard's on the most essential point of all, namely Kierkegaard's belief that it is possible for the Single One to say "Thou" to God without saying "Thou" to man. Despite his aphorisms about the eternal and the indestructible, Kafka knows no ultimate reality that can be reached apart from the world. If he did, his fiction would not concern itself exclusively with the world breaking in on the self and with the person seeking to answer a call that he hears only in the distorted echoes ricocheted to him from the myriad halls of the Trial-Castle world.

Thus the tension between the self and the social is complemented by the tension between social reality and ultimate reality, and the border realm of the social becomes, indeed, the key to K.'s problematic. Through this double tension we can understand K.'s alternation between stubborn rejection of all mediating social forms, such as Momus' protocol, and his clinging to even the smallest social connections with the Castle, such as Frieda, the Barnabas family, the lady from the Castle, the letters from Klamm. Only this double tension enables us to understand why the man who is deathly afraid of "knuckling under" and of "humble work among humble people" is able to accept the ignominious position of school janitor and with it the petty tyranny of the schoolteachers. Ordinary social life is fundamentally boring to K., as it was to Kafka, yet only through some connection with the social can he hope to reach his goal. His goal, however, always remains unclear, both in itself and as to the way of reaching it, and this is because his goal is neither the village nor the Castle but an immediacy from which he is excluded in the former and which he tries in vain to reach through the

---

man life of the village as identical with the world of flux, the Castle as identical with the "eternal" in Kafka's aphorisms—a sundering of social reality and ultimate reality that misses the central significance of *The Castle*.

latter. "There is a goal, but no way: what we call the way is only hesitation."

17

KAFKA:
THE SUFFERING AND
CONTENDING JOB

In Kafka, the Modern Job comes into his own, not only in the heroes of Kafka's novels but in the very point of view from which the novels are written. As Job can get no metaphysical overview that enables him to comprehend the whole of reality but knows God and creation only within his relation to them and from his own point of view—"Where were you when I laid the foundations of the earth? . . . When the morning stars sang together and all the sons of God shouted for joy?" —so Kafka rigorously presents his novels to us only through Joseph K.'s or K.'s perspective and sacrifices the prerogatives of the omniscient, or at least objective and overall, point of view that most novelists retain. To say that a Kafka novel is written only from the hero's point of view does not mean that we see no one else but the hero or that we cannot see some things about the hero and his situation that he himself does not see. What it does mean is that, like Job, Kafka's hero stands face to face with a reality which transcends him and that he sees that reality only from his own point of view. As a result, we too are denied any overall, objective vantage point on K.'s relation to the world. What applies to the perspective from which the events are told applies equally to the meaning of those events: Kafka gives up the position of the objective scientist and still more that of the all-knowing metaphysician in favor of the limited knowledge which arises, as it does for Job, only in personal involvement—in facing and contending. Kafka's hero does not encounter some theological Transcendent or "Wholly Other"; rather, like Job, he confronts a world that cannot be removed into himself.

K., the hero of *The Castle,* is, in many essential respects, a Modern Job. K. does not meet reality through renouncing the finite, as does Kierkegaard, yet he does not simply identify reality with tradition and society, as do Job's friends. Thus he has the unique relation to reality that Kierkegaard's Single One has without the dualism between the world and the transcendent. Like Job, K. demands direct contact with ultimate reality. As Job is not content just to hear about God but wants to see God face to face, so K. is not content with Klamm's environment: he wants to see Klamm face to face and go beyond Klamm into the Castle. Like Job, K. exists in a real two-sidedness of the call and answering the call. K. *must* strive, he cannot do otherwise—not just because of the vicious circle in which he is caught but because of the tension between the self and the social, between social reality and ultimate reality which he in particular knows and embodies but which all men share. K.'s problematic is not just that of modern man. It is the problematic of all men, and in this he is a brother to Job.

Like Job, K. does not feel impelled to choose between the self and what transcends it, as do those Modern Prometheans who hold that man's alienation is to be overcome only by the destruction of the transcendent to which man has bound over his own freedom and creativity. "He may well slay me. I am ready to accept it," says Job. "Yet I shall argue my ways before His face." Like the Job in this passage K. stands his ground. I may not be able to face Klamm, K. says to the landlady. I may run from the room at the very sight of him, but that "is no valid reason in my eyes for refraining from the attempt. If I only succeed in holding my ground, . . . I shall at any rate have the satisfaction of having spoken my mind freely to a great man." Like Job, too, K. contends. "I am here to fight," he says in the variant of the opening. "No, absolutely," he says to the Mayor's question of whether it will be agreeable to him if the latter sends for him in case the Castle reaches a decision or needs to interrogate him further. "I don't want any act of favor from the Castle, but my rights." Like Job, K. dares what other men do not and is condemned by the upholders of tradition as proud and presumptuous. "Oh, Land-Surveyor, who are you, after all, that you dare to ask such things?" cries the landlady. K. wants to compel Klamm to see him and to hear him, as Job wanted some answering word from the God who had become distant from him. "The most important thing for me is to be confronted with him," says K. This desire "to confront the authorities face to face" in no wise means that K. is unaware of the enormous difference in strength between them and himself. But this difference in strength does not cow and intimidate him, any more than it did Job, who knew that he was contending, not with a man like himself, but with a reality utterly beyond his comprehension. K. "made demands, without having the slightest backing," comments Pepi. His dignity, his involvement as a person, the fact that he is fighting for his existence itself give him enough ground to stand on without the social position and favor that Pepi and the landlady assume are the prerequisite for firmness and strength. Although K. submits to the humiliation of working for the teacher, he holds his own before him and never once meets him as anything less than a real person in his own right. Although "he had arrived yesterday, and the Castle had been here since ancient times," he demands what Job demands and what every man alive has the right to demand—the opportunity to confront the Castle directly and with the whole of his existence.

K. is not the Biblical Job, however; he is a *modern* Job, a problematic modern man, and his significance lies precisely in this. K. is an image of modern man. He is an image of modern man as Exile, and, even more, he is an image of modern man as Problematic Rebel. The utter honesty of Kafka's portrayal has removed any possibility of idealizing K. and made him into a poignant and disconcerting mirror of our own problematic. Kafka does not stop at portraying the problematic modern man, however. He presents us again and again with the question of whether there is or can be a way for such a man *and* with the question of whether, in K., he has shown such a way.

To what extent is K. not only an image of modern man but also a modern image of man? Little Hans says he wants to become a man like K. when he grows up. This is not because he sees K. as some ideal figure. On the contrary, it is the very contradictions that he glimpses in K. and in how people regard him that "engendered in him the belief that though for the moment K. was wretched and looked down on, yet in an almost unimaginable and distant future he would excel everybody." K. is not Job—he has not Job's strength and Job's trust in existence—yet he too is not merely problematic. He is a Modern Job—someone who has taken into himself all the tension and the problematic and has shown at least a minimum stance that a man may assume through which he may preserve his own integrity and attempt, at the same time, to answer the wavering call with the uncertain calling. K. is significant for us precisely because he can neither be reduced to the average nor heightened to superman. Those who point a way for modern man which begins by leaving out his problematic offer not hope but despair. Those who settle into the problematic leave only an abyss of nihilism. Those who remain steadfast amid the confusion of the self and the perplexity of the call offer, if not a way forward, at least a holding point until such a way becomes visible. Like Kafka himself, K. is "an end or a beginning." Unlike Gregor Samsa and Georg Bendemann, K. has a ground on which to stand,

and he does stand on that ground and fight.

Suffering is the positive element in this world, indeed it is the only link between this world and the positive.[1]

The thornbush is the old obstacle in the road. It must catch fire if you want to go further.

"The road to love always goes through filth and misery. Yet if one despised the road one might easily miss the goal. Therefore one must humbly suffer the various misadventures of the road. Only thus will one reach one's goal—perhaps." [2]

Whether we think of Kafka's parable of the message from the Emperor in terms of the Gnostic doctrine of the hidden god or of the problematic of modern man who no longer hears a call, the sense of the impossibility of contact between the self and any reality that might call it to meaningful existence could hardly be put more cogently. Yet the last sentence of the parable injects a note of hope into the hopelessness of this situation: "But you sit at your window when evening falls and dream it to yourself." There is a call, and even though you will never hear the welcome hammering of the messenger's fists on your door, you may for all that find some contact with this call in an inwardness which accepts both the reality of the call and the reality of the abyss that separates you from it. Kafka depicted the course of the world in gloomier colors than ever before, writes Martin Buber, yet he also proclaimed trust in existence anew, "with a still deepened 'in spite of all this,' quite soft and shy, but unambiguous." [3]

[1] *Dearest Father*, "The Eight Octavo Notebooks," p. 90.

[2] Janouch, *op. cit.*, pp. 104 f.

[3] Martin Buber, *Two Types of Faith*, trans. Norman Goldhawk (New York: Macmillan Co., 1952; Harper's Torchbooks, 1961), p. 168. Buber sees Kafka as one of the most significant representatives and portrayers of the modern "eclipse of God," or what Buber also calls the "Pauline periods": "Those periods are Pauline in which the contradictions of human life, especially of man's social life, so mount up that they increasingly assume in man's consciousness of existence the character of a fate. Then the light of God appears to be darkened, and the . . . soul be-

Although Kafka did not contend, as did Job, he came close to Job in his struggle to find meaning through his suffering. The day after he entered in his diary the fantasy of the condemned man who is stabbed to death in his room while writing "O loved ones, O angels, at what height do you hover, unknowing, beyond the reach of my earthly hand," Kafka recorded a moving prayer which, even as it suggests the relevance of these fantasies to his own life, also shows his refusal to accept without protest the impossibility of appeal to a higher justice and a higher mercy than that of "The Judgment," "In a Penal Colony," and "A Singular Judicial Procedure":

> Have mercy on me, I am sinful in every nook and cranny of my being. But my gifts were not entirely contemptible; I had some small talents, squandered them, unadvised creature that I was, am now near my end just at a time when outwardly everything might at last turn out well for me. Don't thrust me in among the lost. . . . If I am condemned, then I am not only condemned to die, but also condemned to struggle till I die.[4]

Like Job, Kafka found his existence so intolerable that he longed for death, yet like Job too he did not give up a "ves-

---

comes aware . . . of the still unredeemed concreteness of the world of men in all its horror. . . . Kafka describes, from innermost awareness, the actual course of the world, he describes most exactly the rule of the foul devilry which fills the foreground; . . . His unexpressed, ever-present theme is the remoteness of the judge, the remoteness of the lord of the castle, the hiddenness, the eclipse, the darkness." *Ibid.,* pp. 166 ff. In a commentary on the above passage that also touches on the parable of the imperial message, Fritz Kaufmann writes: "These are times of 'eclipse of God,' in which a life of faith can show itself only in *Hypomene,* as for instance with Kafka—that is, in waiting expectantly for a meaning that here and now is perverted and desecrated into meaninglessness; a meaning to which we nevertheless hold fast, aware of a message which may be the message not of a dead but—already in that it concerns us—of a living God. God is present even in the pain of his absence." Fritz Kaufmann, "Martin Buber's Philosophy of Religion," in *The Philosophy of Martin Buber,* Paul Arthur Schilpp and Maurice Friedman, eds., *The Library of Living Philosophers* (LaSalle, Illinois: The Open Court Publishing Co., 1967).

[4] *Diaries, 1914-1923,* Jul. 20, 1916, p. 161.

tige of faith" in a personal contact that would give meaning
to a life which was itself "the eternal torments of dying."

A first sign of nascent knowledge is the desire for death.
This life seems unendurable, any other unattainable.
One is no longer ashamed of wishing to die: one prays
to be conducted from the old cell that one hates into a
new one that one has yet to hate. There is in this a ves-
tige of faith that during the change the Master may
chance to walk along the corridor, contemplate the prisoner, and say: "You must not lock up this one again. He
is to come to me." [5]

He was like Job too in not simply accepting the comfort of
his friends in his exile but in insisting that his lonely way
had a unique value and meaning of its own.

My situation in this world would seem to be a dreadful
one. . . . But I live elsewhere; . . . the attraction of the
human world is so immense, . . . Yet the attraction of
my world too is strong; those who love me love me because I am "forsaken" . . . because they sense that in
happy moments I enjoy on another plane the freedom of
movement completely lacking to me here. [6]

Like Job, Kafka sensed the abyss that lies behind every moment and struggled to overcome it.

"In such a godless time one must be gay. It is a duty . . .
sorrow has no prospects. And all that matters is prospects, going forward. There is danger only in the narrow,
restricted moment. Behind it lies the abyss. If one
overcomes it, everything is different. Only the moment
counts. It determines life." [7]

Kafka's positive acceptance of his suffering during the illness
that marked the last years of his life mirrors Job's acceptance
when God comes near him again and he finds the meaning
of his suffering in his dialogue with God. "Life has so many
possibilities," Kafka said to Janouch, "and each one only mir-

[5] *The Great Wall of China*, "Reflections," No. 10, p. 256.
[6] *Diaries, 1914-1923*, Jan. 29, 1922, pp. 214 f.
[7] Janouch, *op. cit.*, p. 57.

rors the inescapable impossibility of one's own existence."

His voice broke into a dry convulsive cough, which he quickly mastered. We smiled at each other. "Look," I said, "everything will soon be all right." "It is already all right," Franz Kafka said slowly. "I have said yes to everything. In that way suffering becomes an enchantment, and death—it is only an ingredient in the sweetness of life." [8]

Although this positive acceptance is something which Kafka may have achieved only toward the end of his life, years before, in the very period when he was occupied with *The Trial,* he recorded his conviction that the "unhappiness which almost dismembers me" was not only necessary but was itself indicative of "the existence of a goal to which one makes one's way by undergoing every kind of unhappiness." [9]

Kafka's modern Kabbala has as its most significant corollary a modern exile of the Shekina from the *En Sof,* of the soiled and suffering immanence of God from the hidden transcendence. Unlike the classical Kabbala, however, Kafka's "secret doctrine" has no clear teaching of the "*Yihud*"—a reunification of God and the world. In its place is Kafka's "trust in spite of" —the complaint of a Modern Job who will not give up struggling to find meaning in his suffering but who can never affirm that meaning in the unqualified fashion of the Biblical Job to whom God has come near again. "We were fashioned to live in Paradise, and Paradise was destined to serve us. Our destiny has been altered; that this has also happened with the destiny of Paradise is not stated." [10] Martin Buber comments on this passage: "So must Trust change in a time of God's eclipse in order to persevere steadfast to God, without disowning reality."

"The contradiction of existence becomes for us a theophany," Buber adds. [11] Such "theophany" as Kafka experiences comes not apart from but through the very heart of "the con-

[8] Janouch, pp. 100 f.
[9] *Diaries, 1914-1923,* Mar. 13, 1915, p. 118.
[10] *Parables* "Paradise," pp. 25-27.
[11] Buber, *Two Types of Faith,* pp. 168 f.

tradiction of existence." "Man cannot live without an enduring trust in something indestructible in himself," writes
Kafka.[12] Despite his expressed desire to "raise the world into
the pure, the true, and the immutable," Kafka is no Platonist
and no idealist mystic. What he is concerned about in his
very depths is the meeting of the "sanctum" and the "sputum"
and not the substitution of the one for the other. He is concerned about human existence, and he sees human existence
as standing one's ground and answering the call. That he
knows the eternal accounts for the trust that he has "in
spite of all," but he knows it not apart from existence but in
its very midst.

One may all one's life "be unaware of that indestructible
thing and of one's trust in it. One of the possible ways in
which this permanent unawareness may be expressed is to
have faith in a personal God." [13] What this "faith in a personal God" means to Kafka becomes still clearer in his other
aphorisms: "The word '*sein*' signifies in German both things:
to be and to belong to Him." [14] Being for Kafka is already a
belonging, an attempt to answer the call. Thus being and
believing are inextricably tied together: "Believing means
liberating the indestructible element in oneself, or more accurately, being indestructible, or more accurately, being." [15]
This being means inwardness: "From outside one will always
triumphantly impress theories upon the world and then fall
straight into the ditch one has dug, but only from inside will
one keep oneself and the world quiet and true." [16] But it is as
concerned with the world as it is with the self: it finds its
ground and existence in the relation between the self and
the reality that confronts it—breaking in on it, as in *The
Trial,* calling it, as in *The Castle.* "God can only be comprehended personally. Each man has his own life and his own

[12] With this sentence, writes Max Brod, Kafka has made clear his religious position. Cf. Max Brod, *Franz Kafka. Eine Biographie* (Berlin:
S. Fischer Verlag, 1954), "Neue Züge zu Kafka's Bild," 3rd, enlarged
edition, Chap. VIII, pp. 261 f.
[13] *The Great Wall of China,* "Reflections," No. 48, pp. 265 f.
[14] *Ibid.,* No. 44, p. 264.
[15] *Dearest Father,* "The Eight Octavo Notebooks," p. 78.
[16] *Ibid.,* pp. 66 f.

God. His protector and judge." [17] In this sentence Kafka makes explicit the link between being, believing, calling, and calling to account.

Kafka's statement, "He who seeks does not find, but he who does not seek will be found," [18] is not only a commentary on the wrong sort of striving. It is also a commentary on what comes to "find" the self, to meet it—the world that breaks in on the self and judges it and the world that calls man to existence. Both the judgment and the call come to man through the absurd. His task, therefore, is not to escape from the absurd into inward contemplation but to stand and withstand, to hear and contend. "If I wish to fight against this world," says Kafka, "I must fight against its decisively characteristic element, that is against its transience." [19] Kafka *fights* against the transience of the world, not by leaving the world for some immutable, metaphysical realm but through perceiving and creating, hoping and despairing. It is in existence—his own and that which comes to meet him—that Kafka glimpses the indestructible and the eternal. The indestructible is not the goal of Kafka's striving: "Theoretically there exists a perfect possibility of happiness: to believe in the indestructible element in oneself and not strive after it." [20] Yet his glimpse of the indestructible is inseparable from his striving to answer the call and is essential to it. It is the truth of quietude, of the tree of life, which belongs to eternity—a truth which we only sense, yet one in whose light that other truth which is actually given to us, that of activity, or the tree of knowledge, is extinguished. [21]

Binding together the calling and the call, the self and the world, the transient and the indestructible is a trust in existence which not all the terror and conflict of Kafka's life could destroy. It is a trust that the world will come to you unsummoned.

You do not need to leave your room. Remain sitting at

[17] Janouch, *op. cit.*, p. 93.
[18] *Dearest Father*, "Eight Octavo Notebooks," p. 80.
[19] *Ibid.*, p. 95.
[20] *The Great Wall of China*, "Reflections," No. 66, p. 271.
[21] *Dearest Father*, "The Eight Octavo Notebooks," p. 91.

your table and listen. Do not even listen, simply wait. Do not even wait, be quite still and solitary. The world will freely offer itself to you to be unmasked, it has no choice, it will roll in ecstasy at your feet.[22]

But it is no less a trust that the world calls you and that you can call the world.

Life calls again. . . . . It is entirely conceivable that life's splendor forever lies in wait about each one of us in all its fulness, but veiled from view, deep down, invisible, far off. It is there, though, not hostile, not reluctant, not deaf. If you summon it by the right word, by its right name, it will come.[23]

Kafka's writings do indeed contain a "new secret doctrine," a twentieth-century Kabbala—the paradoxical teaching of the person who finds the meaning of his personal existence in dialogue with the absurd. The "essence of all magic," writes Kafka in the diary entry from which we have just quoted, is that it "does not create but summons." Kafka's works represent just such a summoning magic. They summon modern existence—both its problematic and its hidden splendor. They summon it by its right name, and it comes.

---

[22] *Great Wall*, "Reflections," No. 104, p. 286.
[23] *Diaries, 1914-1923*, Oct. 18, 1921, p. 195.

PART FIVE

ALBERT CAMUS

18

ENCOUNTER WITH THE ABSURD

"CALIGULA," "THE MISUNDERSTANDING," "THE STRANGER":
FROM THE ABSURD REBEL TO THE ABSURD EXILE

In his early play, *Caligula*, Camus portrays a young Roman emperor whose love for his sister Drusilla is metamorphosed on her death into an overwhelming conviction of the absurdity of life. Mourning, for him, takes the form of a determination to force this absurd to its logical conclusions until his indifference to the death of others finds its inevitable denouement in his own death. In other words, *Caligula* is, in the most extreme form imaginable, a portrayal of what Leslie Farber calls the "life of suicide." Having arrived at the conclusion that "men die and they are not happy" and the emotional protest that "things as they are . . . are far from satisfactory," Caligula now wants the moon—the impossible. With his almost godlike power as Roman emperor, he is determined to make the impossible possible or bring down his empire and himself in the attempt. "I wish men to live by the light of truth, and I've the power to make them do so." Before this change, he is pictured as someone who tried to be just and to spare others suffering. Now he wants only injustice and suffering, and he gets them both in full measure. He seeks a freedom that he believes can be won only by the recognition that this world has no importance. But he knows that the road to this freedom is anguish—"How hard, how cruel it is, this process of becoming a man"—and he accentuates this anguish to the utmost by a mad, inhuman logic which tolerates no contradictions. He wants to be a god, to tamper with the scheme of things, "to drown the sky in the sea, to infuse ugliness with beauty, to wring a laugh from pain." If he cannot reduce the sum of suffering and make an end of death, he will make suffering and death so universal as to make an end of life. "He is converting his philosophy into corpses," complains Cherea, the man who ultimately organizes his assassination, "and—unfortunately for us—it's a philosophy that's logical from start to finish." Cherea sees no way to meet this threat but to allow this logic to follow its bent until it founders in sheer lunacy. His fear of Caligula is not just the fear of death but the fear of the absurd meaning of life that Caligula forces on his subjects:

> All I wish is to regain some peace of mind in a world that has regained a meaning. What spurs me on is not ambition but fear, my very reasonable fear of that inhuman vision in which my life means no more than a speck of dust.[1]

Caligula describes himself as single-minded for evil. Deep

---

[1] Albert Camus, *Caligula and Three Other Plays*, translated by Stuart Gilbert (N. Y.: Vintage Books, 1958), p. 22. The three other plays are *The Misunderstanding, The State of Siege,* and *The Just Assassins.*

within himself he is aware of "an abyss of silence, a pool of stagnant water and rotting weeds." Where Scipio, his young poet friend, finds solitude and the beauty of nature, he finds "gnashings of teeth, hideous with jarring sounds and voices." He teaches the hard lesson of indifference, of the equivalence of all things in nothingness. He chooses to play the part of fate, to wear "the foolish, unintelligible face of a professional god." When he pictures his own assassination, which he has done "everything needed" to bring about, he rejoices to see "in all those faces surging up out of the angry darkness, convulsed with fear and hatred, . . . the only god I've worshipped on this earth; foul and craven as the human heart." If Caligula embodies Farber's life of suicide, he also embodies, again in the most extreme form, what Farber holds lies behind this life: willfulness. Contemplating his own approaching death, he says to himself angrily:

> Logic, Caligula; follow where logic leads. Power to the uttermost; willfulness without end. Ah, I'm the only man on earth to know the secret—that power can never be complete without a total surrender to the dark impulse of one's destiny.[2]

He exults in the fact that security and logic cannot go together, that he has used his power to create for his subjects "a world where the most preposterous fancy may at any moment become a reality, and the absurd transfix their lives, like a dagger in the heart." But he does not recognize that what he romantically characterizes as "total self-surrender to the dark impulse of one's destiny" is really the willfulness of the isolated will, separated from the living dialogue that gave it meaning. But meaning is now precisely what he does not want, except in the utterly negative form of the denial that there is any meaning. To Caligula all actions, like all lives, are on an equal footing—because none amounts to anything. Even this negative feeling is not enough to fill the emptiness within.

[2] *Ibid.*, pp. 49-50.

> How strange! When I don't kill, I feel alone. The
> living don't suffice to people my world and dispel
> my boredom. I have an impression of an enormous
> void when you and the others are here, and my eyes
> see nothing but empty air. . . . Only the dead are
> real.[3]

Erich Fromm, with good reason, takes Camus' Caligula as
a prime example of the necrophilous man. But there is an
awareness in Caligula's necrophilia that does not quite fit
the picture. He knows that against him is not only stupidity,
but also "the courage and the simple faith of men who ask
to be happy." He proclaims himself as the man who has
reached "beyond the frontier of pain . . . a splendid, sterile
happiness." Even had Drusilla lived, he could not have
borne to love her, for he was not willing to grow old beside
her. His real suffering is not that death snatched her out of
the blue, but the recognition that grief too cannot last, that
even grief is vanity.

When Caligula confronts himself in the mirror just before
he is assassinated, he weeps because there is nothing in this
world, or in the next, made to his stature. But he also recognizes that his search for the impossible has never done anything but bring him face to face with himself. He has come
to hate himself and with it the "freedom" in which he is
imprisoned. "I have chosen a wrong path, a path that leads
to nothing." He concludes that his freedom is not the right
one, that he has not succeeded in becoming the image of
man that liberates mankind. "We shall be forever guilty."

Writing in 1957 about this play written nineteen years
before, Camus underlines this conclusion:

> If his truth is to rebel against fate, his error lies
> in negating what binds him to mankind. One cannot
> destroy everything without destroying oneself. . . .
> Caligula is the story of a superior suicide. . . .
> Caligula accepts death because he has understood

[3] Ibid., p. 68.

that no one can save himself all alone and that one cannot be free at the expense of others.[4]

This statement "foreshadows" Camus' later image of man, but it is a foreshadowing that is implicit in *Caligula* only in seed. The passages in Camus' 1957 preface to *The Misunderstanding* (1943) seem even more of a retrospective reading-in of a positive meaning than those on *Caligula*. Camus explains the suffocating, claustrophobic atmosphere of the play by the historical and geographical situation in which he lived then: the mountains of central France during the Nazi occupation. He suggests in addition, however, that the play be looked at as an attempt to create a modern tragedy whose morality is not altogether negative:

> A son who expects to be recognized without having to declare his name and who is killed by his mother and his sister as a result of the misunderstanding — this is the subject of the play. Doubtless, it is a very dismal image of human fate. But it can be reconciled with a relative optimism as to man. For, after all, it amounts to saying that everything would have been different if the son had said: "It is I; here is my name." It amounts to saying that in an unjust or indifferent world man can save himself, and save others, by practicing the most basic sincerity and pronouncing the most appropriate word.[5]

Granted that the son would not have been killed if he had not stuck to his foolish notion of making his mother and sister love him before revealing to them that he is the son and brother who left them twenty years before. Yet there is much more of the absurd in this play than Camus' prefatory remarks indicate. The real drama is not so much that of the innocent and provokingly duty-bound husband as it is that between mother and daughter, habitual murderers bound

---

[4] *Ibid.*, p. vi.
[5] *Ibid.*, p. vii.

together by this tie and by a common hopelessness. The mother is reluctant to kill this stranger not because she feels guilty, but because she is weary. "Life is crueler than we," she says, and the daughter, though insisting on going through with the murder, also wants it to be the final one: "Yes, my soul's a burden to me, I've had enough of it. I'm eager to be in that country, where the sun kills every question."

Jan, the son, is accompanied by his wife, Maria, but he will not let her spend the night with him, and he insists on going through with his plan of not making himself known. He justifies himself by saying that it is not so much an idea as the force of things that carries him along. "It takes time to change a stranger into a son." But Maria replies, with acute prescience, "By pretending to be what one is not, one simply muddles everything. . . . There's something . . . something morbid about the way you're doing this." She knows that he is speaking to her with the voice of his loneliness and not his love, and that his desire to redeem himself from exile and estrangement by forcing her to leave him is denying that immediacy of love which has no time for dreams and dreads every separation. On the other hand, her advice to him to speak from the heart could hardly be less appropriate to the heartless situation into which he comes. He wonders, and with good reason, whether he will be made welcome. Although he has a faithful heart which soon builds up memories and attachments if given a chance, his sister rebuffs even the most ordinary sociality, and his mother confesses that she had forgotten her husband before he died and that she only knows her daughter because she has kept beside her all these years. She declares she is too old to love a son. "Hearts wear out, sir." The daughter adds, "If a son came here, he'd find exactly what an ordinary guest can count on: amiable indifference, no more and no less." She is not so explicit as to add, "plus murder," but she warns him that she is in a house where the heart isn't catered to. The bleak years in this little spot of Central Europe have drained all the warmth out of this house and its occupants. Martha is angered at Jan's confiding innocence, and this, her mother points out, is an unsound decline from the indifference that they brought to their task in the past.

When Jan is alone is his room that night, he experiences fear—"fear of the eternal loneliness, fear that there is no answer." He finds an answer, but not the one he is looking for. Martha, who has herself become unsure, is reconfirmed in her determination by Jan's description of the land of sea and sunshine from which he comes and to which she hopes to go by means of his money. She brings him a cup of tea with a sleeping potion in it, and he drinks it before the mother has a chance to come in and stop him. As mother and daughter look at the sleeping man, they rationalize the drowning they are about to carry out by the thought that he, like other men, can never know peace except through the mercy of death. Martha impatiently adds that had he realized sooner that no one would ever find warmth or comfort or contentment in this house, he would have spared them the trouble of killing him. But it is not just the house of which his innocence is unaware, it is also life. They have had to teach him that this world is for dying in.

When Jan's passport reveals his identity after he has been drowned, it is. his turn to teach his mother and sister something about the world in which they live. The mother learns that her heart, which had seemed indifferent to everything, could not help grieving over her son's death, that "in a world where everything can be denied, there are forces undeniable; and on this earth where nothing's sure we have our certainties." A mother's love for her son is now her bitter certainty, and drowning herself is now her only recourse. Martha learns that, though her mother has loved her, she is bound more closely to the son who deserted her so many years before than to Martha, who has stuck by her. Martha says that, even if she had recognized Jan, it would have made no difference, for the only person to whom she lowers her head is her mother. Like Cain, she cries out that she is not her brother's keeper—"What concern of mine was it to look after my brother? None whatever!" But, unlike Cain, she sees herself as the innocent one to whom injustice has been done, for now she is an outcast in her home with no hope of attaining the sun and sea for which she longed.

Her exile is beyond remedy. She has shed blood for her mother's love, and is left with nothing but her "very rightful anger" and her hatred of "this narrow world in which we are reduced to gazing up at God." She is an exile and a rebel, one who will go down to her death protesting and unreconciled.

If *The Misunderstanding* is a sublime and depressing example of what Martin Buber calls "mismeeting," there is hardly a hint in it that in an absurd world meeting is possible. Despite Camus' suggestion to the contrary, the real problem of communication in *The Misunderstanding* could not have been solved by the commonsense directness which would say, "It is I." It is the encounter of smug innocence and bitter, exiled guilt. Between these two there is an abyss which Martha recognizes clearly, which leaves her not remorseful but angry at the brother she has killed; for he has had the happiness that she has been denied. Like a Greek tragedy, *The Misunderstanding* is the story of a family and of terrible things that happen to it that have never before been related, as Maria says. But it is a modern tragedy of the absurd, for all that, with no Greek sense of an order with which one could be reconciled even through suffering and death.

The Stranger was written four years after *Caligula* and a year before *The Misunderstanding*. It is the novel which brought Camus fame, and in its economy and power is unsurpassed in his later works. It is also the novel which is taken most often as the illustration of the philosophy of the absurd which Camus sets forth in *The Myth of Sisyphus*. With the exception of the ending, however, its hero, Meursault, is anything but a philosopher. He lacks that awareness which gives even Caligula a philosophical touch. The sequence of events is very simple. His father deserted his mother when he was small. His mother, whom he has sent to an old folks' home, dies, and he comes to the funeral. He is unable to show any emotion or cry either while he sits by the body all night or at the funeral itself. But he is overcome by the sun and almost faints. The next day he meets a girl named Maria at a swimming pool. He takes her as his mistress the same night. When Maria asks him if he will marry her, he replies perhaps. When she asks him if he loves her, he says no. He makes friends with Raymond, a pimp who lives in his building, but with the same indifference as in his relation with Maria. He sees no reason not to be Raymond's friend, and later he sees no reason not to perjure himself when Raymond asks him to come to the police station with him to defend Raymond against the charge that he has beaten up his Arab girl friend. When Meursault and Maria go to the beach with Raymond and his girl friend and another couple, the Arab brothers of this girl show up and attack Raymond with a knife. Meursault takes away Raymond's revolver so he won't shoot the Arabs, and later himself goes for a walk on the beach. He sees one of the Arabs sitting by a rock in the shadow with a knife glinting in the sun, and now he reenacts what he had earlier thought when Raymond handed him the gun, namely, "that one might fire, or not fire—and it would come to absolutely the same thing." Although he knows he could turn around at any time, he keeps walking toward the rock and, when he gets near, kills the Arab with Raymond's revolver.

Why does Meursault commit this senseless murder? Not, certainly, because he is a fiend, as the jury later suggests on the basis of the fact that he did not weep at his mother's funeral. Nor was he looking for trouble when he went out. His original motive in walking to the shade of the rock is the opposite: "Anything to be rid of the glare, the sight of women in tears, the strain and effort—and to retrieve the pool of shadow by the rock and its cool silence!" The heat itself and the glare of the sun become the chief clue to why he goes forward knowingly to do something he has no wish to do. "It struck me that all I had to do was to turn, walk away, and think no more about it. But the whole beach, pulsing with heat, was pressing on my back." The heat becomes for him an unbearable pressure that leads him to shoot the Arab as a gesture of desperate revolt, a breaking of the unendurable tension.

I was conscious only of the cymbals of the sun

clashing on my skull, and, less distinctly, of the
keen blade of light flashing up from the knife, scar-
ring my eyelashes, and gouging into my eyeballs.

Then everything began to reel before my eyes, a
fiery gust came from the sea, while the sky cracked
in two, from end to end, and a great sheet of flame
poured down through the rift. Every nerve in my
body was a steel spring, and my grip closed on
the revolver.[6]

This apocalyptic breakthrough is something more than a
solar agony and ecstasy. The key to this "something more"
is provided by Meursault's statement: "It was just the same
sort of heat as at my mother's funeral, and I had the same
disagreeable sensations—especially in my forehead, where all
the veins seemed to be bursting through the skin. I couldn't
stand it any longer." What has happened here is nothing
other than Meursault's mourning for his mother. That he
did not weep at her funeral was not because of hardhearted-
ness, but because he identifies himself with her. Like her,
he expects nothing of the world; this lack of expectation is
the clue to his seeming indifference to life. It is not that
he wants nothing, but that—aside from a few immediate
physical sensations—he hopes for nothing. He is a man who
has schooled himself never to demand anything of life, never
to expect anything of it; therefore, he thinks it a matter of
no importance whether he marries Maria or whether he
perjures himself for Raymond. The one time he thinks of
marrying Maria is when she is most like his mother as he
knew her—gossiping with other women—but it is also to escape the "women's talk" which he finds so oppressive that
he leaves the cabin. He identifies with his mother, but he
does not really want her in the form of marriage to Maria;
for he expects nothing out of marriage either.

But why, we must ask, does a man who is so indifferent
to matters that closely concern him give way to an outburst

[6] Albert Camus, *The Stranger*, translated by Stuart Gilbert (N. Y.: Vintage Books,1958), pp. 75-76.

of violence in a matter that does not concern him at all? He explains it as shaking off his sweat and the clinging veil of light, but he also knows that the relief he finds is one that destroys him.

> I knew I'd shattered the balance of the day, the spacious calm of this beach on which I had been happy. But I fired four shots more into the inert body. . . . And each successive shot was another loud, fateful rap on the door of my undoing.[7]

What is this murder-suicide but the involuntary protest of the self which has been pressed in on itself so far that it has no choice but to explode? Like the rebel whom Camus describes in the book of that title, "he confronts an order of things which oppresses him with the insistence on a kind of right not to be oppressed beyond the limit that he can tolerate." Only there is nothing conscious or aware about Meursault's protest. It is the limit which the self sets to the vast, indifferent nothingness which crushes it out of existence.

This same protest is the clue to the one other explosion which Meursault experiences, when the prison chaplain forces his way in on him and tries to bring him to confess before he is executed. Meursault has by no means been indifferent to the certainty of the guillotine. But he has schooled himself with considerable effort to a precarious balance, which the priest now upsets. When the priest asks to be called "Father" and insists that he is on Meursault's side and will pray for him even though his heart is hardened, something breaks in Meursault, and he starts yelling insults at the top of his voice. It is at this point that we discover the deepest ground of the indifference and hopelessness that he shares with his mother—his constant awareness that he will die and that he will die alone. It is better to burn than to disappear, he tells the priest, challenging the latter's ordered universe with the vision of the absurd. He has a certainty that the

[7] *Ibid.*, p. 76.

priest has not—the fact of his present life and of the death that is coming. This certainty makes it a matter of indifference whether he had done x or y, whether he has lived "authentically" or "inauthentically." In the face of the absurd, there can be no image of man, no image of a meaningful direction of personal existence, "nothing, nothing had the least importance, and I knew quite well why." A slow, peristent breeze had been blowing toward him from the years that were to come, *pendant toute cette vie absurde que j'avais menée.* This breeze—the awareness of his future death—has leveled out all the ideas of brotherhood and solidarity that people have tried to foist on him in the equally unreal years he was living through.

> What difference could they make to me, the deaths of others, or a mother's love, or his God; or the way a man decides to live, the fate he thinks he chooses, since one and the same fate was bound to "choose" not only me but thousands of millions of privileged people who, like him, called themselves my brothers. . . . All alike would be condemned to die one day. . . . And what difference could it make it, after being charged with murder, he were executed because he didn't weep at his mother's funeral, since it all came to the same thing in the end?[8]

This leveling down of everything to a common nothingness is reminiscent of Caligula, but in the end of *The Stranger,* Meursault achieves a transformation and even a sort of happiness which were altogether denied Caligula. His anger at the priest has washed him clean and emptied him of hope. Now he is able to understand why his mother took a fiancé at the end of her life.

> With death so near, Mother must have felt like someone on the brink of freedom, ready to start life all over again. No one, no one in the world had any

[8] *Ibid.,* p.152.

right to weep for her. And I, too, felt ready to start life all over again.[9]

His identification with his mother now takes on a positive aspect. He lays his heart open for the very first time "to the benign indifference of the universe." So much farther along is he than the Modern Exile of the nineteenth century that he is not horror-struck by "the heartless voids and immensities of the universe," as is Melville's Ishmael in *Moby Dick*. Instead, he finds indifference a welcome relief from the even worse that he has expected, and he feels a partnership with the inhuman absurd that comforts him. "To feel it so like myself, indeed, so brotherly, made me realize that I'd been happy, and that I was happy still." This new feeling even gives him a tenuous bond to the society that has rejected him. The original exile of his indifference has been reinforced and doubled by the attitude of the jury. Threatened by the fact that Meursault's murder of the Arab was completely unmotivated and absurd, they converted him into a fiend. By so doing, they only widened the gap that separates Meursault from the society that judges and executes him. Now, however, Meursault feels that, just because he expects nothing of his fellowman, he will be less lonely if, on the day of his execution, there should be a huge crowd of spectators who would greet him with "howls of execration." This would be at least a minimal contact.

"THE FALL": THE CRISIS OF MOTIVES

Perhaps the best illustration in contemporary literature of the crisis of motives that results from inner division is in Camus' last novel, *The Fall*. Jean-Baptiste Clamence, the hero of *The Fall*, was once a respected lawyer who contributed his services to worthy causes, loved one woman after another, and felt secure in the approval of himself and the world. Then, as with Kafka's K., the world breaks in on his self-assured existence, in this case in the form of a young

[9] *Ibid.*, p. 154.

woman whom he sees leaning against a bridge on the Seine and does not try to save when she jumps in and cries for help after he walks by. This event so undermines his faith in his own motivation that he leaves his work and the society of those he knows and becomes a "judge penitent," confessing to others in order to get them to confess to him. Unable to assert his own innocence, he takes refuge in the common guilt: "We cannot assert the innocence of anyone, whereas we can state with certainty the guilt of all. Every man testifies to the crime of all the others—that is my faith and my hope." To Clamence, as to Kafka, the Last Judgment takes place every day. The foundation of his world is social guilt, and he tries to bring others with him into "the closed little universe of which I am the king, the pope, and the judge."

Like Dostoievsky's Underground Man, Ivan's Inquisitor, and T. S. Eliot's Prufrock, Camus' "false prophet" is making a confession from hell. Hell is the non-existence to which he retired when he found existence insupportable; it is the world without reality and without grace into which he tries to attract others, whom he knows will have more nasty things to confess in the end than those he himself has told. He identifies himself, both in his past and present unwillingness to commit himself, to risk his life, with the "you" to whom he has talked throughout the book and whom we realize at the end is ourselves:

> Are we not all alike . . . ? Then please tell me what happened to you one night on the quays of the Seine and how you managed never to risk your life. You yourself utter the words that for years have never ceased echoing through your mouth: "O young woman, throw yourself into the water again so that I may a second time have the chance of saving both of us!" A second time, eh, what a risky suggestion! Suppose, *cher maître*, that we should be taken literally? We'd have to go through with it. Brr . . . ! The water's so cold! But let's not worry! It's too late now. It will always be too late. Fortunately![10]

[10] Albert Camus, *The Fall*, trans. Justin O'Brien (New York: Alfred A. Knopf, 1957), p. 147.

Jean-Baptiste Clamence's affirmation of guilt is deeply dis-
quieting because in his very acceptance of the split between
what he had once pretended to be and what he is, he sur-
renders that tension that might have led him back to some
form of real existence. Thus in the end the crisis of motives
becomes inseparable from the problematic of guilt.

"THE PLAGUE":
FROM THE MODERN PROMETHEAN TO THE MODERN JOB

The most impressive example of the way in which the
situation of the Modern Exile leads from the rebellion of the
Modern Promethean to that of the Modern Job is Camus'
The Plague, a novel which combines the spirit of Melville,
Dostoievsky, and Kafka perhaps more than any other in
contemporary literature. If in the world of *The Stranger* social
solidarity proves illusory because of the fact that each man
must die alone, in the world of *The Plague* solitary and un-
committed individuality proves illusory because of the fact
that men die collectively. "The malady experienced by a
single man becomes a mass plague," luring the individual
from his solitude, says Camus in *The Rebel,* and at the
end of *The Plague* we learn that the plague is nothing other
than human existence itself: "What does that mean—'plague'?
Just life, no more than that." The only hero in *The Plague*
is the plague itself, the only plot the course of its rise and
fall, the only reality that of the plague-ridden community of
Oran. The plague is at once natural and social disease. Here
man does not stand over against hostile nature, as Ahab with
Moby Dick; he lives in it. "The plague had swallowed up
everything and everyone. No longer were there individual
destinies; only a collective destiny, made of plague and the
emotions shared by all."

The strongest of the emotions shared by all is "the sense
of exile and of deprivation, with all the cross-currents of revolt and fear set up by these." "People found themselves,
without the least warning, hopelessly cut off, prevented from
seeing one another again, or even communicating with one
another." Exile is the first thing the plague brings to the
town, and it remains the ground upon which each of the

main characters whom Camus sets before us makes his unique response to the plague. The narrator describes the feeling of exile as "that sensation of a void within which never left us, that irrational longing to hark back to the past or else to speed up the march of time, and those keen shafts of memory that stung like fire." Exile, indeed, is nothing other than the absurd as Camus has defined it. It is life without future and without hope. "We had nothing left to us but the past," says the narrator, and adds later, in an echo of *The Stranger,* "Each of us had to be content to live only for the day, alone under the vast indifference of the sky." Love and friendship are gradually killed off in the inhabitants. "Love asks something of the future, and nothing was left us but a series of present moments." To many, existence under the plague is characterized by the identical absurdity that Joseph K. finds in his arrest in *The Trial:* "They had been sentenced, for an unknown crime, to an indeterminate period of punishment."

In the figure of Father Paneloux, the priest whose faith in the objective divine order is shattered by witnessing the death of an innocent child, Camus portrays the nostalgically rational man who cannot stand up to the reality of the absurd. In his first sermon after the onset of the plague, Father Paneloux asserts that the plague is the just punishment of God on a sinful people:

> "Calamity has come on you, my brethren, and, my brethren, you deserved it. . . . The just man need have no fear, but the evildoer has good cause to tremble. For plague is the flail of God and the world His threshing floor, and implacably He will thresh out His harvest until the wheat is separated from the chaff." (86 f.) [11]

He has not yet faced Job's question of the suffering of the innocent. After he goes to work in the wards, however, and sees the plague attack first the eyes of a young boy and then destroy his life itself, Paneloux can no longer escape this question. Like Ivan, he does not give up God but he cannot

[11] All page references are to the Alfred A. Knopf edition of Albert Camus' *The Plague,* trans. Stuart Gilbert (New York: 1957).

accept God's world. He falls ill, but without any specific symptoms of the plague. When Rieux offers him companionship during his illness, he turns away with the statement: "Thanks. But priests can have no friends. They have given their all to God." Clinging to his crucifix with a look of "blank serenity" on his face, he dies. The judgment that is made on his illness and death—"a doubtful case"—applies equally aptly to his life: he was a man who could neither accept nor rebel.

In sharpest contrast to Father Paneloux stands Tarrou, the godless saint who has lost faith in any kind of objective order and attempts to replace the dead God with pure subjectivity. If Father Paneloux is Camus' "god-man," Tarrou is his "man-god." He is the Modern Sisyphus, the man who posits meaning and value *in spite of* the absurd. In this sense he is a rebel, but, as Camus now sees, such a rebel has no ground to stand on. He lacks the resources to meet the plague because he attempts to place meaning in the self alone rather than in the self's relation to the reality that it encounters in its existence. He wishes, like Sartre, to "invent values" rather than to discover them in the rebellion itself through the dialogue with what confronts one.

Ever since he witnessed an execution to which his judge-father had sentenced a man when Tarrou was a child, Tarrou's chief aim in life has been to side with the "victims" rather than the "executioners." Deciding that the social order "was based on the death sentence," he joined a revolutionary group fighting it, only to discover with horror that he was thereby contributing indirectly to other men being sentenced to death by the party. "Mortally ashamed" of having been, "even with the best intentions, even at many removes," a murderer in his turn, he realized that everybody has the plague and resolved "to have no truck with" anything which might bring death to others or justify putting them to death. Tarrou's one ambition is to learn to be a saint, his one engrossing problem "Can one be a saint without God?"

Tarrou himself realizes that this absolute either-or of "victim" versus "executioner" adds to the general exile of the plague the permanent exile of the man who basically desires neither to spread the plague nor to heal it but to be free of it and not to infect others with it. He has become more concerned about his own purity of action and intention—his saintliness—than about the situation in which he finds himself and to which he is called to respond. "I know I have no place in the world of today," he tells Rieux; "once I'd definitely refused to kill, I doomed myself to an exile that can never end. I leave it to others to make history." Unable to accept the fact of the plague and of his own complicity in the social guilt that touches all, he has removed himself from an essential involvement in and commitment to the common life and has thereby undermined the ground of his own existence. He helps Rieux fight the plague only because of a desire to find peace from the contradictions of his life in a saintly service in the cause of others.

> How hard it must be to live only with what one knows and what one remembers, cut off from what one hopes for! It was thus, most probably, that Tarrou had lived, and he realized the bleak sterility of a life without illusions. There can be no peace without hope, and Tarrou, denying as he did the right to condemn anyone whomsoever—though he knew well that no one can help condemning and it befalls even the victim sometimes to turn executioner—Tarrou had lived a life riddled with contradictions and had never known hope's solace. (262 f.)

In Doctor Rieux, the "hero" of *The Plague,* Camus offers us a "third alternative" to his own—and to Dostoievsky's—"god-man" and "man-god." Rieux neither submits to reality as objectively meaningful, as does Paneloux, nor rebels against it on the ground of pure subjectivity, as does Tarrou. His rebellion is neither that of the Modern Promethean nor of the Modern Sisyphus, but of the Modern Job. When Paneloux preaches his sermon explaining the plague as a punishment of God, Doctor Rieux's reaction is that one must fight against creation as one finds it and not just accept it. Like all the evils of the world, the plague can help men rise above themselves. "All the same, when you see the misery it brings, you'd need to be a madman, or a coward, or stone blind, to give in tamely to the plague." Rieux has "never managed to get used to seeing people die," and for him even the religious man can serve God no better than by rebellion against "the order of death."

> "Since the order of the world is shaped by death, mightn't it be better for God if we refuse to believe in Him and struggle with all our might against death, without raising our eyes toward the heaven where He sits in silence." (117 f.)

The fact that Rieux's victories will never be lasting, that the plague is for him "a never ending defeat," is "no reason for giving up the struggle." Rieux does not see this struggle as a romantic rebellion, as does Ahab. It is a matter-of-fact battle against exile.

> The essential thing was to save the greatest possible number of persons from dying and being doomed to unending separation. And to do this there was only one resource: to fight the plague. There was nothing admirable about this attitude; it was merely logical. (122)

It is a rebellion that is compounded with the knowledge of helplessness and impotence and that excludes any possibility of peace.

In Doctor Rieux, Camus combines the Modern Exile and the Modern Rebel and he brings them within the dialogue with the absurd. Rieux is not interested in being a saint but in being a man, and to be human, as Tarrou himself recognizes, is harder than being a saint: it means full involvement, commitment, and response in the situation in which one finds oneself. Doctor Rieux is the healer, the man who shows what it means to be human in a situation in which most men tend to lose their birthright as human beings. Unlike Tarrou, he is not interested in knowing but in curing; unlike Paneloux, he is concerned with health and not with salvation. Both Tarrou and Rieux explicitly point to the "true healer" as the third alternative to the pestilence and the victim, though it is an alternative which Tarrou does not believe is open to him, a "hard vocation" to which he cannot aspire: "I am not with Tarrou, the saint," Camus once said, "but with Rieux, the healer," and the healer, as Rieux himself pictures him at the end of *The Plague*, is the very image of the man who rebels within the dialogue with the absurd:

> He knew that the tale he had to tell could not be one of a final victory. It could be only the record of what had had to be done, and what assuredly would have to be done again in the never ending fight against terror and its relentless onslaughts, despite their personal afflictions, by all who, while unable to be saints but refusing to bow down to pestilences, strive their utmost to be healers. (278)

Camus' dialogical rebel Doctor Rieux stands, like Camus himself, for the meeting with concrete everyday reality rather than for any particular ideology or point of view. He sees the gulf between Paneloux and himself as based not on the fact that Paneloux believes in God and he does not, but on the fact that Paneloux is concerned with absolutes while he deals with the concrete.

> "Paneloux is a man of learning, a scholar. He hasn't come in contact with death; that's why he can speak with such assurance of the truth—with a capital T. But every country priest who visits his parishioners and has heard a man gasping for breath on his deathbed thinks as I do. He'd try to relieve human suffering before trying to point out its excellence." (116)

It is Doctor Rieux who recognizes the plague, who organizes resistance to it, who patiently fights it. Rieux is not an idealist but a realist—a realist of the situation. It is through his unsentimental, day-by-day fight against the plague in a community of men pushed to the limits of their humanity that he is able at the end to "bear witness in favor of those plague-stricken people" and, while leaving a memorial "of the injustice and outrage done them," to "state quite simply what we learn in a time of pestilence: that there are more things to admire in men than to despise." Earlier, Rieux stated that the evil in the world always comes of ignorance, not of malevolence: "On the whole, men are more good than bad," but "there can be no true goodness nor true love without the utmost clear-sightedness." His affirmation at the end of the book, however, is more than a praise of clear-sightedness. It is a witness to humanity wrested from the heart of the inhuman, meaning wrested from the absurd.

Rieux's dialogue with the absurd implies a trust that, though the absurd will never be anything but absurd, meaning may emerge from man's meeting with it. At the end, when the plague has disappeared entirely, Rieux concludes his account with the statement that the plague bacillus has not died but is lying dormant in "bedrooms, cellars, trunks, and bookshelves," biding its time until "the day would come when, *for the bane and enlightening of men,* it would rouse up its rats again and send them forth to die in a happy city." (Italics mine.) Doctor Rieux fights against the plague, and his fight is unremitting and deadly serious, with no chance of permanent victory, no hope of more than a temporary respite. His rebellion, however, is neither a Modern Promethean's affirmation of man and denial of what stands over against man nor a Modern Sysphus' statement of distrust in existence and trust in man. It is a Modern Job's rebellion within the dialogue with the absurd—contending with the absurd yet trusting in the meaning that arises from this contending.

PART SIX

A DEPTH-IMAGE
OF
MODERN MAN

19

MELVILLE, DOSTOIEVSKY, KAFKA,
AND CAMUS

MELVILLE

The problematic of modern man is grounded in his alienation. Melville experiences this alienation in the first instance
as an alienation of man from nature, the nonhuman world
which is either malignant and hostile, as Moby Dick appears
to Ahab, or heartless and indifferent, as the universe appears
to Ishmael. For Ahab this alienation from nature leads, by
way of his Promethean defiance, to an alienation from other
men: in the matter of the whale, Starbuck's face is to him a
"lipless, unfeatured blank." It also leads to an alienation from
himself: his soul flees before his own relentless purpose. In
his one moment of receptive clarity Ahab sees his true self

as driven remorselessly by an inner necessity. In his paradoxical combination of personal freedom and psychological compulsion, Ahab embodies a problematic which we have encountered again and again throughout this book: in Bartleby the Scrivener, that strange precursor of the twentieth-century exile; in the Underground Man, Raskolnikov, Myshkin, Kirilov, Stavrogin, Versilov, and Ivan—Dostoievsky's divided men; in Joseph K., K., and even Kafka himself.

Ahab's dissembling of his madness and his ability to use sane means for a hidden, insane motive—"All my means are sane, my motive and my object mad," says Ahab—are perfectly regular for one type of paranoia; only now we see it not as a case study from outside, but from within. As a result, we can neither say that the evil associated with the White Whale is simply Melville's picture of the universe and forget about "crazy Ahab," pitted "all mutilated" against it, nor can we say that Moby Dick's "intangible malignity" is merely a projection of Ahab's madness and forget about the hostile reality confronting Ahab. We have to enter with Ahab into his madness and stand there facing the horrors he faces so long as the author forces us to go along with him on his search for an "audacious, unmitigable and supernatural revenge." If Melville thus does violence to our secure sense of socially objectified reality, he also forces us to be aware that Ahab has perhaps gone mad because he has come up against an evil greater than any we would dare face, that in his madness he is perhaps aware of some reality that our sanity necessarily excludes, and that before we can again be sure of our own reality we must pit ourselves against it like Ahab and risk, like him, "being eternally stove in."

Although Melville was not mad, he too, like Ahab, "burst his hot heart's shell upon" the maddening, tormenting truth of the evil suffered by man. Melville himself was a man who knew all too well "truth with malice in it" and "all that cracks the sinews and cakes the brain." When Ishmael tells us that the White Whale swam before Ahab "as the monomaniac incarnation of all those malicious agencies which some deep men feel eating in them, till they are left living on with half a heart and half a lung," the unspecified reference of "some deep men" suggests to us not the observer Ishmael, who constantly disclaims profundity, but Melville himself. The passionate protest implicit in these phrases helps us to understand why it was necessary for Melville to go imaginatively to the uttermost extreme with "crazy Ahab" and not just stop short in his imagination with Ishmael and turn back home.

In Ishmael's warning against pushing off from the "insular Tahiti, full of peace and joy, but encompassed by all the horrors of the half known life," Melville is perhaps speaking of those "deep souls" who have had the courage to "push off" from their personal and social centers of safety to face the horror not only of the external world but also of the deep inner world of the unconscious. This is the world of the archetypal unconscious—a world that transcends the personal, like Jung's "collective unconscious," but, unlike it, that has no center, meaning, or way that gives the daring traveler security on his perilous journey. Rather, there is simply that dark horrible world which William Blake's Thel discovers when she leaves her world of innocence, enters the world of experience, sees her own grave plot, and runs shrieking back into the Vale of Har. Here man's life has only two stages, the original innocence and the fall into experience, with no third stage in which man moves through experience to redemption, no hint that our outer and inner experience can itself attain a meaning. Ultimately, the meaning that Melville brought to his own experience of the horror encountered without and within is the form he gave to the book itself. In *Moby Dick*, it may be, he worked through the material of madness without himself going insane, of demonism without becoming demonic. Temporarily, at least, Melville too may have been pushed beyond the limits of the human—like Dostoievsky, he is able to sound the limits of human existence and to bring back to us alive from the world of hell a prize that we, to some extent, can make our own.

By going all the way with Ahab and at the same time turning back with Ishmael and by holding the tension of these two opposing points of view within the form of *Moby Dick* itself, Melville creates an artistic meaning and balance great enough to contain his question, great enough, too, not to attempt an answer. Melville's point of view comprehends both Ishmael's point of view and Ahab's without being identical with either, or being a moderate balance between them such as we find in "The Try-Works." The golden mean is not the moral of this whaling voyage in which Melville, as well as his characters, risked being eternally stoved in. In so far as there is *one* point of view in the book, it is that which holds in tension Ahab's and Ishmael's conflicting directions of movement.[1] This tension is not itself an image of man: it is a literary consciousness that encloses without resolving. The meaning that emerges from *Moby Dick* is that of the artistic form, not of a whole personal existence. It is not a meaning that can be abstracted from the form and given independent objective validity, but neither is it an image of man that, without such abstraction, can point us back toward lived life. The greatness of *Moby Dick* does not lie in its providing us with an image of man, but in its refusing to do so—in the honesty, the intensity of concern, the breadth of scope that put Melville a century ahead of Emerson, Whitman, Thoreau, and even Hawthorne. Of surer tragic stature than Ahab, because more human, is Herman Melville, the man who in his life and his art held in tension Ishmael's "wisdom that is woe" and Ahab's "woe that is madness."

At its deepest level this tension is the tension between the Modern Rebel and the Modern Exile. In *Moby Dick* the contrast between isolated Ahab and companionable Ishmael is ultimately not so important as that between Ahab the Modern Promethean and Ishmael the Modern Exile. Ahab, for all his inner division, is too much of a nineteenth-century romantic rebel to be a really modern man. That Melville lends his mind, his imagination, and his heart to both rebel Ahab and exile Ishmael gives him a modernity that his hero taken

[1] "Melville, withdrawing from the contest the better to be able to visualize it objectively, found himself deeply engaged in the hunt in two separate identities. By projecting, say, his own loneliness into Ishmael and his own obsessed bitterness into Ahab, Melville gave his drama a double authenticity of experience as well as a high dramatic quality quite beyond the powers of his previous works." (Ronald Mason, *The Spirit above the Dust: A Study of Herman Melville* [London: John Lehmann, 1951], p. 134.)

by himself does not possess. That Melville cannot unite the rebel and the exile into one figure, however, nor bring the conflict between them into anything other than an artistic unity points to the problematic of modern man that lies beneath the surface even of this greatest and most artistically mastered of Melville's works.

At the foundation of Melville's world, as at the foundation of ours, lies the crisis of "confidence" which Melville so tirelessly explicated in *The Confidence Man*. The question with which Melville leaves us is the question at the heart of our own problematic: Is it possible for modern man to trust in existence? Must we, too, like Ahab find behind the mask "inscrutable malice," or wonder, like Ishmael, whether reality is not actually empty and impersonal—"the heartless voids and immensities of the universe that threaten us with annihilation"? And if we cannot trust, can we live without trust? The artistic consciousness that held in tension Ahab and Ishmael in *Moby Dick* was itself a form of affirmation, but it was a tension that Melville could not sustain, one that was succeeded by the bitterness of *Pierre* and *The Confidence Man*, the intolerable solitude of "Bartleby," and the ironic resignation of *Billy Budd*. At the heart of Melville is the problematic of modern man.

DOSTOIEVSKY

In Melville's *Moby Dick*, the rebel and the exile remain separate to the last in the figures of Ahab and Ishmael. In Dostoievsky, the rebel and the exile are also present, but with greater dialectical interplay and less clarity of distinction. The dualism that Melville finds between man and the universe Dostoievsky removes into the human heart: "God and the devil are fighting there, and the battlefield is the heart of man." Moreover, Dostoievsky is too realistic and psychological, too fundamentally antiromantic to create any pure types. From underneath his famous rebels an exile always peers forth. Dostoievsky's "Byronic" hero quickly unmasks himself as an "anti-hero": his concern with Napoleon serves to set in relief the fact that he himself is "not Napoleon, but a louse." Dostoievsky's starting point is not the romantic hero, even ironically regarded, as in Stendhal, but the Underground Man, and the romantic rebellion of the Underground Man, where it occurs, is never more than a convulsive attempt to escape alienation, an attempt to break out of the "underground" into some kind of real existence. The romantic hero like Ahab who can persist to the end in his noble rebellion and his defiance no longer exists here. All we have is the sick society and the "anti-hero."

Dostoievsky provides us with many exemplars of the Modern Exile. Shatov, who tries to recover his roots through Russian nationalism and closeness to work and the land, still knows himself in exile, believing in Christ and *hoping* to believe in God. Ippolit's attempted suicide is as much an expression of his exile as is his lonely death. Kirilov loves a Christ who was abandoned by God; he is tormented all his life by a God in whom he does not believe; and he kills himself in a hopeless attempt to overcome man's original exile and restore mankind to paradise. Stavrogin kills himself out of sheer emptiness and despair, and Ivan ends in hopeless inner division. Even Ivan's rebellious Inquisitor is an exile, a suffering, lonely figure taking on himself the knowledge that others cannot bear. From the soil of this alienation—from the "funk hole" of the Underground Man—there spring again the Modern Promethean and the Modern Job.

When these are combined into one figure, as with Ivan Karamazov, there emerges the Problematic Rebel—the Rebel-Exile in whose face is reflected the problematic image of modern man. Dostoievsky has carried through the tragedy of Ivan with honesty and realism. Of the three brothers, Ivan remains the least positive and the most problematic, but he is also the most modern, more modern, perhaps, than his creator himself. In Ivan, the end product of the Underground Man and the most impressive teacher of the man-god, Dostoievsky has brought the problematic of modern man to the point of its highest tension—and left it unresolved. Alyosha imagines a choice between God and the devil for a man whose sickness lies precisely in his being torn between these extremes. Alyosha's alternatives of submitting to God and perishing in hatred reflect the impossible tension between submission and rebellion, conscience and nihilism, in Ivan himself.

The fact that the novel shows no way forward for Ivan, no way toward wholeness and integration, may be set down to the realism and honesty with which Dostoievsky depicts Ivan's tragedy. What constitutes a serious charge against Dostoievsky, however, is that there is no point of view in the novel that assesses broadly enough the tragedy of Ivan's inner division. The division between pride and meekness in Raskolnikov receives a specious resolution in his "conversion" and the defeat, for the time being at least, of his pride. Stavrogin's inner division is resolved on the negative side in complete despair and suicide. Ivan's inner division is not resolved at all. Still less than Raskolnikov, Stavrogin, and Versilov can Ivan choose between his two selves, and it is as much his honesty and integrity as his sickness and irresoluteness that prevent this choice. He *cannot* sacrifice one side of himself to the other, for either side—submission or rebellion—is only a half, and by itself even less than half. Neither the triumph of the one nor of the other offers him a way to wholeness.

Our question at the end, therefore, is not "Did Ivan end in a stalemate because he did not choose the right way forward or did not choose at all?" but "*Is* there a way forward for the divided man like Ivan?" In this sense the honesty and humanity of Dostoievsky's *portrayal* of Ivan transcends the honesty and humanity of the *point of view* that Dostoievsky offers us toward Ivan's tragedy—the alternative of the man-god and the god-man.

Zossima, like Dmitri, stresses an emotional affirmation, an ecstasy which takes the place of the slow, hard work of shaping the tough, resistant material of life into an image of meaning and grace. Whereas the man-god Ivan has pressed to the extreme of isolated consciousness and absolute self-affirmation, the god-man Zossima has pressed to the extreme of an already existing perfection of mutual love, or one that is easily and directly attainable. This either-or cannot be an answer for us, for our real existential situation is one of never-ending tension between our existence as separate persons and our existence as persons in direct and indirect relations with other men. We are not allowed the separating-out of the elements that leads in an Ivan to complete isolation and in a Zossima to complete and untroubled connection. Profound as they are as analyses of the dichotomous situation in which nineteenth-century man found himself, both Dostoievsky's man-god and his god-man must be seen ultimately as not doing justice to the problem of man. The need of modern man is for a really human image that will help him to preserve and enhance his humanity. He cannot be helped by an image that forces him to sacrifice one element in himself to another—to choose between rebellion and submission, social and spiritual freedom, social and spiritual equality, individual consciousness and cosmic solidarity.

"Hurrah for Karamazov!," the repeated shout with which The Brothers Karamazov ends, is not just an affirmation of Alyosha but of all the Karamazovs—of the sentimental Dmitri, the divided Ivan, the buffoon Fyodor, and even the insect-like Smerdyakov, the most purely unsympathetic and thoroughly evil character in the book. This affirmation is based less on an actual redemption of evil than on an attitude of the god-man toward evil—a love, faith, and joy that accept and include all opposites and see evil as a part of the oneness of the universe. This faith enables Alyosha to help Captain Snegiryov, Kolya, and Ilusha, to be sure, but it does not enable him to love Rakitin and Smerdyakov or to help Fyodor. The affirmation with which The Brothers Karamazov ends is all the more remarkable because of the depths of evil which the novel contains. It looks as deeply as Dostoievsky's earlier novels into the abyss of evil that we find unrelieved in them. God and the devil share an equal rule over the Karamazov world with the advantage slightly in favor of the devil. The dialectic between evil and good which is at the center of the novel does not mean so much a transformation of evil into good, however, as a coincidentia oppositorum—a movement back and forth between good and evil in which each retains its own nature yet is finally contained in a greater whole—the paradise on earth of the god-man. For Ivan, Smerdyakov, Rakitin, and Fyodor, this greater whole does not even exist. For the Zossima of the Exhortations it exists through an affirmation that tends to look away from the tragic contradictions of personal existence, and for Alyosha through a natural grace and trust that even the crisis over Zossima has not been able to shatter.

The most significant representative of this coincidence of opposites is Dmitri, for in him the opposites are as real as the affirmation. But Dmitri's Dionysian emotions swing too easily from love to hate and from self-exaltation to self-abasement to be fully convincing. Though he suffers and weeps throughout the book, he does not seem to be very much further along toward a unified way of life at the end of the book than he was at the beginning. Dmitri is Dostoievsky's most faithful image of man. In him alone the either-or's of rebellion and submission, pride and meekness, man-god and god-man are eschewed in favor of the whole, real man whose heart, after his "conversion" as before, remains the battlefield between God and the devil. Yet though Dmitri represents man in his contradictory nature, the very childlikeness and good-heartedness that make him more endearing and less problematic than Stavrogin and Ivan also stand in the way of his being *by himself* Dostoievsky's full image of man. Mitya's "old man" does not include Ivan and the man-god, nor does the "new man" that he becomes after his suffering include Alyosha and the god-man, despite the resemblance of his conception of the "new man" to the teachings of Father Zossima.

Dmitri is an image of man caught in the tension of opposites, an image of the breadth of man but not of his depths and his heights. Dmitri's statement "God and the devil are fighting . . . and the battlefield is the heart of man" offers us a broader and more human understanding of man than Ivan's man-god or Zossima's god-man. Yet in the mouth of Dmitri it does not mean so much a reconciliation of opposites as a tormented antinomy at the very heart of existence. It is this antinomy that Dostoievsky himself lived and suffered. That he could accept its tension with the honesty and awareness that he did and that he could emerge from this tension with as much affirmation as he showed in his portrayal of Zossima and Alyosha is truly remarkable. Yet the opposites in *The Brothers Karamazov* remain all too real. Though the affirmation which encloses them removes some of their terror, the evil which Dostoievsky portrays remains evil in the hearts of most of the persons who bear it—untransformed and unredeemed.

We cannot criticize Dostoievsky for the fact that he saw the world in terms of opposites, still less for the fact that he had too much artistic honesty and integrity to offer us a sentimental redemption of evil in a tragic situation where none was possible. What we must criticize him for, however, is that he mistook one of his two opposites for the whole, that he offered Zossima and the god-man as the answer to Ivan and the man-god, that he thought Zossima's affirmation of life as a paradise an all-encompassing reality which could include *both* Ivan's Inquisitor and his Christ, *both* Dmitri's "ideal of the Madonna" and his "ideal of Sodom."

If the depths of evil and tragedy that Dostoievsky faces point back to the age-old problem of evil, they also point forward to the problematic of modern man. No modern writer has given us so much insight into this problematic as Dostoievsky. The series of figures whose tortured depths he has revealed is breathtaking: the Underground Man, Raskolnikov and Svidrigailov, Myshkin and Ippolit, Shatov and Kirilov and Stavrogin, Dolgoruky and Versilov, Ivan and Dmitri. Even more astounding is the sweep and greatness of Dostoievsky's final and most profound portrayal of man in *The Brothers Karamazov*. No other modern writer has achieved such a statement about man as Dostoievsky has through his development of Ivan, Alyosha, and Dmitri. Taken separately, they constitute a remarkable portrayal of three significant types of man. Taken together, they constitute the most positive response in modern literature to the "death of God" and the absence of a meaningful image of man, the most impressive attempt to create a modern image of man.

There is no question that Dostoievsky wished to understand Alyosha not only as the chief hero of the book and the one through whom he most often expressed his own judgment on other characters, but also as an image of man for modern man. Alyosha is odd, even eccentric, Dostoievsky writes in his preface, and that might seem "to interfere with rather than help in the uniting of the strands and in the finding of some sort of common meaning in the general confusion."

> If you do not agree with this last thesis, . . . then I . . .
> might become encouraged about the significance of my
> hero, Alexey Fyodorovich. For not only is an eccentric
> "not always" a particularity and a separate element, but,
> on the contrary, it happens sometimes that such a person,
> I dare say, carries within himself the very heart of the
> universal, and the rest of the men of his epoch have for
> some reason been temporarily torn from it, as if by a gust
> of wind.[2]

Alyosha is a representative of mystical community and loving humility in contrast to the individualistic separateness and
intellectual pride of the Westernized Ivan.[3] Ivan's life centers
around ideas, Alyosha's around people. Ivan's humanitarianism is abstract, intellectual, and condescending; Alyosha's
love of humanity is direct, personal, and mutual. While Ivan
is, first to last, a complex enigma, Alyosha is and remains basically simple. Alyosha and Ivan are the exact embodiment of
the contrast that Martin Buber makes in "The Way of Man"
between the man who "by nature" or "by grace" has "a soul
all of a piece, and accordingly performs . . . works all of a
piece" and the man who has "a divided, complicated, contradictory soul" whose inhibitions, disturbances, and restlessness
express themselves in his action.[4]

It is the latter, however, and not the former who represents
the problematic of modern man. We must ask, therefore,
whether the "all of a piece" Alyosha offers an image of man
to the "divided, complicated, contradictory" Ivan. If Ivan has
too much of the negative and not enough of the positive to be
an image of man in the full sense of the term, Alyosha has too
much of the positive and not enough of the negative. Not
that Alyosha is a purely ideal or unconvincing character, but
in his own way he is as much of an exception as the superman to the problematic man who stands in need of a direc-

---

[2] Dostoievsky, *The Brothers Karamazov*, "From the Author," p. xix.
[3] Cf. *Die Urgestalt*, pp. 160 f.
[4] Martin Buber, *Hasidism and Modern Man*, ed. and trans. by Maurice
Friedman (New York: Harper Torchbooks, 1966), p. 148.

tion-giving image. Taken together, Zossima and Alyosha represent Dostoievsky's most complete portrayal of a positive image of man.[5] Yet this god-man, in his humility and active love, is an image of saintliness that sidesteps the contradictions and problematic of modern man. Attractive as the gentle, loving, and realistic Alyosha is, he is too little realized as a person with problems of his own to offer a way to modern man.

None of the brothers offers us a modern image of man. Ivan remains torn by his inner contradictions and his ideological dichotomies. Alyosha experiences Dmitri's lust and Ivan's rebellion only as modified impulses. Dmitri begins and ends the most human of the three brothers. But he neither experiences the depths of the problematic of modern man, as do Stavrogin and Ivan, nor attains any way forward that bespeaks a decisive change and promises a "new man." Nor can the three taken together equal an image of man for the simple reason that each is real in himself and cannot be added to the others as parts of a whole. If they were three aspects of one man, then they would indeed include the full range of man—the movement through tragic contradiction and inner turmoil to the highest reaches of human existence. As it is, however, they represent panels in a triptych painting rather than movements in a symphony. None of them is great enough to encompass Dostoievsky's own image of the depth, the breadth,

[5] On the basis of the internal evidence and of his letters, we may assume that Zossima and Alyosha represented Dostoievsky's own highest image of man. That we may assume this without violating M. M. Bakhtin's principle that Dostoievsky's characters are independent voices rather than expressions of a single consciousness and a single point of view is shown by Bakhtin himself: "Dostoievsky's is a world of consciousnesses illuminating one another, a world of concomitant formulations of the meaning of man. Among them he seeks the loftiest formulation, the one most deserving of faith, and he perceives it not as his own true thought, but as another true man and his word. In the image of the ideal man or in the image of Christ there is offered to him a solution to his ideological searches. This image or this loftiest voice is to crown the world of voices, organize, and subject it. It was the image of man, with his voice that is not the author's voice, which was the final ideological criterion for Dostoievsky—not to remain true to his own convictions and not the truth of his own convictions taken in the abstract, but to remain true to the faith-commanding image of man." (Bakhtin, *op. cit.*, pp. 88 f., quoted in Seduro, *op. cit.*, pp. 218 f.)

and the height of man. None of them includes the problematic of modern man as Dostoievsky himself understood it coupled with an image of human existence in which that problematic becomes part of a meaningful direction of personal life. It is Dostoievsky's tragedy that even in the greatest of his novels, he did not know how to create a character whom he could bring from inner contradiction to personal wholeness, from negation and rebellion to affirmation and meaning. This tragedy itself deepens our understanding of the problematic of modern man.

KAFKA

If the note of the Modern Exile is sounded in Kafka so much more strongly than that of the Modern Rebel, this is, in part, because the crisis of the person in the modern world removes the ground for that unqualified rebellion which was still possible for the romantic hero or the Modern Promethean. The need of the self for confirmation, the problematic of the calling and the call, the tension between personal and social confirmation, the impossibility of either separating or identifying social reality and the reality that speaks through the medium of the social—all these make impossible those simple contrasts between the self and the other, the "autonomous individual" and the "mass society," the "Single One" and the "crowd," the "insider" and the "outsider," the "beat" and the "square" with which the problematic of the Modern Rebel has been obscured and the real crisis of the person in our age ignored. Kafka knows that the person does not exist as a self-evident, self-sufficient reality any more than he can be subsumed under his social role or group category. The person in the modern world exists as pure paradox: responding with a calling of which he is never sure to a call which he can never clearly hear. For Kafka it cannot be a question of overthrowing the "authoritarian" in favor of the "humanistic," as it is for Erich Fromm, but of discovering the human again and again in the very heart of the bewildering social hierarchy, personal meaning in the midst of the impersonal absurd.

Because it grows out of the personal existence of an honest, perceptive, and deeply problematic man, the meaning inherent in Kafka's works is by its very nature a meaning for the problematic of modern man. Kafka himself formulates with striking clarity this representative quality of his own existence:

> It is not inertia, ill will, awkwardness—even if there is something of all this in it, because "vermin is born of the void"—that cause me to fail, or not even to get near failing: family life, friendship, marriage, profession, literature. It is not that, but the lack of ground underfoot, of air, of the commandment. . . . I have brought nothing with me of what life requires, so far as I know, but only the universal human weakness. With this—in this respect it is gigantic strength—I have vigorously absorbed the negative element of the age in which I live, an age that is, of course, very close to me, which I have no right ever to fight against, but as it were a right to represent. The slight amount of the positive, and also of the extreme negative, which capsizes into the positive, are something in which I have had no hereditary share. I have not been guided into life by the hand of Christianity—admittedly now slack and failing—as Kierkegaard was, and have not caught the hem of the Jewish prayer shawl—now flying away from us—as the Zionists have. I am an end or a beginning.[6]

Kafka, who embodies as few others the problematic of modern man and the loneliness of the Modern Exile, is also the man who more than any other has sought the way forward through the very heart of the absurd. The question which Kafka poses us is expressed most succinctly in his statement: "I am an an end or a beginning." If we see Kafka only in terms of his problematic, we shall join those who regard him as "an end"—a neurotic, a nihilist, an enemy of culture, or a desperate believer "fleeing humanity," in Camus' words, "in order to try to enter . . . the desert of divine grace." [7] But if

---

[6] *Dearest Father,* "The Eight Octavo Notebooks," pp. 99 f.
[7] Camus' absurd is often not that of Kafka, as is shown by Camus' own interpretation, or, as we would think, misinterpretation, of Kafka. Beginning with the penetrating insight that "Kafka expresses tragedy by the everyday and the absurd by the logical," Camus ends with the

we see in Kafka the humor and the trust and the steady movement toward meaning in the teeth of contradiction and despair, we shall glimpse the sense in which Kafka is "a beginning" for modern man.

CAMUS

Camus' call to face the absurd in *The Myth of Sisyphus* still represents the defiant protest of the Modern Promethean rather than the open contending of the Modern Job. Camus' very definition of the reality we confront as absurd depends upon his *expectation* of rationality:

> A horde of irrationals has sprung up and surrounds man until his ultimate end. In his recovered and now studied lucidity, the feeling of the absurd becomes clear and

---

critique of Kafka's work as representing "the emotionally moving face of man fleeing humanity, deriving from his contradictions reasons for believing, reasons for hoping from his fecund despairs, and calling life his terrifying apprenticeship in death." Aside from a misguided tendency to identify Kafka with Kierkegaard, the cause for this misreading of Kafka seems to lie in Camus' own conception of the absurd as a much more fixed and set reality than it is for Kafka, a reality which imposed limits not only to reason and congruity but to meaning of any kind. For the Camus of this stage one could not say, as one can of the later Camus, that meaning comes through the heart of the absurd. Rather, it is subjective revolt against and in spite of the absurd in which Sisyphus forever shoulders anew his futile burden and, precisely because he lives without hope and illusion, knows happiness as inseparable from the absurd. "The struggle itself toward the heights is enough to fill a man's heart. One must imagine Sisyphus happy." The absurd "drives out of this world a god who had come into it with . . . a preference for futile sufferings" and "makes of fate a human matter, which must be settled among men." Camus sees the exile in Kafka, but he fails to see the rebel, the Modern Job, and the reason for this failure is that he begins with the either-or thinking of the Modern Promethean which assumes that the rebel must deny and put aside any relation with the transcendent if he is to remain true to himself: "The Land-Surveyor's last attempt is to recapture God through what negates him, to recognize him, not according to our categories of goodness and beauty, but behind the empty and hideous aspects of his indifference, of his injustice, and of his hatred. That stranger who asks the Castle to adopt him is at the end of his voyage a little more exiled because this time he is unfaithful to himself, forsaking morality, logic, and intellectual truths in order to try to enter, endowed solely with his mad hope, the desert of divine grace." (Camus, *The Myth of Sisyphus*, p. 133.)

definite. . . . This world in itself is not reasonable, that is all that can be said. But what is absurd is the confrontation of this irrational and the wild longing for clarity whose call echoes in the human heart. . . . Man stands face to face with the irrational. He feels within him his longing for happiness and for reason. The absurd is born of this confrontation between the human need and the unreasonable silence of the world.[8]

When we speak of dialogue with the absurd, it is not, therefore, the absurd of the early Camus that we mean—the product of a disappointed expectation born of a nostalgia for lucidity more characteristic of modern rationalism than of man as man. We mean, rather, the affirmation of a concrete reality that we can meet yet cannot comprehend as it is in itself apart from that meeting. This latter meaning of the absurd—the meaning Camus himself arrived at in *The Plague* —offers us a realistic approach to the "world" of modern science. The dialogue with the absurd means here an open-minded and courageous standing one's ground before a world which man cannot image and to which he can ascribe no independent, objective meaning.

In his essay "Neither Victims nor Executioners" Camus clearly rejects the either-or of the Modern Promethean in favor of the Modern Job. Though his plea for abolition of the death penalty and his declaration that he will never sanction murder as a means to social or political ends bring Tarrou to mind, the basic position which Camus takes is that of Rieux—neither acceptance of evil nor cutting oneself off from history to avoid it.

These evils are today the very stuff of History, so that many consider them necessary evils. It is true that we cannot "escape History," since we are in it up to our necks. But one may propose to fight within History to preserve from History that part of man which is not its proper province."[9]

[8] *The Myth of Sisyphus*, pp. 16, 21.
[9] Albert Camus, "Neither Victims nor Executioners," trans. by Dwight Macdonald, in Paul Goodman, ed., *The Seeds of Liberation* (New York: George Braziller, 1964), pp. 41 f.

Camus calls on men to take up Rieux's task of healer in the never-ending struggle to wrest meaning from the dialogue with the concrete situation, from the absurdities of history and society.

> Some of us should . . . take on the job of keeping alive, through the apocalyptic historical vista that stretches before us, a modest thoughtfulness which, without pretending to solve everything, will constantly be prepared to give some human meaning to everyday life.[10]

This path is possible for us only if we move from the absolute silence imposed by ideologies to the mutual limitation and communication of dialogue. "Mankind's long dialogue has just come to an end," writes Camus, in "a vast conspiracy of silence."

> We live in a world of abstractions, of bureaus and machines, of absolute ideas and of crude messianism. We suffocate among people who think they are absolutely right, whether in their machines or in their ideas. And for all who can live only in an atmosphere of human dialogue, this silence is the end of the world.[11]

In opposition to all ideologies, Camus calls for "a political position that is modest—i.e., free of messianism and disencumbered of nostalgia for an earthly paradise." In the face of a tragedy which has become collective, Camus calls for a "civilization of dialogue" in which the dialogue and universal intercommunication of men will be defended against fear, silence, spiritual isolation, slavery, injustice, and lies.

This progression from ideology to dialogue means the progression from the Modern Promethean to the Modern Job. The Modern Promethean, like Captain Ahab and Ivan, is the man of monologue pure and simple, the romantic hero who does not need to listen to anyone else. The Modern Job is the man who has learned from his very rebellion a measure and

[10] *Ibid.*, p. 42.
[11] *Ibid.*, pp. 26 f. That Dwight Macdonald consistently translated "le dialogue" as "sociability" rather than as "dialogue" suggests how little he understood Camus' third alternative to being a victim or an executioner! I have restored the original meaning in the passages I quoted.

limit which means the recognition of the validity of the other person's point of view, the dialogue between man and man. "In order to exist, man must rebel," writes Camus in *The Rebel*, "but rebellion must respect the limit it discovers in itself—a limit where minds meet and, in meeting, begin to exist." Unlike Zarathustra and Dostoievsky's man-god, Camus' rebel is in no danger of putting himself in the place of God. He begins with the affirmation of the man who stands facing him as well as of himself, the recognition that his own existence is limited by the existence of the other: "Each tells the other that he is not God; this is the end of romanticism." So far from rebellion being the highest expression of individualism, as it is for the romantic hero and the Modern Promethean, it is the beginning of human solidarity: "I rebel—therefore we exist." Thus in contrast to the Modern Promethean who demands the choice *between* rebellion and dialogue, Camus' image of the Rebel represents a fusion of the two.

> The mutual recognition of a common destiny and the communication of men between themselves are always valid. Rebellion proclaimed them and undertook to serve them. . . . It opened the way to a morality which, far from obeying abstract principles, discovers them only in the heat of battle and in the incessant movement of contradiction. . . . Nothing justifies the assertion that these principles have existed eternally. . . . But they do exist, in the very period in which we exist. With us, and throughout all history, they deny servitude, falsehood, and terror. . . . The mutual understanding and communication discovered by rebellion can survive only in the free exchange of . . . dialogue.[12]

The source of values is now no longer the Modern Sisphyus' subjective affirmation in spite of the absurd, but the dialogue itself—the struggle with the concrete situation within which the Modern Job stands his ground and rebels.

[12]Albert Camus, *The Rebel, An Essay on Man in Revolt*, trans. Anthony Bower (New York: Vintage Books, 1956), pp. 283f.

20

THE PROBLEMATIC REBEL:
AN IMAGE OF MODERN MAN

From our study of Melville, Dostoievsky, Kafka, and Camus there has emerged a depth-image of modern man the significance of which extends far beyond the personal existences and immediate cultures that these authors represented and reflected. Although this image can make no claim to comprehensiveness, it can claim to have delineated some of the most basic and lasting aspects of that torrent of existence in which modern man is swept along and of which he has become ever more keenly aware. The image of modern man that has emerged is an indivisible totality. We can point toward it, but we cannot define it. This whole book, indeed, is nothing but an attempt to point to this image. This does not pre-clude our approaching it from several different vantage points, as we have in our discussion of the "death of God," the alienation of modern man, the Modern Exile, the Modern Promethean, the problematic of modern man, and the Modern Job. These vantage points are not separate realities, how-ever, but only different ways of illuminating the total image.

THE "DEATH OF GOD" AND THE ALIENATION OF MODERN MAN

Although the meaning of Prometheus' rebellion is insepa-rable from the Greek order *on the strength of which he re-belled*, to modern man Prometheus has become the symbol of rebellion *against* all order, divine or social. Similarly, Job, the Biblical rebel who, in spite of his exile from God, trusts, and because of it contends, has become to modern man the symbol of an absolute exile that no dialogue with God may overcome, or of a metaphysical rebellion that aims to "do away" with God on the ground of the problem of evil. In the era of the "death of God," when men can no longer believe in a cosmic order or in a creating and revealing God, Pro-metheus and Job live on divorced from their original context and transformed into the Modern Rebel and the Modern Exile.

The "death of God" does not mean that modern man does not "believe" in God, any more than it means that God him-self has actually died. Whether or not one holds with Sartre that God never existed at all or with Buber that God is in "eclipse" and that it is we, the "slayers of God," who dwell in the darkness, the "death of God" means the aware-ness of a basic crisis in modern history—the crisis that comes when man no longer knows what it means to be human and becomes aware that he does not know this. This is not just a question of the relativization of "values" and the absence of universally accepted mores. It is the absence of an image of meaningful human existence, the absence of the ground that enabled Greek, Biblical, and Renaissance man to move with some sureness even in the midst of tragedy.

At the fountainhead of some of the most important religious movements of our time stands Søren Kierkegaard. Yet Kierkegaard's famous "knight of faith" itself bears witness to the "death of God." In *Fear and Trembling* Kierkegaard presents two images of man. One is Agamemnon—the tragic hero or "knight of infinite resignation" who sacrifices his daughter Iphigenia for the sake of the safety of the Greek ships, thus subordinating his individuality to the universal order. The other is Abraham—the "knight of faith" who is commanded by "an absolute relationship to the Absolute" to "suspend" the ethical principles enjoined by the universal order and sacrifice his son Isaac. Kierkegaard's "knight of faith" stands, like Job, in a unique relationship to God, not mediated by any order or universal law. In every other respect, however, he differs decisively from Job, as from the Biblical Abraham on whom he is modeled. He does not reach the finite directly but through a dialectic in which he first renounces the finite for the infinite and then regains the finite through "faith by virtue of the absurd." Thus he substitutes for Abraham's and Job's direct trust in God a faith of tension and of paradox. He obeys, moreover, instead of contends, for to Kierkegaard the relationship of the man of faith to God can always mean only a "hearkening," never a withstanding. What is more, Kierkegaard's "knight of faith" must choose *between* God and creation. There is no longer a possibility of finding God in creation. He rejects society and culture for the lonely relation of the "Single One" to God, thereby losing any check on the reality of the voice that addresses him. In its very affirmation of faith, as a result, Kierkegaard's concept of the "knight of faith" is a consequence and an expression of the "death of God": it entails the loss of faith in the universal order and in the society that purports to be founded on it; the "suspension of the ethical" and the relativization of ordinary ethical values that follows from it; the rejection of creation—the world and society—as an obstacle to the relationship with God; and the paradoxical "leap of faith" that is necessary to attain any sort of contact with God.

The "death of God" means the alienation of modern man, as Albert Camus has tirelessly pointed out in his discussion of the "absurd":

> In a universe suddenly divested of illusions and lights, man feels an alien, a stranger. His exile is without remedy since he is deprived of the memory of a lost home or the hope of a promised land. This divorce between man and his life, the actor and his setting, is properly the feeling of absurdity.[1]

The absurd, to Camus, is born of the confrontation of the human longing for happiness and for reason with the irrational silence of the world. The absurd means life without hope and without illusion: "I want to know whether I can live with what I know and with that alone." "Knowing whether one can live *without appeal* is all that interests me." In conscious contrast to Kierkegaard, Camus asserts that "the absurd . . . does not lead to God . . . the absurd is sin without God."

From the "death of God" and the alienation of modern man arise the other aspects of the image of modern man that we have considered—the Modern Exile and the Modern Promethean, the problematic of modern man, and the Modern Job. The Greek Exile was an exile from the order, the Greek Rebel a rebel within and on the basis of the order. The Biblical Exile was an exile from God, the Biblical rebel a Job who contended with God. Both Oedipus and Job touch deeply upon the problem of evil, both question at its base man's relationship to *moira* or his dialogue with God. Yet both end in a reaffirmation of that relationship of God, man, and the world which characterized their particular heritage and tradition. The Renaissance Exile, similarly, may have been portrayed as an exile from the "joys of heaven," as in *Doctor Faustus*, but that rebellion which placed him in exile was founded upon a new hope in the unlimited possibilities of human development—a new faith in a striving that seemed to be without upward limit.

The modern Rebel-Exile, in contrast, has neither the Greek, Biblical, nor Christian base on which to stand, nor has he the

---

[1] Albert Camus, *The Myth of Sisyphus and Other Essays*, trans. Justin O'Brien (New York: Alfred A. Knopf, 1955), p. 6.

hope of his Renaissance counterpart. He knows himself as in exile, but he no longer knows anything definite that he can speak of as being in exile *from*. The "infinite spaces" of Pascal and the "heartless voids and immensities" of Melville's Ishmael have taken the place of *moira*, the Garden of Eden, the dialogue with God, and the Christian Heaven. Similarly, although he "rebels" against a "Transcendent" that he believes has alienated from him his own creative freedom, modern man knows that this Transcendent is "dead" already, that he is "condemned to be free," that he is a "rebel without a cause."

Whether one reacts to the "death of God" with the bitter resignation of Hardy's Jude the Obscure or with the Promethean "will to power" of Nietzsche's Zarathustra, the alienation that both experience is the same. Underneath the Modern Promethean who hopes to overcome man's alienation can always be found the Modern Exile—"the world's outcast," as Nietzsche's Zarathustra calls him. Despite Faust's inner conflict, Goethe's Faust still stands within a harmony between nature, culture, and spirit. In Nietzsche's *Thus Spake Zarathustra* these spheres have come apart: the "higher" man, the bearer of the spirit's "holy Yea," knows himself as alienated not only from nature but also from modern society and culture. He is necessarily a lonely figure in his fight against all those manifestations of modern life that suffocate the spirit and prevent man from surpassing himself.

Zarathustra often affirms evil as a part of the upward progress of the spirit:

I tell you: one must still have chaos in one, to give birth to a dancing star. I tell you: ye have still chaos in you. $(11)^2$

—For there is a salt which uniteth good with evil; and even the evilest is worthy, as spicing and as final overfoaming. (259)

"Man must become better and eviler"—so do *I* teach. The evilest is necessary for the Superman's best. (322)

[2] All page references are to the Modern Library Edition of Friedrich Nietzsche's *Thus Spake Zarathustra*, trans. Thomas Common (New York: 1927).

But Zarathustra is no more able than Faust to include within this dialectical view that evil which does not represent energy and creative force but denial and inertia. There comes a "time when man will no longer give birth to any star . . . the time of the most despicable man, who can no longer despise himself." This is "the last man."

> "We have discovered happiness"—say the last men, and blink thereby.
>
> They have left the regions where it is hard to live; for they need warmth. One still loveth one's neighbour and rubbeth against him; for one needeth warmth . . .
>
> A little poison now and then: that maketh pleasant dreams. And much poison at last for a pleasant death . . .
>
> No shepherd, and one herd! Everyone wanteth the same, everyone is equal: he who hath other sentiments goeth voluntarily into the madhouse. (11 f.)

These "last men," these "superfluous ones," arouse in Zarathustra a "great disgust at man" which almost strangles him:

> But I asked once, and suffocated almost with my question: What? Is the rabble also *necessary* for life?
>
> Are poisoned fountains necessary, and stinking fires, and filthy dreams, and maggots in the bread of life?
>
> Not my hatred, but my loathing, gnawed hungrily at my life! Ah, ofttimes became I weary of spirit, when I found even the rabble spiritual! . . .
>
> Like a cripple become deaf, and blind, and dumb—thus have I lived long; that I might not live with the power-rabble, the scribe-rabble, and the pleasure-rabble. (104)

In Thomas Hardy's novel *Jude the Obscure,* the rebellion of the hero serves only to accentuate his exile, and this exile is linked in explicit fashion with the "death of God." Jude, a boy from the lower classes, spends his life vainly trying to get a university education which, in nineteenth-century England, is reserved for the higher classes. The social order which here takes the place of the Greek *moira* is just as inexorable, but it does not have the meaning that the latter has. Man is alien from this order and cannot be reconciled with it. Jude's work fails, his children hang themselves, Sue, his common-law wife whom he loves, leaves him, and Arabella, his vulgar and unloving first wife, takes possession of him again only finally to desert him. As the abandoned Jude lies dying, he recites Job's curse of the day of his birth while the cheers of the crowd at the fair to which Arabella has gone punctuate Jude's last speech with ironic accompaniment. Here the undermining of the very meaning of existence comes at the end and not at the beginning, as in the Book of Job. Job's exile becomes the symbol of the exile of modern man.

In contemporary literature Camus' novel, *The Stranger,* is a classic presentation of the "death of God" and the Modern Exile. The "stranger," Meursault, can have no meaningful contact with any person or anything. Meursault is not a Doctor Faustus but an Ishmael. He knows that it is "better to burn than to disappear," better to have a future in whatever form than to have no future at all. He is proof against the social conspiracy of all those "cocksure" people who try to conceal from others and from themselves the shattering effect that the certainty of lonely death has on the illusion of social solidarity.

THE MODERN EXILE

Both in "Moby Dick" and "The Whiteness of the Whale" there is a suggestion of the White Whale as absolute in the sense of infinite and immortal. This absolute, particularly in the latter chapter, brings to mind the Hindu Brahman—the neuter nondualistic and impersonal reality which is beyond good and evil alike and in some sense contains them both. This absolute is quite as capable of destruction as it is of creation and preservation. Melville's absolute, however, unlike the Hindu Brahman, is not identical with the real self of man but simply over against man. It has neither purpose nor divinity. It does not include man in any order which it underlies but, on the contrary, destroys all order, reduces cosmos to chaos, meaning to contingency, value to brute fact. In the end, therefore, the comparison with the Hindu absolute can only force us to still sharper contrast. To all nondualism Melville here opposes the strongest possible dualism.

Melville's "almighty forlornness" stands opposed to any form of idealism or mysticism that tends to abolish the gulf between man and the world. Man is the creature whose existence is limited in space and time and who knows it; the creature whose life is conditioned by his knowledge of death. He has to face the infinite and know that it is infinite and he is finite. But this is just what specifically modern man cannot bear. For modern man can no longer believe, as primitive man could, that he is one with a natural-spiritual order; nor can he believe, as Biblical man could, that the world is the creation of a creator in relationship to whom his own existence finds its meaning; nor, as the Greek man could, that there is an order with which he can become reconciled even if at the expense of tragic suffering; nor, as Emerson and the transcendentalists tried to believe, that the universe is all one great soul, and the whale and the sharks are nothing but thoughts peopling the soul. As a man of modern consciousness, he is cut off from all that. Fully aware of his individuality and his individual mortality, he exchanges the consolations that are inaccessible to him for the defiance of the Modern Rebel or the forlornness of the Modern Exile.

"The Ugliest Man," in Nietzsche's *Thus Spake Zarathustra*, murders God, because he cannot bear the crushing weight of an infinity above him that has no essential relation to him, an "Other" that is merely other.[3] Even the compassion of such a deity suffocates human existence in the same way as the White Whale suffocates Ahab. Job says to God, "Thou wilt seek me, but I shall not be" (Job 7:21), but he believes that he can find a meaning to his finite, mortal existence in his relationship to God. Ishmael, unlike Job, cannot find any meaning in the face of man's death and finiteness.

At the end of *Bartleby the Scrivener*, as we have seen, the employer links Bartleby with Job by answering the grub-

[3] Cf. Romano Guardini, *Welt und Person*, "Gott und 'der Andere,'" pp. 23-27.

man's question, "He's asleep, ain't he?," with the quotation, "With kings and counsellors." Here Job stands not for the Biblical rebel but, as in the ending of Thomas Hardy's *Jude the Obscure*, for the Modern Exile. What Bartleby and Jude have in common with the Biblical Job is the experience of the most terrible exile: that sense of abandonment that undermines the very meaning of existence and makes life insupportable. But for Job the cursing of his existence, even though it means a denial of the creation and by implication of the Creator, does not mean the "death of God." Even when Job contends most bitterly with the God who has turned away from him, he still trusts and he still remains in dialogue. In *Jude the Obscure* and in "Bartleby," in contrast, the exile is linked with the "death of God." In both, the Modern Exile is alien from the social order and cannot be reconciled with it. As the hapless and abandoned Jude lies dying, he recites Job's curse of the day of his birth while the cheers of the crowd at the fair punctuate his speech with ironic accompaniment. The allusion to Job's curse after the death of Bartleby is subtler but no less effective, and it has the same purport. In both the undermining of the very meaning of existence comes at the end and not at the beginning, as in the Book of Job. Job's exile, unredeemed by any reestablishment of trust, becomes the symbol of the exile of modern man.

In the extreme form in which we see it in Bartleby, this exile means a destruction of confidence in existence itself. In this respect "Bartleby" presages Melville's bitter novel *The Confidence Man* in which the distrust of the creature is explicitly linked with the distrust of the Creator, misanthropy with infidelity.

It is the inability to trust in existence that lies at the core of the remarkable resemblance between Bartleby and Kafka's "Hunger Artist." Bartleby eats almost nothing except ginger-nuts when he is in the office, and in the Tombs he declares, "I prefer not to dine to-day . . . It would disagree with me; I am unused to dinners." On the employer's second visit, the grub-man asks him whether Bartleby will dine today or whether he lives without dining. The employer replies, "Lives without dining," and closes the eyes of "the wasted Bartleby," who though apparently sleeping is actually dead. This brings to mind the death of Kafka's Gregor Samsa, the routine-bound traveling salesman who, after his metamorphosis into a gigantic insect, starves to death because he cannot find any food that he can eat or any confirmation from his family that could lead him to want to eat. But the parallels with "A Hunger Artist" are more striking still. The hunger artist would have "stuffed" himself had he only found "food" he liked—had he found some way open to a meaningful existence. This coincides exactly with the prophetic first question which the grub-man puts to the employer concerning Bartleby: "Does he want to starve?" Bartleby *wants* to starve because he can find no way to live, no access to real life, to authentic existence. In him the exile of modern man has become absolute and irrevocable. The only way that remains open to him is death.

It is death, and death in the peculiarly modern emphasis that Freud and Heidegger give to it, that is the focus of the epilogue of this novella. In this epilogue Bartleby's exile is broadened into the exile of modern man, whose hyper-intensive awareness of death is the exact corollary of the alienation and rootlessness of his existence and the ten-uousness of his sense of self. It is death which produces the "pallid hopelessness" not only of Bartleby but of the Modern Exile in general. Like Camus in *The Myth of Sisyphus*, the Modern Exile sees death as the final term of absurdity set to his own attempts at a meaningful existence. It is death, too, which reduces all attempts at communication be-tween persons to permanent silence. "On errands of life, these letters speed to death" summarizes the entire hope-less attempt at human dialogue and communication be-tween Bartleby and his employer and, by the same token, between man and man. The final comment of the narrator of Bartleby" is also one of solidarity: "Ah Bartleby! Ah humanity!" implies the recognition of the common bond that fate and death have imposed upon all men, the bond that links even the safest and smuggest of men with Bartleby, the pitiful, unheroic figure who anticipates the Modern Exile.

If Meursault can say, What does it matter if I took one way or another since each ends in death? Bartleby may ask, with equal justice, What does it matter to me if there exists an image of authentic existence if I am barred from responding to it? What does it matter to me if there is a "way of man" if I cannot walk on it? When it comes to the image of man, the exception casts doubt on the rule. If even one man can live as Bartleby lived, then the "meaning" and "authenticity" which we claim as the birthright of all men becomes a contingent matter and the way of man becomes absurd. "The true way is like a rope stretched one foot above the ground," writes Kafka. "It seems more fit to stumble over than to walk upon."

The exile wants to become a member of the community and to find the confirmation for the calling that will answer his call; he cannot do so, however, precisely because his position as an exile puts him in the wrong relationship to the community and to those who might confirm him. A man like K. is thus excluded from the "true way" by his very nature and situation. But can there be a true way which is not available to the unique person who must follow it? "What does it matter if God is made man in Christ," says Meister Eckhart, "if Christ is not born in my soul?" Surely I haven't suffered," cries Ivan Karamazov," "simply that I, my crimes and my sufferings may manure the soil of the future harmony for somebody else?" What does it matter if there is a "true way" if the Modern Exile, through no fault of his own, is unable to find and follow it!

Must we conclude that if there is no way of man for Bartleby, then all possibility of authentic humanity goes under with him? Bartleby's "I prefer not to" is not only negative. It is also positive—the last effort of the drowning self to preserve its existence as a self. In this sense, even his defeat and death may be for us an image of the outermost limit of a common human condition—a condition which forces us to go through the anguish of the Modern Exile but need not leave us there. This condition is the inescapable but nonetheless genuine personal struggle of each one of us. Each of us, in his unique tension of compulsion and responsibility, must try to find a way forward which will be true—true both to ourselves and to the situation to which we must respond. In this struggle, and in it alone, there remains a possibility of authenticating our humanity.

THE MODERN PROMETHEAN: NIETZSCHE'S ZARATHUSTRA

The "allienation" of modern man has been a recurrent theme in nineteenth- and twentieth-century thought from Hegel, Feuerbach, and Marx to Nietzsche, Sartre, and Fromm. To many of those who have used this term, this alienation is something that can be overcome: by rejecting the transcendent God of Christianity for "the dialogue of I and Thou," as in Feuerbach; by destroying capitalism and restoring the means of production to the workers, as in Marx; by taking on oneself the responsibility for creating values, as in Nietzsche and Sartre. The Modern Promethean not only proclaims that God *is* dead, but also that he *had* to die—to give man back his true existence. The Modern Promethean is one of the basic forms through which the Modern Exile has attempted to rebel against his alienation.

"Dead are all the Gods: now do we desire the Superman to live," says Nietzsche's Zarathustra. The "death of God" means that there is now no longer any absolute to which man can appeal for reality, meaning, and value. Man must himself create meaning through his own will to power: "The Superman is the meaning of the earth. Let your will say: The Superman *shall be* the meaning of the earth!" Man overcomes his own exile through refusing any longer to accede to the alienation of reality from the human world: "There is needed a holy Yea unto life: *its own* will, willeth now the spirit; *his own* world winneth the world's outcast." The highest virtue is now remaining true to the earth, the most dreadful sin to blaspheme it by rating "the heart of the unknowable higher than the meaning of the earth!" All gods are "human work and human madness" created by the suffering and impotent "Backworldsmen."

Weariness, which seeketh to get to the ultimate with one leap, with a death-leap; a poor ignorant weariness, unwilling even to will any longer: that created all gods and backworlds. . . .

But that "other world" is well concealed from man, that dehumanised, inhuman world, which is a celestial naught; and the bowels of existence do not speak unto man, except as man. (29 f.)

Evil do I call it and misanthropic; all that teaching about the one, and the plenum, and the unmoved, and the sufficient, and the imperishable! . . . Of time and of becoming shall the best similes speak. (91 f.)[4]

To begin with human existence as the ground of reality and of knowledge is to reject that "eternal reason-spider and reason-cobweb" that leads the rationalist to see all existence as rational and objectifiable.

All being would ye *make* thinkable: for ye doubt with good reason whether it be already thinkable.

But it shall accommodate and bend itself to you! So willeth your will. Smooth shall it become and subject to the spirit, as its mirror and reflection. (122 f.)

If there is no objective order, there is also no universal way, but only the unique path that each must find for himself: " 'This—is now *my* way,—where is yours?' Thus did I answer those who asked me 'the way.' For *the* way—it doth not exist!" By the same token, without a God there is no longer any equality of men.

"Ye higher men,"—so blinketh the populace—"there are no higher men, we are all equal; man is man, before God—we are all equal!"

Before God!—Now, however, this God hath died. Before the populace, however, we will not be equal. (320)

We only understand the rebellion of the Modern Promethean fully when we learn *how* God died. In Chapter 66, "Out of Service," Zarathustra asks the old pope if it is not true that God choked to death on his sympathy for man, that

---

[4] Friedrich Nietzsche, *op. cit.*

he could not endure man's crucifixion. This picture of an immanent God, deprived of all transcendence, does not prevent Zarathustra from indicting and doing away with God on the ground of the problem of evil!

> He was also indistinct. How he raged at us, this wrathsnorter, because we understood him badly! But why did he not speak more clearly?
>
> And if the fault lay in our ears, why did he give us ears that heard him badly? If there was dirt in our ears, well! who put it in them?
>
> Too much miscarried with him, this potter who had not learned thoroughly! That he took revenge on his pots and creations, however, because they turned out badly—that was a sin against *good taste*. (291 f.)

In the next chapter we learn of still another "death of God." The "Ugliest Man" has murdered him because he could not endure the witness who beheld him through and through. To the Ugliest Man, God's very compassion represents a hostile infinite that makes impossible his existence, God's understanding an invasion that robs him of freedom and of self.

> "But he—*had* to die: he looked with eyes which beheld *everything*,—he beheld men's depths and dregs, all his hidden ignominy and ugliness.
>
> His pity knew no modesty: he crept into my dirtiest corners. This prying, over-intrusive, over-pitiful one had to die.
>
> He ever beheld me: on such a witness I would have revenge—or not live myself." (297)

Here at last we have reached the Modern Promethean whose sense of alienation leads him to an either-or which demands the destruction of the "Other" as the indispensable prerequisite of his own existence. The "Other" cannot be tolerated because *no* other can be understood except as alien and hostile—to oneself or to man. No longer is it conceivable that a Job might witness at one and the same time for God and for himself. The Modern Promethean *cannot* trust and contend: he must sacrifice himself to the "Other" or the "Other" to himself. Rather than have a God who created evil, Zarathustra states, it is "better to have no God, better to set up destiny on one's own account, . . . *better to be God oneself!*" (Italics mine.) It is not just God's being the creator of evil that the Modern Promethean cannot tolerate: it is his being God, and therefore infinite, while man remains limited and finite. "That I may reveal my heart entirely unto you," says Zarathustra to his friends, "*if* there were gods, how could I endure it to be no God! *Therefore* there are no gods."

THE PROBLEMATIC OF MODERN MAN
Personal Freedom and Psychological Compulsion

The modern Rebel-Exile is an uncertain figure underneath whose romantic gestures is revealed not only the alienation but the problematic of modern man. This problematic in no way invalidates the Modern Rebel, but it transforms his meaning. It is no longer possible to see him as a pure type or to divorce his heroic gestures from the inner conflicts and complexities which bring us into the realms of personal freedom and psychological compulsion, inner division, the crisis of motives, the problematic of guilt, and the paradox of the existence of the person in the modern world. On a deeper level still this problematic points us again to the traditional question of evil, but this time in terms of the special way in which modern man experiences this question—in a world where it is no longer possible to take for granted an order with which man may be reconciled, a God with whom man may contend, a macrocosm which man contains in essence in himself and whose potentialities he may unfold. Thus the most significant effect of that alienation of modern man that underlies both his exile and his rebellion is the problematical nature of his situation in the modern world.

One of the most important aspects of this problematic is the complex intermixture of personal freedom and psychological compulsion, a paradoxical phenomenon that can only be understood from within. The characters of Melville, Dostoievsky, and Kafka show more clearly than any case history the impossibility of ignoring the reality of such compulsion, on the one hand, or reducing man to a deterministic system, on the other. "The real battle is the battle over the image of man," says Ludwig Binswanger of his argument with his life-long friend Sigmund Freud. Freud's genetic approach reduces human history to natural history, says Binswanger, and in so doing misses that in man which is specifically human. An image of man that sees him as "at bottom a driven or drive-dominated creature," necessarily focuses on what man has to be and leaves out what he may and should become, his own freedom in relation to the psychological given. "Even the neurotic is not only a neurotic and man in general is not only one compelled." Existence does not lay its own ground, Binswanger points out, but it is still left with freedom in relation to that ground.[5]

The problem of the relation of personal freedom to psychological compulsion cannot be solved by the attempt to reduce man to a bundle of instinctual drives, unconscious complexes, the need for security or any other single factor. Each psychoanalytic school has attempted to find a key to man, and each, in so doing, has lost man. Motivation is inextricably bound up with the wholeness of the person, with his direction of movement, with his struggles to authenticate himself. This wholeness of the person in his dynamic interrelation with other persons Dostoievsky guards as no psychoanalytic theory ever has. In Dostoievsky we never see a metaphysical freedom or free will separate from conditioning factors; rather, we see the free will shining through and refracted by the sickness which shapes and exasperates so many of Dostoievsky's characters.[6] At the age of eighteen Dostoievsky

[5] Ludwig Binswanger, "The Case of Ilse" and "The Case of Ellen West" in *Existence: A New Dimension in Psychiatry and Psychology*, eds. Rollo May, Ernest Angel, Henri F. Ellenberger (New York: Basic Books, 1958), pp. 225, 314 f.

[6] Vyacheslav Ivanov sees the relation of compulsion to freedom in Dostoievsky as a lower level of empirical determinism and a higher level of free will that simply uses but is in no wise determined by the lower: "Dostoievsky presents each individual destiny as a single, coherent event taking place simultaneously on three different levels. . . . On the two lower levels is displayed the whole labyrinthine diversity of life . . . the changeability of the empirical character even within the bounds of its determination from without. On the uppermost, or metaphysical, level . . . there is no more complexity or subjection to circumstance: here

wrote to his brother: "Man is a mystery. Even if you were to spend your whole life unraveling it, you ought not say that you had wasted your life. I occupy myself with this mystery, for I want to be a man."[7] The fact that so many psychiatrists, including Freud, have praised Dostoievsky for his psychological acumen has led some to assume that Dostoievsky either holds a theory of psychological determinism himself or provides evidence for it. Dostoievsky is interested in mental sickness, as Samuel Smith and Andrei Isotoff have pointed out, but not in its genesis à la Freud.

> So far from holding to the doctrine of close-linked . . . causation for psychic events, he emphasizes the waywardness and unpredictability of impulse which motivates the actions of his persons. . . . The closeness of his observation, since borne out by psychiatrists, is no evidence that he had the same notions on causation in psychic dynamics as the analysts have developed.[8]

To Dostoievsky the view which reduces free will to psychological determinism is as untrue as that which accords man a metaphysical free will untouched by conditioning forces. The Underground Man is both free and not free at

---

reigns the great, bare simplicity of the final . . . decision . . . for being in God; or for . . . flight from God into Not-being. The whole tragedy played out on the two lower levels provides only the materials for the construction, and the symbols for the interpretation of the sovereign tragedy of the God-like spiritual being's final self-determination: an act which is solely that of the free will." (Vyacheslav Ivanov, *Freedom and the Tragic Life: A Study in Dostoievsky.* [New York: Noonday Press, 1957]), pp. 38 f. Ivanov's material and metaphysical levels do not so much solve the problem that Dostoievsky presents us as sidestep it. Although we may agree with Ivanov that Dostoievsky's "searching . . . has a single aim: to ascertain the part played by the intelligible act of will in the empirical deed," we cannot agree with any *a priori* formulation that answers this question in the abstract rather than in terms of each character and each situation. Dostoievsky does not present us with "empirical" and "metaphysical levels," but with an image of the wholeness of man in all his complexity and contradictoriness.

[7] Quoted in Zenta Maurina, *Dostojewskij. Menschengestalter und Gottessucher* (Memmingen: Maximilian Dietrich Verlag, 1952), p. 129, my translation.

[8] Samuel Stephenson Smith and Andrei Isotoff, "The Abnormal from Within: Dostoievsky," *Psychoanalytic Review*, XXII (1935), pp. 390 f.

once. No general theory of psychogenesis and no general knowledge of a person will tell us in advance what will be his actual mixture of spontaneity and compulsion in any particular situation. Hence Dostoievsky's contribution to the problematic of modern man is in this respect superior to Freud's psychogenic determinism. This does not mean that Dostoievsky's characters must be taken at face value or even as Dostoievsky himself may have intended them. On the contrary, even in those characters that he intended to make most ideal, like Myshkin, and in those ideas that he most cherished, like suffering, guilt, and the responsibility of each for all, abysses open before us that lead us into the problematic of modern man.

Fathers and Sons: The Divided Man

That deep inner division which characterizes the problematic of modern man can only partially be illumined through understanding the intermixture of personal freedom and psychological compulsion, for this tells us only of the psychological accompaniment and not of the interhuman reality of which that psychological division is the product. A deeper insight into the divided man can be obtained through understanding his close connection with the image of man and the relationship between father and son in which that image first arises.

The father is the first and often the most lasting image of man for the son. It not infrequently happens, however, that the father is not really present for the son, either because he is dead or absent or inattentive, or because he is in no sense a father, or because he is too weak or despicable for a son to be able to emulate him. In such a case the need for the father as the image of man remains and often leads to a lifetime search for a father who will supply an image of man as the actual father has not. Freud and modern psychoanalysts in general have only seen one aspect of this father-son relationship and have reduced it to fear of castration, introjection of the father's ideals and conscience, or even identification. The aspect which they have missed is the need that the son has for a relationship with the father which will help him find direction in the choices he must make between one way of life and another. This need is not for identification but dialogue, and it is not a conditioned formation or reaction but a free and even spontaneous response. At the same time, the other, conditioned reaction does enter in, and the relationship of father to son, even in the most "normal" cases, must also be seen as a blend of the conditioned and the free, the "psychological" and the personal, as is the problematic of Stavrogin and Versilov, of which we have spoken.

It is illuminating to consider the extent to which the relationship to the father has been at the center both of the life and the writings of the three men with whose work we are particularly concerned in this book: Melville, Dostoievsky, and Kafka. Throughout almost all their works one theme remains constant—that of the son in search of a father who is either dead or absent or who has betrayed him or does betray him.

The Crisis of Motives and the Problematic of Guilt

The inner division which results from the alienation between fathers and sons is as much a commentary on the absence of a modern image of man as on the breakdown of the specific father-son relationship. At the heart of this breakdown, in fact, is the inability of the father to give his son a direction-giving image of meaningful and authentic human existence. The inner division in the son that results expresses itself at times, as we have seen, in the bifurcation into opposing selves and opposing father images. It may also, as we have seen, express itself in a crisis of motives when the son, unable to accept the father, suppresses his awareness of the side of him that resembles his father in favor of an ideal self-image. Ivan Karamozov has two contradictory images of man, two incompatible sets of motivations: the one represented by his "Grand Inquisitor," a noble man with high humanitarian motives, the other by the lackey devil of his hallucinations, who embodies all the mean and trivial emotions and attitudes which he has not wanted to recognize in himself. In all Dostoievsky's divided men the inner conflict takes the form of a crisis of motives. Motives which in the past might have been taken at their face value—humility, love, friendship—must now be looked at more carefully. For, as Dostoievsky saw even before Freud, they may, in fact, mask resentment, hatred, or hostility. When modern man thinks of the humility of St. Francis, he may also see the masochistic Marmeladov allowing his wife to drag him by the beard, or of Dostoievsky's "Eternal Husband" who, after ministering to the sick friend who has taken his wife, tries to kill him in his sleep.

For Nietzsche, too, men dissemble without knowing it, unaware of the ignoble lust that conceals itself behind the noble ideal. Zarathustra labels as "Tarantulas" those socialist and humanitarian "preachers of *equality*" whose demand for "justice" masks a secret desire for revenge. The man "who will never defend himself" is the man of *ressentiment* who "swalloweth down poisonous spittle and bad looks, the all-too-patient one, the all-endurer." The chaste are those who seek in chastity the satisfaction of lust that has been denied them elsewhere.

> And how nicely can doggish lust beg for a piece of spirit, when a piece of flesh is denied it! . . .
> Ye have too cruel eyes, and ye look wantonly towards the sufferers. Hath not your lust just disguised itself and taken the name of fellow-suffering? (56 f.) [9]

Friendship, similarly, is often merely an attempt to overleap envy, and the love of one's neighbor nothing but the bad love of oneself.

> Ye call in a witness when ye want to speak well of yourselves; and when ye have misled him to think well of you, ye also think well of yourselves. . . .
> The one goeth to his neighbour because he seeketh himself, and the other because he would fain lose himself. (63 f.)

That modern psychoanalysis has attempted to find a rational pattern behind these hidden motivations that Dostoiev-

[9] Nietzsche, *op. cit.*

sky and Nietzsche have unmasked in no way reduces the problematic nature of the mistrust that impels such unmasking and of the bad faith—with others and with oneself —that is unmasked. Both the bad faith and the mistrust mean essentially the fragmentation of the self. Modern man knows his alienation nowhere so intensely as in the alienation from himself that results from this inner division and conflict. In the modern age it is no longer possible to accept any person, not even oneself, at "face value." Yet it is equally impossible simply to explain away the reality of a person by reducing him to the psychologically determined being pictured by one or another school of psychoanalysis. What confronts us again and again in others and in ourselves, in the characters of our literature and in the authors who create them is the bewildering intermixture of personal freedom and psychological compulsion, and the specific form which this intermixture takes differs with each person and with each unique situation.

Man as called and called to account; life as in need of justification before eternity; the world as confronting the self and placing a demand on it; the absurd as the paradoxical way through which the self finds such meaning in existence as is open to it; "the fight between you and the world" in which one does not cease to contend yet backs the world; the suffering that must be borne as a part of one's meeting with the world; the balance between the reality of what transcends the self and the need of the self for narrowing its circle and avoiding distraction; sin as failing to answer the call and answering it in a wrong, impatient way; our existence as a tension and mid-point between the "sanctum" and the "sputum"; the confusion produced by hearing at the same time the call of eternity and its opposite; life as a commission and a task in which we do not know who commissions and what is the task; our accountability for our total personal existence; and our guilt for not answering or answering in the wrong way a call that we can never clearly hear—all these enter into Kafka's unique understanding of the problematic of guilt.

If one takes seriously the last words of *The Trial,* one

may question whether the deepest level of *The Trial* is not guilt but shame. Why, after all, do Kafka and his hero Joseph K. speak of a shame so great that it might outlive one if it were not that deeper than any sense of personal guilt, and certainly than any sense of guilt for a specific action, lay shame for his father and for himself? A man may defend himself against specific accusations of guilt, but when he has a sense of "boundless guilt" rooted in a deep feeling of worthlessness, a shame for his very existence, he can only take all accusations on himself. Everything that happens to such a person confirms his essential shame at being himself, and no amount of external success or social confirmation will do more than enable him to forget it temporarily. The only "immortality" such a man may know is the very shame which may do him to death but will not die itself, so much is it the very air that he breathes, the all too narrow and constricting ground upon which he walks! This "boundless guilt" represents that area in the depths where existential shame and existential guilt meet and interfuse. Kafka and Joseph K. are ashamed for their very existences: having one's throat cut like a dog leads one to question not just the specific actions that lead one into this cul-de-sac but one's whole life.[10] But by the same token, it means a recognition of personal, existential guilt for what one's life has been. Since this guilt is not just a matter of specific acts, there is no point where one can accurately draw a line and say, "These acts were avoidable and these not; these acts are a subject for guilt and these for shame." An important aspect of the problematic of guilt lies in this interrelationship of existential shame and existential guilt.

The Paradox of the Person in the Modern World

The most far-reaching consequence of the alienation of mod-

[10] Following Helen Lynd's distinction between guilt and shame, we should not find it difficult to interpret much of Kafka's attitude toward his parents and himself as an expression of that sort of irreducible, un-rationalizable shame that is so closely associated with the body and the sense of self, with the relation of the child to its parents and to itself. (Cf. Helen Merrel Lynd, *On Shame and the Search for Identity* [New York: Science Editions, 1961].)

ern man and the deepest level of his problematic is neither his inner division nor the complex intermixture of freedom and compulsion that this division gives rise to, but the crisis of the person in the modern world. Indeed, inner division, the crisis of motives, the problematic of guilt, and the confusing interplay of free person and unfree "second self," already herald this crisis. It is in Kafka above all that the later stages of this crisis have become clear.

Despite the loneliness of Kafka and of his heroes, there is a sense in which they are representatives of the problematic of modern man. Not all men are artists, yet each man has need of the personal confirmation that can come only when he knows his "calling"—his existence in the fullest sense of the term—as an answer to a call. No man is able simply to confirm himself. He may be able to do without the admiration of crowds, but he cannot do without that silent dialogue, often internalized within himself, through which he places his efforts within the context of a mutual contact with what is not himself. He needs to feel that his work is "true"—both as a genuine expression of the reality that he encounters in his life and as a genuine response to some situation or need that calls him.

The artist, of course, exists in a specially sharpened paradox of confirmation. He has sacrificed the possibility of a more direct confirmation through his relations with others or a more certain confirmation through his social role for the loneliness and uncertainty of trying to create something unique that only he can create. His designation as an "artist" offers no confirmation, for unless he succeeds in this unique creation his art is meaningless and his attempt to except himself from the ordinary calling of mankind a presumption. He must make upon his public the impossible demand that only the truly great artist can get away with, namely, that they give him complete freedom to create and at the same time that they confirm his work as meaningful for their lives. No man can *know* himself to be a "great artist," but only that he is called or even compelled to create. No man, consequently, can become an artist without the risk of ending his life like the hunger artist—ignored or even scorned by the world while unconfirmed by himself. Kafka's hunger artist is a paradigm of the problematic of the modern man who strives to answer a call of which he is not sure in a way of which he cannot be certain.

As the artist must risk himself to establish that he is an artist and perhaps fail in that risk, so every man must risk himself to establish himself as the person that he is and risk failure in so doing. Paradoxically, this means that while the "calling" is in its original meaning an answer to a call, one may have to take the first step oneself and assert that one is called before the call comes. Everyone, no matter how great his training, experiences a moment of uneasy relation between his personal and professional self when he first steps forward as a "doctor," a "psychotherapist," a "minister," a "teacher," a "lawyer," or even a "husband," a "wife," a "father," or a "mother." At this moment the question, "What am I doing taking on this role?" may well produce an invisible inner panic that has nothing to do with competence or "self-confidence." This is the sense of incongruity that comes when one part of oneself is consciously "role-playing" while another part looks on and asks whether one can, in all good faith, identify oneself with this role. If the person who takes this venture can make it "stick," he will then be confirmed by others in his "calling" and soon will come to identify himself so much with his social role that his self-image will be unthinkable without it. The transition from not having a role in society to having one is soon forgotten, but it is instructive in the nature of the confirmation that the person is seeking.

The problematic of the "calling" that runs throughout *The Castle* is that before K. can find the calling that will answer the call, he must hear the call that will confirm his calling. There is also another problem, a still deeper one than that of the artist who demands confirmation as the unique artist that he is from a public insensible to the unique —that of the tension between personal and social confirmation. The man who makes the assertion that he is a doctor or minister "stick" does not necessarily thereby receive personal confirmation. It may happen, on the contrary, that the more successful he is in his social role, the less he feels confirmed as a person. This is bound to be the case when his social role remains "role-playing" and is never integrated in any thoroughgoing fashion with his existence as a person. This is particularly true of those whose social roles elevate them above the populace and make it necessary for them to pretend to attitudes, convictions, and ideals that they do not really hold. But it is also likely to be true of anyone who, in his desperate need for the confirmation of others, prefers to sacrifice his personal integrity rather than run the risk of not being established in a definite, socially approved role.

The man who enters the transition stage stands, therefore, in the tension point between personal and social confirmation. He cannot resolve this tension by renouncing social confirmation, for no man can live without it: everybody must play a social role, both as a means to economic livelihood and as the simplest prerequisite for any sort of relations with other people in the family and society. On the other hand, he cannot resolve the tension by sacrificing personal confirmation, for this suppression of a basic human need results in an anxiety that may be more and more difficult to handle as the gap between person and role widens. To stand in this tension, however, is to insist that one's confirmation in society also be in some significant sense a confirmation of oneself as a unique person who does not fit into any social category.

It is in precisely this tension that K. stands: "Never yet had K. seen vocation and life so interlaced as here, so interlaced that sometimes one might think they had exchanged places." This interlacing can either mean an integral relation between personal and social confirmation or it can mean the opposite—such an insistence on social role that one's personal existence itself seems to derive from that and nothing else.

One reason why K. cannot receive this confirmation, as we have seen, is that he himself must establish his calling: the message of the Emperor is for him alone; no one else knows what it says or can help him in answering it. A second is that the man who seeks meaning inevitably finds himself in the paradox of losing it as soon as he finds it. Like Maurice Maeterlinck's bluebird which becomes a blackbird as soon as it is caged, "meaning" quickly becomes empty when it is cut off from the living waters that it was meant to channel. Man is driven to seek meaning by the very absurdities and contradictions of existence and by the fact that as a self-conscious man he is not simply carried along by the stream of life but stands on the bank and watches it flow. Yet the meaning he seeks is that of the stream. When he brings it up on the bank with him, like a fish that he has caught, it gasps and dies for want of the oxygen that it can find only in the stream. The artist is in a better position than the philosopher, for his art remains more closely bound to the concrete. Nonetheless, he too falls within this paradox: all art is an attempt to find the right dialectic between detachment from the concrete and pointing back to it. The artist like Kafka who stakes out a new art and a new realm of meaning must move in "fear and trembling," therefore, quite as much as Kierkegaard's "knight of faith."

The artist creates out of his whole existence and cannot circumscribe the part of his existence which belongs to his wrestling with meaning and that which does not. What is more, since he is engaged in creating unique meaning he cannot have any sure ground on which to stand but must constantly be exposed to the despair that comes when he doubts his own struggle or when existence itself seems to shift beneath him, making all his images and formulations invalid.

In *The Castle* the social is an amorphous realm between the self and the call, a neutral strip, or "no man's land," whose borders on either side are constantly fluctuating. The fluctuation of these borders constitutes the central problematic of *The Castle* in which all its other problematic aspects are included. The problem of the calling, as we have seen, is not merely that a calling is only meaningful as a response to a call and that a call is needed to confirm the calling, but also that the confirmation needs to be personal as well as social, social as well as personal. The impossibility of identifying social and personal confirmation, on the one hand, and of separating them, on the other, is paradigmatic of the whole situation of the self. The self experiences the vertigo of being a free and directing consciousness, on the one hand, and an "eddy in the social current"—to use George Herbert Mead's phrase —on the other. This is a contrast of which Kafka himself was all too painfully aware, and his hero K. is a masterful portrayal of the confusion of the anxious and at the same time reflective man who fights for his freedom and independence yet recognizes both the necessity of social binding and the extent to which he himself is not so much an individual as a social unit. If this paradox is heightened in K. and the resulting confusion is consequently greater, it is, nonetheless, an ambiguity that is inseparable from the very existence of the self and that no human being can escape. The harder a man tries to fight his way through this ambiguity, in fact, the deeper his confusion must be if he is both honest and aware.

The other border is between the social and the ultimate reality—what we might call "ontological reality" in order to distinguish it in some way from the social without erecting it into a separate metaphysical or theological realm. Here too the self experiences great confusion, this time from the side of the call. The call seems to come through the social, yet in such a way that it not only becomes indistinct but often highly dubious. It tempts one to believe, as a result, either that there really is no call or that it comes to one from some metaphysical, religious, or eternal realm quite outside the social. The problematic of the social, as a result, becomes essential to understanding both the self and the call.

What is true of *The Trial* is also true of *The Castle*: the self finds meaning in its existence not through identifying society and social confirmation with the call nor through turning away from them to some pure call that one hears apart from the world. It finds meaning, rather, through answering with its existence the call that comes to it through the absurd—through the bigoted villagers and the endless, senseless hierarchies of Castle officials, the call that can reach it in no other way. The intermixture of social and ultimate reality that we have already glimpsed in the problem of justice in *The Trial* and in the tension between personal and social confirmation in *The Castle* is also basic to the relations between village and Castle in K.'s search to answer his call. K.'s ambivalent attitude to marriage and the community is not to be explained simply by the notion that the village is his goal and the Castle the means to that goal or by the notion that the Castle is his goal and the village is the means to the Castle. He never sees any "ultimate reality," he never hears the call except as it is mediated through social reality. He hears the call in such a way, what is more, that he can neither separate social and ultimate reality, on the one hand, nor accept social reality as simply reality, on the other.

Kafka's unique contribution to the problematic of modern man is his probing of the paradox of existence as a person in the modern world. Kafka offers us an image of modern man confronting a transcendent reality which can neither be dismissed as unreal nor rationalized as anything less than absurd. Kafka's hero is neither able to affirm meaning *despite* what confronts him, as do Nietzsche's Zarathustra, Sartre's Orestes, and Camus' Sisyphus, nor to fix meaning *in* what confronts him, as do Plato's philosopher or Kierkegaard's "knight of faith." Unable to believe any longer in an objective absolute or order through which his personal destiny is determined or in a Biblical God who calls him, he nonetheless knows himself as a person face to face with reality which transcends him. This reality demands from him response and punishes a failure to respond even while it offers neither confirmation nor meaning in return for response nor any guidance as to which response is "right" and which "wrong."

Put in the simplest terms, Kafka explores what it means to continue to be "I" in a world that offers neither confirmation nor personal meaning to the "I." He is no individualist, for he sees the person as existing in relation to a world that calls him into existence. Yet he clings too tenaciously to what is given the person in his concrete existence ever to describe who calls or even to assert that anyone does call. He sees the person in the modern world as pure paradox: the self needs a personal meaning for its very existence and continuity as self, yet it is confronted by an absurd reality which seems by its very nature to offer no personal meaning.

THE PROBLEMATIC REBEL

That Kafka is centrally concerned with the problem of evil and that his writings constitute one of the most salient commentaries on this problem in our time cannot be doubted from the explicit evidence of the aphorisms and diaries as well as the implicit evidence of his stories. But his concern is an existential and not a metaphysical one, and it is embodied in his writings not in metaphysical symbols and religious allegories but in depictions, however weird and distorted, of the concrete situation of modern man. The problematic of modern man leads us to the perennial problem of man, not by way of universal and timeless metaphysical concepts, however, but by way of the paradoxes and complexities of the concrete situation of modern man. Crisis is not unique to modern man: man has always been in crisis. Yet the crisis of modern man is, nonetheless, unique—in its intensity, in its manifold and all-pervasive nature and, most important for us, in the fact that it is *our* crisis, which we cannot avoid or see around. There is no way for us to move toward contact with reality except through the heart of this crisis. We must take unto ourselves the problematic of modern man and shape from it an image of meaningful human existence, an image that neither leaves out this problematic nor simply reflects it, but wrestles with it until it has found a way forward.

Melville, Dostoievsky, and Kafka do not themselves offer us such an image. Melville gives a merely aesthetic enclosure to the tension between Ahab and Ishmael; Dostoievsky leaves us with a bifurcated image—a problematic man-god for whom there is no way forward and a god-man who does not include the problematic of modern man; while Kafka, perhaps because he is more honest than Dostoievsky as well as more modern, offers us an image of man which is positive only to a minimal degree. Ahab, Ivan, and K. remain, nonetheless, the three greatest exemplars in modern literature of the Problematic Rebel—our depth-image of modern man.

FROM THE MODERN PROMETHEAN TO THE MODERN JOB

The first response to the situation of the Modern Exile is the rebellion of the Modern Promethean, who tries to recover the true existence from which he has been alienated by denying the reality of the "other" that confronts him, the reality that transcends him and stands over against him. From this rebellion there arises the Modern Rebel-Exile, an uncertain figure who brings us into the heart of the problematic of modern man. Out of the paradox of the person in the modern world, in which this problematic culminates, there grows the Modern Job—the second form in which modern man has rebelled against his situation as an exile.

Although the Problematic Rebel is not in itself an image of meaningful human existence, we can glimpse such an image in the figure that has emerged in the course of our study of the Problematic Rebel—the Modern Job. Ahab and Ivan echo Job's protest against innocent suffering and an existence deprived of meaning. Yet both remain essentially Modern Prometheans, seeking to affirm the self and man through destroying or denying the reality that confronts them. K., in contrast, not only contends but also affirms: he takes his rebellion into his dialogue with the absurd. The Modern Promethean still harbors a touch of nineteenth-century romanticism—the grand gesture with which Ahab defies Moby Dick, Ivan's Inquisitor judges Christ, or Sartre's Orestes denies the power of Zeus. The Modern Job stands on the other side of romanticism. The Modern Job begins with the world of Kafka's Castle, which cannot be captured by any direct assaults; with the Nazi occupation of France—Camus' model for *The Plague;* with the scientific extermination of six million Jews and a million gypsies. He is "the Job of the gas chambers" in the name of whom Martin Buber contrasts the Greek tragic hero who is overcome before "faceless fate" with those who "contend . . . with God."[11]

If the Modern Promethean is marked by the either-or which holds that man must destroy the reality that faces him in order to recover his alienated freedom, the Modern Job is marked by the "both-and" which faithfully affirms what confronts

[11]Martin Buber, *On Judaism* ed. Nahum Glatzer (New York: Schocken Books, 1967), "The Dialogue between Heaven and Earth," pp. 224 f.

him as the "given" of his own existence and at the same time does not submit to it but opposes and contends with it. The choice of the Modern Promethean is between submission and rebellion, that of the Modern Job between this very either-or, in which submission and rebellion are the two sides of the same coin, and that other rebellion which holds the tension between the affirmation of oneself and the faithful confronting of what faces one. Although the Modern Job in the full sense of the term does not appear as such in the works of Melville or Dostoievsky any more than in Thomas Hardy or any other nineteenth-century writer, some of the separate elements that go to making up this figure do appear —Job's complaint against innocent suffering, his contending, his meeting a limit that transcends him and that he cannot remove into himself. Occasionally the contending appears without the affirming, as in Ivan, or the affirming appears without the contending, as in Father Zossima.

THE MODERN JOB

Taken together, Kafka's K. and Camus' Rieux enable us to discern within the general image of modern man as Problematic Rebel the more specific image of the Modern Job. What carries over from the original Job to a Captain Ahab and an Ivan is the questioning, the struggling, and the contending but not the dialogue itself, while Father Zossima and Alyosha have Job's trust without the contending. In Kafka's K. and Camus' Rieux, on the other hand, there is both dialogue and contending. This dialogue means an affirmation of relationship rather than a denial of it, even though it is Heraclitus' "harmony" of the bow and the string rather than Plato's harmony of the musical chord. In discussing *The Castle* we have preferred to speak of a dialogue in which ultimate reality addresses K. only through absurd social reality, rather than to decipher the Castle into God and the village into the community. In *The Plague* too there is a reality that speaks through the absurd, and Rieux is an illustration of the one attitude which remains open to this reality. Father Paneloux, by accepting suffering and evil as objective divine order, runs aground on the rock of the absurd. Tarrou, by recognizing the absurd and rejecting it, excludes any meaning other than that of his own saintliness. Rieux, by remaining in dialogue with the absurd—neither accepting it nor cutting off from it but fighting with it and receiving from it—attains the meaning that the absurd has to give us.

At the heart of Job's contending lies the question of trust in existence—he begins not by cursing God but by cursing the day of his birth. It is not his belief in God that is undermined but his trust in existence: if he affirms his relationship with God throughout yet refuses to give up his demand for justice, it is because his trust in existence is at stake. It is this same problem of trust in existence that is at the center of the struggle of the Problematic Rebel—Ahab, Ivan, and K. In Ahab and Ivan, however, the trust has broken. Finding it impossible to hold together human values and the absurd, they have "turned their ticket in." K. has not. He insists on the reality of the goal even while he suspects that "the true way" is only a "wavering," more a "stumbling block" than a way forward. Similarly Rieux, even while he accepts the never-ending struggle with the plague as the inescapable human condition, also affirms that some meaning may emerge from that struggle. Standing one's ground before what confronts one rather than giving way before it or trying to escape it mark the Modern Job as much as they do the original one. The question of trust in existence which is at the heart of Job's dialogue with God is equally at the heart of K.'s and Rieux's dialogue with the absurd.

To the Modern Job, unlike the Modern Promethean, it need not matter whether this rebellion be expressed in terms of the "atheism" of a Camus or the "theism" of a Buber. The basic attitude is essentially the same. In both, dialogue and rebellion are inseparably coupled. "The dialogical leads inevitably to Job's question to God," writes Martin Buber. "My God will not allow to become silent in the mouth of his creature the complaint about the great injustice in the world, and when in an unchanged world his creature yet finds peace because God has again granted him his nearness, . . . that is a peace that is compatible with the fight for justice in the world." [12]

Kafka's special contribution to understanding the problematic of modern man, as we have seen, is the image of man as striving to answer a call that he neither certainly nor distinctly hears and that he does not know how to answer. This means, on the one hand, that Kafka abjures the path of the metaphysicians and the theologians, who are able to speak of

[12] From "Responsa," "Theology, Mysticism, Metaphysics," Chap. VI, trans. Maurice Friedman, in *The Philosophy of Martin Buber, loc. cit.* That the Modern Job really means an essential affinity of spirit between these two men and not just an external resemblance is borne out by statements that each has made about the other. "Camus acknowledges a profound respect for Buber," writes R. W. B. Lewis on the basis of a remark made by Camus to him, "and Camus is even willing to say that for himself 'the sacred' is just that presence felt in the silence during a moment of genuine awareness. . . . Only in what Buber calls a condition of being aware is even a transitory moment of communion accomplished." (R. W. B. Lewis, *The Picaresque Saint* [Philadelphia and New York: J. B. Lippincott, 1959] p. 103. Cf. p. 302, footnotes 32 and 33 to Chap. III.) In a letter to me of Nov. 9, 1961, Buber points, by implication, to what we might characterize as the distinction between the atheism of a Modern Promethean like Sartre and that of a Modern Job like Camus: "I would not call Camus an atheist. He was one of the men who are destroying the old images. You know how I feel about them." The reference Buber is making is to the conclusion to his essay, "Religion and Philosophy": "The religious reality of the meeting with the Meeter, who shines through all forms and is Himself formless, knows no image of Him, nothing comprehensible as object. It knows only the presence of the Present One. Symbols of Him, whether images or ideas, always exist first when and insofar as Thou becomes He, and that means It. . . . They always quickly desire to be more than they are, more than signs and pointers toward Him. It finally happens ever again that they swell themselves up and obstruct the way to Him, and He removes Himself from them. Then comes round the hour of the philosopher, who rejects both the image and the God which it symbolizes and opposes to it the pure idea, which he even at times understands as the negation of all metaphysical ideas. This critical 'atheism' (*Atheoi* is the name which the Greeks gave to those who denied the traditional gods) is the prayer which is spoken in the third person in the form of speech about an idea. It is the prayer of the philosopher to the again unknown God. It is well suited to arouse religious men and to impel them to set forth right across the God-deprived reality to a new meeting. On their way they destroy the images which manifestly no longer do justice to God. The spirit moves them which moved the philosopher." (Martin Buber, *Eclipse of God. Studies in the Relation between Religion and Philosophy*, trans. Maurice S. Friedman et. al. [New York: Harper Torchbooks, 1957], pp. 45 f.)

God or the Absolute as if they have some knowledge of ultimate reality as it is in itself, apart from their relation to it. It
also means, however, that he abjures the negative metaphysics of a Nietzsche, a Sartre, or a Jung who, because they cannot
believe in any absolute simply independent of man, deny it
altogether or remove it into the immanence of the human
psyche. Instead, Kafka as artist stands where his hero stands
—as a man face to face with a reality that he cannot avoid
facing yet can see only from the ground on which he, the concrete, existing person, stands. "Our art is a dazzled blindness
before the truth:"—writes Kafka—"The light on the grotesque
recoiling phiz is true, but nothing else."[13] In *The Castle* "the
light on the grotesque recoiling phiz" is K.'s meeting with the
reality not himself *seen from his point of view*. It is his striving to find the calling that will answer the call, to hear the
call that will confirm his calling.

Melville, Dostoievsky, and Kafka are alike in their concern
for the problem of evil. In Kafka, however, this concern never
becomes a separate metaphysical dimension divorced from
human existence. In *The Trial*, for example, the choice between "ostensible acquittal" and "indefinite postponement"
that is open to the accused man reminds us at one and the

[13]*The Great Wall of China*, "Reflections," No. 61, p. 269. Eliseo Vivas
uses this aphorism as the starting point for his essay, "Kafka's Distorted
Mask," *The Kenyon Review*, X, No. 1 (Winter 1948), pp. 51-69, also in
The Kenyon Critics, 1951. Vivas stresses the encounter of Kafka's heroes
with what transcends them but then chides Kafka for his failure to affirm
a theological transcendent in a way that again violates our principle that
Kafka offers us no universal picture of reality that may be grasped apart
from K.'s relation to it. Wilhelm Emrich rightly insists that Kafka's writings are neither allegories nor symbols, even in Goethe's sense, for in
Kafka the phenomena do not directly reveal the universal. Yet he himself proceeds to a total allegory of freedom and binding, impersonal and
personal love, in which the realm of Count West West stands for death,
snow death, warm water life, Klamm impersonal eros, Pepi collective
love, etc. This allegory is more convincing than Ronald Gray's in that
it is total and less external and that it points to an existential reality
that was at the same time close to Kafka's own life. But it comes too
close to being a "key" to the "real meaning" behind *The Castle* to be
consistent with Emrich's own principles of interpretations, and it violates
those that we have suggested: it presents one stratum as the total reality,
and it offers an objective totality seen from above that transcends the
given of the novel seen from K.'s point of view.

same time of the Gnostic cosmologies in which the majority of men are trapped in the darkness of an unredeemed world, the totalitarian state in which no reprieve is ever permanent for the hunted man, nor any acquittal ever secure, and the reality of each man's personal existence in which one is never done with being personally responsible, and in that sense accountable.

This startling juxtaposition of images from such different phases of human experience as the Gnostic, the totalitarian and the existential yields an insight into Kafka's attitude toward justice and toward the problem of evil that is implicit in it. If we take seriously the proposition that Kafka is not talking exclusively about one or another aspect of reality—the psychological, the social, the religious—we come upon the illuminating discovery that he had found a way of dealing with justice and guilt at the meeting point of all of these spheres. The intermixture of psychological, social, and ontological reality is basic, in fact, to Kafka's understanding of the problem of justice, whether in the family, in society, or in the relation of man to the world or to God. Kafka's own experience of being treated unjustly as a child undoubtedly gave him a keen awareness of justice and at the same time a realization of an arbitrary element in human destiny and social relations, an irreducible absurd that makes much talk of family, social, or religious justice a pretense or an illusion. Even where justice exists and is effective, it is often a merely superficial readjustment alongside the fundamental and irreducible injustice of each man's unique situation—the "given" of his physical and mental capacities and his position in one family and social group or another, the ostracism of the one who does not "fit in," the domination of the less forceful (Kafka, Gregor Samsa, Georg Bendemann) by the more forceful (the father). Kafka, in other words, removes Job's question to where it belongs—right in the middle of the personal and social reality in which we live, that reality in the face of which our rational conceptions of justice are often thin abstractions. The very meaning of justice changes, in this context, from Aristotle's distributive and corrective justice based upon the fundamental similarity of one man to another to the special, personal "justice" which is the lot of each man individually, based upon the unrepeatable irreducible uniqueness of his situation. "We unfold (not less deeply bound to humanity than to ourselves) through all the sufferings of this world," writes Kafka. "In this process there is no place for justice, but no place either for . . . the interpretation of suffering as a punishment."

For modern man meaning is not accessible either through the ancient Prometheanism that extends man's realm in an ordered cosmos or through the Renaissance Prometheanism that makes man a little world that reflects the great. Still less is it accessible through the Modern Prometheanism that defies what is over against man while striving at the same time to control, subdur, or destroy it, as Ahab strives to destroy Moby Dick. Today, meaning can be found, if at all, only through the attitude of the man who is willing to *live* with the absurd, to remain open to the mystery which he can never hope to pin down. In the world of "the plague" no room is left for the self-deifying postures of a Faust, an Ahab, or a Zarathustra. Nor is there room for that anthropomorphic approach to the absurd which led the early Camus to a stoic rebellion against a world that will never again assume the appearance of rationality longed for by the lucidity of subjective consciousness from Descartes to Sartre.

Our contrast between the Modern Promethean and the Modern Job by no means implies that the former is a *problematic* rebel and the latter not. On the contrary, if we are to take him seriously as an image of modern man, the Modern Job must include this problematic. But if this is so, we must make a fundamental distinction between the two figures whom we have used as exemplars of the Modern Job—K. and Rieux. K. lacks the firmness and sureness that makes the contending and the affirmation of Rieux so clear-cut, while Rieux has relatively little of the problematic of modern man. This latter fact becomes immediately evident if we contrast Rieux's sureness that he knows what healing is and that he can at times heal and the overpowering conviction of Kafka's "country doctor" that he cannot help his patient and that he has gone irremediably astray in trying to help him. Thus neither of these figures is a Modern Job in the full sense of the term: in neither are both the rebellion and the problematic brought in full strength into the dialogue with the absurd. Taken together, nonetheless, Kafka's K. and Camus' Rieux point the way toward the Modern Job—an image of modern man that is at the same time an image of meaningful existence. They show us the direction in which such a figure must develop if he is to bring into the dialogue with the absurd the tension of the Problematic Rebel—the paradox of the person in the modern world. This dialogue implies both trust and contending, but it does not mean *either* denial *or* affirmation on principle. We stand our ground and meet what comes with clear-sighted trust—in each new situation that confronts us affirming where we can affirm and withstanding where we have to withstand.

Since the death of God, declares Jean-Paul Sartre, man must accept complete responsibility not only for his actions but also for the values which he himself is forced to invent. Having done away with God, man is "condemned to be free," but it is this freedom and its maintenance through a minimum of self-deception which make up the only values that Sartre recognizes.

> If I've discarded God the Father, there has to be someone to invent values. . . . To say that we invent values means nothing else but this: life has no meaning *a priori*. Before you come alive, life is nothing; it's up to you to give it a meaning, and value is nothing else but the meaning that you choose.[14]

> Even if he let himself be carried off, in helplessness and in despair, even if he let himself be carried off like an old sack of coal, he would have chosen his own damnation; he was free, free in every way, free to behave like a fool or a machine, free to accept, free to refuse, free to equivocate; to marry, to give up the game, to drag this dead weight about with him for years to come. He could do what he liked, no one had the right to advise him,

[14] Jean-Paul Sartre, *Existentialism*, trans. Bernard Frechtman (New York: Philosophical Library, 1947), p. 58.

there would be for him no Good nor Evil unless he brought them into being. All around him things were gathered in a circle, expectant, impassive, and indicative of nothing. He was alone, enveloped in this monstrous silence, free and alone, without assistance and without excuse, condemned to decide without support from any quarter, condemned forever to be free.[15]

Here the Modern Promethean reveals himself—the man who chooses as an image of man for all men the denial of all meaning transcending the self or arising from the self's meeting with being in favor of a "meaning" which man himself "invents."

Albert Camus, in contrast, portrays a number of genuinely different images of man, to each of which he lends validity, yet commits himself in *The Plague* to one image above all others—that of the dialogical rebel Doctor Rieux. If we compare Doctor Rieux with Matthieu Delarue, the hero of Sartre's novel *The Age of Reason*, we are impelled to a contrast between the man who is responsible only to himself and his own freedom and for that reason is unable to act (Delarue) and the man who is responsible to and for the situation in which he finds himself (Rieux). The former means futile suffering with no commitment except to the abstract ideal of not being committed. The latter means suffering *and* action through commitment to the concrete demands of the hour. This commitment is not a limitation of human freedom within a specific mode of conduct. It is, rather, the most practical possible assertion of freedom by a man who knows that only through commitment in the present will there be real freedom in the future. It is not a prescription for others that chooses the image of man for them, as Sartre would have it. It is a witness to an attitude that may be meaningful for any Problematic Rebel in his own personal encounter with "the plague"—the attitude of the Modern Job.

The fact that Camus wrote *The Stranger*, *The Myth of Sisyphus*, and *The Fall* as well as *The Rebel* and *The Plague*

---

[15] Jean-Paul Sartre, *The Age of Reason* (New York: Bantam Books 1959), pp. 275 f.

is indicative of what we mean by speaking of a progression *through* the Modern Promethean to the Modern Job. The tension between these two types of rebels still constitutes the image of modern man. But in the Modern Job the approach of the Modern Promethean is no longer romanticized into a program and a *Weltanschauung*. It is realistically recognized and dealt with as an integral part of the problematic of modern man. It must be taken up as such into the greater wholeness of the Modern Job if a meaningful modern image of man is to emerge. In the Modern Job the problematic becomes a ground, the paradox of the person a stance, exile and rebellion a way.

Bibliography

Bibliography

BOOKS BY HERMAN MELVILLE

Clarel: A Poem and Pilgrimage in the Holy Land. Vols. XIV and XV of *The Works of Herman Melville.* London: Constable & Co., 1924.

The Confidence Man: His Masquerade. New York: Grove Press, 1949.

Journal of a Visit to London and the Continent 1849-1850. Edited by Eleanor Melville Metcalf. Cambridge, Mass.: Harvard University Press, 1948.

Moby-Dick. Edited by Newton Arvin. New York: Rinehart & Co., 1948.

Pierre, Or the Ambiguities. New York: Grove Press, 1929. (Evergreen Books E-55).

Four Short Novels. New York: Bantam Books, 1959. (*Benito Cereno; Bartleby the Scrivener; The Encantados or Enchanted Isles; Billy Budd Foretopman.*)

BOOKS ENTIRELY OR PARTLY ABOUT "MOBY-DICK"

Arvin, Newton. *Herman Melville.* New York: William Sloane Ass., 1950.

Auden, W. H. *The Enchafèd Flood.* London: Faber & Faber, 1951. Chapter III, pp. 83-120.

Baird, James. *Ishmael.* Baltimore: The Johns Hopkins Press, 1956.

Brasswell, William. *Melville's Religious Thought*. Durham, N.C.: Duke University Press, 1943.

Chase, Richard. *Herman Melville: A Critical Study*. New York: Macmillan, 1949.

Feidelson, Charles, Jr. *Symbolism and American Literature*. Chicago: University of Chicago Press, 1953.

Hicks, Granville. 'A Re-Reading of *Moby Dick*.' *Twelve Original Essays on Great American Novels*, ed. Charles Shapiro. Detroit: Wayne State University Press, 1958.

Hillway, Tyrus, and Mansfield, Luther S. (ed.) *Moby-Dick Centennial Essays*. Dallas: Southern Methodist University Press, 1953.

Howard, Leon. *Herman Melville*. Berkeley: University of California Press, 1951.

Kazin, Alfred. *The Inmost Leaf, A Selection of Essays*. New York: Noonday Press, 1959. Chapter 20, pp. 197-207.

Levin, Harry. *The Power of Blackness: Hawthorne, Poe, Melville*. New York: Alfred A. Knopf, 1958.

Mason, Ronald. *The Spirit above the Dust: a Study of Herman Melville*. London: John Lehmann, 1951.

Matthiessen, F. O. *American Renaissance*. London and New York: Oxford University Press, 1941. Pp. 392-466.

Mumford, Lewis. *Herman Melville*. New York: Harcourt Brace, 1929.

Myers, Henry Alonzo. *Tragedy: a View of Life*. Ithaca, N.Y.: Cornell University Press, 1956. Chapter III, pp. 57-77.

Olson, Charles. *Call Me Ishmael*. New York: Reynal & Hitchcock, 1947.

Percival, M. O. *A Reading of Moby Dick*. Chicago: University of Chicago Press, 1950.

Pommer, Henry F. *Milton and Melville*. Pittsburgh, Pa.: University of Pittsburgh Press, 1950.

Rosenberry, Edward H. *Melville and the Comic Spirit*. Cambridge, Mass.: Harvard University Press, 1955.

Rourke, Constance. *American Humor*. New York: Harcourt Brace, 1931. Pp. 191-200.

Sedgwick, William Ellery. *Herman Melville: The Tragedy of Mind*. Cambridge, Mass.: Harvard University Press, 1944.

Stern, Milton R. *The Fine Hammered Steel of Herman Melville.* Urbana, Ill.: University of Illinois Press, 1957.

Sundermann, Karl-Heinrich. *Herman Melville's Gedankengut. Eine kritische Untersuchung seiner weltanschaulichen Grundideen.* (Inaugural dissertation, Philosophische Fakultät. University of Berlin.) Würzburg: Buchdruckerei Richard Mayr, 1937.

Thomas, Lawrence. *Melville's Quarrel With God.* Princeton: Princeton University Press, 1952.

Thorp, Willard (ed.). *Herman Melville: Representative Selections.* New York: American Book Co., 1938.

Vincent, Howard P. *The Trying-Out of Moby Dick.* New York: Houghton Mifflin, 1949.

Williams, Stanley T. "Bibliographical Essay on Melville." *Eight American Authors.* New York: Modern Language Association, 1956.

Winters, Yvor. *Maule's Curse.* Norfolk, Conn.: New Directions, 1938. Pp. 53-89.

Wright, Nathalia. *Melville's Use of the Bible.* Durham, N.C.: Duke University Press, 1949.

ARTICLES ABOUT "MOBY DICK"

Abele, Rudolph von. "Melville and the Problem of Evil," *American Mercury,* Vol. LXV (1947), pp. 592-98.

Belgion, Montgomery. "Heterodoxy on *Moby-Dick?*" *Sewanee Review,* Vol. LV (Jan.-March, 1947), pp. 108-25.

Bell, Millicent. "Pierre Bayle and *Moby Dick,*" *Publications of the Modern Language Association,* Vol. LXVI (1951), pp. 626-648.

Bewley, Marius. "A Truce of God for Melville," *Sewanee Review,* Vol. LXI (Autumn, 1953).

Cook, Charles H. "Ahab's Intolerable Allegory," *Boston University Studies in English,* Vol. I (1955), pp. 45-52.

Dale, T. R. "Melville and Aristotle: The Conclusion of *Moby-Dick* as a Classical Tragedy," *Boston University Studies in English,* Vol. III (1957), pp. 45-50.

Dix, William S. "Herman Melville and the Problem of Evil," *Rice Institute Pamphlet,* Vol. XXXV (July, 1948), pp. 81-107.

Duffy, Charles. "A Source for the Conclusion of Melville's *Moby Dick*," *Notes and Queries*, Vol. CLXXXI (November 15, 1941), pp. 278-279.

Fiedler, Leslie A. "Out of the Whale," *Nation*, Vol. CLXIX (November 19, 1949), pp. 494-496.

Gary, L. M. "Rich Colors and Ominous Shadows," *South Atlantic Quarterly*, Vol. XXXVII (1938), pp. 41-45.

Geiger, Don. "Melville's Black God: Contrary Evidence in The Town-Ho's Story," *American Literature*, Vol. XXV (1953), pp. 464-471.

Hall, James B. "*Moby-Dick*: Parable of a Dying System," *Western Review*, Vol. XIV (Spring, 1950), pp. 223-226.

Hubben, William. "Ahab, the Whaling Quaker," *Religion in Life*, Vol. XVIII, No. 3, pp. 363-373.

Hull, William. "*Moby-Dick*: An Interpretation," *Etc.*, Vol. V (Autumn, 1947), pp. 8-21.

Hyman, Stanley Edgar. "Melville the Scrivener," *New Mexico Quarterly*, Vol. XXXIII (1953), pp. 381-415.

Kazin, Alfred. "The Inmost Leaf," *New Republic*, Vol. CXI (December 18, 1944), pp. 840-841.

―――― "Ishmael and Ahab," *Atlantic Monthly*, Vol. CXCVIII (November, 1956), pp. 81-85.

―――― "On Melville as Scripture," *Partisan Review*, Vol. XVII (January, 1950), pp. 67-75.

Mabbott, T. O. "A Source for the Conclusion of Melville's *Moby Dick*," *Notes and Queries*, Vol. CLXXXI (July 26, 1941), pp. 47-48.

Miller, Perry. "Melville and Transcendentalism," *Virginia Quarterly Review*, Vol. XXXIX (1953), pp. 566-575.

Olson, Charles. "Lear and *Moby Dick*," *Twice a Year*, Vol. I (1938), pp. 165-189.

Osbourn, R. V. "The White Whale and the Absolute," *Essays in Criticism*, Vol. VI (1956), pp. 160-170.

Skard, Sigmund. "The Use of Color in Literature," *Proceedings of the American Philosophical Society*, Vol. XC (1946), pp. 163-249.

Slochower, Harry. "*Moby-Dick*: The Myth of American Expectancy," *American Quarterly*, Vol. II (February 1, 1950), pp. 259-269.

Stewart, George R. "The Two Moby-Dicks," *American Literature*, Vol. XXV (1953), pp. 417-448.

Walcutt, Charles. "The Fire Symbolism in *Moby-Dick*," *Modern Language Notes*, Vol. LIX (1944), pp. 304-310.

Watters, R. E. "The Meanings of the White Whale," *University of Toronto Quarterly*, Vol. XX (January, 1951), pp. 151-168.

——— "Melville's Isolatoes," *Publications of the Modern Language Association*, Vol. LX (1945), pp. 1138-1148.

——— "Melville's Metaphysics of Evil," *University of Toronto Quarterly*, Vol. IX (January, 1940), pp. 170-182.

Wright, Nathalia. "Biblical Allusion in Melville's Prose," *American Literature*, Vol. XII (May, 1940), pp. 185-199.

Young, James Dean. "The Nine Gams of the *Pequod*," *American Literature*, Vol. XXV (1953), pp. 449-463.

BOOKS BY DOSTOIEVSKY

The Brothers Karamazov. Translated by Constance Garnett. Introduction by Marc Slonim. New York: Modern Library, 1950.

Crime and Punishment. Translated by Constance Garnett. New York: Modern Library, 1944, 1945.

Der Unbekannte Dostojewski. Edited by René Fülöp-Miller and Friedrich Eckstein. Munich: Piper & Co., 1926.

The Devils. Translated by David Magarshack. New York: Penguin Classic L 35, 1953.

The Diary of a Writer. Translated by Boris Brasol. New York: George Braziller, 1954.

Die Urgestalt der Brüder Karamasoff. Dostojewskis Quellen, Entwürfe und Fragmente Erläutert von W. Komarowitsch. Munich: R. Piper & Co., 1928.

Dostoevsky: Letters and Reminiscences. Translated by S. S. Koteliansky and Middleton Murry. London: Chatto & Windus, 1923; New York: Alfred A. Knopf, 1923.

The Idiot. Translated by Constance Garnett. New York, Bantam Classic, 1958.

Letters of F. M. Dostoevsky to His Family and Friends. Translated by Ethel Colburn Mayne. London: Chatto & Windus, 1914; New York: Macmillan, 1914.

A Raw Youth. Translated by Constance Garnett. Introduction by Alfred Kazin. New York: Dial Press, 1947.

Short Stories of Dostoevsky. Translated by David Magarshack. New York: Modern Library.

Stavrogin's Confession. Translated by Virginia Woolf and S. S. Koteliansky. With a Psychoanalytic Study by Sigmund Freud. New York: Lear Publishers, 1947.

Stavrogin's Confession and the Plan of the Life of a Great Sinner. Translated by S. S. Koteliansky and Virginia Woolf. Richmond, England: L. & V. Woolf, 1922.

BOOKS ENTIRELY OR PARTLY ABOUT DOSTOIEVSKY

Berdyaev, Nicholas. *Dostoevsky.* Translated by Donald Attwater. New York: Sheed & Ward, 1934; Meridian Books, Living Age Books, 1957.

Brasol, Boris. *The Mighty Three: Poushkin, Gogol, Dostoievsky.* New York: William Farquhar Payson, 1934. Pp. 196-295.

Buber, Martin. *Israel and the World: Essays in a Time of Crisis.* New York: Schocken Books, 1948. Pp. 197-213.

Camus, Albert. *The Myth of Sisyphus.* Translated by Justin O'Brien. New York: Alfred A. Knopf, 1955. Pp. 104-112.

Carr, Edward Hallett. *Dostoevsky: A New Biography.* Boston and New York: Houghton Mifflin, 1931.

Dostoevsky, Aimée. *Fyodor Dostoievsky, A Study.* London: W. Heinemann, 1921.

Dostoevsky, Anna. *Dostoevsky Portrayed by His Wife: The Diary and Reminiscences of Madame Dostoevsky.* Translated and edited by S. S. Koteliansky. London: G. Routledge & Sons, 1926; New York: E. P. Dutton, 1926.

Evdokimof, Paul. *Dostoievsky et le Problème du Mal.* Paris: Valence. Imprimeries Réunies, 1942.

Fueloep-Miller, René. *Fyodor Dostoevsky.* Translated by Richard and Clara Winston. New York: Charles Scribner's Sons, 1950.

Gide, André. *Dostoevsky.* Translated by and with Introduction by Arnold Bennett. New York: Alfred A. Knopf, 1926.

Guardini, Romano. *Religiöse Gestalten, In Dostojewskis*

Werk. Munich: Hegner Bücherei, bei Josef Kösel, 3rd ed., 1947.

Halperin, George. *Tolstoy, Dostoevsky, Tourgenev.* Chicago: Chicago Literary Club, 1946.

Hesse, Hermann. *Blick in Chaos; Drei Aufsätze.* Bern: Verlag Seldwyla, 1921. In Sight of Chaos. The Brothers Karamazov. Thoughts on Dostoevsky's Idiot. Translated by Stephen Hudson, Zurich, 1923. (These essays appeared separately in *Dial,* Vol. LXXII [1922], pp. 607-618; *Living Age,* Vol. CCCXIV [1922], pp. 606-613; and *English Review,* Vol. XXXV [1922], pp. 108-120, 190-196.)

Howe, Irving. *Politics and the Novel.* New York: Meridian Books and Horizon Press, 1957. Chapter 3, "Dostoevsky: The Politics of Salvation."

Hromádka, Joseph L. *Doom and Resurrection.* Richmond, Va.: Madrus House, 1945. Chapter 3, "Descensus ad Infernos."

Hubben, William. *Four Prophets of Our Destiny: Kierkegaard, Dostoevsky, Nietzsche, Kafka.* New York: Macmillan, 1952. Pp. 45-80.

Ivanov, Vyacheslav. *Freedom and the Tragic Life. A Study in Dostoevsky.* Foreword by Sir Maurice Bowra New York: Noonday Press, 1952.

Jackson, Robert Louis. *Dostoevsky's Underground Man in Russian Literature.* The Hague: Mouton, 1958.

Komarovitsch, W. "Explanations and Commentaries in F. M. Dostojewski," *Die Urgestalt der Brüder Karamasoff.* Munich, P. Piper & Co., 1928.

Lavrin, Janko. *Dostoevsky: A Study.* New York: Macmillan, 1947.

Lloyd, J. A. T. *Fyodor Dostoevsky.* New York: Charles Scribner's Sons, 1947.

Lubac, Henri de, S. J. *The Drama of Atheist Humanism.* Translated by Edith M. Riley. New York: Sheed & Ward, 1950.

Mackiewicz, Stanislau. *Dostoevsky.* London: Orbis, 1948.

Maurina, Zenta. *Dostojewskij. Menschengestalter und Gottsucher.* Memmingen: Maximilian Dietrich Verlag, 1952.

Merejkowski, Dmitri S. *Tolstoi as Man and Artist; With an*

Essay on Dostoevsky. New York: G. P. Putnam's Sons, 1902.

Modern Fiction Studies, Special number on Dostoevsky. Vol. IV, No. 3 (Autumn, 1958). Louise Dauner, "Raskolnikov in Search of a Soul"; Simon O. Lesser, "Saint and Sinner —Dostoevsky's 'Idiot' "; Nathan Rosen, "Breaking Out of the Underground"; Victor E. Amend, "Theme and Form in 'The Brothers Karamazov' "; Carl Niemeyer, "Raskolnikov and Lafcadio"; George Gibian, "The Grotesque in Dostoevsky"; Maurice Beebe and Christopher Newton, "Dostoevsky in English: A Selected Checklist of Criticism and Publications."

Murry, J. Middleton. *Fyodor Dostoevsky: A Critical Study.* London: Martin Secker, 1916.

Nigg, Walter. *Religiöse Denker. Kierkegaard, Dostojewskij, Nietzsche, Van Gogh.* Berlin-Munich: Gebrüder Weiss, 1952.

Pfleger, Karl. *Wrestlers With Christ.* Translated by E. I. Watkin. New York: Sheed & Ward, 1936. Pp. 183-220.

Rahv, Philip. *Image and Idea.* New York: New Directions, 1949. Two essays on *The Possessed* and on "The Legend of the Grand Inquisitor."

Roe, Ivan. *The Breath of Corruption: An Interpretation of Dostoievsky.* London: Hutchinson, 1946.

Roubiczek, Paul. *The Misinterpretation of Man. Studies in European Thought of the Nineteenth Century.* New York: Charles Scribner's Sons, 1949. Chapter 10, "The Return to Man."

Seduro, Vladimir. *Dostoievsky in Russian Literary Criticism, 1846-1956.* New York: Columbia University Press, 1957. See in particular Chapter 15, "M. M. Bakhtin on Dostoyevski's Polyphonic Novel."

Sewall, Richard B. *The Vision of Tragedy.* New Haven: Yale University Press, 1959. Pp. 106-126.

Shestov, Leo. *In Job's Balances. On the Sources of the Eternal Truths.* Translated by Camilla Coventry and C. A. McCartney. London: J. M. Dent & Sons, 1932. Pp. 3-82.

Simmons, Ernest J. *Dostoevsky. The Making of a Novelist.* London: John Lehmann, 1950.

Simon, Ernst, "Religious Humanism," in Arnold Bergstraesser (ed.), *Goethe and the Modern Age*. Chicago: Henry Regnery, 1950, pp. 304-325.

Slonim, Marc. *The Epic of Russian Literature: From its Origins through Tolstoy*. New York: Oxford University Press, 1950. Pp. 272-308.

Soloviev, Eugenii. *Dostoievsky: His Life and Literary Activity*. London: George Allen & Unwin; New York: Macmillan, 1916.

Steiner, George. *Tolstoy or Dostoevsky*. New York: Alfred A. Knopf, 1959.

Stocker, A. *Ame Russe. Réalisme Psychologique des Frères Karamazov*. Geneva: Collection Action et Pensée 18, Edition du Mont Blanc, 1948.

Troyat, Henry. *Firebrand; The Life of Dostoevsky*. New York: Roy Publishers, 1946.

Vatai, Laszlo. *Man and His Tragic Life. Based on Dostoievsky*. Translated by Laszlo Kecskemethy. New York: Philosophical Library, 1954.

Woodhouse, C. M. *Dostoievsky*. New York: Roy Publishers, 1951.

Yarmolinsky, Avrahm. *Dostoevsky: His Life and Art*. New York: Criterion Books, 1957.

Zander, L. A. *Dostoevsky*. Translated by Natalie Duddington. London: S.C.M. Press, 1948.

Zernov, Nicolas. *Three Russian Prophets: Khomiakov, Dostoevsky, Soloviev*. London: S.C.M. Press, 1944. Pp. 82-115.

Zweig, Stefan. *Three Masters: Balzac, Dickens, Dostoievsky*. London: George Allen & Unwin, 1930. Pp. 99-234.

ARTICLES ABOUT DOSTOIEVSKY

Alexander, Franz. "The Neurotic Character," *The International Journal of Psychoanalysis*, Vol. XI (July, 1930), pp. 308-311.

Beardsley, Monroe C. "Dostoyevsky's Metaphor of the 'Underground,'" *Journal of the History of Ideas*, Vol. III (1942), pp. 265-290.

Beebe, Maurice. "The Three Motives of Raskolnikov: A Reinterpretation of *Crime and Punishment*," *College English*, Vol. XVII (December, 1955), pp. 151-158.

Blackmur, R. P. "A Rage of Goodness: *The Idiot* of Dostoievsky," *Accent*, Vols. III-IV (1942), pp. 30-45.

——— "In the Birdcage: Notes on *The Possessed* of Dostoievsky," *Hudson Review*, Vol. I (Spring, 1948), pp. 7-28.

Buber, Martin. "Guilt and Guilt Feelings," translated by Maurice Friedman, *Psychiatry*, Vol. XX, No. 2 (May, 1957), pp. 123 f.

Eastman, Richard M. "Idea and Method in a Scene by Dostoevsky," *College English*, Vol. XVII, No. 3 (December, 1955), pp. 143-150.

Gibian, George. "Traditional Symbolism in *Crime and Punishment*," *Publications of the Modern Language Association*, Vol. LXX, Part I (December, 1955), pp. 979-996.

Guardini, Romano. "Dostoyevsky's Idiot, a Symbol of Christ," translated by Francis X. Quinn, *Cross Currents*, Vol. VI, No. 4 (Fall, 1956), pp. 359-382.

Hesse, Hermann. "The Brothers Karamazov or the Downfall of Europe: Thoughts on Reading Dostoevsky," translated by Harvey Gross, *Western Review*, Vol. XVII (1953), pp. 185-195.

Matlaw, Ralph E. "Recurrent Imagery in Dostoevsky," *Harvard Slavic Studies*, Vol. III (1957), pp. 201-225.

——— "Structure and Integration in *Notes from the Underground*," *Publications of the Modern Language Association*, Vol. LXXIII, Part I (March, 1958), pp. 101-109.

Mortimer, Ruth. "Dostoevsky and the Dream," *Modern Philology*, Vol. LIV (November, 1956), pp. 106-116.

Ramsey, Paul. "God's Grace and Man's Guilt," *Journal of Religion*, Vol. XXI (January, 1951), pp. 21-37.

——— "No Morality Without Immorality: Dostoevsky and the Meaning of Atheism," *Journal of Religion*, Vol. XXXVI (April, 1956), pp. 90-108.

Smith, Samuel Stephenson, and Isotoff, Andrei. "The Abnormal from Within: Dostoevsky," *Psycho-Analytic Review*, Vol. XXII (1935), pp. 361-391.

Strakowsch, H. E. "Dostoevsky and the Man-God." *Dublin Review*, Vol. CXIX (Second Quarter, 1955), pp. 142-153.

Traschen, I. "Dostoevsky's *Notes from the Underground,*" *Accent,* Vol. XVI (Autumn, 1956), pp. 255-264.

Tsanoff, Radoslav Andrea. "The Problem of Life in the Russian Novel," *Rice Institute Pamphlet,* Vol. IV (1917), pp. 121-272. Lecture 3: "From Darkness Into Light: Fyodor Dostoyevsky," pp. 180-209.

Wernham, James C. S., "Guardini, Berdyaev, and the Legend of the Grand Inquisitor," *The Hibbert Journal,* Vol. LIII (October, 1954), pp. 157-164.

BOOKS BY KAFKA

Amerika. New York: New Directions, 1946.

Beschreibung Eines Kampfes. Novellen, Skizzen, Aphorismen, Aus Dem Nachlass. Berlin: S. Fischer; New York: Schocken Books, 1946. Vol. V. of *Franz Kafka. Gesammelte Werke.* Edited by Max Brod.

Briefe. Edited by Max Brod. New York: Schocken Books, 1958.

The Castle. Translated by Willa and Edwin Muir. New York: Alfred A. Knopf, 1956.

Dearest Father, Stories and Other Writings. Edited by Max Brod. Translated by Ernest Kaiser and Eithne Wilkins. New York: Schocken Books, 1954.

Description of a Struggle. New York: Schocken Books, 1958.

The Diaries of Franz Kafka, 1910-1913. Edited by Max Brod. Translated by Joseph Kresh. New York: Schocken Books, 1948.

The Diaries of Franz Kafka, 1914-1923. Edited by Max Brod. Translated by Martin Greenberg with the co-operation of Hannah Arendt. New York: Schocken Books, 1949.

The Great Wall of China. Stories and Reflections. Translated by Willa & Edwin Muir. New York: Schocken Books, 1946.

Letters to Milena. Edited by Willi Haas. Translated by Tania and James Stern. London: Secker & Warburg, 1953.

Parables and Paradoxes. In German and English. New York: Schocken Paperback, 1961.

Selected Short Stories of Franz Kafka. Translated by Willa and Edwin Muir. Introduction by Philip Rahv. New York: Modern Library, 1952.

The Trial. Translated by Willa and Edwin Muir. Revised and with additional materials translated by E. M. Butler. New York: Alfred A. Knopf, 1957.

BOOKS ENTIRELY OR PARTLY ABOUT KAFKA

Anders, Günther. *Franz Kafka.* Translated by A. Steer and A. K. Thorlby. In Erich Heller (ed.), *Studies in Modern European Literature and Thought.* London: Bowes, 1960.

Brod, Max. "Additional Note" to *The Castle,* 1st ed. Translated by Edwin and Willa Muir, New York: Alfred A. Knopf, 1946.

Brod, Max. *Franz Kafka. Eine Biographie.* Berlin and Frankfurt: S. Fischer, 1954. 3rd edition.

Camus, Albert. *The Myth of Sisyphus and Other Essays.* Translated by Justin O'Brien. New York: Alfred A. Knopf, 1955. Pp. 124-138.

Eisner, Pavel. *Franz Kafka and Prague.* Translated by Lowry Nelson and René Wellek. New York: Arts Inc. (Golden Griffin Books), 1950.

Emrich, Wilhelm. *Franz Kafka.* Bonn: Athenäum, 1958.

Flores, Angel (ed.). *The Kafka Problem.* New York: New Directions, 1946.

Flores, Angel (ed.). "The Kafka Number," *The Quarterly Review of Literature,* Vol. II, No. 3 (1945).

Flores, Angel, ·and Swander, Homer (eds.). *Franz Kafka Today.* Madison, Wisconsin: University of Wisconsin Press, 1958.

A Franz Kafka Miscellany. Edited by Dorothy Norman. New York: Twice a Year Press, 1940.

Fromm, Erich. *The Forgotten Language.* London: Gollancz, 1952. Pp. 213-224.

Glatzer, Nahum N. "Franz Kafka and the Tree of Knowledge," in *Between East and West. Essays in Memory of Bela Horovitz.* Oxford: East and West Library, 1958. Pp. 48-58.

Goodman, Paul. *Kafka's Prayer.* New York: Vanguard Press, 1947.

Gray, Ronald. *Kafka's Castle*. Cambridge: Cambridge University Press, 1956.

Heller, Erich. *The Disinherited Mind. Essays in Modern German Literature and Thought*. Cambridge: Bowes & Bowes, 1952; Philadelphia: Dufours, 1953. Pp. 157-181.

Janouch, Gustav. *Conversations with Kafka*. Notes and Reminiscences by Gustav Janouch with an Introduction by Max Brod. Translated by Goronwy Rees. London: Verschoyle; New York: Frederick A. Praeger, 1953.

Krieger, Murray. *The Tragic Vision*. New York: Holt, Rinehart & Winston, 1960, "Franz Kafka: Nonentity and the Tragic." Chap. 5, Sec. 1.

Neider, Charles. *The Frozen Sea; A Study of Franz Kafka*. New York: Oxford University Press, 1948.

Pearse, Andrew, and Rajan, B. (eds.). *Focus One, Symposium on Kafka and Rex Warner*. London: Dennis Dobson, 1945.

Politzer, Heinz. *Parable and Paradox*. A Study of Franz Kafka. Ithaca, New York: Cornell University Press, 1962.

Rahv, Philip. *Image and Idea; Fourteen Essays on Literary Themes*. New York: New Directions, 1949. "The Hero As Lonely Man" and "The Death of Ivan Ilyich and Joseph K."

Russell, Francis. *Three Studies in Twentieth Century Obscurity*. Aldington, Ashford, Kent: The Hand and Flower Press, 1954. Pp. 45-65.

Scott, Nathan A. *Rehearsals of Discomposure. Alienation and Reconciliation in Modern Literature. Franz Kafka, Ignazio Silone, D. H. Lawrence, and T. S. Eliot*. New York: King Crown's Press; London: Lehmann, 1952. Pp. 11-65.

Slochower, Harry. *No Voice Is Wholly Lost*. New York: Creative Age Press, 1945. "Secular Crucifixion," pp. 103-125.

Tauber, Herbert. *Franz Kafka; An Interpretation of His Works*. Translated from German by G. Humphreys Roberts and Roger Senhouse. New Haven: Yale University Press, 1948.

Weltsch, Felix. *Religion und Humor im Leben und Werk Franz Kafkas*. Berlin-Grünewald: F. A. Herbig, 1957.

West, Rebecca. *The Court and the Castle: Some Treatments*

of a Recurrent Theme. New Haven: Yale University Press, 1957.

ARTICLES ABOUT KAFKA

Anders, Günther. "Franz Kafka, Ritual Without Religion," *Commentary*, Vol. VIII (December, 1949), pp. 560-569.

Arendt, Hannah. "Franz Kafka: A Revaluation," *Partisan Review*, Vol. XI (1944), pp. 412-422.

────── "The Jew as Pariah; A Hidden Tradition," *Jewish Social Studies*, Vol. VI, No. 2 (1944), pp. 99-122.

Auden, W. H. "The Wandering Jew," *New Republic*, Vol. CIV (February 10, 1941), pp. 185-186.

Barnes, Hazel E. "Myth and Human Experience," *Classical Journal*, Vol. LI (December, 1955), pp. 121-127.

Belgion, Montgomery. "The Measure of Kafka," *The Criterion*, Vol. XVIII (October, 1938), pp. 13-28.

Burnham, James. "Observations on Kafka," *Partisan Review*, Vol. XIV (1947), pp. 186-195.

Burns, Wayne. "Kafka and Alex Comfort: The Penal Colony Revisited," *Arizona Quarterly*, Vol. VIII (Summer, 1952), pp. 101-20.

Church, Margaret. "Time and Reality in Kafka's *The Trial* and *The Castle*," *Twentieth Century Literature*, Vol. II (July, 1956), pp. 62-69.

Collignon, Jean. "Kafka's Humor," *Yale French Studies*, No. 16 (Winter, 1955-1956), pp. 53-62.

Daniel-Rops. "In the Labyrinth: A Note on Kafka," *Manitoba Arts Review*, Vol. III (1942), pp. 3-13.

Fraiberg, Selma. "Kafka and the Dream," *Partisan Review*, Vol. XXIII (Winter, 1956), pp. 47-69.

Glicksberg, Charles E. "Art and Disease," *Nineteenth Century*, Vol. CXLV (March, 1949), pp. 180-190.

Goldschmidt, H. L. "Key to Kafka," *Commentary*, Vol. VIII (August, 1949), pp. 129-138.

Greenberg, Clement. "The Jewishness of Franz Kafka," *Commentary*, Vol. XIX (1955), pp. 320-324.

Hesse, Hermann. "The Exorcism of the Demon," *Symposium*, Vol. IV (1950), pp. 325-348.

Hodin, J. P. "Memories of Franz Kafka," *Horizon*, Vol. XVII, No. 97 (January, 1948), pp. 26-45.

Kauf, Robert. "Once Again—Kafka's 'Report to an Academy,'" *Modern Language Quarterly*, Vol. XV (December, 1954), pp. 359-366.

Kazin, Alfred. "Kafka, Twentieth Century Man of Sorrows," *New York Herald Tribune* Books Section (April 3, 1947), p. 3.

Madden, William A. "A Myth of Meditation: Kafka's 'Metamorphosis,'" *Thought*, Vol. XXVI, No. 101 (Summer, 1951), pp. 246-266.

Margeson, John. "Franz Kafka, A Critical Problem," *University of Toronto Quarterly*, Vol. XVIII (October, 1948), pp. 30-40.

Neider, Charles. "Kafka Mirrors Our Uncertainties, Frustrations, Fears," *New York Times Book Review* (August 6, 1945), pp. 6, 30.

―――― "Two Notes on Franz Kafka," *Rocky Mountain Review*, Vol. X, No. 2 (Winter, 1946), pp. 90-95.

Ong, Walter J. "Kafka's Castle and the West," *Thought*, Vol. XXII (September, 1947), pp. 439-460.

Pearce, Donald. "Dante and *The Castle*," *Northern Review*, Vol. I, No. 5 (February-March, 1947), pp. 2-8.

Politzer, Heinz. "Franz Kafka's Letter to His Father," *Germanic Review*, Vol. XXVIII (October, 1953), pp. 165-179.

―――― "From Mendelssohn to Kafka; The Jewish Man of Letters in Germany," *Commentary*, Vol. III (April, 1947), pp. 344-351.

―――― "Messenger of the King," *Commentary*, Vol. VIII, No. 1 (July, 1949), pp. 93-96.

―――― "Prague and the Origins of Rilke, Kafka, and Werfel," *Modern Language Quarterly*, Vol. XVI, No. 1 (March, 1955), pp. 49-62.

―――― "Recent Trends in Kafka Criticism," *Books Abroad*, Vol. XXVII, No. 2 (Spring, 1953), pp. 143-144.

Reed, Eugene E. "Moral Polarity in Kafka's *Der Prozess* and *Das Schloss*," *Monatshefte*, Vol. XLVI, No. 6 (November, 1954), pp. 317-324.

Reiss, H. S. "Franz Kafka's Conception of Humor," *Modern Language Review*, Vol. XLIV (October, 1949), pp. 534-542.

Rubinstein, William C. "A Hunger Artist," *Monatshefte*, Vol. XLIV (January, 1952), pp. 13-19.

——— "A Report to an Academy," *Modern Language Quarterly*, Vol. XIII (December, 1952), pp. 372-376.

Sokel, Walter H. "Kafka's 'Metamorphosis,' Rebellion and Punishment," *Monatshefte*, Vol. XLVIII (April-May, 1956), pp. 203-214.

Stallman, Robert W. "Kafka's Cage," *Accent*, Vol. VIII, No. 2 (Winter, 1948), pp. 117-125.

Tyler, Parker. "Kafka's and Chaplin's Amerika," *Sewanee Review*, Vol. LVIII (Spring, 1950), pp. 299-311.

Urzidil, John. "Franz Kafka, Novelist and Mystic," *Menorah Journal*, Vol. XXXI (October-December, 1943), pp. 273-283.

Vivas, Eliseo. "Kafka's Distorted Mask," *Kenyon Review*, Vol. X, No. 1 (Winter, 1948), pp. 51-69.

Walker, Augusta. "Allegory, a Light Conceit," *Partisan Review*, Vol. XXII, No. 4 (Fall, 1955), pp. 480-490.

Warshow, Robert. "Kafka's Failure," *Partisan Review*, Vol. XVI, No. 4 (April, 1949), pp. 428-431.

Wolff, Kurt. "On Franz Kafka," *Twice A Year*, Nos. VIII-IX (1942), pp. 273-279.

Index

Index

Abraham, 67, 396, 457

Adam and Eve, 5, 6, 7

Aeschylus, 35, 102, 211

Aglaia Ivanovna (Epanchin) (Dostoievsky's *The Idiot*), 228

Ahab, Captain (*Moby Dick*): as divided man, 130-34; and Gnostic rejection of creation, 198; and Job, 143-47, 271, 484-85, 486; and Melville, 53, 440; as Modern Job, 147-48; as Modern Promethean, 53, 62, 67, 69, 95-96, 98-129, 484, 490, 183, 211, 440; and monological man, 164, 453; and the problem of evil, 71-77, 88, 441; and psychological compulsion, 438, 439; and Romantic Superman, 190, 431; and Starbuck, 78, 437; and sundering of truth and reality, 60, 80; and Trancendentalism, 58

Ahab, King (in the Bible), 147-48

Alyona (*Crime and Punishment*), 163, 191-92, 194

Amalia (*The Castle*), 313-15, 318-20, 365-66, 387

Antigone, 29-34

Antigone, 29-33, 35

Apollo, 24-25

Aristotle, 22, 26-27, 127-28, 489

Arnold, Matthew, 4

Arvin, Newton, 111

Bacon, Francis, 107

Bakhtin, M. M., 172 n, 448 n

Barnabas (*The Castle*), 313-15, 319, 335 n, 391, 396-98

Bartleby ("Bartleby the Scrivener"), 82-92; as divided man, 134-36; as the Modern Exile, 462-65

"Bartleby the Scrivener" (Melville), 82-92, 441

Bauer, Felice, 323, 330-31, 344

Bazarov (Turgenev's *Fathers and Children*), 173

Bendemann, Georg, 331, 339-44, 351, 403, 489

Berdyaev, Nicholas: and Dostoievsky, 172 n, 194, 200-201, 212, 214 n, 255; and Gnostic Personalism, 110 n

Bernard, Claude, 259-60

Bible, the Hebrew, 6-22, 203, 276-77, 300

Biblical God, the, 5-22, 110, 203, 482

Billy Budd, 81 n, 90, 136-41

Billy Budd, Foretopman (Melville), 81 n, 136-42, 441

Binswanger, Ludwig, 470

Birth of Tragedy, The, 5

Blake, William, 186, 439

Blanchot, Maurice, 325 n

Bloy, Leon, 300

Brandenfeld, Frieda (Kafka's "The

Judgment"), 340, 344
Bridge Inn Landlady. *See* Gardena
Brod, Max, 316, 322, 333–34, 376, 384
Brothers Karamazov, The, 168–69, 168 n, 229, 238–81, 442–49
Buber, Martin: and Ahab, 123; and Alyosha and Ivan, 447; and The Book of Job, 18 n, 3, 4; and Camus, 447 n; and Camus' *The Misunderstanding*, 420; and the "eclipse of God," 94, 456; and Existential guilt, 347–48; and Freud, 348; and human knowledge, 36 n; and Kafka, 14, 286 n, 292 n, 347–48, 404, 404 n; and the Modern Job, 407, 484, 486, 487 n; and Stavrogin, 173, 179 n, 347–48; and *The Trial*, 347–48, 348 n, 356 n
Bucephalus, Doctor (Kafka's "The New Advocate"), 304–5, 311
Buddha, The, 108
Bulkington, 53–54, 69, 102, 125, 129, 131
Bürgel (*The Castle*), 316, 320–24, 323 n
"Burrow, The" (Kafka), 293–96

Cain, 7, 204
Caligula (Camus), 413–17, 420, 424
Camus, Albert: and Bartleby, 82, 85–86; and crisis of motives, 425–26; and depth image of the modern man, 4; and guilt, 426–27; and Kafka, 450, 450 n; and the Modern Exile, 288, 413–25, 427–30, 452; and the Modern Job, 428, 430–33, 452–54; and the Modern Promethean, 5, 427, 451 n, 482
Carpenter, the (*Moby Dick*), 72–73
Castle, The (Kafka), 310, 312–27, 331–33, 335 n, 344; and guilt, 365–67, 376; and Kafka's relations to women, 331–33, 344; and the Modern Exile, 310, 312–27; and the Modern Job, 484–88, 488 n; and paradox of the person, 378–99, 401–3, 408, 478–82; and problematic of modern man, 335 n

Charvat, William, 69 n
Chase, Richard, 146 n
Christ: and Billy Budd, 137; and Dostoievsky, 448 n; and Faustus, 39–40; and Kirilov, 187; and "Legend of the Grand Inquisitor," 198–208, 243, 264, 264, 446; and Meister Eckhart, 465; and Rogozhin and Myshkin, 230; and Shatov, 442; and Zossima, 277
Claggart (*Billy Budd*), 137–38, 140
Clamence, Jean Baptiste (Camus' *The Fall*), 159, 425–27
Confidence Man, the, 93–94, 270
Confidence Man, The (Melville), 92–94, 441, 463
"Country Doctor, A" (Kafka), 301–4, 309, 374–75, 490
Connolly, Cecil, 294
Copernicus, 70
Creon, 24–25, 28–33

Dasha (Dostoievsky's *The Devils*), 174, 180
Delarue, Matthieu (Sartre's *The Age of Reason*), 492
Descartes, Rene, 250, 490
Devils, The (Dostoievsky), 170–81, 287; and Existential guilt, 247; and freedom and compulsion, 220–25; and Mother Earth, 168; and polyphony of voices, 172 n; and Zossima, 273
Diary of a Writer, The (Dostoievsky), 275
Doctor Faustus, (Marlowe) 38–41, 45, 47, 107, 458
Dolguruky, Arkady (Dostoievsky's *The Raw Youth*), 225–27, 239, 248
Dostoievsky, Fyodor: and absolute value of man, 194; and alienation of modern man, 4; and crisis of motives, 473–75; and denial of creation, 272 n; and depth image of modern man, 4; and the divided man, 214 n–215 n; and fathers and sons, 238–40, 470; and freedom and compulsion, 223–24, 226–27, 233, 334–35; and "Man-God," 262; and the Gospel of John, 198; and

Grand Inquisitor, 199–201; and guilt, 236–37; and image of man, 286–87, 445, 446–48, 448 n; and Job, 5, 277–78; and "The Life of a Great Sinner," 175, 175 n; and love of God and love of man, 196; and "Man-God," 182, 454; and the Modern Exile, 288, 441–43; and Mother Earth, 167–68, 170; and *The Plague*, 427, 430; and polyphony, 172 n; and problematic of modern man, 172, 216, 266, 444, 449; and the problematic rebel, 189; and Prometheus, 5; and psychological compulsion, 469–72; and the rape of a little girl, 169; and Rousseau, 173; and *Sobornost* (organic reciprocity), 272–76; and suffering, 217, 234, 267–68; and tension of opposites, 242, 255, 445–46

"Dream of a Ridiculous Man, The" (Dostoievsky), 177

Donne, John, 68

Dymant, Dora, 331

Ecclesiastes, 9–10, 21–22, 76

Eckhart, Meister, 465

Eliphaz, the Temanite, 14

Employer, the ("Bartleby"), 82–92, 134–35

Emrich, Wilhelm, 323 n, 335 n, 488 n

Erlanger (*The Castle*), 316, 320–21

Fall, The, 425 n–27, 493

Farber, Leslie, 135–36, 413–15

Faust, 37, 41–48, 215

Faust (Goethe), 41–48, 116, 225, 459–60, 490

Faustus, Doctor, 38–43, 461

Fear and Trembling (Kierkegaard), 280

Fedallah, 65, 107, 116

Flaubert, Gustav, 376

Francis, Saint, 474

Freud, Sigmund: and death, 464; and distrust of other people, 354; and Dostoievsky, 233, 471; and the ego, 154; and guilt, 348; and image of man, 470; and the Modern Promethean, 492; and

psychological compulsion, 472

Frieda (*The Castle*): and K. and the authorities, 391; and K.'s call, 384–85, 387; and K. as Land Surveyor, 381–82; and K. as Modern Exile, 316–20, 325–26, 335 n; and K. and Single One, 394; and K. and the village and the Castle, 397–98, 397 n

Fromm, Eric, 133, 416, 449, 466, 492

Gabriel (*Moby Dick*), 147–48

Gardena (landlady of Bridge Inn, *The Castle*); and K. and the authorities, 390; and K.'s call, 385, 387; and K. as Modern Exile, 315, 326; and K. and the Modern Job, 402; and K. and the Single One, 394–95

Georg Bendanna (Kafka's "The Judgment"), 87

Glatzer, Nahum, 323 n, 397 n

Gnostics: and Dostoievsky's "Man-God," 197; and evil, 105–6, 300; and Fedallah, 65; and Ishmael as Modern Exile, 75; and Job, 21; and Kafka's "In The Penal Colony," 356 n; and Psalm 82, 12, 356 n; and the redeemer God, 110–11; and *The Trial*, 358. 360, 489

Goethe, Johann Wolfgang von, 41, 56 n, 209

Grand Inquisitor, the (*The Brothers Karamazov*): and contempt for man, 190, 211, 213; and denial of creation, 208–9; as father figure to Ivan, 240; and a harmonious "ant heap," 156; and human nature, 201; and Ivan Karamazov, 206–7, 272 n, 473; and Ivan's devil, 209–10, 215; and Ivan's guilt, 243; and the metaphysical rebel, 204–5; and the Modern Exile, 442; and problem of evil, 274, 277; and rejection of creation, 198; and temptations of Christ, 199–200, 202–04; and totalitarian dictator, 199–202; and Zossima, 264

Gray, Ronald, 323 n, 488 n

Gray, Thomas, 20
"Great Wall of China, The" (Kafka), 309–12, 313
Gretchen (Goethe's *Faust*), 46–48
Guardini, Romano, 183, 188, 198, 207
Grushenka (*The Brothers Karamazov*), 255–56, 258, 260–61, 265–66, 280–81

Haemon (*Antigone*), 31–33
Halperin, George, 167
Hans, (*The Castle*), 317–19, 403
Hardy, Thomas, 5, 459, 485
Hawthorne, Nathaniel, 54 n, 93, 440
"Hebraism and Hellenism" (Arnold), 4
Hegel, Friedrich, 466
Heidegger, Martin, 464
Heller, Erich, 388
Heraclitus, 23, 485
Hoffman, Frederick J., 336 n, 346 n
"Hunger Artist, A" (Kafka), 305–8, 375, 377–78, 463–64, 478
"Hunter Gracchus, The" (Kafka), 300–301

Idiot, The (Dostoievsky), 184–85, 227–35
"In the Penal Colony" (Kafka), 330, 337–38, 356 n
"Investigations of a Dog" (Kafka), 307–9, 311, 377–78
Ishmael (in the Bible), 67, 80–81
Ishmael (*Moby Dick*): and Calvinist predestination, 118 n; and Captain Ahab, 103, 124–25, 131, 136; and evil, 130; and Job, 462; and Job's Whale, 143–46; and Melville, 53, 56 n, 438–40; and Merseault (*The Stranger*), 425, 461; and Moby Dick, 105–6; and the Modern Exile, 67-71, 73–82, 88, 437, 441, 459; and the Monkeyrope, 119; and sundering of truth and reality, 58–64
Isotoff, Andrei, 471
Ivanov, Vyacheslav, 470 n

Jacob, 16
Jan (Camus' *The Misunderstanding*), 418–19
Jane Eyre (Charlotte Bronte), 384
Janouch, Gustav, 290–91, 365, 370, 372, 375–76, 406
Jeremiah (in the Bible), 81 n
Jeremiah (*The Castle*), 318, 391
Jesus: and Billy Budd, 137–38; and Grand Inquisitor, 274; and Ivan's Christ, 199, 208; and Kafka, 383; and Kirilov, 184; and Myshkin, 235
Jisenska, Milena, 330–31, 333, 376
Job, 12–22; and alienation of modern man, 456–58; and Bartleby, 192; and Captain Ahab, 108; and Captain Ahab, Ivan, Father Zossima, and Alyosha, 485; and Dmitri, Ivan, and Alyosha, 267–81, 468, 489; and Faust (Goethe), 46; and Faustus, 39, 44; and Grand Inquisitor, 204; and Ishmael, 71; and Ivan Karamazov, 215; and Kafka, 400–403; and Moby Dick, 143–47; and *Moby Dick*, 51; and the Modern Exile, 462–63; and the Modern Job, 486, 487 n; and modern man, 4–5, 183; and *The Plague*, 428
Job, Book of, 10–22, 41, 100, 272, 461
Jonah, 97–98
Joseph K. (*The Trial*), 331, 347–72, 379, 428, 476
Jude the Obscure (Hardy), 460–61, 463
"Judgment, The" (Kafka), 85–87, 330–31, 339–44, 349–51, 357 n
Jung, Carl, 439, 488, 492

K. (*The Castle*): and the Modern Exile, 312–27; and the Modern Job, 400–403, 451 n, 465, 485–88, 491; and paradox of the person, 378–99, 478–82
Kafka, Franz, 4–5, 82, 85, 87, 238; and fathers and sons, 473; and guilt, 346–73, 475–76; as Modern Exile, 285–327, 465; and the Modern Job, 400–10, 425–26, 427, 449–51; and paradox of the person, 374–99, 477–83; and problem of evil, 488–90; and psychological

compulsion, 328–45, 469

Kant, Immanuel, 250

Karamazov, Alyosha: and Fyodor Karamazov, 240, 242; and Ivan 195, 197–98, 205, 207–8, 212–14, 243; and Job, 266, 270, 278–81, 442, 444–48, 448 n; and Zossima, 239

Karamazov, Dmitri, 193, 240; and fathers and sons, 240, 242–46, 251–61, 263; and Job, 267–69, 443–46, 448

Karamazov, Fyodor: and Alyosha, 262–63; and Dmitri, 244, 252, 256–57; and his sons, 240, 242, 254, 258; and Ivan, 213, 245–47, 251, 253; and Zossima 205, 241

Karamazov, Ivan: and Alyosha, 281; and crisis of motives, 473; and denial of creation, 272 n, and the divided man, 447–48; and fathers and sons, 240, 242–53, 255–57, 258–61; and Job, 269, 271, 272, 276, 277–79, 484–86; as "Man-God," 172, 188, 192–215, 224, 238, 240; and the Modern Exile, 465; and the Modern Job, 269; and the Modern Promethean, 269, 453; and problematic of modern man, 442–46; and problem of evil, 268–69, 270, 274

Karamazovs, The, 253–55, 264, 268, 444

Katya Ivanovna *(The Brothers Karamazov)*, 184, 197, 243, 246, 251, 259–60

Kaufmann, Fritz, 405 n

Kazin, Alfred, 81, 94 n

Kierkegaard, Soren; and Alyosha, 280; and Camus, 458; and Captain Ahab, 123; and Ivan Karamazov, 271; and Job, 457; and K. *(The Castle)*, 393–94, 396, 397 n, 401 and Kafka, 331, 398, 450, 451 n, 480, 482

King Lear (Shakespeare), 126

Kirilov (Dostoievsky's *The Devils*): as "Man-God," 272, 272 n, 442; as Modern Exile, 172 n, 173, 180–81, 182–88, 199, 207, 211

Klamm *(The Castle)*: and Barnabas, 386; and the Castle, 398,

401; as a Castle official, 385; as impersonal Eros, 488 n; and K., 315–18, 323, 335 n, 380, 391–93, 395–96; and K. as Land-Surveyor, 389; and K. as Modern Job, 402; and K.'s call, 383

Laius, 24

Land-Surveyor, the. *See*: K.

"Letter to His Father" (Kafka), 328–29, 328 n, 329 n, 335–38, 340

Lisa (Dostoievsky's *The Devils*), 174–75

Lisa (Dostoievsky's *Notes from the Underground*), 157–61, 217

Lizaveta (Dostoievsky's *Crime and Punishment*), 163–64

Lorrain, Claude, 177

Lubac, Henri de, 191

Luther, Martin, 387

Lynd, Helen Merrel, 476 n

Macbeth (Shakespeare), 126

Macleish, Archibald, 5

Maeterlinck, Maurice, 480

Manfred (Byron), 95, 124

Marcionites, 207. *See* also Gnostics

Marlowe, Christopher, 38, 40

Marmeladov *(Crime and Punishment)*, 474

Marx, Karl, 466

Mapple, Father, 96–98, 102

Matthiessen, F. O., 116

Matryosha (Dostoievsky's *The Devils*), 176–78, 180, 222–23

Mead, George Herbert, 481

Melville, Herman: and Ahab, 122–26, 130, 133; and alienation of man, 437–38; and *Billy Budd*, 138–42; and the "dead God," 71; and depth image of modern man, 4; and divided man, 137; and Dmitri Karamazov, 254; and Emersonian Trancendentalism, 55; and Existential judgment, 148; and Existential truth, 59' and fathers and sons, 238; and freedom and compulsion, 134; and Gnosticism, 110; and Hawthorne, 93; and the heart, 112–13; and the image of man, 286; and Job, 143–45; and Kafka, 286–

88; and Modern Exile, 82, 94, 461–63; and Modern Promethean, 5; and Pantheism, 56; and *The Plague*, 427; and the point of view of *Moby Dick*, 52–53, 58–59, 77, 439–40; and problematic of modern man, 92, 441, 473; and romantic suffering, 190; and search for the father, 136–37; and search for truth, 54 n; and tragedy, 127–28; and the whiteness of the Whale, 69 n

Mephistophilis, 39–42, 44–47, 209

"Metamorphosis, The" (Kafka), 296–300, 306–7, 339–40, 342–43, 349

Meursault (Camus' *The Stranger*), 86–87, 89, 420–25, 461, 464

Milton, John, 6, 95

Misunderstanding, The (Camus), 417–20

Moby Dick: and Ahab, 69–70, 99, 102, 105–6, 108, 113; and the chase, 116–17, 120–23; and evil, 130, 437–38; and Ishmael, 68, 103–6; as a Job's whale, 143–44, 146–48; and Stubb, 124; and sundering of truth and reality, 52–53, 57, 61

Moby Dick, 51–82, 88, 93, 95–134, 143–48, 437–41

Modern Exile, the: and awareness of death, 464; and Bartleby, 82, 88, 463, 465; and Camus, 4; and Dr. Rieux, 431; and Dostoievsky, 442; and Existential mistrust, 94; and Ishmael, 53, 67, 81, 440; and Job, 463; and Kafka, 288, 449–50; and Melville, 461–62; and Meursault, 425; and *Moby Dick*, 51, 88; and the Modern Promethean, 459, 483–84; and *The Plague*, 427; and the romantic rebel, 124

Modern Job, the: and Alyosha, 278–81; and Camus, 4, 451–54, 487 n, 492–93; and Captain Ahab, 147; and Dr. Rieux, 430, 433, 485–86, 490–92; and Dostoievsky, 277–78; and Ivan Karamazov, 269–72; and K., 485–86, 490–91; and Kafka, 400–10, 451 n, 484,

487–90; and Martin Buber, 484, 486, 487 n; and the Modern Promethean, 485, 490; and *The Plague*, 427, 484; and Zossima, 272–76

Modern Promethean, the: and Camus, 493; and Captain Ahab, 53, 67, 102, 123, 128–29, 147; and choice between submission and rebellion, 485; and Dr. Rieux, 433; and Dostoievsky's Modern Exiles, 442; and individualistic rebellion, 454; and Ivan Karamazov, 193, 214–15, 269, 271; and K., 401; and meaning for modern man, 490; and *Moby Dick*, 128; and modern crisis of the person, 449; and the Modern Exile, 459, 466; and the Modern Job, 486; and monological man, 453; and the *Myth of Sisyphus* (Camus), 451; and Nietzsche's Zarathustra, 183, 466–69; and 19th century Romanticism, 484; and *The Plague*, 427; and Sartre, 487 n, 491–92

Modern Rebel, the, 51

Momus (*The Castle*), 385, 390, 392, 395, 398

Myshkin, Prince (Dostoievsky's *The Idiot*), 185, 217, 227–35, 472

Myth of Sisyphus, The (Camus), 420, 450 n, 451, 464, 492–93

Napoleon Bonaparte, 189–92, 441

Nastasya Filippovna, 227–31, 234

"Neither Victims nor Executioners" (Camus), 452–53

Nietzsche, Friedrich: and alienation of modern man, 456; and crisis of motives, 475; and Grand Inquisitor, 202; and Ivan Karamazov, 196, 271; and Ivan's devil, 209; and Job, 22; and Kafka, 309; and the Modern Promethean, 183, 467–69; and Prometheus, 5; and Raskolnikov, 189, 191; and the Underground Man, 154

Nigg, Walter, 189

Notes from the Underground (Dostoievsky), 152–61, 217–19, 234

Oedipus, 6, 22-29, 40, 204, 458
Oedipus at Colonus, 28
Oedipus the King, 22-29, 31, 40
Olga (*The Castle*), 313-15, 317, 319, 366-67, 387, 391, 394
Otto, Rudolph, 14 n

Paneloux, Father (*The Plague*), 428-30, 432, 485
Paradise Lost (Milton), 6, 95
Pascal, Blaise, 19, 70-71, 459
Pepi (*The Castle*), 317, 321, 326, 387, 390, 420, 488 n
Percival, M. O., 99 n
Pierre (Melville), 71, 441
Pip (*Moby Dick*), 71-72, 88, 109, 118, 121, 126-27
Plague, The (Camus), 427-33, 452; and the Modern Job, 484, 486, 487 n, 490-93
Plato, 55, 205-06, 482, 485
Platonist, the sunken-eyed young (*Moby Dick*): and Bulkington, 69, 454; and Captain Ahab, 102; and Emerson, 55; and Ishmael, 61, 64, 76; and Melville, 56, 56 n, 58; and Pantheism, 66, 106; and truth, 131; and unendurable infinity, 99
Poetics, The (Aristotle), 27, 128
Politzer, Heinz, 328 n
Polyneices, 28-29
Porfiry (Dostoievsky's *Crime and Punishment*), 164, 235-36, 239
Priest, the (*The Trial*), 361-64
Prometheus: and Biblical man, 6; and Captain Ahab, 95, 102, 107, 111-12, 117, 127, 129; and Father Mapple, 98; and Faustus, 41; and Grand Inquisitor, 204; and Greek image of man, 4, 33-37, 51; and Ivan Karamazov, 215, 271; and Job, 16; and "Man-God," 210-11; and modern man, 456; and the Modern Promethean, 5; and Nietzsche, 22
Prufrock (T. S. Eliot), 159
Psalm 82, 17, 356 n

Queequeg (*Moby Dick*), 66, 76-79

Raskolnikov (Dostoievsky's *Crime and Punishment*): and guilt, 235-36, 239, 251, 255, 258, 443, 446; as "Man-God," 188-94, 196, 199, 211, 215; as Modern Exile, 161-71; and psychological compulsion, 219-20, 247
Raw Youth, The (Dostoievsky), 238-40
Razumihin (Dostoievsky's *Crime and Punishment*), 162-63, 166
Rebel, The (Camus), 427, 454, 493
"Report to an Academy, A" (Kafka), 292-94
Rieux, Doctor (*The Plague*), 429-33, 452-53; as Modern Job, 485-86, 490-93
Rogozhin, Parfyon (Dostoievsky's *The Idiot*), 228-31, 234, 279
Rose (Kafka's "A Country Doctor"), 301-3

Samsa, Gregor ("The Metamorphosis"): and Bartleby, 464; and K., 403; and Kafka, 377; and Kafka's escape from father, 339-40; and the Modern Exile, 296-300, 306-7; and the problem of justice, 489
Sartre, Jean-Paul: and alienation of modern man, 466; and "death of God," 456, 491; and Dostoievsky, 212; and Faust (Goethe), 44; and Ivan Karamazov, 271; and Kafka, 482, 488; and Martin Buber, 487 n; and the Modern Promethean, 492; and subjective consciousness, 490; and Tarrou (*The Plague*), 429
Satan (Milton's *Paradise Lost*), 124
Schiller, Friedrich, 254
Shatov (Dostoievsky's *The Devils*), 172 n, 173-74, 185, 187, 207, 442
Shelley, Percy Bysshe, 5
Shigalyov (Dostoievsky's *The Devils*), 156, 199, 201, 203, 211
Simmons, Ernest, 189
Simon Magus, 37
"Singular Judicial Procedure, A" (Kafka), 357 n
Smerdyakov (*The Brothers Karamazov*), 197, 210, 212-14, 242-48,

251

Smith, Samuel, 471

Sonia (*Crime and Punishment*), 161-62, 170-71, 191, 217, 220, 265

Sophocles, 22, 26, 28

Starbuck (*Moby Dick*): and Captain Ahab, 72, 99-102, 112, 114-19, 126, 134, 147; and destruction of the Pequod, 76; and the Leviathan, 145-46; and the Modern Exile, 73

Stavrogin, Nicholas (Dostoievsky's *The Devils*): and Dmitri Karamazov, 255; and Dostoievsky, 287; and Existential guilt, 347-48; and fathers and sons, 239; and Ivan Karamazov, 245; and "Man-God," 214, 215 n; and the Modern Exile, 169, 171-81, 442-43; and problematic of modern man, 445-46; and psychological compulsion, 220-27

Stranger, The (Camus), 85-86, 104, 420-25, 428, 461, 492

Stubb (*Moby Dick*): and Captain Ahab, 109, 117; and destruction of the Pequod, 76; and the Doubloon, 121; and evil, 265; and Moby Dick, 120, 124; and Pip, 71

Sullivan, Harry Stack, 220

Svidrigailov (Dostoievsky's *Crime and Punishment*): and Ivan Karamazov, 215; and Ivan's devil, 209-10, and "Man-God," 192; and Raskolnikov, 168-71, 168 n, 193, 219-20, 239; and Stavrogin, 177

Swander, Homer, 397 n

Tarrou (*The Plague*), 429-32, 452, 486

Tempest, The (Shakespeare), 81

Thrasymachus (Plato's *Republic*), 201, 206

Tikhon, Father, 174-76, 175 n, 178-79, 179 n, 214, 221, 239

Tillich, Paul, 348 n

Tiresias, 24, 32

Titorelli (*The Trial*), 356, 358-59

Trial, The (Kafka): and *The Castle*, 379; and "The Great Wall of China," 310; and judgment, 339; and Kafka, 376, 407; and Kafka's "Letter to his Father," 335; and Kafka's relation to women, 331-32, 334; and "The New Advocate," 305; and *The Plague*, 428; and problematic of guilt, 347-72; and problem of evil, 488-89; and problem of justice, 481-82; and psychological compulsion, 329 n; and relationship of Existential guilt and Existential shame, 475-76; and the world breaking in on the self, 408

Underground Man, the (Dostoievsky): and alienation of modern man, 442; and Berdyaev, 215 n; and Dmitri Karamazov, 254, 258; and Dostoievsky, 442; and Ivan Karamazov, 193-95, 215; and the Modern Exile, 152-61; and psychological compulsion, 216-19, 224, 226, 471-72; and pure consciousness, 250; and Raskolnikov, 164-65, 190; and Stavrogin, 171; and suffering, 235

Vere, Captain (*Billy Budd*), 90, 136-42

Verkhovensky, Peter (Dostoievsky's *The Devils*), 184-85, 187-88, 221, 224, 287

Verkhovensky, Stepan Trofimovitch (Dostoievsky's *The Devils*), 239, 287

Versilov (Dostoievsky's *The Raw Youth*): and Anna, 174; and fathers and sons, 239; and freedom and compulsion, 224-27; and Ivan Karamazov, 248, 443; and "Man-God," 211; and visions of the Golden Age, 177, 188

Vivas, Eliseo, 448 n

Weizsäcker, Viktor vom, 136

Werfel, Franz, 292 n.14

White Whale, the. See: Moby Dick

Wright, Nathalia, 146 n

Yeats, W. B., 73 n

Zarathustra (Nietzsche): and alienation of modern man, 459-60; and crisis of motives, 474-75; and Ivan Karamazov, 194; and Kafka, 482; and Kirilov, 183; and the Modern Promethean, 462, 466-69, 490; and Raskolnikov, 190-91; and *The Rebel*, 454; and the Underground Man, 159

Zeus: and Creon, 32; and *moira*, 23; and Prometheus, 6, 33-36, 98, 117, 215; and rape of Lida and Europa, 314

Zossima, Father: and Alyosha, 239-42, 257-58, 262, 264-65; and Dostoievsky's image of man, 448, 448 n; and "God-Man," 217, 443-46; and guilt, 236-37; and Ivan Karamazov, 195-96, 211-12; and Job, 272-81